LEBANON IN CRISIS

Contemporary Issues in the Middle East

With contributions from

M. GRAEME BANNERMAN

HALIM BARAKAT

NICKI J. COHEN

JAMES F. COLLINS

JOHN K. COOLEY

HARRY N. HOWARD

PAUL A. JUREIDINI

FRED J. KHOURI

RONALD D. McLAURIN

MOHAMMED MUGHISUDDIN

ITAMAR RABINOVICH

ROBERT W. STOOKEY

ABRAHAM R. WAGNER

LAWRENCE L. WHETTEN

LEBANON
IN CRISIS

Participants and Issues

Edited by
P. EDWARD HALEY and LEWIS W. SNIDER

SYRACUSE UNIVERSITY PRESS • 1979

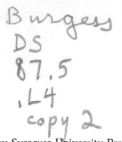
Copyright © 1979 by Syracuse University Press
Syracuse, New York 13210

Library of Congress Cataloging in Publication Data
Main entry under title:

Lebanon in crisis.

   (Contemporary issues in the Middle East)
   Includes bibliographical references and index.
   1. Lebanon—History—Civil War, 1975-   —Addresses, lectures, essays. 2. Lebanon—History—Civil War,
1975-   —Diplomatic history—Addresses, essays,
lectures. 3. Near East—Politics and government—
1945-   —Addresses, essays, lectures. I. Haley,
P. Edward. II. Snider, Lewis W. III. Series: Contemporary issues in the Middle East series.
DS87.5.L4   956.92'04   79-11204
ISBN 0-8156-2210-4
ISBN 0-8156-2213-9 pbk.

Manufactured in the United States of America

CONTENTS

TABLES

EDITORS' PREFACE

THE LEBANESE WAR was first and last a tragedy for the people of Lebanon, who died and were maimed by the tens of thousands before the guns could be stilled. This terrible human loss rails in the mind and will not be quieted. Why did the explosion occur when it did? How and why did those directly involved in the war become involved? What was the fighting about? Why did it take three deathly years to stop the killing and wounding of soldier and civilian, militant and innocent? What causes the fighting to start again and again? Why is it still continuing? Our first concern in this book was to find answers to these questions.

Although finding answers requires an understanding of Lebanese society and politics, it also requires much more, for the answers lie as much in Damascus and Cairo and Jerusalem—in the rivalries and ambitions of the major Arab governments and Israel—as they reside in Palestinian camps or the Muslim and Christian sectors of Beirut—in the arcane and vicious recesses of religious, communal, and ideological politics in Lebanon. And what part of the answer may be found in the policies of Washington and Moscow? What part of the blame for the tragedy is theirs? What of the United Nations and the Arab League? Could not these august bodies have acted to stop the fighting?

If these questions are at the heart of this book, other concerns added interest and urgency to our endeavor. We hope this book will serve as a guide for those who wish to understand the Lebanese conflict—expert and general reader alike—and for those, as well, who would work to bring peace to that tormented land and its wounded, sorrowing people. Of vital importance to Lebanon, that very specific peace and understanding also have a general significance. From the beginning, the tragic war in Lebanon has also been part of a larger Arab-Israeli conflict. Lebanon today is the most explosive arena in which that larger struggle is conducted. A spark in Lebanon—an ill-timed political step, an ill-considered raid or reprisal—could ignite a much larger war between Syria and Israel, with the risk of superpower confrontation and worldwide economic dislocation. The promptness with which Presidents Sadat and Carter and Prime Minister Begin turned to Lebanon after the Camp David meetings ended in October 1978 suggest that they recognize that the success of their efforts to conclude a general Middle East settlement will depend in part on their ability to bring peace to Lebanon.

The contributors to this book identify the main causes of civil strife in Lebanon and the principal Lebanese participants in the fighting: their dreams, their strengths and weaknesses, their objectives, and their actions. With the authors' help one begins to understand the tragedy—its beginnings, the agonizing prolongation, the repeated foreign interventions —and one turns to address the many important questions raised by the Lebanese conflict. What forces in Lebanon and the Middle East led to the explosion and to Palestinian, Syrian, and Israeli intervention? Why did a number of states abstain from any involvement whatever or play an indirect or a very limited role? What has the conduct of the nations and movements and organizations considered in the book revealed about their capabilities, their ability to influence others, and their intentions and interests in Lebanon, in the Middle East, and in international politics? Will the active participants or the bystanders intervene in Lebanon again and in the Middle East, and what forms will their intervention take? How has the conflict affected the parties themselves and their relations with one another? What are the connections between the Lebanese conflict and a general Middle East peace settlement?

In Part I the contributors examine the Lebanese War itself, its origins, development, and effects in the Middle East. Halim Barakat analyzes the sociological, economic, institutional, and political factors that led to the civil war. His sobering appraisal of the primary and contributing causes of the conflict suggests that Lebanon is more likely to slide back into another round of self-destruction than to achieve lasting political, social, and economic recovery from the war. John Cooley emphasizes the impact of the Palestinian Arabs on the fragile Lebanese political system and the no-win situation in which the Palestinian guerrilla organizations found themselves. Lawrence Whetten provides a careful account of the actual fighting. He found all the Lebanese combatants dependent on foreign nations for weapons and ammunition. Not only does this place a heavy moral and political burden on the outside suppliers for the prolonged fighting and heavy civilian casualties, but it also makes peace and unity in Lebanon hostage to the willingness of those same outsiders to restrict weapons supplies.

In his essay on Syria and the Lebanese conflict, Itamar Rabinovich observes that Syria intervened in order to control the outcome of the war and to enhance her ability to act autonomously in inter-Arab affairs and in her dealings with Israel, a need felt all the more acutely in Damascus because of Anwar Sadat's peace moves toward Jerusalem. Syria's intervention stopped the radicalization of Lebanon but mired her army in an occupation that seems unending, thereby weakening her in the face of Israel without gaining the support of Egypt, Iraq, or Libya. The position of Israel grew stronger because of the extremely heavy political and military losses suffered by the Palestinians and because of the growth in Arab disunity and her open alignment with the Christians and anti-Palestinian Muslims in Lebanon. She has achieved a substantial delay in serious negotiations and now, stronger than ever, must feel little need to volunteer important concessions of any kind. Although too little is known of the Camp David agreements to allow conclusive judgments to be made, Israel appears to have agreed to nothing more at Camp David than the provisions of the earlier Begin plan for Gaza and the West Bank. Most of the military arrangements in Sinai also appear to have been agreed before the summit. As Fred J. Khouri observes, the rebuilding of peace and unity in Lebanon now waits on the conclusion of an Arab-Israeli peace settlement acceptable to all the major parties. At this writing it does not appear that the Camp David agreements will lead to a general peace of this kind. The prospect for Lebanon, therefore, remains bleak and dangerous.

Israel's active intervention in Lebanon is viewed by Lewis Snider, P. Edward Haley, Abraham Wagner, and Nicki Cohen as strongly influenced by Israel's perceived security requirements and pessimistic outlook about the possibility of achieving an acceptable final settlement. Graeme Bannerman's analysis of Saudi Arabia's behind-the-scenes role reveals the newfound influence of the oil-rich monarchy in inter-Arab affairs. The end of Jordan's political isolation and the strengthening of its position in inter-Arab politics is discussed by Ronald McLaurin and Paul Jureidini. Jordan's apparent gains are seen partly as an outcome of the war and partly a result of Amman's policy of attentive inactivity where Lebanon was concerned. Mohammed Mughisuddin emphasizes the effect of Cairo's search for a negotiated settlement of the Arab-Israeli conflict on Egypt's response to the fighting in Lebanon. In addition he calls attention to Egypt's desire to regain its position of leadership in the eastern Arab world and to block Syrian challenges to that position.

Regional questions are addressed in the essays by Fred J. Khouri and Lewis Snider. Khouri argues that the civil war, and particularly Israel's continued intervention in southern Lebanon, has diminished the chances for a negotiated settlement of the Arab-Israeli conflict in the foreseeable future, and so diminished the chances for Lebanon's recovery. The impact of inter-Arab relations on the Lebanese conflict and how that conflict, in turn, affected inter-Arab relations is the main subject of Snider's essay. Snider identifies the apparent losers and winners as a result of the fighting in Lebanon and assesses their changing positions in the Arab political arena.

The reaction of the United States, the Soviet Union, and Great Britain to the Lebanese war and the handling of the conflict in the United Nations and the Arab League are treated in Part II. For the Soviet Union and the United States the paradox of superpower and cautious, even reticent, diplomacy from the sidelines receives special attention. After spending billions in economic and military aid and confronting the United States during the October War, the USSR could do little more than plead and scold to get her way in Lebanon. James Collins found the Soviet Union powerless to prevent the Lebanese conflict from disrupting her plans to harmonize the actions of the Arab "progressives"—Syria, Libya, Iraq, and the Palestinians—to defeat the American step-by-step diplomacy, and, by returning to Geneva negotiations, to claim a share equal to that of the United States in Middle Eastern affairs. Unable to control Syrian intervention or to protect the Palestinians, the Soviets played a small part in the Lebanese conflict and must have welcomed the end of the fighting as gratefully as a winded boxer greets the bell. There would be other rounds and better opportunities for the USSR, as the hostile reaction to Sadat's trip to Jerusalem and the Camp David agreements have shown.

The paradox is even more striking in the case of the United States, for in 1958 she had launched a combined military intervention with Britain to thwart both Nasser and the Soviet Union. In 1975 and 1976 the United States found herself reduced to the part of messenger between Israel and Syria and a makeweight used by the local states to counter Soviet and Israeli power. Robert Stookey's study of American policy during the Lebanese civil war shows the Ford Administration to have been unprepared for the sudden spread of the fighting and the collapse of government in Lebanon. Distracted by the fall of Vietnam and Cambodia and intent on its early, unsuccessful efforts to conclude Sinai II, the administration at first opposed all outside intervention. When its meager initiatives failed, along with those of the French and other outsiders, the Ford Administration welcomed the Syrian peacekeeping efforts and helped Syria and Israel avoid a military collision in Lebanon. While the Lebanese war may have damaged United States policy less than Soviet policy, that outcome appears to have been less the result of conscious decisions and use of influence than of good fortune, Anwar Sadat's secure position in Egypt, and Hafez al-Assad's discretion. One should not underrate the importance of helping Israel and Syria avoid another war, but the United States, like the USSR, could find few means to influence the development or outcome of the Lebanese civil war.

An analysis of British policy is included in Part II, both to illuminate the present kinds of European involvement in Lebanon and the Middle East and to anticipate the growth of European influence in the region. P. Edward Haley notes that all signs point to the expansion of British—and French—influence in the Middle East. The Lebanese war offers a convenient base from which to measure that increase and to evaluate the instruments used to achieve it. Already the British have added an imaginative wrinkle to the customary agreements on arms sales, trade, and economic aid: en route to Camp David the foreign ministers of Egypt, Israel, and the United States met in a moated English castle in an attempt to revive the bilateral Egyptian-Israeli peace negotiations.

Like the chapters on the superpowers and Britain, the essay by Harry N. Howard on the United Nations and the Arab League centers on the reasons for their cautious and limited involvement in the Lebanese conflict. Professor Howard reveals the devastating effect of the fighting on the humanitarian activities of the United Nations in Lebanon. Throughout the civil war the highest officials of the UN sought without success to bring that agency into action in the establishment of an enduring cease-fire. Eventually, this ready concern bore fruit in the dispatch of a UN force to southern Lebanon.

The essays were assigned and the authors chosen for the collection in an attempt to treat the Lebanese conflict and this moment in Middle Eastern and international affairs as comprehensively as possible. The book is intended to be accessible to students and general readers and to offer information and analysis of use to the regional expert as well. Inevitably there has been some overlap in the substance of the various chapters. In part the overlap was intentional in that certain issues or actors—the Palestinian resistance organizations, the Arab-Israeli conflict—are treated from different perspectives and in relation to different sets of questions. In part it was unavoidable, for the editors did not require the contributors to agree in their assessments of the conflict or in their forecasts for the future.

Even without a requirement of unanimity readers will be interested to note the extent to which the contributors agree on a wide range of issues of great importance. One would like to be able to add that the authors are optimistic about the return of peace to Lebanon and to the

Middle East. Unhappily, they agree here, too, in a generally pessimistic outlook. Their common findings may be summarized as follows. Caught at last in the Arab-Israeli conflict and an internal struggle for reform and social justice, Lebanon exploded in prolonged violence and death. Lebanon remains divided and embittered, perhaps irreconcilable, with all her major religious and political groups looking outside the country—mainly to Syria, Israel, Libya, and Iraq—for money, arms, and protection.

One of the illuminating observations to emerge from the book as a whole is that the roles formerly played by the great powers—that of supporting one side in a local conflict against another side supported by a rival Great Power—were played by regional powers. Stalemated by each other, the major powers were elbowed aside and their "traditional" parts in local conflicts assumed by Israel, Syria, and Saudi Arabia. These countries, along with Egypt, behaved very much as Britain, Austria-Hungary, Germany, and czarist Russia acted over the Eastern Question in the nineteenth century. The parallel should not be overdrawn, but it is there. The Great Powers in the nineteenth century were concerned with furthering their own territorial and strategic interests in the Eastern Mediterranean and the Balkans at the expense of their Great Power rivals should the Ottoman Empire finally disintegrate. Tragically, Lebanon assumed a similar position for some of the surrounding Middle Eastern powers.

We would add our special thanks to Mary Craig for her cheerful and prodigious efforts in typing the manuscript and in many other ways. Claremont Men's College provided grants to Professor Haley that allowed him free time for writing and editorial chores and helped pay some of the costs of preparing the manuscript for publication.

Our collaboration has been easy and fruitful. We hope for a time when a sequel can be written, a chronicle not of the descent into anarchy, civil war, and despair in Lebanon and the Middle East but of the steady, blessed realization of peace and justice.

Claremont, California   P. Edward Haley
Fall 1978   Lewis Snider

CONTRIBUTORS

M. Graeme Bannerman is with the Near East Section at the Bureau of Intelligence and Research at the U.S. Department of State, Washington, D.C.

Halim Barakat is Associate Professor of Sociology and Arab Studies at Georgetown University and is affiliated with the University's Center for Contemporary Arab Studies. He is author of *Lebanon in Strife: Student Preludes to the Civil War.*

Nicki J. Cohen was a research assistant at Analytical Assessments Corporation, Marina del Rey, California, and is currently working on her Ph.D. in psychology at the University of Minnesota.

James F. Collins is with the Soviet Office at the Bureau of Intelligence and Research, U.S. Department of State, Washington, D.C.

John K. Cooley was Middle East correspondent for the *Christian Science Monitor* from 1965 to October 1978, and was stationed in Beirut during most of the fighting. He is currently the *Monitor's* Defense Correspondent in Washington. He is author of *Green March, Black September: The Story of the Palestinian Arabs.*

P. Edward Haley is Associate Professor of Political Science and International Relations and Director of the International Relations Program at Claremont Men's College, Claremont, California. He is author of "Britain and the Middle East" in *The Middle East in World Politics.*

Harry N. Howard is a retired U.S. Foreign Service Officer and Adjunct Professor in the School of International Service, American University, Washington, D.C. He is author of *The Partition of Turkey, The Problem of the Turkish Straits, The United Nations and the Problem of Greece,* and *The King-Crane Commission.*

Paul A. Jureidini is Vice-President of Abbott Associates, Inc., Alexandria, Virginia, and a specialist in Middle Eastern political and security affairs. He has been involved in numerous studies of the Middle East, particularly of Lebanon and the Fertile Crescent, for the U.S. government. He is co-author of *The Palestinian Movement in Politics.*

Fred J. Khouri is Professor of Political Science at Villanova University, Villanova, Pennsylvania. He has visited many Palestinian refugee camps and trouble spots along the Arab-Israeli demarcation and cease-fire lines. His book, *The Arab-Israeli Dilemma,* is now in its second edition.

Ronald D. McLaurin is Senior Staff Member with Abbott Associates, Inc., Alexandria, Virginia. He is co-author of *Foreign Policy Making in the Middle East: Domestic Influences on Policy in Egypt, Iraq, Israel, and Syria* and author of *The Middle East in Soviet Policy.*

Mohammed Mughisuddin is Dean of International Programs and a member of the faculty of the School of International Service at American University in Washington, D.C. He is also consultant to Abbott Associates, Inc., co-author of *Foreign Policy Making in the Middle East,* and editor of *Conflict and Cooperation in the Persian Gulf.*

Itamar Rabinovich is Chairman of the Department of Middle Eastern and African History at Tel-Aviv University and is affiliated with the university's Shiloah Center for Middle Eastern and African Studies. He is author of *Syria Under the Ba'th 1963–66* and co-editor of *From June to October: The Middle East between 1967 and 1973.*

Lewis W. Snider is Assistant Professor of International Relations and Government at Claremont Graduate School, Claremont, California, and Staff Consultant on Middle Eastern security matters for the Analytical Assessments Corporation. He is author of *Arabesque: Untangling the Pattern of Supply of Conventional Arms to Israel and the Arab States and the Implications for United States Policy on Supply of "Lethal" Weapons to Egypt.*

Robert W. Stookey is a retired U.S. Foreign Service Officer and an Associate of the Center for Middle Eastern Studies, University of Texas at Austin, Texas. He is author of *Mexico and the United States, 1821–1973: Conflict and Coexistence* and *America and the Arab States: An Uneasy Encounter.*

Abraham R. Wagner is President of Analytical Assessments Corporation, Marina del Rey, California, and consultant to the U.S. Departments of Defense and State. He also served in the Israeli prime minister's office, 1973–74. He is author of *Crisis Decision-Making: Israel's Experience in 1967 and 1973* and co-author of *Foreign Policy Making in the Middle East: Domestic Influences on Policy in Egypt, Iraq, Israel and Syria.*

Lawrence L. Whetten is Resident Director of the University of Southern California's Graduate Program in International Relations in Germany. He is author of *The Canal War: Four Power Conflict in the Middle East* and editor of *The Future of Soviet Military Power* and *The Political Implications of Soviet Military Power.*

LEBANON IN CRISIS

PART I

The Lebanese War and the Middle East

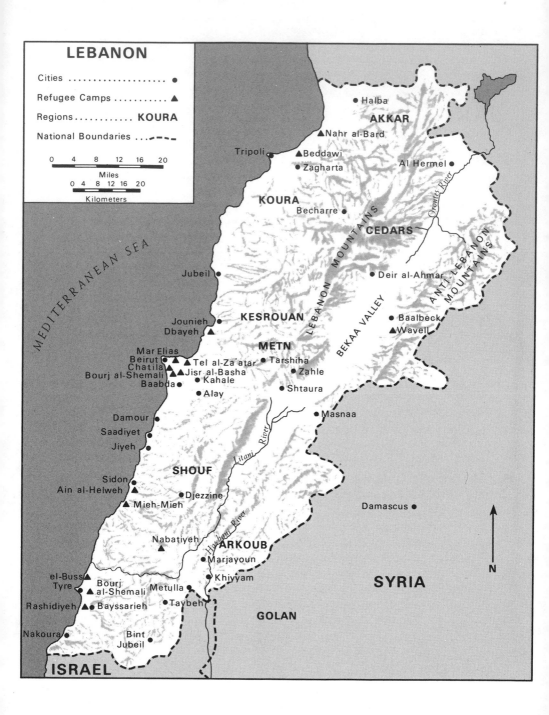

LEBANON

Cities .... •
Refugee Camps .... ▲
Regions .... KOURA
National Boundaries ...--- ---

Miles
0 4 8 12 16 20

Kilometers
0 4 8 12 16 20

MEDITERRANEAN SEA

• Halba

AKKAR

▲ Nahr al-Bard

Tripoli •
▲ Beddawi
• Zagharta

Al Hermel •

KOURA

Becharre •

CEDARS

Deir al-Ahmar •

Jubeil •

KESROUAN

Jounieh •
Dbayeh ▲

Baalbeck •
Wavell ▲

METN

Mar Elias
Beirut • ▲
Chatila ▲ ▲ Tel al-Za'atar   • Tarshiha
Bourj al-Shemali ▲ ▲ Jisr al-Basha   • Zahle
Baabda • • Kahale
• Alay   • Shtaura

Damour •

Saadiyet •

Jiyeh •

• Masnaa

SHOUF

Litani River

Sidon •
Ain al-Helweh ▲
▲ Mieh-Mieh

• Djezzine

Damascus •

Nabatiyeh ▲

ARKOUB

Hasbani River

• Marjayoun

• Khiyyam

SYRIA

el-Buss ▲
Tyre • ▲ Bourj
al-Shemali
Rashidiyeh • ▲ Bayssarieh

Metulla •

• Taybeh

N

Nakoura •

Bint
Jubeil

GOLAN

ISRAEL

LEBANON MOUNTAINS

ANTI-LEBANON MOUNTAINS

BEKAA VALLEY

Orontes River

THE SOCIAL CONTEXT

Halim Barakat

> A certain hunter . . . came one day upon a cave in the mountains, where he found a hollow full of bees' honey. So he took somewhat thereof and carried it to the city, followed by a hunting dog which was dear to him. He stopped at the shop of an oilman and offered him the honey for sale. . . . As he emptied it that he might see it, a drop fell to the ground, whereupon flies flocked to it and a bird swooped down upon the flies. Now the oilman had a cat, which pounced upon the bird, and the hunter's dog sprang upon the cat and killed it; whereupon the oilman ran at the dog and killed it and the hunter in turn sprang upon the oilman and killed him. Now the oilman was of one village and the hunter of another; and when the people of the two villages heard what had passed, they took arms and rose on one another in anger, and the sword continued to play amongst them until many of the people died, none knows their number, save God almighty.
>
> *Arabian Nights,* Night 528

THE WAR in Lebanon was the result of several highly interconnected internal and external conditions that have been in the making for a long time.

Distinction should be made between causal and contributing forces: the former are directly connected with the civil war and inherently rooted in the existing social and political structures of the country, while the latter aggravated the internal conflicts and set the process of confrontation into motion, triggered a set of events already in the making that awaited only the proper time and place.[1]

The causal forces include (1) the mosaic social structure of Lebanon composed of fragmented, hierarchically arranged communities; (2) a pyramidal social class structure characterized by great gaps between the deprived and the privileged; (3) a weak, inefficient, and corrupt central government; (4) a rigid, sectarian political system unable to transform or even modify itself; and (5) a prevailing condition of social unrest and anomie generated by the dynamics of Lebanon's laissez faire economic system and sudden prospects for limited prosperity.

The contributing forces included (1) the armed presence of the Palestinian resistance movement; (2) the Israeli raids; and (3) the urgent search for a peaceful solution to the Arab-Israeli conflict.

Both the causal and contributing forces (which will be described in detail) contributed to the polarization of Lebanese society into two camps: the camp of rightist Lebanese (mostly Maronite Christians) supported, manipulated, or encouraged by several Arab reactionary governments, Israel, Iran, and the West; and an alliance of Palestinian resistance movements and the Lebanese leftist nationalist movements supported on and off by a few Arab governments and some socialist groups and countries.

The rightist camp was composed of (1) the Phalange (Al-Kata'ib), a highly organized political party led by Pierre Gemayel and his sons Bashir and Amin;[2] (2) the party of the Free Nationalists (often named in Western literature as the Liberal party) led by ex-president of the Lebanese Republic, Camille Chamoun and his sons Dany and Dory;[3] (3) the Maronite order of Monks headed by Cherbel Kassis; (4) the militia of ex-president Suleiman Frangieh and his son Tony, who was killed in a Phalangist attack in June 1978; and (5) factions of the Lebanese army and other smaller organizations.

Arrayed against these groups was a Lebanese nationalist progressive front composed of (1) the Progressive Socialist party, headed by Kamal Jumblatt, who was killed in an ambush in the spring of 1977; (2) the Syrian Social Nationalist party; (3) the Lebanese Communist party; (4) the Organization of Communist Action; (5) Al-Mourabitoun—a Nasserist movement; (6) the Arab Ba'ath socialist party; (7) the Arab Lebanese army; and (8) other smaller organizations. The Lebanese nationalist progressive front allied itself with the Palestinian resistance movement.

The choosing of sides paralyzed the Lebanese army and then split it, neutralizing pro-government forces and several traditional leaders. Among the most significant neutralized organizations was the Nationalist Bloc of Raymond Edde and the traditional Muslim leadership (such as Saeb Salem, Rashid Karameh, Takieddine Solh, Kamel As'ad and others).

The complexity of the Lebanese conflict—that it was more than religious strife, or Palestinian-Lebanese conflict, or purely class struggle— is suggested by the following facts.

1. The rightist camp controlled by Maronite leaders received substantial support from a number of Muslim leaders, factions, and countries.

2. A significant segment of Lebanese Christians has sided with the leftist camp.

3. The rightist camp has attacked a number of Lebanese Christian communities, groups, and individuals.

4. Several Lebanese groups, political parties, movements, and leaders joined and supported the leftist camp.

5. Some Arab nationalist parties and groups supported the isolationist rightist movement.

6. Some poor Christians have fought on the rightist side.

7. Some upper class Muslims have fought on the leftist side.

8. Groups on both sides were involved in indiscriminate attacks, torture, and killing using the Lebanese I.D., which specifies one's religion, as the only evidence to justify their acts.

9. The leftist groups included diverse groups and organizations (some being basically nationalist, socialist, and religious-traditionalist in orientations). The Palestinian resistance movement included also groups and organizations of such diverse orientations.

10. Splits in the rank of the rightists camps have resulted in brutal encounters such as the massacre of Frangieh's family in the spring of 1978.

The most reliable method of classifying the participants in the Lebanese civil war, then, is not by religion or class but by the division between those who seek basic and comprehensive change from those who would maintain the existing order.

CAUSAL FORCES

Causal forces are those conditions and characteristic behavior patterns directly connected with the civil war and inherently rooted in the Lebanese social and political structures. Five such causal forces were already identified. They are described in detail in the following sections.

The Mosaic Social Structure of Lebanon

Lebanon consists of diverse religious communities organized in a hierarchical manner accommodating their own conflicts and interests within the confines of a system that promotes sectarian identities and loyalties and opposes the development of belief in a common national fate. Some religious communities enjoy more social and economic privileges than others, and sectarian loyalty disguises and denies social injustice and even suppresses awareness of it out of the realm of consciousness. Consequently, relationships between the diverse religious communities have wavered between conflict and accommodation without the benefit of a vision for assimilation and development of national or ideological consciousness. On the contrary, the Lebanese elites and their agencies of socialization (including the educational systems) followed a policy of divisiveness by promoting religious loyalties and interests. Though a limited system of checks and balances, such as the National Pact of 1943 has been introduced; this system promoted the dominance of some religious groups (particularly the Maronites) over others and secured the needed conditions for self-perpetuation of the traditional elites.

Lebanon has continued to be fragmented on the basis of dominant traditional loyalties, governed by an inefficient and corrupt oligarchy, and lacking a core uniquely of its own. To be more specific, Lebanon has continued to be characterized by the following dominant features:

1. There is lack of consensus on fundamentals such as on a constitution, a popular national pact, a political order for the country, and, above all, on the national identity of Lebanon. The Lebanese have continued to be divided on the question of whether or not Lebanon constitutes a nation. Some, predominantly Christian Maronites, conceive of Lebanon as an independent, separate, sovereign, complete, and eternal entity. For them, however, Lebanon is a national home for the Christians in the sense that their loyalty is mostly to the area of Mount Lebanon and not to the rest of the country, and in the sense that they insist on the sectarian system that guarantees their dominance. A prominent theoretician of the Lebanese Right, Charles Malik, speaks of the "security and self-mastery of Lebanon's Christian community," and of "Lebanon being the home of the Lebanese everywhere," or "the historic uniqueness and apartness of Lebanon in the whole of Asia, Africa and the Middle East." When majoritarian democracy is proposed, Malik inquires, "Must the fate of the Christians . . . be ineluctably sealed by sheer determinism of numbers?" He further adds: "The Christians of Lebanon cherish their freedom; they cherish their own mastery over themselves and over their destiny. . . . In the rule of numbers they will soon be in the minority and that is what instills fears in their hearts . . . and this is what the Christians refuse to concede;" hence his insistence also that "Lebanon remains

the one fatherland at once for the Lebanese residing in it and the Lebanese overseas."[4]

On the other hand, for a large number of Lebanese, particularly the Muslims, the present arrangement of Lebanon was imposed by French mandate in 1920. To them Lebanon is an integral part of the Arab nation. Still others, mostly Orthodox Christians and Druze, see Lebanon as an integral part of Greater Syria. In the present civil war Lebanese subscribing to Syrian nationalism and Arab nationalism fought alongside the leftists and Palestinian resistance organizations against fellow Lebanese subscribing to a purely Lebanese national identity. The Syrian and Arab nationalists call Lebanese nationalists isolationists and accuse them of wanting to isolate Lebanon from other Arab countries and to dissociate its cause from their cause.

The lack of consensus on the national identity of Lebanon is accompanied by and coincides with disagreement on many other ideological issues including social and political reform, relations with the West, support of the Palestinian cause, and socialism. This may partly explain why Lebanese nationalists are more inclined to the Right and prefer to maintain the status quo, while the Syrian and Arab nationalists are more inclined to the Left and prefer to transform the existing order or to replace it with another order. The lack of consensus on fundamentals among the Lebanese has rendered Lebanon a mosaic and fragmented society without a core or a focus and has doomed it to constant tensions and conflicts including violent confrontations such as those of the 1958 and 1975–76 civil wars.

2. There is a lack of extensive and open dialog. The Lebanese ruling elites used a number of what theorists of consociational democracy call conflict-regulating practices, including purposive depoliticization. Sensitive issues were purposefully kept out of discussion even in times of national elections. Competition was based on personalities, family names, and whole lists headed by traditional leaders without any programs for reform. The ruling elites have often asserted emphatically the existence of real unity among the Lebanese communities. Such a policy of denying reality and facade building prompted the Lebanese journalist Ghassan Tueini to point out that "the treatment of confessionalism should start with a confession of its existence. The Christians say two things and the Muslims say two things: what they say to themselves and what they say to others."[5]

A hypocritical dialog has characterized relationships between religious communities, and mutual apprehensions have barred self-criticism

and self-examination. The Lebanese Maronite Christians in particular
tended to accept the status quo and fight for it even at those times when
they would privately admit some faults. The Lebanese Muslims tended to
reject the status quo without much clarity as to their vision for the country and with little commitment to secularism.

   3. There is a lack of loyalty to the country. The Lebanese, regardless of their religious affiliations, have been more loyal to religion, family, and locality than to the country as a whole. In fact, Lebanese nationalism is more a manifestation of religious identification. During the civil
war the Christians dropped the cedar symbol of Lebanon and replaced it
with the cross. It was clearly indicated also that once their privileges
were threatened, the Maronites preferred partition of the country (not
unlike the story of the false mother in the Bible).

   The Christian rightists complain that Muslims are not loyal to Lebanon and that they would prefer to see Lebanon united with other Arab
countries. It is true that Arab nationalism, which is accepted by a significant proportion of Lebanese Christians, is the dominant sentiment
among Lebanese Muslims. After all, Lebanon was carved out of Syria in
1920 against the will of the Muslim community and the Christian Arab
and Syrian nationalists in the country and in the heartland of Mount
Lebanon. Furthermore, the Muslims have been relegated to the status of
second class citizens, as will be shown later. In fact, the Christian rightists are not loyal to the country as a whole but to their own religious
community. The Christian rightists have always expected the Muslims to
give up their notion of Arab nationalism and declare their "final and absolute allegiance" to Lebanese nationalism. The working paper of the
Lebanese front, for example (Phalangist party, the party of Free Nationalists of Chamoun, ex-president Suleiman Frangieh, and the Maronite
order of monks), to the Lady of the Well conference declared that "there
is no place in Lebanon of the future for any group or community that
does not subscribe to complete and absolute loyalty to Lebanon." The
working paper of the Phalangists to the same conference adds, using
Christian religious terms, "all Lebanese must renew their act of faith in
Lebanon the eternal."[6]

   4. There is geographical representation of the different religious
communities. Lebanese religious communities live in isolated regions of
their own, rendering the society a mosaic even in shape and form. Some
districts and many villages are exclusively inhabited by one religious
community. Even where different religious groups live in the same city,
town, or village, they tend to live in separate neighborhoods.

   5. There is a joining of religion and the state. Instead of moving to-

wards secularism after independence, Lebanon further legitimized the sectarian system inherited from the French mandate and earlier Ottoman millet system. Political representation, employment in all branches of government including the courts and public education system, and legislation in the areas of personal status such as marriage and inheritance are based and governed by sectarian affiliation. Among the consequences of the mingling of religion and the state are absence of civil marriage and lack of intermarriage between the different religious communities.

6. There are conflicting reference groups. The different Lebanese religious communities model themselves after, and identify with, different outside countries and movements. The Christian Lebanese, and more particularly the Maronites, have constantly looked to Western nations for protection and inspiration. They have exposed themselves most willingly and freely to Western influence even in instances where they realized that such influences might be harmful to Arab causes. On the other hand, the affinities of Lebanese Muslims and some Christians are with the Arab nation, and they seek (since the Palestinian disaster) the protection and support of socialist countries. Because Lebanese look to competing protectors, conflicts between the West and socialist countries or between different Arab countries (especially when linked to East-West issues) are projected on the Lebanese stage.

One interesting development in this area is the great disappointment of rightist Christians with Western response to the Lebanese civil war. Such a disappointment is expressed most bitterly by Charles Malik who has always been seen by his opponents in Lebanon as an agent of the West and an ardent anti-Communist. He concluded that Europe and the United States refused to aid Lebanon "because the spirit in Europe and America is in general overwhelmed with cynicism, materialism, hedonism and pettiness. Pornography is nauseating . . . the search is for money and more money . . . and the scourge of drugs has not much abated, if at all, in America, and in Europe it is taking a turn for the worse."[7]

7. The educational system reflects and reinforces the stratified social mosaic of Lebanon. The Lebanese educational systems are as diversified as the country's social situation. There have been as many systems and philosophies of education as there have been religious communities, for each sect has its own autonomous private schools without any government supervision. Private schools demanded and acquired educational autonomy, though they have received government financial assistance. The different private schools—missionary, commercial, national, and foreign—followed different philosophies of education and used different

languages for instruction (mainly Arabic, French, and English) even on elementary levels. The private schools are mostly attended by Christian students and public schools (intended for those who could not afford the expensive education of private schools) mostly by Muslim students.

In the best of times, these seven characteristics rend Lebanese society and dim the prospects for unity, let alone harmony, between the dominant groups. Yet, these conditions alone might not have been sufficient to bring about a civil war; other developments have coexisted and contributed in turn to violent encounters. Here, however, it should be pointed out that the conflicting loyalties have encouraged outside interference and helped traditional leaders remain in power.

Pyramid Class Structure and Poverty Belts

Lebanese society is characterized by a pyramidal social class structure. The majority of the Lebanese are relatively poor, a smaller proportion are middle class, and very few are ultrarich. A government-sponsored study conducted by a French research team revealed that 9 percent of Lebanese families were miserably poor, another 41 percent poor, and an additional 32 percent earned moderate income. The rest were the "well-to-do," constituting 14 percent, and "the rich," 4 percent. The wealthiest 4 percent received 32 percent of the total gross national product of Lebanon, or more than the lower half of the population who received only 18 percent of the country's GNP, and only a little less than 82 percent of the population who received only 40 percent of the GNP.[8] Since the study appeared, critics have constantly referred to "the 4 percent class" ruling Lebanon and monopolizing its wealth.

Lebanon has also been characterized by two poverty belts, one surrounding the country itself and one surrounding Beirut. They became increasingly a miniature of the country itself. The poverty belt surrounding the country included the southern region, the Akkar region of the north, and the Bekaa (the eastern part of the country). These impoverished areas surround the prosperous Christian Mount Lebanon. Poor educational opportunities, roads, and hospitals, and a lack of commercial and industrial enterprises and other facilities at least partly explain the huge rural-urban migration to form another poverty belt around the city. The Israeli raids on the south have contributed in turn to the immensity of village-city migration. Several areas around Beirut such as Ghbeiri, ash-Shiyah, and an-Nu'ba have become overcrowded, poverty-stricken slums. Quite often one single room would house ten or more persons, and swarms of children filled the narrow, dirty streets and alleys.

The gap between the poverty belts and Mount Lebanon and other rich neighborhoods of Beirut has increased in recent years. For instance, the country's student enrollment in pre-university schools has been increasing at a yearly rate of 9.6 percent in elementary schools and 24 percent in secondary schools since the mid-fifties, but at different rates among districts. The rate of increase in Mount Lebanon has been 18 percent in elementary schools and 57 percent in secondary schools, while in the south the rates of increase have been 8 percent in elementary schools and 16 percent in secondary schools. Furthermore, the proportion of students in private schools increased between 1955 and 1968 in the Beirut district from 66 percent to 86 percent, and in Mount Lebanon from 58 percent to 78 percent, while in the other districts this proportion remained the same (about 4 percent). The gap is not just a question of quantity only, but of quality also. The proportion of students attending public schools has decreased in Mount Lebanon and increased in the other districts. The private schools are becoming extremely expensive and thus destined to serve only the well-to-do, while the lower classes can afford to send their children only to public schools.

What should be noted here is that the poverty areas were overwhelmingly inhabited by Muslims (and particularly Shi'ites), while Mount Lebanon is overwhelmingly inhabited by Christians. Thus social class and religion overlap, a situation which blurs the nature of the split in Lebanese society. What is seen by some as religious strife is seen by others as class struggle. The Muslims, and particularly the Shi'ites, suffer most acutely from poverty and low social and political status. Most significant positions in the socioeconomic and political structures in Lebanon are occupied by, and in many instances reserved for, the Christians and particularly the Maronites. In this way the Lebanese religious communities and not just individual Lebanese become arranged into hierarchical, stratified structures of privileged and deprived communities. Such splits were aggravated by the increasing inflation immediately prior to the civil war.

It should be noted also that the disinherited Lebanese found themselves sharing the same destiny with the Palestinians living in refugee camps. In certain instances, they coexisted in the same areas such as Tel al-Za'atar. Such conditions aggravated one another and contributed to further polarization between forces for change and forces for preserving the existing alienating order.

Weak Central Government

In a study on cabinet politics in Lebanon, Elie Salem pointed out that "the crisis [more accurately the civil war] of 1958 revealed beyond doubt that in the moment of truth local leaders and established families held greater control of their followers than did the central government. Each religious and ethnic group has its own pyramid of power and its own internal source of strength, and it is with these pyramids that the cabinet must deal and at times even negotiate."[9] In 1969 Lebanon lived without government for seven months during which Lebanese would not have noticed the difference had they not been constantly reminded by the press that there was no government; hence the rhetorical comment of Ghassan Tueini in an editorial of his paper, *an-Nahar*, "The government does not exist, and whatever part of it exists it has no authority, and whoever has authority it is not the government."[10] The rightists, traditional leaders, and tycoons of free economy have preferred this situation and ideologically justified it by indicating that Lebanon's strength lies in its weakness. They would be critical of "absence of government" only when the leftists, nationalists, and Palestinians took advantage of such a situation.

The weakness and corruption of the central government manifested itself in several aspects and areas of Lebanese daily life such as (1) protection of outlaws by political leaders, even by those who held official positions of responsibility; (2) settlement of feuds and conflicts (including those involving criminal and civil offenses) without interference of court or central authorities; (3) smuggling by political elites or with their partnership with full knowledge of authorities (at one time a secret airport for smuggling was uncovered); (4) widespread evasion of taxation by businesses, professionals, and others to the extent that taxation was almost limited to salaries and custom duties (themselves often corrupt); (5) establishment of private militias; (6) direct interference by foreign powers in Lebanese internal affairs and free movement of foreign agents including those of Israel and other enemies of Arab countries; (7) use of Lebanon as a stage for conflicting Arab groups, governments, and movements, as shown in violent encounters and establishment of private media of communication and propaganda; (8) greater importance of informal than formal roles, in that top political leaders preferred to be outside while nominating their followers even to cabinet positions; (9) the playing of conflicting roles, such as being a minister of interior and leading a fighting militia at the same time as in the case of Chamoun during the civil war, which prompted Premier Rashid Karameh to accuse him of being simultaneously "the guard and thief"—*hamiha haramiha*; (10) lack of authority on the part of the government to collect data or conduct census at private institutions, such as private schools refusing to give estimates of the number of students and staff to the ministry of education, though they could be receiving financial help from the government; and (11) difficulty of enforcing laws and imposing solutions even when solutions were reached.

In short, the Lebanese political system has been a unique form not of governing but of nongovernment. Several states have always existed within the state. The Palestinian armed presence was only one of several sovereignties within the state. The civil war of 1975–76 has proved that the central government has no role in times of crisis. With a strong central government, Lebanon could have been spared the bitter course of the civil war itself. In the face of these facts, it is ironic that the Lebanese rightists have been proposing decentralization as a way out of the desperate impasse.

The Problem of Political Rigidity

Though the Lebanese political system proved flexible in allowing for anarchy and free enterprise in several areas, it proved rigid in its resistance to political reform, to circulation of leadership, and to representation of emerging powers. The sectarian formula allocated the parliamentary, cabinet, and administrative posts to the various religious communities in accordance with an arbitrary population ratio based on the 1932 census by the French. Because the religious ratios changed in favor of the Muslims, Christian elites refused to allow a new census, attacked any suggestion for amendment of the constitution, and insisted that the president of the republic be Maronite. The rightist Christians demanded that Lebanese citizenship and voting rights be given to immigrants and their descendants, but the government failed to adopt a consistent policy on naturalization and citizenship. While some groups were granted citizenship, others were deprived of it.

The largest increase in population has been among the Shi'ites, who have been badly underrepresented. The Sunni Muslims have also felt that they are losing rather than gaining power with time. The office of the premier, reserved for Sunni Muslims, has been gradually undermined by the Maronite president of the republic. Instead of a fairer distribution of power, the decision-making process has been increasingly centralized in and monopolized by the presidency. Immediately prior to both the 1958 and the 1975–76 civil wars, the position of premier was particularly weakened causing uproar in the Muslim community.

The political system also proved unresponsive to public opinion and to demands for reform. A research survey conducted by Iliya Harik and the author in two voting districts of Beirut in 1972 showed that the majority of the Muslim (86 percent) and Christian (61 percent) respondents favored ending Maronite monopoly over the office of president of the republic, and that they believed it should be accessible to all Lebanese, regardless of their religious affiliation. Previous public opinion polls by *an-Nahar* showed also that the Lebanese preferred that the president be elected by popular vote and not by the parliament.

The Lebanese political system also proved rigid in not allowing the liberals and the emerging bourgeoisie to share in power. The contention for power between the Lebanese oligarchy and the emerging liberal bourgeoisie ended in the defeat of the latter, and Lebanon continued to be ruled by traditional leaders. The Lebanese oligarchy has maintained its power, and political positions have been inherited like family names. Some children could not wait for the death of the father, hence the phenomenon of voting both father and son into parliament, and having the father and the son in the same cabinet. Some liberal professionals and newly prosperous businessmen were able to reach the parliament and cabinet but only under the wing and at the disposal of the traditional leaders, and quite often by buying their nominations on the tradition leaders' slates. Once in power, these professionals and businessmen could be re-elected or could maintain their positions by adhering to the policies of the traditional leaders, who continued to rule the country even when not holding formal positions. During the period prior to the civil war, some traditional za'ims refused to hold formal positions (nominating their followers instead), preferring the informal role of running the show from behind the screen.

Liberals and liberal policies failed in the sixties and the seventies. Fuad Chehab's liberal regime failed in its attempts at administrative reforms. Also suffering failure were the policies of the liberal technocrats who were appointed in the early 1970s—men such as journalist Ghassan Tueini, economist Elias Saba, physician Emile Bitar, engineer Henry Eddeh, and others—who tried to introduce such minor reforms as imposing higher taxes on luxury items, reducing the soaring prices of medical drugs, enforcing laws governing taxation, improving public schools, and reforming educational curricula. All these attempts at reform failed, and all these ministers had to resign; in one instance, a minister was expelled from office when he refused to resign.

The inability of the political system to transform itself is also reflected in the great disparity between popular support for progressive parties and their representation in parliament and cabinet (the Communists, the socialist organizations, the Syrian Social Nationalists, and other leftists were not represented). The system proved unable to accommodate the liberals, let alone the radicals. The regime vehemently rejected the demands of the Lebanese nationalist and progressive movement voiced by Kamal Jumblatt: secularization, reform of electoral laws, amendment of the constitution, reorganization of the army, and lifting restrictions on naturalization. Simply, the system proved closed, rigid, and static in a highly dynamic situation. It did not possess the ability to transform itself and face challenging and overdue problems. On the contrary, it marvelled in its ability to generate new problems.

Social Unrest and Anomie

Lebanon, as a gate to the Arab East, served as headquarters for business, financial, and administrative activities prompted by the discovery of oil in the area. During the last quarter century, the country witnessed sudden prosperity and a great rat race for procuring the biggest share of the fortune in the shortest time possible, legitimately if possible, illegitimately if necessary. The intensity of the need for achievement generated by the new conditions resulted in sharp rivalries, lack of mutual respect, infringements on the rights of others, and fascination with status symbols. This situation was further aggravated by inequities in opportunity, scarcity of legitimate means, lack of law enforcement, absence of authorities, and total free economy. Illegitimate means became justifiable (or even defined as clever and reflecting "Lebanese genius") as long as they could lead to success. Even ardent rightists (such as Gemayel and Malik) at one and the same time condemned the "immorality of the Lebanese" and took pride in the free and competitive system of Lebanon and "the ambitions of its sons" without seeing any connection between such behavior and the existing order which they defended.

Prosperity was confined to few areas and few families. Though the country became the finance center for the whole Middle East, profits were not invested in the country, and few development projects were undertaken, particularly outside Mount Lebanon and some parts of the capital. In an interesting editorial in *an-Nahar* (January 8, 1973) Ghassan Tueini described Lebanon as "the donkey of prosperity."

> The talk about prosperity . . . is sad not only for the poor for whom prosperity became showcases filled with the most desired things whose prices they don't even dare to inquire about, let alone the ambition to buy them . . .
>
> The talk about prosperity is sad not only for the poor, but to the rest of the Lebanese including those who have been spending like crazy . . . taken in by the great desire for consumption. . . .
>
> They brag about . . . billions deposited in banks . . . [It] reminds the Lebanese of the story of a donkey that was loaded with gold on a long journey . . . it is precisely the same story with due respect to the Lebanese people. Perhaps, what is most annoying in the story . . . is that the gold which the donkey cannot benefit from . . . is this time the sweat and toil of the donkey itself and of its own making . . . as if banks exist to enrich the rich with the savings of the poor.
>
> . . . Is prosperity to increase the wealth of the rich and the poverty of the poor? Is it possible that the day might come when, without need to destroy the showcases, prosperity will be shared by all?

The violence shown in the current civil war was partly an attempt to steal the gold and destroy the showcase. The fact of the matter is that the privileged rarely give up their privileges and share the wealth of the country with the rest. Whenever threatened, they themselves initiate violence in defense of their privileges. The violence of the deprived is a desperate reaction to the violence of the privileged. Furthermore, it should be noted that the laissez faire economic system contributed to the emergence of a class of Lebanese who have been able to improve their economic condition in times of crisis and anarchy. Several factors that contributed to the sustenance and re-eruption of the civil war were looting, arms trade, and smuggling. Such acts have been widespread, well organized, and even rationalized to the extent of legitimation. This situation also partly explains the fierce fighting in commercial districts and the latest inter-rightist fights.

Many observers failed to comprehend the extent of social unrest and anomie in Lebanon. This lack of comprehension may explain why so many outsiders were surprised by the Lebanese capacity for atrocities. Comments have circulated that the easy-going, spoiled, neatly dressed, fun-oriented Lebanese youths were not expected to harbor that much hatred, toughness, and cruelty. The behavior exhibited by the Lebanese lay not simply in them but also in the conditions surrounding their life.

CONTRIBUTING FORCES

In the 1950s the emergence of Nasserism and the subsequent unity of Egypt and Syria, the Western offensive to prevent this unity and eliminate Nasser, and the Israeli invasion of the Suez Canal aggravated the internal Lebanese situation and helped bring about the 1958 civil war. Similarly, in the 1970s the emergence of the Palestinian resistance movement and its armed presence in Lebanon, the Western offensive for a Middle East peace settlement and the elimination of Palestinian resistance, and the Israeli raids into Lebanon aggravated the situation in Lebanon and helped cause the 1975–76 civil war. In both cases Lebanon proved vulnerable to external influence because of its delicate internal balance and the intensification of its social and political problems.

The causal forces described above in detail have been shown to stem from the very structure of the society and the political system based on it. A set of circumstantial conditions acted as contributing forces in triggering the civil war in April 1975, and in sustaining it for a year and a half. These circumstances included the armed presence of the Palestinians in Lebanon, the search for a peaceful solution to the Arab-Israeli conflict, and the constant Israeli raids. Because of the focus of the present chapter on the internal social situation of Lebanon, these circumstances will be described in brief and in so far as they have aggravated the internal contradictions.

Palestinian Armed Presence

refer to p. 11

The armed presence of the Palestinians in Lebanon served as a catalyst, contributing both to the articulation and diffusion of radical ideas and to the willingness of nationalist and progressive groups to unite and press for fulfillment of overdue demands. Initially, the emergence of the Palestinian resistance movement was seen as a healthy reaction of Arab society to the defeat of the June War of 1967. Without its emergence, the Arab world would have been desolate and condemned as dead for not responding to such a trying challenge to its very existence and control over its destiny. Consequently, the Palestinian resistance was acclaimed all over the Arab world as a savior, a hope for the future, a phoenix emerging from its ashes to rejuvenate Arab society. The support it received was overwhelming, and its magnitude started to decrease only after Arab ruling classes and rightist elements realized they would have to pay a price for their support.

The Lebanese conservatives were particularly alarmed after the Israeli raid on Beirut International Airport, and by the end of 1968 they began their move to restrict the movement of the commandos. The Lebanese army (controlled by Maronite officers) had to make a choice between resisting Israeli raids or containing the Palestinian resistance movement. They decided to contain the Palestinians, and this cast the army as a repressive instrument controlled by the Christian ruling elites rather than as a national army entrusted with the task of defending the country against foreign invasion. Because it had lost its image as the army of the country as a whole, when civil war broke out the army could not stop the raging conflict. Instead, it split into different factions bent on destroying one another.

The rightist parties, which flourished mostly in Maronite communities, were also alarmed and began to solidify their ranks and strengthen their militias with the encouragement of the army. An increasing reference to the Palestinians as foreigners or strangers (*Ghourabā'*) began to circulate, and wall inscriptions appeared in Christian quarters saying, "No to the Resistance," "No to Syria," "No to Arabism," "No to the coward strangers" (*al-Ghourabā' al-Joubnā'*). Exactly reversed inscriptions appeared in Muslim quarters saying, "Yes to the Resistance," "Yes to Arabism."

As a reaction to this new threat, the Palestinian resistance movement feared the repetition of the September massacre of 1970 in Jordan. They tried to coordinate with the rightists (by establishing joint committees and by frequent visits and meetings between Yasir Arafat and other Palestinian leaders and Gemayel, Chamoun, and other rightist elements). The Palestinian resistance movement sought also to strengthen its alliance with the leftist nationalist groups in Lebanon. Throughout the first year of war, the Palestine Liberation Organization (PLO) tried to keep out of the fighting. Constant rightist attacks on Palestinian camps pushed them into battle, for the rightists hoped to demonstrate that the war was a Palestinian-Lebanese war and not a Lebanese civil war. In fact, the majority of the Lebanese sympathized with the Lebanese leftists' defense of the Palestinian cause, which merged with their own cause.

Israeli Raids

The constant Israeli raids aimed, among other things, at driving a wedge between the Lebanese and the Palestinians. They threatened the Lebanese economy, drove thousands of peasants from the south into the cities and particularly Beirut, embarrassed the Lebanese army and demonstrated its inability to defend the country and its citizens. and pushed the Palestinian resistance movement to fortify their camps. The fact that Palestinian leaders were also attacked and killed in their apartments further complicated the situation. Three top Palestinian leaders (Kamal Nasser, Yusaf Najjar, and Kamal Radwan) were assassinated in their homes in Beirut by Israeli commandos without meeting any interference from the Lebanese army (in the spring of 1973). The Lebanese premier then resigned in dispute with the president over the army's reluctance to defend the country. The results were a series of difficulties between the presidency and the Muslim communities for appointing weak premiers and further centralization of power in the hands of the Maronite rightist president.

Simply, the Israeli raids contributed to the intensity of Lebanese internal conflicts. The raids divided the Lebanese themselves, turned many Lebanese against the Palestinians, and added to further polarization. Once the civil war started, Israel began directly to support the rightists, helped to keep the war going, and indirectly pressured Syria towards siding with the rightists.

Search for a Peaceful Solution to the Arab-Israeli Conflict

The search for a peaceful settlement of the Arab-Israeli conflicts (which has been posed as an alternative to popular armed struggle) required that radical elements be contained or eliminated and replaced with "moderate" leadership. Several Arab governments, the West, Israel, and rightist political parties in Lebanon followed a policy of containing the Palestinian resistance movement, of promoting moderate leadership that would be willing to negotiate a settlement, and of splitting the Arab world against itself. Arab governments, political movements and organizations, and Arab public opinion became effectively divided for and against the proposed peaceful settlement. Unlike the North Vietnamese and Viet Cong, Arabs oversimplified the issue by putting it in either/or terms. Opting for a peaceful solution meant rejecting popular armed struggle for liberation, and opting for armed struggle meant refusal to engage in dialog and to project an image of Arabs as peace seekers. Instead of confronting Israel, Arabs became engaged in negating one another.

The Lebanese rightists, who have been anxiously hoping for a peaceful settlement, received support and encouragement from a number of Arab governments and Israel. Israel was particularly involved and worked hard to sustain the civil war which served to (1) decimate the Palestinian resistance; (2) distract and divide the Arab countries; (3) strengthen its grip over newly occupied Arab lands; (4) end Israel's isolation; (5) destroy the notion of establishing secular-democratic-pluralistic states; (6) prevent leftist victories; and (7) promote the establishment of other religious homelands in the area.

In regard to Arab governments, the normal pattern has been to interfere immediately to stop violent confrontations within or between Arab countries. The existence of a plan for a peaceful solution which required containing the Palestinian resistance government and radical elements may explain why those Arab governments who were seeking such a peaceful settlement allowed the civil war to drag for so long and finally to culminate in the Syrian military intervention on the side of rightists to prevent a leftist victory. The same fact may explain why the Western countries did not interfere to end the war which they might have done under different circumstances. Arab regimes can at times be most militant against each other and most compromising with their real enemies.

THE PALESTINIANS

John K. Cooley

LEBANON: The Reluctant Sanctuary

At MIDMORNING on January 6, 1978, President Elias Sarkis of Lebanon faced the assembled members of the Beirut diplomatic corps, suitably arrayed before him in tailcoats for a solemn occasion. Sarkis gave them some of the plainest talk heard from him since his election, as a compromise candidate acceptable to Syria and the major Lebanese and Palestinian factions, to the Lebanese presidency.

At his desk in his palace office at Baabda, before receiving the diplomats, Sarkis had read his morning newspapers and the latest intelligence summary signed by Colonel Jean Abdo, chief of the Deuxieme Bureau: Egyptian and Israeli military men were about to meet in Cairo to discuss peace. Within ten days, the foreign ministers of Egypt and Israel and U.S. Secretary of State Cyrus Vance would be sitting down in Jerusalem to discuss the future of the Palestinian people. In Lebanon the rightist Lebanese front leaders were discussing again the "expulsion" of the 400,000 or so Palestinians in Lebanon, and their distribution among the other Arab states or their resettlement in a Palestinian state.

"From the beginning of the Middle East crisis," Sarkis reminded his ambassadorial guests, "Lebanon has taken a frank, clear attitude calling for just peace based on protecting the just right of the Palestinian people to their land. We are following with total interest the moves taking place . . . to find a solution to this dispute. . . . The Palestinian people have not abandoned their legal rights to their land; nor have we abandoned our right to every inch of our territory or conceded any measure of our sovereignty." (Nonetheless, as he spoke, Palestinians controlling enclaves near the Israel border in south Lebanon were exchanging fire with the troops of the Lebanese front—in areas where no Lebanese soldier had ventured since the end of the civil war in November 1976).

"As for our attitude on aspects of the settlement which concern us,"

Sarkis went on, leaning forward for emphasis, "it is our own prerogative to express it. . . . Regarding reports about solutions being drawn up that involve resettling the Palestinian people or leaving them where they are, we affirm that any solution which does not consider the Palestinian problem as the crux of the Middle East crisis will not be a sound solution."

"At any rate, Lebanon will not accept any kind of settlement providing for the Palestinians to remain on its territory, because it is aware that this would encroach upon the very core of its interests, would be beyond Lebanon's ability and would harm the Palestinian issue itself. . . . The peace which we desire in this region will be based only on justice, and it will be an injustice to solve the Palestinian problem on the basis of creating a new problem for Lebanon and its people."[1]

Only a day later, at a rally in Beirut attended by Palestine Liberation Organization (PLO) chairman Yasir Arafat and his principle deputy, Salah Khalaf (Abu Iyad) of al-Fatah, Khalaf gave the PLO's view: "Referring to the reported plans of repatriation of the Palestinians in southern Lebanon, the Palestine revolution rejects all forms of repatriation because it accepts no substitute for Palestine."[2] In short, neither the chief of what remained of the Lebanese state, nor the leaders of the PLO, were prepared to discuss either making the Palestinians' presence in Lebanon a permanent one, or moving them to places other than their own home country, that is, a Palestinian state created by a peace agreement.

For Lebanon there had been nothing new or strange about the influx of Palestinian Arabs fleeing their homes and lands to the south. From 1948 on Lebanon, after all, had been a country of asylum, a hospitable haven for the oppressed of all its neighboring lands, during the time of the Crusades, as during the long centuries of Ottoman Turkish occupation that followed. After the 1894–95 massacres of Armenians in Turkey, a first wave of Armenians arrived, and more came in 1915. Since U.S. President Woodrow Wilson's concern for human rights had led him to encourage promises, never kept, of "national homes" for Kurds as well as Armenians, new waves of both those peoples had found homes in Lebanon.

However, Lebanon had seen nothing in modern history on the scale of the arrival of the Palestinians after 1948, and the even larger numbers of Syrians who began to arrive in the 1960s. By January 1, 1970, when the stage was nearly set for the Jordan civil war and the new migration of the defeated Palestinians fleeing the Hashemite armies, Palestinians and Syrians represented more than three-fourths of the entire foreign population in Lebanon. This population represented, in turn, about 23.5 percent of the total resident population, or 564,051 persons.[3]

President Sarkis' remarks in January 1978 carried weight. One of the bloodiest civil wars in history had been fought, from April 1975 to November 1976, partly over the fate and future of the Palestinians in Lebanon. The country and its economy had been laid waste, some 50,000 of its people had been killed, and hundreds of thousands of others, Lebanese, Palestinians, and brother Arabs, had been wounded. The regional role of Lebanon as an arena of freedom for the different Palestinian groups and for all of their activities, from terrorism to works of scholarship and charity, had given way to Syrian tutelage. As before the war, the fate and future of the Palestinians in Lebanon still lay very much in doubt. With this doubt there was also the danger of a new and much deadlier regional war (if the peace efforts which began with President Sadat's November 1977 visit to Jerusalem failed), in which Lebanon would likely be the first and most decisive battlefield. A foretaste of that possible war came with the Israeli invasion of southern Lebanon in March of 1978.

The Coming of the Resistance

On an early morning in 1952, the two Lebanese gendarmes at the border post between Kafer Kelaa, Lebanon, and Metulla, Israel, yawned as they sipped their tea. A young Palestinian had just slipped across the border in a nearby field in the company of two smugglers, who had acted as guides. The Palestinian came from Jaffa, where he had lost his home, his family, and all that he owned, except his hopes for the future. (Later, after completing his education in Beirut, and at a university in the United States, he became a highly respected member of the American academic community. But that is another story, and there are scores of others like it.)

The Lebanese gendarmes purposely looked the other way. One reason was that they were getting a cut of the smugglers' take from their crossing, as was the custom. Another was that there was a conscious policy on the part of the Lebanese authorities, just then, to look the other way and admit illegal Palestinian refugees, even though, by that day in November 1952, fully 100,642[4] had fled into Lebanon and were eking out an existence there, one way or another.

By 1970 Palestinian sources estimated that 240,000 people of Palestinian origin were living in Lebanon, though many of these had managed to acquire nationalities and passports of other Arab countries, mainly Lebanon, Syria, and Jordan, since their arrival. In that same year, the Palestine Research Center estimated the number of Palestinians living in refugee camps, including those drawing rations and other benefits, including schooling, from the United Nations Relief and Works Agency for Palestine Refugees (UNRWA) at 130,500 persons. The Lebanese Interior Ministry found in the same year that there were 150,915 Palestinians, whereas the Central Directorate of Statistics put the number outside the refugee camps at 43,000.[5]

From these differing but parallel figures, it seems fair to conclude that Lebanon's Palestinians numbered about 200,000 before the civil war of 1975, or between 7 and 8 percent of the whole population. (UNRWA listed 201,171 refugees registered in Lebanon in 1977.) The proportion outside the camps, something less than 90,000, included students and professional men and women (especially lawyers, physicians, teachers and university professors, artisans, and technically skilled tradespeople such as garage and shop-owners) who had managed to acquire an Arab nationality. They were, therefore, not wholly deprived of political, economic, and civil rights as were the stateless refugees, who usually possessed only the identity cards carried by stateless persons in its special variant for Palestinian refugees, issued by the United Nations. Those Palestinians outside the camps, especially the elite at the upper end of the educational and social ladder, were among the firmest supporters, and in many cases the leaders, ideologues, or financiers of the Palestinian guerrilla movement.

However, it was from the camp population that the guerrilla movement drew the main body of its volunteers. It was often in the various camps where these volunteers were trained for guerrilla missions inside Israel and the occupied territories. In the case of the Popular Front for the Liberation of Palestine (PFLP) this included training for transnational or international terrorist missions abroad, such as airplane skyjackings or sabotage. Often there was cooperation with other international terrorist groups such as the Japanese Red Army, the Latin American Tupomaros and Monteneros, the Irish Republican Army (IRA), and many others.

Since most of the Palestinians entering Lebanon came from northern Palestine before 1948, or northern Israel after that, the closeness of the frontiers was important in determining the patterns of their movements and settlement. Most of the 1948 refugees were temporarily settled in transit camps built in southern Lebanon by the French mandate authorities in 1935 to care for refugees from Turkey and Armenia, many of them Kurds. Only in 1950 did the Lebanese government begin to transfer the Palestinians to camps scattered throughout Lebanon.

In 1968 when the guerrilla movement began to establish itself and to conduct operations from Lebanon, the main camps and their populations were as follows.[6]

1. Mar Elias. A small camp inside the Beirut city limits, Mar Elias housed mainly Christian Palestinians who arrived from Haifa and Jaffa by sea during the last months of the Palestine mandate and the first months of Israel's existence in 1948. The original ninety families were settled in the Greek Orthodox monastery of Mar Elias (St. Elie). In 1952 the Greek Orthodox partriarchate converted the monastery into a school. The refugees were moved to a camp in the nearby woods. It contained 889 people in 1968, according to UNRWA, but by 1977 only 430 remained. Another 26,893 UNRWA-registered Palestinians lived in West Beirut.

2. Chatila. This camp is located in Beirut's western suburbs, adjoining the thickly populated Sabra district of Beirut (which became a stronghold of the Palestinians and their mostly poor Muslim Lebanese allies) and fronting in one place on the main road to Beirut airport. Most came from Palestinian border villages and from Jaffa. They were first settled in transit camps in the Lebanese villages of Jiyeh and Berjeh, then transferred to the wood of umbrella pines known as Chatila. The 1968 population of 4,892 had approximately tripled in size by the outbreak of the fighting in 1975. Chatila became the headquarters base of the PFLP, though other organizations including the Syrian-based al-Sa'iqa and the Iraqi Arab Liberation Front used it at times, creating often explosive situations and conflicts inside the camp. On several occasions it was attacked by Israeli aircraft.

3. Bourj al-Barajneh. Most of the people in this sprawling collection of huts, shacks, tents, and permanent buildings spread out over a wide area flanking the main road to Beirut airport, came from the village of Tarshiha, later renamed Maalot by the Israeli settlers, in northern Palestine. In 1968 they numbered 7,189, but this had increased to nearly 20,000 by the outbreak of the civil war in 1975. UNRWA-registered refugees in 1977 totaled 8,384. Bourj al-Barajneh has been involved in all of the major confrontations between the guerrillas and the Lebanese (later the Syrian) armies. It was shelled by Lebanese forces in 1969. During the heavy fighting of May 1973, Lebanese airforce jets strafed the camp to silence rocket and artillery fire directed from it onto Beirut airport. The camp's strategic position, astride the main approach to the airport, and

its heavy defenses have also made it a target of a few Israeli air attacks.

4. Tel al-Za'atar (Karameh). This was to become the beleaguered stronghold of the Palestinians during the 1975–76 fighting, blockaded, besieged and finally conquered by the Lebanese rightist forces which surrounded it in August 1976. Originally, its population, located in the area of the Tabet Forest and the industrial villages of Dekwaneh and Makaless, east of Beirut proper, came from northern Palestine and most were peasants. There were also Bedouin from the Lake Tiberias region, adjoining Syria. Their number, 7,403 in 1968, had swelled to between 15,000 and 20,000 by the outbreak of fighting in 1975. The camp and its adjoining neighborhoods were fortified by a system of underground bunkers, casemates, and entrenchments. In the eyes of the Lebanese rightist Christian forces, it was "the headquarters of international Communist subversion in Lebanon," as Camille Chamoun once described it to the author. After its fall and the massacre of many of the camp's survivors in August 1976, the area was cleared by the rightist Lebanese forces, and many of the Lebanese who had to leave its surroundings returned to their homes. The Palestinian survivors of the camp were dispersed among other camps and towns of southern Lebanon, including a new emergency camp, Bayssarieh, established about halfway between Sidon and Tyre, just inland from the main coastal road.

5. Jisr al-Basha. Located on high ground east of Beirut, partly overlooking Tel al-Za'atar, this camp was captured by the rightists before the fall of Tel al-Za'atar. They used it for command posts and artillery positions during the bombardments and final assault on Tel al-Za'atar. Most of the original camp dwellers were Christian Palestinians from Haifa, Jaffa, and Akka (St. Jean d'Acre), and in 1968 they numbered 1,236. This number had more than doubled by the time the inhabitants were killed, made prisoners, or dispersed by the Lebanese rightist forces in 1976.

6. Dbayeh. Refugees here came mainly from the Christian village of Banneh, northern Palestine. The camp is northeast of Beirut, on the road to Jounieh, and its inhabitants numbered 2,448 in 1968. They were joined by economically better off Lebanese Christians of the Greek Orthodox faith, who often sympathized with the Palestinians, and built substantial houses and villas. There was a considerable settlement of these people, including the prominent Lebanese banking family of Michel Saab, living here when the rightists attacked and overran the camp in January 1976. Some of the inhabitants were allowed to remain, under rightist military control. The guerrilla organizations had only a token presence in this camp, which had never been attacked by Israeli forces.

7. Nahr al-Bard (Cold River). Inhabitants of this camp originally

came from northern Palestinian villages, and most were Muslim. They had set out for Syria, but Syria refused to admit them. In 1968 the camp, located about eight miles north of Tripoli on the main highway to Syria, numbered 10,076, and 13,197 in 1977, according to UNRWA figures, which listed 4,863 other Palestinians not in camps in Tripoli in 1977. The camp became a major headquarters of the guerrilla organizations, especially the PFLP, the Popular Democratic Front (PDF), and al-Fatah. It was raided by Israeli aircraft on several occasions and was the target in February 1973, of combined Israeli sea and airborne operations resulting in many casualties. Guerrillas of nationalities other than Palestinian, including Turks, were captured by Israeli forces here and taken back to Israel, where some stood trial and were imprisoned.

8. Beddawi. Located just outside the northern city limits of Tripoli on the main highway to Nahr al-Bard and Syria, this camp originally housed people from northern Palestine, mainly Muslims. They settled initially in the city of Tripoli itself, but in 1955 floods destroyed their shelters. They numbered 5,445 in 1968, and 7,203 in 1977. They, too, were the targets of destructive Israeli air attacks. Militia of the various guerrilla organizations were present in the camp, and like Nahr al-Bard they engaged in some fighting with Syrian army regulars and al-Sa'iqa. They also became involved in fighting between pro-Syrian and pro-Iraqi forces in 1976.

9. Ain al-Helweh. This was the principal and largest camp in Lebanon, located on the southeast edge of the city of Sidon. Its people were mainly Muslims from northern Palestine. Many permanent structures were built in the camp, which had the full range of UNRWA services until that organization began heavy budget cuts just after the Lebanese civil war. Its population, 17,029 in 1968, grew to possibly 25,000 by the outbreak of the civil war in 1975 and temporarily doubled during the March 1978 Israeli invasion, after being listed by UNRWA in 1977 as 21,788. The camp dwellers and the armed guerrilla movements, especially al-Fatah, the PFLP, and the PLO's military police, the Palestine Armed Struggle Command (PASC), intervened in the affairs of Sidon and fought against both Israeli and Syrian attacks (after the Syrian intervention in Lebanon in the spring of 1976). Because Ain al-Helweh is located near the major Lebanese army barracks and headquarters for the southern region, there was often friction and fighting with the Lebanese army during times of tension, as in 1969, 1973 and, finally, in February 1975, when the killing of the popular Muslim parliamentary deputy of Sidon, Ma'arouf Sa'ad, helped to ignite civil war. Some 19,260 Palestinians lived in Sidon province outside the camps in 1977, according to UNRWA.

10. Mieh-Mieh. This is one of the oldest camps, located three miles east of Sidon. The inhabitants came in 1948 mostly from Haifa, Jaffa, and the northern Palestinian villages of Tireh and Mayrun. They were mixed Christian and Muslim and numbered 1,871 in 1968, and 2,085 in 1977, according to UNRWA. Mieh-Mieh, attacked several times by Israeli aircraft, never became a large camp. There was only a small guerrilla presence.

11. El-Buss. This was one of the original transit camps, built in 1935–36 by the French authorities for Armenian refugees at the northern entrance of Tyre. The Palestinians who entered in 1948 and 1949 came from Haifa and Akka (St. Jean d'Acre) and were mainly Christians. It numbered 3,911 people in 1968, and UNRWA counted 4,643 in 1977. There was a considerable guerrilla presence during the civil war and afterwards, and the camp suffered much damage and many casualties from Israeli air and sea attacks, especially in the fighting of March and April 1978.

12. Bourj al-Shemali. Just two miles east of the Tyre seafront, this camp became part of the defense system associated with Rashidiyeh, the principal guerrilla stronghold facing the Israeli border, about thirteen miles away. Its inhabitants, 7,159 in 1968, but perhaps three times that many in 1978 (though UNRWA listed only 9,368 in 1977), came from northern Palestinian villages and originally migrated to the mainly Armenian village of Anjar, near the Syrian border in the Bekaa Valley, and in southern Lebanese border villages until moved to Bourj al-Shemali in 1955. Like its larger neighbor Rashidiyeh, it has been repeatedly bombed, strafed, and shelled by the Israelis and is consequently one of the camps where the presence of all the guerrilla organizations has been heaviest. Israeli troops stopped short of capturing it in their 1978 drive.

13. Rashidiyeh. This transit camp was built by the French in 1936 and enlarged by UNRWA in the 1950s to accommodate refugees then living in Camp Gourand, near Baalbeck in the northern Bekaa. Its people came from northern Palestine and include a large cross-section of the former Arab population there. Israeli reports often described it as the main bastion of the guerrillas in the south of Lebanon, but the size and strength of its defenses have often been exaggerated. It has been bombed, strafed, and shelled by Israeli naval units and land-based artillery time and time again. The author witnessed the aftermath of a heavy Israeli air raid on this and the nearby Lebanese village of Azziye November 9, 1977, and the use of U.S.-supplied cluster bombs in March 1978. President Sadat of Egypt later said the November 1977 bombing led him to believe the Israelis were preparing a major offensive, and so helped influ-

ence him to visit Jerusalem on November 19–21, 1977, and begin his peace offensive. The camp has better-than-average housing and good UNRWA primary and secondary school facilities. UNRWA's figure for the permanent camp population in 1977 was 13,165.

14. Nabatiyeh. There are several camps, close together, spread over hillsides and plateaus near the big market town of Nabatiyeh, a Lebanese center of mainly Shi'a Muslims and of Palestinians who live integrated with them. Their original people came from the Lake Tiberias region.

Israeli reports often alleged they were bases for guerrilla operations on the border, about nine miles away. The camps have been three times almost totally destroyed by Israeli planes and artillery, the last in March 1978. Each time, UNRWA and private charities and relief agencies, as well as the welfare services of the PLO and al-Fatah, have rebuilt the school, the clinic, and many of the houses and shelters. The population in 1968 was 3,937 people (3,538 in 1977), many, if not most, of whom were dispersed and partially replaced by others following the various Israeli attacks and by the warfare between Palestinians and the Lebanese rightist forces which developed in south Lebanon after the civil war ended elsewhere in November 1976. This was also on the "red line" drawn by the Israeli army command in warnings, transmitted through the United States to Syrian and other Arab peace-keeping forces in Lebanon, not to penetrate any closer to the Israeli border.

15. Wavell. Refugees in this camp came from northern Palestine in 1948. It is located near the entrance of the city of Baalbeck, in the northern Bekaa Valley, within sight of some of Baalbeck's ancient temples and ruins. Its inhabitants numbered 3,937 people in 1968, and were increased by another 1,000 or so by 1975, then fell to 3,875 in 1977, according to UNRWA. The PFLP and other guerrilla groups trained here. Israeli planes hit it several times, and the inhabitants offered some resistance to the Syrian occupation of the Bekaa Valley in the summer of 1976. Outside the Wavell camp some 4,159 Palestinians were registered by UNRWA in the Bekaa Valley in 1977.

THE CAIRO AGREEMENT

Serious confrontation between Lebanese and Palestinians began on August 28, 1969, when fighting erupted in the Nahr al-Bard camp. A declaration of concern about Lebanon's stability was made by U.S. Under Secretary of State Joseph Sisco on October 12, 1969. Heavy fighting broke out between guerrillas and the Lebanese army in southern Lebanon, spreading to most of the refugee camps and to the Bekaa on October 18, after some 120 guerrillas, according to the government figure, had tried to establish a base at Majdel Salim, a southern village, and were challenged by the army. Syria indirectly intervened in the fighting on October 23. This day saw the first major involvement of al-Sa'iqa, the guerrilla organization commanded by Zuheir Mohsin and directly under the control of the military wing of the Ba'ath party in Damascus. Al-Sa'iqa groups attacked several Lebanese army positions at border posts, including the main one at Masnaa. Guerrillas attacked and occupied police posts in Muslim districts of Beirut. Even heavier fighting occurred in Tripoli, where Muslim political organizations made common cause with the guerrillas. On October 25, 1969, the Lebanese government formally requested the mediation of President Nasser, through Nasser's powerful ambassador in Beirut. After mediation by Yusuf Sayegh, Palestinian professor of economics at the American University of Beirut, Yasir Arafat, by now the undisputed head of al-Fatah and chairman of the PLO, met with General Emile Bustany, the Lebanese army commander-in-chief in Cairo on November 2, 1969. On the next day, a joint communique of the PLO and the Lebanese government announced conclusions of a "secret" accord known at first as the "Cairo Agreements."

More honored in the breach than in the observance, the Cairo Agreements, or Agreement as it later came to be called, were published in various newspapers and periodicals, though no serving Lebanese government ever acknowledged that the published texts were authentic. In essence, the Palestinian resistance movement was granted the right of security and administrative control inside the refugee camps in Lebanon. The Palestinians in Lebanon were authorized to "participate in the Palestinian revolution through armed struggle." Commando movements were permitted passage, in certain designated border areas and through certain designated corridors, for operations into Israel. The western half of the frontier, within artillery and rocket range of Israel's northern Galilee heartland towns like Nahariyeh and Safed, was supposed to be immune, as was the coastal highway that crossed the Israel border at Ras al-Nakoura, and which was used by United Nations truce observers, clergymen, and the few other travellers permitted to cross the border legally. In effect, the Cairo Agreement legitimized the armed Palestinian presence in Lebanon. It tried to reconcile and regulate this presence with Lebanese sovereignty, an exercise which turned out to resemble an attempt to square the circle. There was supposed to be coordination between Lebanese and Palestinian authorities (exercised through the PLO's PASC). The resistance movement was supposed to accept the ultimate sovereignty of the Lebanese state.[7]

Signing of the Cairo Agreement was followed by Karameh's successful formation of a new cabinet on November 25, 1969, giving the new interior minister, none other than Kamal Jumblatt, one of the chief Lebanese sympathizers of the guerrillas, the mission of regulating government-resistance relations. By February 1970, Jumblatt had reached an understanding with the guerrillas to "freeze" their operations across the Israeli border, to stay at least one kilometer from south Lebanese villages, and to halt military training in the refugee camps. Palestinian-Lebanese coordinating committees were formed to implement these understandings and the Cairo Agreement itself. On May 20, 1970, the Lebanese government formally amended the agreement by new regulations prohibiting the firing of rockets from Lebanese territory, laying minefields along the 1949 armistice line with Israel (which Israel and Lebanon both considered their international frontier), and bearing arms in towns and villages. The main Palestinian groups, al-Fatah and al-Sa'iqa, accepted, though the Popular Front for the Liberation of Palestine, a radical group led by Dr. George Habbash, which was then preparing to precipitate civil war with the Jordan royal army and was already preparing for collaboration with international terrorist groups, did not.[8]

From the Rent-A-Car Raid to the Yom Kippur War

On April 10, 1973, Israeli intervention in Lebanon again set the Lebanese-Palestinian conflict ablaze. Landing by night on a Beirut beach, an Israeli assassination unit kept a rendezvous with seven Israeli secret agents who arrived with European passports, passing themselves off as tourists, and rented cars (from a car rental agency near the author's apartment) in which they transported the Israeli hit team to their objectives in four Beirut neighborhoods. Their most spectacular deed was the murder, in their own apartments, of three al-Fatah leaders, PLO spokesman Kamal Nasser, Abu Yussouf, and Kamal Radwan, the latter two with high operational responsibilities in al-Fatah. Several innocent bystanders and two Lebanese military policemen were killed or wounded. An office building of the PDF was attacked and partially demolished by explosives.

Prime Minister Saeb Salem resigned, blaming the army commander-in-chief, Maronite General Iskander Ghanem, for the failure of the army to defend Beirut, and demanded General Ghanem's dismissal. Funerals of the victims and kidnappings of army personnel, mainly by the PFLP, exploded into major violence and a state of emergency was declared. On May 3, as fighting spread to the camps near Beirut, the Lebanese air force intervened to silence artillery and rocket fire from Bourj al-Barajneh camp, which had closed the airport. In a radio message President Frangieh said he would not allow a "Black May" in Lebanon like the "Black September," but he would also not allow the Palestinians to act as an "occupying army."[9]

On May 17 a new Lebanese-Palestinian agreement, known as the Melkart Protocols (concluded at Beirut's Hotel Melkart) was signed by Lebanese and PLO officers. Contrary to Lebanese newspaper reports at the time, it did not alter the content of the Cairo Agreement but only reinforced it. PDF Secretary-General Nayyaf Hawatmeh said, "The aim of the resistance movement is not to conclude new agreements, but to implement the one concluded in Cairo in 1969."[10] The Palestinian figures for casualties in the month of fighting that followed the Israeli assault were 108 dead, 234 wounded, and 1,160 houses either destroyed or damaged by shelling and bomb explosions.[11] A realization spread through Lebanon that this had been truly a prelude to civil war, and that worse was probably to come.

The outbreak of the new Arab-Israel war in October 1973, temporarily eased the situation in Lebanon. Guerrilla units in the south took part in the shelling of some Israeli settlements. Palestine Liberation Army (PLA) military units and some other guerrilla units supported the Syrian army in the fighting in the Golan Heights. The Lebanese authorities welcomed statements by the resistance movement of its intentions to establish a Palestinian state in the West Bank and Gaza, statements which heralded the eventual end of a Palestinian presence in Lebanon. On October 30, 1973, a week after the end of the war, the guerrillas again suspended operations against Israel on the southern border.

PRELUDE TO CIVIL WAR

Although the next period was a relatively calm one for Palestinian-Lebanese relations, there were nevertheless many signals of the coming storm. The Muslim Lebanese sympathizers of the Palestinians protested the efforts of the rightists, especially the Phalange and Camille Chamoun's National Liberal Party (NLP), to accelerate the military training of their party militias. On September 17, 1973, Pierre Gemayel, the Phalange leader, claimed the absolute right of his party to continue its training and mobilization program and Nasri Maalouf, the minister of defense, endorsed this right. On September 18 two ministers who were friends of Kamal Jumblatt resigned, according to Jumblatt in protest against the failure of Premier Takieddine Solh to prohibit arms imports by the Phalangists and the Chamounists. Solh himself resigned September 25.

A plus factor for Lebanese-Palestinian relations, though a transitory one, was the Rabat Arab summit conference of October 1974, which recognized the PLO as "sole legitimate representative of the Palestinian people" and appointed President Frangieh (of all people) to plead the Palestinian cause on November 14, 1974, before the United Nations General Assembly session in New York, which was also addressed by Yasir Arafat in his famous "gun and olive branch" speech.

During 1974 there was a strong tendency by Arafat's PLO leadership, al-Fatah, to curb cross-border activity. This neither prevented "wildcat" actions by the groups of Habbash, Hawatmeh, or Jabril, nor did it inhibit Israeli reprisal action, as on May 16, 1974, when the Israelis bombed villages and two refugee camps in south Lebanon following the PDF attack on an Israeli school at Maalot, northern Galilee, the previous day.

Relations between the guerrillas and the Lebanese government began to deteriorate again in January 1975. The Israelis carried out a number of destructive "preventive attacks" against Lebanese and Palestinian targets in the south, and on January 20 Lebanon called for a meeting of the Arab Defense Council to seek pan-Arab aid. Four days later Pierre Gemayel sounded a portent of things to come by a note to President Frangieh criticizing Lebanon's attitude of compromise toward the Palestinian military activity, and on February 20 he called for a referendum on this, claiming that 60 percent of the Lebanese population, at least, backed his party's demands for firmer Lebanese government control.

THE STORM BREAKS

Camille Chamoun fully supported Gemayel's campaign for restraints on the resistance movement. In February 1975, Chamoun's dabbling in business produced an explosive mixture which acted as one of the detonators of the civil war. He was the moving spirit in forming the "Protein Company," a fishing concession which would modernize deep-sea fishing off Lebanon and, the poor Muslim fishermen of Sidon and Tyre feared, put most of the fishermen out of work. During a mass demonstration on February 26 against the government's granting of a license to the company, Ma'arouf Sa'ad, a popular former Sunni Muslim parliamentary deputy of Sidon, was fatally wounded by a bullet thought to have been fired by a Lebanese soldier. Clashes erupted in Sidon March 1 in which five soldiers and eleven civilians were killed, and a Lebanese-Palestinian committee was organized to try to calm the situation in Sidon, in which the Ain al-Helweh refugee camp was heavily involved.

The stage was now set for the final and crucial explosion: a Lebanese-Palestinian one.

On Sunday, April 13, 1975, a bus carrying Palestinians and Lebanese from Chatila and Sabra back to the Tel al-Za'atar camp, after a ceremony commemorating guerrillas killed in a raid inside Israel, passed through Ain al-Rammaneh, a Christian neighborhood closely adjoining the Muslim one of ash-Shiyah. Pierre Gemayel was taking part in the benediction of a new Maronite church in Ain al-Rammaneh, and the bus ran into heavy fire. There were other, simultaneous Phalange-Palestinian incidents elsewhere. Each side accused the other of provocation and of firing the first shot. Sunni Muslim Premier Rashid Solh, when he resigned a month later, declared: "It is clear that the Phalangist party is entirely responsible for the massacre perpetrated April 13 and the consequences it engendered."[12] In any case, twenty-seven of the bus passengers, eighteen of whom belonged to the Iraqi-based Arab Liberation Front, were killed and nineteen others wounded. Word of the shooting spread. Throughout Beirut the political parties and Palestinians mobilized their militias and took up positions. At a meeting of leftist leaders, as fighting spread to many districts, Kamal Jumblatt called for expulsion of the Phalangist cabinet members, dissolution of the Phalange party, and "punishment of those responsible for the butchery." These demands were echoed by a special meeting of the PLO executive committee under Arafat, which blamed a "plot against the resistance" by "foreign powers."

Fighting spread to the areas soon to become the "traditional fronts" of the civil war in Beirut: Dekwaneh, Tel al-Za'atar, Ain al Rammanah-Shi'ah, and Hret Harayk, adjoining the Bourj al-Bourajneh camp on the approaches to the airport. Despite mediation efforts by Arab League Secretary-General Mahmoud Riyadh, who arrived in Beirut April 14, and a Phalangist agreement to surrender for trial by the authorities two of its militants involved in the April 13 shooting, both sides began using artillery and heavy weapons. By April 16 Premier Solh announced the first of a series of hundreds of "cease-fires" and this first, purely Palestinian-Lebanese round of the war slowly subsided, leaving, according to the Lebanese newspapers, about 300 dead, many hundreds wounded, and 1,500 houses, commercial establishments, and factories either destroyed or damaged. The Chamber of Commerce and Industry estimated May 5 that economic losses already totaled about 500 million Lebanese pounds (between $100 and $200 million).

This first phase of the conflict ended with the shortlived military government formed, on President Frangieh's orders, by retired Brigadier General Noureddine Rifai on May 23, 1975. It collapsed and resigned three days later under protests from the leftists, Muslim religious and political leaders, and numerous Christian ones, especially Raymond Edde, who demanded immediate creation of a new government under Rashid Karameh. Syrian Foreign Minister Abdel Halim Khaddam arrived on May 25 amid a general strike and new violence throughout most of the country. Karameh formed a new government on May 28, but without the collaboration of the leftists and Muslims who refused to sit in a cabinet with Phalangist ministers.

In June, after a series of nasty kidnappings, incidents of torture, and reprisals involving some Palestinians, but this time more of a Lebanese intercommunal character, fighting again broke out on a large scale, and heavy artillery was used against many sections of the city and the Palestinian refugee camps outside it. After repeated new political intervention by the Syrians, and amid strong efforts by Arafat to keep the PLO out of the fighting except when called upon to defend Palestinian camps and positions, Karameh succeeded in forming a cabinet of "national salvation" of six members, including the main fighting factions. On July 6 a secret organization calling itself the Revolutionary Socialist Action Organization claimed responsibility for the kidnapping of U.S. Army Colonel Ernest Morgan and demanded distribution of food and building material to the beleaguered slum quarter of Karantina, under siege by the rightists, as ransom for his release. The demands were met and Morgan was released, with the PLO and the guerrilla organizations decrying the crime and disassociating themselves from it.

During this period Arafat and the PLO leadership repeatedly pledged they would respect Lebanese sovereignty under the Cairo Agreement and would not get involved in Lebanese affairs or support one faction against another. At the same time, al Fatah and al-Sa'iqa did get involved to the extent that they armed some Muslim and leftist groups and helped defend certain Muslim districts such as Karantina and Nabaa in east Beirut. They also gave some tactical support, mainly with rocket-firing units, to assaults against Phalangist and Chamounist positions, without committing the main body of the guerrillas, that is, al-Fatah's "strategic reserve" of perhaps 12,000 well-armed and well-trained men.[13] At the same time, the Arafat mainstream leadership, using the machinery of conciliation set up by the Melkart Protocols, acted as a mediator, helping to arrange cease-fires and agreeing to help police them with PASC and al-Fatah troops.

More active militarily were the "rejection front" groups, including the PLFP, the PDF, Jabril's PFLP-General Command, and the Arab Liberation Front, which at this stage, in 1975, was cooperating with al-Sa'iqa, the Syrian guerrilla organization whose strength on the ground was second only to that of al-Fatah. The rejectionists' political doctrine opposed Egyptian President Sadat's cooperation with the United States and his two disengagement agreements with Israel which had followed the October 1973 war, Sinai I in January 1974, and Sinai II in September 1975, both of which Libya, Iraq, and Syria also strongly opposed. Support in arms and money to the "rejectionist" organizations by these Arab governments lent a strong dimension of external interference to the Lebanese-Palestinian aspect of the civil war.

The "rejectionist" groups, especially the Arab Liberation Front, made common cause with such Lebanese leftist organizations as the one in Tripoli headed by Farouk Mokkadem, a picturesque figure who had strong ties with the Algerian leadership and many of the "political men" of the Palestinian movement in Lebanon. There was also involvement by both al-Fatah and rejectionists in the first battles for control of the city center and hotel district of Beirut in September and October 1975. The author personally saw al-Sa'iqa and al-Fatah weapons-carriers and rocket-launchers being brought in, together with some elite snipers, to assist in repelling the Phalangist attack toward the western city in late October, and also to participate in the assault on the Holiday Inn, Phoenicia, and St. George hotels, then held by the Phalangists.

On October 12, 1975, the PLO took a new step toward political involvement in the war when it joined the Lebanese leftist groups and the Syrian government in denouncing the idea (following a cease-fire meeting between Arafat and Chamoun October 11) of Lebanese army intervention. The Arab League, on Kuwaiti initiative, had tentatively decided to "Arabize" the crisis. It was strongly hinted that this meant Syrian intervention on the side of the Left. Israeli Prime Minister Yitzhak Rabin warned October 12 that "Israel's defence would be jeopardized if the Syrian army intervenes in Lebanon."[14]

A new stage of the war, with the active and open involvement of most of the Palestinian organizations, began on January 4, 1976, when the Phalangist, Chamounist, and Cedar Guards militia began the blockade of the Tel al-Za'atar and Jisr al-Basha refugee camps in East Beirut. By this time, such events as "Black Saturday" on December 6, 1975, when over 200 Muslim hostages were taken and murdered by the Phalange in reprisals for murders of four Phalangist militiamen, and a new leftist offensive against the fortified hotels, had consummated the partition of Beirut and Lebanon as a whole into two well-defined zones: the eastern Christian and the western, "Islamo-Progressivist" or leftist sector.

It was at this point, too, that Syria began to waver in its support to the leftists, who were obviously gaining ground and strength. Motivated by the fear that the leftists might succeed in the more extremist and revolutionary goals of groups like the PFLP, and establish some kind of a people's republic—which in alliance with the PLO could take the initiative of war or peace with Israel out of the hands of a Syria ill-prepared to fight another war with Israel—President Hafez al-Assad began to cut down Syrian pressure on behalf of the Left and to swing the balance in the other direction. The first visible sign of this was refusal by al-Sa'iqa to take part in the general leftist assault (though al-Fatah did so) on the hotel and downtown districts of Beirut in December 1975.

Another prelude to the rightist blockade of the Palestinian camps was a violent diatribe by President Frangieh on December 16, 1975, against the Palestinian movement, accusing it of violating all its agreements with Lebanon and implying that it bore a heavy responsibility for the civil war.[15] By this time, some Palestinian spokesmen were joining Lebanese Muslim and leftist leaders in demanding the resignation of President Frangieh before completion of his normal term of office in September 1976. Fighting now spread into the Bekaa Valley and to many other parts of Lebanon, with the Palestinians in their camps often being caught up in it, generally in self-defense, but sometimes in offensive moves with their leftist allies.

The start of the blockade of Tel al-Za'atar in January 1976—the camp area was totally surrounded by the rightist forces which stopped food and fuel supplies—was accompanied by a new political move to escalate the Palestinian-Lebanese conflict. After a meeting of the Maronite military chiefs on January 3, Pierre Gemayel denounced the Cairo Agreement as "the root of all the catastrophes which have overtaken Lebanon."

On January 6 the PLO decided to take no further part in meetings of a co-ordination committee which was supposed to supervise the various and ephemeral "cease-fires." On the same day, Syrian Foreign Minister Abdel Halim Khaddam, fearing partition might be the goal of the Christian Right as well as of some of the revolutionary Left, issued a solemn warning that "Syria will not tolerate the partitioning of Lebanon" and would absorb Lebanon at the first serious attempt at partition.[16] In efforts to raise the siege of Tel al-Za'atar, the Left began its most violent offensive of the war, as the Phalangist daily newspaper, al-Amal, warned January 9, "The fighting which is currently raging . . . marks the beginning of the war for liberating all of Lebanon" from the Palestinians and their allies. "If our generation does not achieve victory," al-Amal added, "those which follow shall surely vanquish, and partition—if ever it must come to pass—will be nothing more than the provisional difference between Free and Occupied Lebanon."

On January 12 the rightists surrounded the small Palestinian camp of Dbayeh, north of Beirut. In a diversionary offensive, the leftists, especially the Lebanese Communist party militia and the forces of Kamal Jumblatt, encircled Damour, one of the main fiefdoms of Camille Chamoun's NLP, and threatened to conquer the entire mountainous Shouf region. This is part of the historical entity of Mount Lebanon which, though its population included Druze as well as Christians, is claimed by the Christian advocates of partition. Dbayeh fell the next day, and the Palestinian command, accusing the army of making its capture easier for the rightists, decided to throw forces onto the leftist side in the sieges of Zagharta, Suleiman Frangieh's birthplace in the mountains near Tripoli, and the Christian town of Zahle, in the Bekaa, and to continue to press the attack on Damour. The war's first attack by two planes of the Lebanese air force, on January 16, 1976, was intended to relieve a military convoy near Beirut on its way to help the defenders of Damour. However, it provoked a merciless new drive by the leftist Palestinian forces in the south and the overrunning of Karantina and the massacre of many of its inhabitants by the rightists, who burned and razed the slum with bulldozers on January 19. Damour and Jiyeh fell to the leftist-Palestinian coalition and were occupied, looted, and destroyed with the leftists pressing on toward Saadiyet, Camille Chamoun's seaside home and stronghold.

Chamoun accused the Syrian army of invading Lebanon and called for United Nations intervention. What had happened was that the Palestine Liberation Army (PLA), officered by both Syrians and Palestinians and normally under PLO control but actually under Syrian army command, had sent 2,000 troops across the border into the Bekaa. Israel, apparently reassured by the United States, which was closely in touch with both sides, did not threaten intervention, explaining in a government statement that it had "sufficient proof that Syria would not intervene directly in the Lebanese conflict."[17] Syrian political intervention then took the form of formation of a new Syrian-Lebanese-Palestinian Higher Military Committee, supposed to work out and enforce a general cease-fire and "return to normal." Chamoun's residence at Saadiyet was looted and burned, and the leftists were in complete control of the strategic coastal highway to the Israeli border.

Through Syrian mediation, President Frangieh was able to announce on February 14 a new Lebanese "constitutional declaration" designed to end the civil war, to increase Muslim political rights, and to affect other reforms but preserve the country's confessional system in government. A further agreement was supposed to confirm the Cairo and Melkart documents concerning the Palestinians. All of these documents were virtually forgotten within a matter of days, as fighting flared on all fronts. A sign of things to come was the position of al-Sa'iqa, the only group to announce its unreserved support of what was, after all, an attempt at a "Syrian solution."

The next step in the civil war was the disintegration of the Lebanese army. Lieutenant Ahmed Khatib, a Sunni Muslim from the Shouf region, announced in January that several units had rallied to the standard of "The Lebanese Arab Army."

Garrisons, barracks, and several crucial artillery positions overlooking the Litani River valley and the Israeli border in south Lebanon followed Lt. Khatib's lead. They arrested Maronite commanders, replacing them with Muslims, and at least forty tank crews joined the mutiny with their tanks.[18] Christian units sided with the Right, as Major Ahmed Maamari, a Muslim officer from Tripoli, joined Khatib. Various other groups of officers issued manifestoes or declarations calling for reform, and Brigadier General Hanna Said, the Maronite appointed commander-in-chief by Frangieh, offered an amnesty for those rejoining the ranks. It was too late: the army was split wide open.

SYRIA INTERVENES AGAINST THE PALESTINIANS

On March 11, 1976, as the author gathered family and a few possessions together to evacuate them to Athens, armed bands of Palestinians in

West Beirut and the rightist militiamen in East Beirut had made a mock-ery of any remaining semblance of law and order. That night Brigadier General Azziz al-Ahdab, the Muslim commander of the Beirut garrison, seized Beirut's radio and television stations and demanded President Frangieh's resignation within forty-eight hours. Frangieh completely ig-nored Ahdab, and only the Palestinians in West Beirut appeared to sup-port his "television coup" wholeheartedly. It was significant that when the original coup took place, an al-Fatah military contingent accompa-nied Ahdab to the television station.[19] On March 15 Khatib's Lebanese Arab Army announced it was joining forces with Ahdab, and three days later the Palestinians joined them in new offensives in downtown Beirut, and in a new area: the Upper Metn, a Christian and Druze mountain zone north of Beirut and adjoining Kesrouan province, part of the Maronite central mountain stronghold. By March 23 an effort to appease Frangieh's foes by a cabinet decision to amend the constitution, making election of a new president possible six months before the old one's term expired, had not stopped the fighting, and Frangieh's place was under bombardment. On March 24 President Sadat called for his resignation. Instead of resigning, Frangieh fled his palace in Baabda for a new strong-hold, Zouk Mikhail, in mountains above Jounieh.

These events forced President Assad's hand. From this time on, Syria swung openly to the rightist side, opposing the leftist Palestinian offensive which might ultimately have threatened to drag Israel and the big powers openly into the war and expose Syria to new dangers.

On March 22, as he advanced up the road toward Frangieh's palace at Baabda, Major Yacoub Daher, commanding several motorized infan-try and artillery units of the leftist army, suddenly found his way blocked by well-entrenched troops and tanks of the Syrian-commanded Palestine Liberation Army. Instead of challenging their heavy firepower, Daher backed down and was content to shell Baabda from a distance of nine miles. But the handwriting was now on the wall: on March 31, the Leba-nese branch of the Syrian Ba'ath party for the first time attacked Jum-blatt, calling him a "traitor" and "mercenary." Syria then delivered a ten-day ultimatum to all parties to stop fighting, backed by a statement from King Hussein of Jordan, Syria's ally. On April 9 Syrian regular troops occupied the Masnaa and Deir al-Achayer frontier posts. While in Da-mascus on March 26, the author reported that President Assad had con-sulted with both Hussein and King Khalid of Saudi Arabia and would move new troops into Lebanon only with their approval:[20] he now had it.

In succession, Jumblatt, Arafat, and the rightist Lebanese leaders were summoned to Damascus. Before the end of April, Syrian-commanded PLA units had invested West Beirut, and a new system of joint Syrian-Lebanese-Palestinian committees was supposed to be polic-ing the cease-fires. Parliament was convoked for May 8 to elect a new president of the republic under the amended constitutional provision. On election day al-Sa'iqa had begun to fight pitched battles with the leftist-Palestinian alliance. Al-Sa'iqa and other Syrian elements escorted Sarkis, who was holed up in the Carlton Hotel near the seafront, to the Mansour Palace, near the "green line" now dividing the partitioned city, where Sarkis was elected president by sixty-six votes on the second ballot, with twenty-nine deputies absent. (Raymond Edde was the opposing candi-date of the Left.)

Heavy fighting now erupted between the Syrian and pro-Syrian forces on one side and the Palestinian, leftist Lebanese, and Iraqi or pro-Iraqi forces on the other, especially in Tripoli. On May 11 Israeli Prime Minister Rabin observed: "Syria is currently in a state of war with al-Fatah. Its forces killed last week in Lebanon more al-Fatah elements than the Israeli army has killed in two years."[21] There were many local and in-ternational mediation attempts to end the new Syrian-rightist alliance. Some were made by Libyan Prime Minister Abdel Salem Jalloud, Colo-nel Muammar al-Qaddafi's personal emissary, whose dramatic appear-ances on the Lebanese stage became a familiar feature of the war. Libya was now pumping large quantities of arms and money to the Palestinians and leftists, especially the PFLP and the independent Nasserites, or Mourabitoun (Guardians).

Though Washington, where Secretary of State Henry Kissinger had several times called the Syrian intervention "constructive," continued to minimize the new entries of Syrian troops, 4,000 more Syrian regulars and 200 tanks entered the Bekaa June 1 and engaged the Palestinian-leftist troops throughout that area, while Soviet Prime Minister Alexei Kosygin, visiting Damascus, muttered about "imperialist intervention" in Lebanon.[22] By June 4 the PLO and all the leftist groupings had formed a joint military command to resist the Syrians, while the Maronite leaders, meeting the next day, decided to support them.

The Palestinians and their allies in Lebanon now became both vic-tims of and actors in the larger Arab drama outside the borders of Leba-non. Iraq joined Libya in arming and financing its own chosen leftist groups, mainly the Arab Liberation Front (Palestinian, but controlled by the Iraqi Ba'ath party). Sometime between April and June, President Sadat of Egypt transferred a 1,000-man brigade of the PLA from Egypt to fight with al-Fatah (after earlier having given some aid and encourage-ment to the rightists). Each Arab leader felt it his duty to support the faction which was fighting against his own rivals or enemies (Iraq vs. Syria; Syria vs. Egypt; Libya vs. Egypt; the Palestinians vs. almost everyone else). As Hassan Sabry al-Kholy, the Egyptian diplomat dispatched by the Arab League as mediator and political advisor to the first contingent of Arab peace-keeping forces, put it to the author: "Lebanon became a hired stage, with the actors disregarding normal rules or morality, and completely oblivious of who had hired the stage or why."

On this stage the American CIA, the French SDECE, the British intelligence services, the Soviet KGB, Israeli intelligence (now openly helping the Christian side with arms and training), and all the Arab intelligence services became involved. The various Lebanese and Palestinian gangs and factions fought neighborhood battles which were often petty and parochial, scarcely aware of how they were being manipulated by the larger outside interests.

Only twenty-four hours after the Christian Right had agreed, on June 15, to allow entry of Arab peace-keeping forces, provided no PLO, Iraqi, Libyan, or Algerian forces were included, United States Ambassador to Lebanon Francis Melloy (only in Beirut since May 12) and his economic advisor and chauffeur were kidnapped and murdered as their car approached the "green line" on a trip to meet with President Sarkis in East Beirut. No group claimed the deed, and the PLO denounced it. There was some evidence that a leftist gang was involved, and the Party for Arab Socialist Action, a Lebanese group linked to the PFLP expressed approval without actually claiming responsibility. The murders involved an incredible breakdown and neglect of normal security precautions—by now, the beleaguered U.S. embassy in the author's old neighborhood on West Beirut's seafront was guarded by PLA and Lebanese Arab Army elements—and U.S. embassy communications were poor, to say the least.

The PLO announced arrest of the murderers, suggested they acted for an "outside power" and said they would be handed to the Arab peace-keeping force for punishment, when the peace-keeping force arrived. They never were. President Ford expressing "shock and revulsion," met with the U.S. National Security Council, and Secretary Kissinger began planning a new evacuation by sea, the second, of Americans remaining in Lebanon, then about 1,400. He acknowledged the U.S. was playing the "honest broker" between Israel and Syria, at the moment when Hassan Sabry al-Kholy was beginning his work of peacemaker between the warring parties. On June 20 the USS *Spiegel Grove*, covered by a seven-ship task force of the U.S. Sixth Fleet, including a ship carrying 1,000 battle-ready Marines, approached the coast. Aboard a U.S. aircraft carrier planes were armed with rockets and bombs for an air-strike, if needed, to rescue the *Spiegel Grove* in case it was attacked. The operation was smooth and peaceful, and Secretary Kissinger thanked the Palestinians for their contribution to its security.

It was on President Sadat's initiative in the Arab League that 1,000 Arab peace-keeping troops, half Syrians and half Libyans,* of an agreed force of 6,000, arrived in Lebanon June 21, as Sadat met with King Khalid and Arafat in Riyadh (a meeting paving the way for the October 1976 summit which eventually stopped the war). The next day Arafat relieved the chief of the Palestine Liberation Army, General Musbah al-Budeiry, who was under Syrian orders, of his command. Arafat took over the command himself.

"Bowing to Syrian pressure," London *Daily Telegraph* correspondent John Bulloch wrote, "the Leftists ended their offensive; largely because the Palestinians, who always did most of the fighting, made it plain they would not go on."[23] The rightists now proceeded to close their ring of steel around Tel al-Za'atar and Nabaa, and on June 29 captured Jisr al-Basha camp, overlooking Tel al-Za'atar. The PLO appealed to Arab, Communist, and third-world nations for help in raising the siege, and Camille Chamoun's NLP claimed that Libyan, Cuban, Soviet, and other foreign volunteers were fighting with Tel al-Za'atar's 15,000 Palestinian defenders. Abu Iyad of al-Fatah warned July 3 that Tel al-Za'atar's fall would mean the end of all hope of a political solution and that the "Viet Namization of Lebanon and the rest of the region," a favorite slogan of the PFLP's George Habbash, would follow. Inter-Arab complications in Lebanon deepened on July 5, when Libyan and newly arrived Sudanese troops of the peace force clashed near Beirut airport, following charges by Sudanese President Ja'afaar al-Numeiry that the Libyans were behind an attempted coup to overthrow him in Khartoum.

On July 14 Phalangist military commander William Hawk was killed on the Tel al-Za'atar front and replaced by Bashir Gemayel, one of Pierre Gemayel's sons. The PLO insisted that an end to Palestinian fighting with the Syrians must be dependent on a Syrian retreat from their most advanced mountain position, in Sofar, and from south Lebanon, where they had met unexpectedly heavy Palestinian resistance in Sidon, and on lifting of the siege of Tel al-Za'atar. But on July 20 President Assad replied that Syrian troops would leave Lebanon only if "the country's legal authorities so demanded."[24] Syrian troops, resisted by the Palestinians in the Wavell camp, entered Baalbeck in the Bekaa Valley and set afire a tank farm at the U.S.-owned oil refinery near Sidon. The active Soviet ambassador in Beirut, Alexander Soldatov, assured Arafat and Jumblatt that the Soviet Union planned "urgent action" to help the leftists and Palestinians.

The author arrived in Beirut July 14 and discovered the Soviet overture to the Palestinians and how much was really behind it: Moscow broadcasts and Soviet diplomats and newsmen were assuring the Palestinians that the Soviets would "lean hard" on the Syrians by cutting down arms, fuel, and spare parts supplies. However, as one Palestinian ruefully admitted, "It's unlikely that Moscow really will do this." They have too good a thing in Syria to lose. And they don't want to see Assad following the example of Sadat and moving further toward the United States." Later, a quasi-official Russian admitted to me: "The USSR and Syria have too much interest in keeping up their good relationship to really jeopardize it now. The Palestinians are in a militarily difficult position. They should compromise. But Syria must meet them halfway, and we are telling them this."[25]

At the same time, the PLO hardened its position and rejected any more compromises by Arafat with Damascus until the Syrians began to withdraw from Lebanon, until the rightist blockades on Tel al-Za'atar and other regions were lifted, and until the Arab peace-keeping forces moved in to protect the Palestinian refugee camps. On July 27 the Palestinians provided shore security cover for another U.S. evacuation, again protected by the Sixth Fleet: the U.S. Navy transport *Coronado* took 208 foreigners to Athens. One of them was U.S. Ambassador Talcott Seelye, returning to Washington to report to Kissinger, after having been unable to cross the dangerous "green line" for even a single meeting with the rightists. A new cease-fire accord July 29 between Arafat and the Syrians was the first major Palestinian concession tacitly recognizing Syria's predominant role in Lebanon, but it remained unimplemented like all the others.

Day after day the rightist artillery pounded Tel al-Za'atar, but the camp held firm. After long, patient efforts by Hassan Sabry al-Kholy and International Red Cross Committee delegate Jean Hoefliger, the rightists on August 3 and 4 permitted Red Cross personnel to enter the camp and take out a few of the worst wounded. They reported appalling conditions inside, after a direct artillery hit on a building burying alive and killing over 500 people, including many children. As the author and other newsmen watched from the rightist command post in Jisr al-Basha, the rightists violated the cease-fire while it was still supposedly in force and opened fire on the camp while Hoefliger and the Red Cross party were still inside. They barely escaped with their lives. On August 6 the evacuation of wounded was suspended when the convoy was hit by bullets.

On August 6 the rightist command announced the fall of the leftist enclave of Nabaa, and the usual looting and killing took place there. On August 12 as 12,000 survivors fled Tel al-Za'atar, which now lacked water, food, and basic medicines as well as ammunition, the rightists launched a final assault on the camp, despite assurances given Hassan Sabry al-Kholy and others the day before that they would observe a cease-fire to permit evacuation of more wounded.[26] Many of the camp's residents were massacred after the surrender. Those who survived were dispersed to other Palestinian refugee camps and areas in south Lebanon, inside the zone still controlled by the leftist-Palestinian alliance with Tyre, now blockaded and harassed by the Israelis, its main outlet to the sea. In a news conference after the camp's fall, Jumblatt accused Syria of supporting the rightists in the battle, announced formation of a new "popular Liberation Force," and said further negotiation was impossible. Thereupon Hassan Sabry al-Kholy left for Damascus and Cairo and began efforts to convene an Arab summit conference.

ISRAEL INTERVENES

Israel's concern with ending the armed Palestinian presence on her northern borders drew her gradually into open involvement. By early summer considerable transfers of tanks, vehicles, artillery, and other military equipment had been made by Israel to the rightists. The author and many other eyewitnesses saw armored personnel carriers and tanks, still with Israeli Defense Forces markings in Hebrew, in action at Tel al-Za'atar and elsewhere. Israeli patrols frequently crossed into south Lebanon to discourage Palestinian activity in the region and to protect the Israeli "open fence" border crossings which, since early summer, had permitted Lebanese, mainly Maronites, but also some of the poor Shi'a residents of the south, to enter Israel for work, business, medical treatment, and visits to relatives. Israel began buying tobacco and other farm products from the southern Lebanese. Meetings were disclosed between Israeli officers and Ahmed al-Khatib's leftist Lebanese Arab Army units, now largely a rag-tag band still stationed or roaming in parts of south Lebanon, at Khatib's request.

Chaim Landau, an opposition deputy in the Israeli Knesset, warned August 4 that meeting the leftists was a political blunder which might help to legitimize the PLO as a negotiating partner with Israel. By mid-August hundreds of Lebanese were commuting to work in Israel; Lebanese farmers were selling their crops and buying supplies there; and Israeli army medical clinics were treating and immunizing Lebanese children and adults. All this, of course, assured a steady and detailed flow of information about the Palestinians and the course of the war to Israeli intelligence.

As Syria further reinforced its troops in Lebanon, bringing the number close to 20,000, a coordinated Syrian-rightist offensive to expel al-Fatah and Jumblatt partisans and their allies from mountain positions north of the main Beirut-Damascus highway began in mid-August. On August 17 al-Fatah forces retaliated with harassing attacks and sabotage against Syrian forces occupying the Bekaa and the northern province of Akkar. When the Palestinians infiltrated back into the southern border area, especially around the village of Ein Ebel, Israeli artillery supported the rightist drive to flush guerrillas out of border villages, though Israeli military censors prevented reporting of this by correspondents in Israel.

On September 4 Abu Hassan, chief of al-Fatah security, visited President-elect Sarkis, Maronite Patriarch Khoreish, and the Phalangist military commander to begin discussing a Palestinian withdrawal from the mountains. The next day, Abu Iyad of al-Fatah made a first public declaration supporting Sarkis. Meetings then began between Abu Iyad, Khaled al-Hassan, and other al-Fatah representatives with the Syrians and foreign Arab envoys, including the Tunisian and Kuwaiti foreign ministers. These meetings prepared the long road back toward a Syrian-Palestinian reconciliation, one of the main preconditions for the general peace agreement for Lebanon which Arab summit diplomacy, at Saudi Arabian insistence, was beginning to slowly and painfully hammer out. Fighting raged on most fronts on September 24, when President Sarkis was sworn into office before sixty-seven parliamentary deputies meeting at the Park Hotel in Shtaura under Syrian military protection.

On September 8 the Soviets began publicly backtracking on their support for the leftist-Palestinian camp. They criticized "ultra-leftist elements" for rejecting all peace proposals, though the Moscow newspaper *Pravda* tried to balance this by repeating the Soviet call for Syrian troops to quit Lebanon. On August 28 the PLO had announced a general conscription of all Palestinians in Lebanon and other Arab states between ages of eighteen and thirty to fight in Lebanon. The rightists and Israelis thereupon redoubled their sea blockade to prevent personnel and supplies from reaching the Palestinians in south Lebanon. Beginning September 6, the Arab League granted to the PLO the status of a full member (which it had never enjoyed, despite the fact that the Arab League itself created the PLO in 1963). The PLO was not given voting rights in the league. It maintained its refusal to establish a provisional government-in-exile, as urged by President Sadat and others for years.[27]

Syria's relations with the Palestinians, however, sank to a new low September 26 when a four-man guerrilla team in Damascus occupied the Semiramis Hotel and held its occupants hostage. The Syrian army stormed the hotel, with loss of life, and immediately hanged the three surviving guerrillas. Syria first accused al-Fatah of organizing the operation then switched the accusation to its eastern enemy, Iraq. The PLO denied any involvement but blamed Abu Nidal, an al-Fatah dissident "rejectionist" and terrorist leader who had taken refuge in Baghdad after being condemned to death by an al-Fatah court.

THE RIYADH AND CAIRO CONFERENCES

Two days later the Syrian army launched a major offensive against the leftist-Palestinian alliance in Mount Lebanon. Arafat asked for outside Arab intervention. By September 30 the Syrians had occupied the entire Upper Metn area. The offensive now turned into a pincer movement, as the rightists attacked from the direction of Kahale, a Maronite village on the road to Beirut toward Aley. The Palestinians, Jumblatt partisans, and Communists repulsed them with heavy losses. With the help of Kholy, back in Lebanon in his mediator's role, a cease-fire was imposed October 11.

New Syrian offensives near Jezzine in the south and against Bhamdoun and Aley, on the main highway to Beirut, brought Saudi Arabian diplomatic pressure to a head, and an urgent Arab summit conference was convoked October 16 in Riyadh. Among the Riydah decisions which were finally to silence the guns in all of Lebanon, except the south, in the following month, the Palestinians were enjoined to comply with the 1969 Cairo Agreement. This time, their compliance was to be guaranteed by the Arab states, with, as their muscle, a 30,000-man, mainly Syrian, Arab peace-keeping force, under political authority of the Lebanese president. The peace force would separate combatants, collect heavy weapons, punish truce violators, and aid the Lebanese government in restoring public order, utilities, and protecting military installations. The Syrians and the Palestinians were officially reconciled, as were presidents Sadat and Assad.

However, it took nearly another month of fighting to enforce the Riyadh decisions, which were ratified by an enlarged summit in Cairo attended by President Sarkis. This conference settled the composition of the Arab peace-keeping force October 26. On the same day the PLO announced it had begun to withdraw all Palestinian forces from the mountains to south Lebanon. This, indeed, was destined to be the arena for the following chapters of the Lebanese drama.

THE CONFLICT IN THE SOUTH

Fighting and some of the heaviest shelling of the civilian areas of Beirut and other Lebanese cities, continued up until the very end: the entry of Syrian deterrent forces into Beirut, Tripoli, and Sidon, by November 21. Israeli warnings, transmitted through the U.S., prevented the Arab peace-keeping forces from moving south of Nabatiyeh.

The presence of strong rightist forces in the southern villages, given Israeli fire support when necessary, and the continued presence of the Palestinians set the theme for the fighting which has continued in south Lebanon until this writing, in the summer of 1978. This rightist presence was at first limited to the village of Koleiya, with about 6,000 inhabitants, mainly Maronites, in the district of Marjayoun, where some troops had remained loyal to General Hanna Said (a native of Koleiya) after the mutiny of Lieutenant Khatib. They were joined by other soldiers from Koleiya, who were transported by sea from Jounieh, the rightist "capital," to Haifa in Israel and secured control of the adjoining village, Khraibeh, where several hundred Orthodox Christians lived.

The rightists later extended control to Rmeish, in the Bint Jbeil district, where 4,500 Maronites lived under great economic hardship (most were small farmers whose fields lay close to the Israeli border), and which became one of the first villages to collaborate with the Israelis when the "open fence" was first opened. The rightist Lebanese front first set up a roadblock there on August 28, 1976. Next, the front moved into the Maronite village of Debel (3,000 people), Ain Ebel (6,000) and Alma Shaab (4,000). In a clash on August 31, 1976, with four al-Fatah guerrillas who were killed, the front's supporters demonstrated the necessity to protect the villages from the Palestinians.

Heavy fighting broke out in September between these villages, and the Palestinians, who had artillery positions in and near Marjayoun and the majestic, mountain-top medieval Crusader castle of Beaufort, overlooking the Litani river gorges. On October 16, 1976, the day of the Arab summit conference in Riyadh, the front launched an attack from the Christian border villages against the Muslim Shi'a village of Hanin and occupied it. This made impossible the defense of several other Shi'a villages, Aita Shaab, Ramieh, and Yarin, which were in turn occupied by the Christians. Fighting then erupted between these new Christian positions and the Palestinians, who were dug into the main border town of Bint Jbeil and the hamlets of Ain Ata, Tireh, and Rashaf. Marjayoun barracks and the town itself fell on October 18 to the Christians, who advanced into other villages held by Palestinians at the foot of Mount Hermon, facing Marjayoun and the Israeli border. The Christians always enjoyed Israeli artillery and occasionally, infantry and tank support. The Palestinians counterattacked and took the Christian town of Aishieh, Jezzine district, and the Christians accused them of massacring fifty of its inhabitants.

Due to repeated Israeli warnings not to cross the "red line," usually understood to be the Litani River, the Syrian deterrent forces were obliged to stand idly by as the Christians and Palestinians slaughtered each other south of the Litani. This situation continued until January 23, 1977, when a small Syrian force advanced to within one mile north of Nabatiyeh. Though this is well above the Litani line, Israel threatened to intervene, and the Lebanese front took the opportunity to launch new attacks. They seized the Muslim border hamlet of Adayssieh, giving them control of a crucial road junction adjoining Israel and leading to the towns of Taybeh, Blida, Meiss al-Jebel, and several others. By February 20, 1977, the rightists had Khiyyam and Ibl Saki, threatening the Arkoub region where, under the Cairo Agreement, the Palestinians have the right to keep their forces.

The rightist leaders indicated in March 1977, that they would be agreeable to "internationalizing" the southern question by admitting U.N. troops, since Israel would not permit Arab troops in the area. Kamal Jumblatt's murder on March 16 and the reprisals which followed raised tension but had no lasting effect. The last straw for the rightists was appointment by President Sarkis of Brigadier General Victor Khoury, whom Chamoun and Gemayel opposed, as new Lebanese army commander-in-chief on March 28. With heavy Israeli artillery support, the front seized Taybeh and a string of villages controlling the western sector of the Israeli border up to Ras al-Nakoura on the Mediterranean, but without taking some of the Muslim villages. The Palestinians halted them at Aintaroun, near Bint Jbeil. But the Palestinians were now bottled up in a narrow, five-mile area stretching from Blida to Bint Jbeil. If the rightists captured Bint Jbeil, this would link the two territorial strips controlled by them along the border: to the east, from Blida to Khraibeh and to the west, from Ain Ebel to Ras al-Nakoura.[28] An agreement signed at Chtoura between all parties on July 23 provided for entry of the Lebanese army into the area and re-establishment of Lebanese sovereignty with evacuation of all but an unspecified number of Palestinians allowed to remain, under the Cairo Agreement. But despite strenuous U.S. diplomatic efforts, led by Ambassador Richard Parker, the postwar government of Premier Selim Hoss was unable to secure agreement of all the parties: Syria, the PLO, the Lebanese rightists, who are supplied by Israel, and Israel itself. South Lebanon, where Israeli planes struck in new air raids against the Palestinian camps on November 9 and 16, 1977, just before President Sadat's peace journey to Jerusalem, remained a battleground. The scene was set by these events for the large-scale Israeli invasion of south Lebanon of March 15, 1978.

How the rightist Lebanese political leaders then viewed the future of the Palestinians in Lebanon was expressed dramatically, and with hyperbole, to the author by Camille Chamoun: "Through infiltration, the number of Palestinians in Lebanon has reached 600,000, despite, or, more accurately, because of the civil war, and the events of 1970 in Jordan. Perhaps it is only 500,000, though President Sarkis told me 600,000."

"Can we go on with one-sixth of our population foreigners? We obviously cannot. Therefore, what Lebanon and the world both need are a Jordanian-type solution in which the Palestinians would have their own state on the West Bank, federated or confederated with Jordan. The continued presence of the Palestinians here adds to the bifurcation of our country. Syria is now the senior partner and we (Christians) are their friends. That could change, if President Assad should disappear. Our future should not depend upon Syria. Our friendship with them will not last if they stay in Lebanon too long, and *Israel will not tolerate a Syrian strategic base in the country.* How long can we go on living in a bifurcated state, where two different civilizations are trying to live side by side, but where even a minor administrative appointment stirs up a fuss?"[29]

At a two-day conference January 21–22, 1978, in Zagharta, the rightist Lebanese front parties reiterated that the Palestinian presence— their figure was 400,000 Palestinians—was an "obstacle to national reconciliation."[30]

The stark fact was that in 1978, as President Sadat's peace efforts hung in the balance, neither Lebanon herself nor the Palestinians living there had control of their own destinies. President Sarkis presided over a government which had little power to govern. The PLO command in Lebanon was rent by internal dissension. It was partly in an effort to unify their ranks, and partly an attempt to put the PLO back on the world map as a fighting force, that al-Fatah carried out its most spectacular attack ever inside Israel on March 11, 1978, and so touched off Lebanon's first full-scale Israeli-Palestinian war, with United Nations intervention and other consequences which might prove to contain the seeds of a new round of major war in the Middle East.

Eleven al-Fatah guerrillas, setting out from two points on the Lebanese coast, landed on a beach about thirteen miles south of Haifa March 11, shooting an American woman photographer they found on the beach. Seizing a bus and sixty-three hostages, they set out for Tel Aviv, firing at vehicles and people as they passed and forcing their way through two police roadblocks. At Hertzelia, north of Tel Aviv, a final clash with Israeli army units resulted in explosion of the bus and the killing of nine guerrillas (two had already been lost en route from Lebanon) and thirty-seven Israelis. Eighty-two Israelis and two guerrillas were wounded, the latter two captured. It had been the al-Fatah unit's intention to shoot their way through to Tel Aviv and seize the Hilton Hotel and its occupants, and to demand liberation of Palestinian prisoners in Israel.

On the night of March 14, about 15,000 Israeli troops supported by armor and air strikes invaded southern Lebanon along the entire length of the border. They encountered about 2,000 Palestinians who were swept back to a depth of about six miles within twenty-four hours. Israeli aircraft attacked targets both north and south of the Litani River, including a dock and village area adjoining Beirut airport which the Israel military command said had been used by the Palestinian boats. The refugee camps in the Tyre area came under heavy bombardment from air, land, and sea.

By March 16 the Israeli military command, claiming that their wish for a cease-fire had not been respected, ordered a push northward to the Litani, except for the extreme western end where they deliberately left open an "escape hatch" north of Tyre. The main coastal highway and the

Litani bridge, linking Tyre with the north, were under fire but were used by a large majority of the 200,000 Lebanese who poured northward out of their devastated villages and farms. The southern Palestinian refugee camps were largely evacuated and given over to the fighters, who tried to defend them against the constant Israeli air strikes.

Syria's reaction and that of its peace-keeping troops, who kept well north of the Litani, were prudent. Syria at first called on members of the U.N. Security Council to "assume their responsibilities" but later announced that al-Sa'iqa was participating in the fighting and that the Arab deterrent force would provide air defense for the force's positions in Lebanon. Syria authorized Iraqi reinforcements and supplies to cross its territory to south Lebanon.

On March 19 a conference of the "steadfastness front" countries (Syria, Libya, Algeria, South Yemen, and the PLO) reaffirmed positions they had taken at earlier summit conferences in Tripoli (December 1977) and Algiers (February 1978), opposing Sadat's peace initiative and calling for closed ranks against Israel. Syria made it clear in various statements that it would not be drawn into war against Israel, except at the time and place of its own choosing. Algeria, Libya, and Iraq announced the departure of volunteers to fight with the PLO. The Syrian peace-keeping forces seem to have generally admitted them and facilitated their movement south.

Egypt condemned both the al-Fatah attack and the Israeli response and on March 17 officially declared support for dispatch of United Nations Interim Forces (UNIFIL) to Lebanon. Egyptian commentators taunted President Assad of Syria for having concluded a tacit "non-intervention agreement" with Israel, accusations repeated by President Sadat March 25. Sadat also claimed that President Assad, Israeli Prime Minister Begin, and Camille Chamoun, as leader of the Lebanese front, had agreed to set up a "Maronite state" guaranteed by the Israelis in south Lebanon.

On March 15 King Khalid of Saudi Arabia demanded President Carter's intervention to end the "odious Israeli aggression" in south Lebanon. In Jordan Palestinians in refugee camps and towns rioted for the first time since 1971, and King Hussein, paying homage to the Palestinian resistance in south Lebanon, channeled off some of their energies by authorizing Palestinians in Jordan to fight as volunteers.

The United States at first avoided any stand, leading to Palestinian accusations that it had given the Israelis a "green light" for the operation. But on March 16 the State Department, at President Carter's request, asked the Israelis to withdraw. More than this, Washington took the initiative in asking for a U.N. Security Council resolution, which brought about a resolution calling for total Israeli withdrawal from Lebanon and establishment of the UNIFIL force, to be staffed by French, Iranian, Norwegian, Swedish, and later Nepalese and Fiji contingents, reaching a strength of about 4,000 by June 1978. New demonstrations and riots broke out among West Bank Palestinians against the Israeli moves in Lebanon, and the Israeli repression of them was severe.

Many other Western and Third World countries, which had condemned the March 11 terrorist attack, and others (like the Soviet Union and its east bloc allies) which had not done so, called on Israel to withdraw.

The shape of Israel's future wishes for the south of Lebanon became clear on March 27, when Major Saad Haddad announced formation of the "Army of South Lebanon," in which he hoped to enroll Shi'a Muslim volunteers under Christian command and Israeli protection (an operation which largely failed: when the author visited the Israel-occupied zone before it was evacuated by the Israelis in June 1978, Haddad's men were nearly all Christians, remnants of the old Lebanese army, and Phalangists).

As UNIFIL troops moved in, and Syria maintained its passive role to the north, fighting gradually died down to skirmishes between the Israelis and Palestinian infiltrators. On April 8 the U.S. State Department confirmed congressional reports that the Israelis had used "cluster" or fragmentation bombs in south Lebanon. On the next day Washington said Israel should "accelerate" its withdrawal. By April 11 Israel had completed the first phase of its withdrawal southward, and by April 14 this was extended. U.N. Secretary-General Kurt Waldheim conferred with Arafat and with President Sarkis in Beirut April 17 and said Arafat had promised the PLO would "cooperate" with UNIFIL efforts to secure total Israeli withdrawal.

By May and June, as unostentatious but steady U.S. pressure continued, it was clear that the Israelis meant to pull out completely (as pledged by Prime Minister Begin April 18), but to turn over control of their six-mile "security zone" inside Lebanon, including the three Maronite enclaves and territory linking them, to Major Haddad's men. By June 15, 1978, this had been accomplished, and the UNIFIL forces were not permitted into the Christian enclaves, a situation bitterly protested by U.N. Secretary-General Waldheim and General Emmanuel Erskine, the Ghanaian U.N. commander to the Israelis.

Meanwhile, severe factional fighting broke out among the Christians in north Lebanon. The old rightist Lebanese front of the civil war

virtually fell apart. Still, however, the Maronite leadership called for expulsion of the Palestinians from Lebanon and their dispersion among the
other Arab states. Arafat and the PLO command made it equally clear,
on every possible occasion, that they considered the Cairo Agreement
still in force, and that this gave the PLO the right to stay in (or return to)
south Lebanon, which it was doing by summer of 1978.

A new Middle East war involving Lebanon would almost certainly
see the Maronites actively enlisted as allies of the Israelis. This might bring
about the genocide of the Palestinians, caught between the jaws of a two-
pronged Israeli-Maronite trap. Such an eventuality might mean the final
destruction of Lebanon, as the modern world has known it. By contrast,
a successful Arab-Israel settlement in the Middle East, which provides
the Palestinian homeland envisaged by President Carter in his Clinton,
Massachusetts speech in March 1977, might be the start of Lebanon's
salvation.

THE LIMITS OF MILITARY POWER: Syria's Role

Itamar Rabinovich

AMONG THE EXTERNAL ACTORS in the Lebanese civil war of 1975–76, it was Syria which played the most prominent, intricate, and controversial role. The prominence of Syria's role is displayed in an ironic fashion by the fact that as a result of the war it can now hardly be regarded as an external actor in Lebanese politics. The intricacy of Syria's policy in Lebanon, evidenced by the several shifts it underwent, was shaped by the importance of Syria's direct interests in Lebanon and by the interplay between that policy and the Ba'ath regime's domestic, regional, and international policies. The controversy concerning Syria's role in Lebanon has now entered its second phase. Between January and October 1976, it was primarily a matter of political argument, when Syria's conduct in Lebanon gave rise to strong criticism—domestic, Arab, and Soviet. Since October 1976, the polemics have shifted to the rapidly growing body of literature, academic and other, which has been generated by the Lebanese civil war.

It is partly as a byproduct of this debate that the general outline of Syria's policy in Lebanon has become comparatively clear and well documented. Syria's political system tends to be secretive, but the need to defend their conduct in Lebanon forced President Assad and other Ba'ath spokesmen to explain Syrian policy in unusual detail. Consequently, a study of Syria's role during the recent Lebanese crisis affords also a rare insight into the decision-making process in the Syrian Ba'ath regime as well as into some of the major issues with which its leaders are preoccupied.

FOREIGN POLICY ENVIRONMENT

Syria's decision to intervene directly and overtly in the Lebanese War, taken in January 1976, may be analyzed from two vantage points: as the culmination of the build-up of Syria's position in Lebanon, which began in the early 1970s, and as the product of the particular circumstances which the outbreak and the development of the war created in the latter part of 1975. In both cases Syria's long-standing claims and interests in Lebanon constitute an essential background.

An irredentist claim to all, or part of, Lebanon's territory has been a permanent feature of the Syrian state's attitude to its western neighbor since the 1920s. The maximalist claim to the whole of Lebanon was inspired by nationalist ideologies, Syrian or Arab, which viewed the Syrian and Lebanese states as part of a broader entity centered in Damascus. The minimalist claim is based on the belief that the detachment of territory from Syrian provinces in 1920 to create Greater Lebanon was an unjust and unlawful act which ought to be rectified.[1]

One of the compromises involved in the achievement of independence was Syrian acceptance of Lebanon's existence in its 1920 boundaries. Thus since the 1940s Syrian governments normally refrained from making explicit demands on Lebanon's territory. Still, Syria maintained an implicit claim to a special relationship with Lebanon, for instance by avoiding the establishment of normal diplomatic relations. The underlying assumption was that it would be unnatural for two parts of the same (undefined) entity to conduct their relations through diplomatic channels.[2]

This attitude was nourished and perpetuated by the existence of a significant body of opinion inside Lebanon which continued to challenge its legitimacy as well as by the importance of Syria's interests in Lebanon. The nature and scope of these interests underwent several changes during a thirty-year period, as did their perception by various Syrian regimes. Thus the economic interdependence of the two states, which had formerly been parts of a single system, steadily declined in importance. In recent years Syria's economic interests in Lebanon concerned mainly the 400,000 or so Syrian workers in that country. But Syria's political and military interests grew, rather than diminished in importance and diversity.

Politically, Syria's rulers have been primarily interested in risks to stability of their regimes, actual or potential, which emanate from Lebanon. Lebanon is a natural center for political exiles and refugees from Syria, and several coups, successful and abortive, against various Syrian governments were planned in and launched from Lebanon. Lebanon was also an all-Arab political center where several political parties and a comparatively free press conducted their activities. Successive Syrian regimes and particularly Ba'ath ones displayed a keen interest in both. In addition to the general interest which was natural to a regime and a party subscribing to a pan-Arab ideology, there were foci of particular interest: the pro-Syrian and pro-Iraqi factions of the Ba'ath and independent newspapers, which on more than one occasion stirred trouble in Syria by publishing damaging reports or documents.

Since the late 1960s two fresh aspects have been added to Syria's political interest in Lebanon. One concerned the Palestinian organizations who established their political headquarters and eventually the bulk of their manpower in Lebanon. As a major participant in Palestinian politics and as a champion and protector of the PLO (or parts of it), Syria kept a close watch on the fortunes of the Palestinians in Lebanon and maintained a direct link with the autonomous Palestinian enclave in southeast Lebanon. Syria also developed a close relationship with the Shi'ite community—a large and disaffected segment of Lebanon's population which presented Syria's leaders with more than the ordinary prospect of political cooperation. By endorsing the Lebanese 'Alawi community as part of them—as they eventually did in 1973—the Lebanese Shi'ites could draw comfort from the political standing of the 'Alawi members of Syria's ruling group, who encountered great difficulties in making themselves acceptable to the Muslim Sunni population in Syria.[3]

For Syria's military planners Lebanon's territory is of great importance. Syria's line of defense (both before and after June 1967) could be outflanked by an Israeli force coming through Lebanon's territory and attacking Syria from its soft western underbelly. In offensive terms Syrian (or other Arab) troops stationed in Lebanon could activate a dormant front, improve Syria's posture vis-à-vis Israel, and force the Israelis to allocate to the Lebanese border units which would otherwise have been deployed or used on the Syrian front.

The Expansion of Syrian Influence in Lebanon

Until the early 1970s Syria was unable to acquire influence in Lebanon commensurate with the importance of its interests. This began to change at that period as a result of three developments: (1) the emergence of a stable and effective regime in Syria which, under the leadership of Hafez al-Assad, conducted a successful foreign policy; (2) the progressive weakening of the Lebanese state and apparent inability of the Lebanese political system to cope with the crisis which finally led to the outbreak of the civil war; and (3) the decline of Egypt's position as a regional power.

Syria's newly acquired position in Lebanon manifested itself primarily in the bilateral relationship between the two countries. Thus Syria intervened effectively in the elections of 1972, provided political asylum to the leaders of the Deuxieme Bureau, and gradually replaced Egypt as the external center—demanding allegiance and extending support—for both Sunni and Shi'a politicians. In May 1973, Syria exercised direct pressure on the Lebanese government so as to prevent the Lebanese army from pursuing its effort to contain the Palestinian organizations. The process of cabinet formation during that year clearly revealed that Syria had acquired a virtual veto power over major political decisions within the Lebanese political system.

During the two years which followed the October War, the development of Syria's policy in Lebanon was integrated into the broader framework that was then afforded by the more systematic formulation of the Assad regime's regional and international policies. When he first assumed power, Assad sought primarily to bring Syria out of her regional isolation and almost exclusive dependence on the Soviet Union in the international arena. Later, both opportunities and constraints led Syria to pursue a more ambitious policy. That policy was predicated on the unprecedented domestic stability of the Assad regime's first years and on the vacuum created by the decline in Egypt's regional position. Its direction was also influenced by the course of the October War and its political and military sequels in 1973 and 1974. These developments underline the importance of the American and Saudi positions in the Middle East and the unreliability of the Egyptian alliance.

Syria now sought to develop an independent power position from which to conduct her regional and international policies in an autonomous fashion. It was to rest on Syria's influence in her immediate Arab environment comprising Lebanon, Jordan, and the PLO. The political and military dimensions of this influence were closely interwoven. As the leader of such a prospective bloc or grouping, Syria was certain to acquire a decisive say in inter-Arab affairs. As a more significant actor in the Arab-Israeli conflict, Syria would also acquire important assets in her future dealings with the superpowers and with such regional powers as Saudi Arabia, Egypt, and Iraq. Militarily, a paramount position in Lebanon and a close coordination could endow Syria with most of the benefits associated with the notion of an Eastern Front even without Iraqi acquiescence. At a time when it was being supplied by the Soviet Union while Egypt was not, Syria could be thinking of developing a military capability equivalent to, and possibly independent of, that of Egypt in future conflicts with Israel.

The pursuit of that policy became evident in 1975. In addition to its growing influence in Lebanon, Syria was in the process of formalizing her alliance with Jordan and proposed also a unification of political and military commands with the PLO. These measures were in part calculated to prevent separate Egyptian deals with Israel, and they were given further impetus when Egypt and Israel signed the Interim Agreement over the Sinai in September 1975.[4]

SYRIA

It was in the context of implementing the Eastern Front strategy that Syria had to formulate its policy toward the civil war which broke out in Lebanon in April 1975, and grew both in scope and intensity during the summer. The outbreak of the Lebanese civil war and the course it took confronted the Syrian leadership with a difficult dilemma. The importance of Syria's interest in Lebanon and its closeness presented both great opportunities and great risks. As a power seeking to establish its hegemony over Lebanon and the PLO, Syria could view the civil war as a welcome development. A political system Syria disliked was being successfully challenged by a revisionist coalition. Several of the groups composing the anti-status quo coalition—leftist, Muslim and Palestinian elements —were allied with or kindred to Syria. Gains made by this coalition could well increase Syria's influence in and over Lebanon and consequently over the PLO.

But other considerations were as powerful. The situation in Lebanon could deteriorate in a number of ways. A clear cut victory by the pro-status quo coalition and a resulting distress of Syria's clients and allies could create strong pressure on Syria to intervene on their behalf. Such an intervention could lead to a premature and disadvantageous collision with Israel. Or, conversely, a decisive success of Syria's allies could create pressures on the U.S. and Israel to intervene on behalf of the pro-status quo, or, more narrowly, Christian forces. Again, the danger of an uncontrolled deterioration to war would be considerable. In more general terms, Syria realized the complexity of the situation in Lebanon and the political risks of intimate involvement in such a situation. After all, Hafez al-Assad took power in Syria only five years earlier in the aftermath of Syria's disastrous involvement in a rather similar crisis in Jordan.[5] The policy which Syria formulated and pursued between April and

December 1975, rested on two major foundations. It extended support to its allies (mainly in the form of arms supplies) and tried to bring an end to the conflict by mediating between the two warring coalitions and by seeking to devise a compromise formula.

Transition to Direct Intervention

Syria's policy of indirect intervention reached a deadlock in January 1976. This was brought about by two major developments. First, the Phalangists and some of their allies, having realized that they could not defend the status quo in the entirety of Lebanon, opted for a partition and the establishment of a virtual Christian state in part of Lebanon.[6] Second, the PLO, which until that time remained formally out of the war and in practice was only partially involved in it, decided to throw its full weight behind the anti-status quo coalition.

The potential consequences and repercussions were most alarming from Syria's point of view. The notion of Lebanon's partition along sectarian lines and particularly the establishment of a separate Christian state were an anathema to Arab nationalist thinking. An exacerbation of the sectarian issue could have a spillover effect into Syria, where confessionalism was as sensitive, though less overt, an issue. Nor were the prospects of a separate radical Muslim state or a Muslim-Palestinian takeover in Lebanon welcome to Syria. The alternative appeared to be a direct Syrian intervention in Lebanon that would decide the issue militarily, establish Syrian supremacy, and enable Syria to impose a political solution to the crisis. The danger of American and Israeli reaction could be averted by coordinating Syria's moves with the United States and by using Syrian units of the PLA that would be more palatable to Israel than full-fledged Syrian units.[7]

Implied in this line of thinking were two new factors which affected both Syria's decision to intervene in the Lebanese civil war and the subsequent involvement of Syria's policy in Lebanon. One was the new relationship which began to develop between Syria and the United States in the wake of the October War. The latter saw an opportunity to reestablish at least a working relationship with Damascus, to draw Syria away from the Soviet Union, and to tie it more firmly to Saudi Arabia and Egypt. Syria sought to bolster its independence vis-à-vis the Soviet Union and to obtain American support for its policy in the Arab-Israeli conflict and for its regional ambitions. Its leadership concluded after two years of postwar diplomacy that Syria should establish a direct dialog with the United States rather than depend on Egyptian mediation or follow the Egyptian lead. The situation in Lebanon provided an excellent opportunity to further both aims. A successful intervention and the imposition of a stable settlement in addition to their other merits would underscore Egypt's weakness in the Arab *Mashriq* (Eastern Arab World) and demonstrate that matters in that area had to be arranged through Syria. The notions then underlying the American approach to the recently concluded Sinai interim agreement would be shown to be untenable.[8] A second factor concerned the change which had taken place in Syria's own outlook on the Lebanese civil war and the Lebanese political system. As a regime with long term ambitions seeking to stabilize the situation in Lebanon (though to its own benefit), the Ba'ath regime came to realize that it had to cooperate with elements situated on both sides of the dividing line in the Lebanese crisis. This realization was facilitated by the changes which had taken place within the Ba'ath regime in the preceding years.

Changing Complexion of the Ba'ath Regime

The regime established by Hafez al-Assad in November 1970, has in a number of ways represented a continuation of the two preceding Ba'ath regimes in Syria to which Assad himself had been an important partner. But in several significant aspects Assad's rise to power signified a departure from the image and practice of the previous seven years. The changes derived from a variety of sources: Assad's personality, the lessons of past failures, a reaction to past excesses, and, perhaps most important, the fact that much of the revolutionary potential which brought the Ba'ath to power and generated many of the reforms and changes of the 1960s had been largely spent by the early 1970s. As a result, a more pragmatic and conservative mood came to prevail in Syria which affected both the domestic politics and foreign policy of the country. It is only against this background that the gradual rapprochement between the Syrian Ba'ath regime and the generally conservative Christian Lebanese leadership can be understood. The dialog was first prepared by younger and dynamic elements such as the Phalangist Karim Pakandouni, but in time a working relationship was established with the three elder leaders of the pro-status quo camp—Camille Chamoun, Pierre Gemayel and Suleiman Frangieh. Syria's relationship with Suleiman Frangieh, it should be noted, was of a special nature. As a semifeudal leader of north Lebanon's Maronites, Frangieh had traditional ties in the 'Alawi area, just south of his own region. When he fled from Lebanese justice in the 1950s, following a bloody feud with the rival Duwayhi clan, Suleiman Frangieh established a close relationship with the Assad family. This relationship, illustrative of the importance of personal and family relations in Middle Eastern politics, has remained an important feature of Syria's position in Lebanon.

Dynamics of Intervention, January–June 1976

Syria's original direct intervention in the Lebanese civil war took place in January 1976, when units of the Palestine Liberation Army (which included regular Syrian army units) entered Lebanon. The issue was decided militarily (for the short run, at any rate) as expected. Syria then proceeded to impose on the defeated pro-status quo coalition and on the apparently victorious anti-status quo coalition a compromise political solution. Syria's plan for a reform of the Lebanese system and a solution of the crisis which transpired in January was presented in full on February 15. President Frangieh, who returned from Damascus, announced the "new national charter" whose text was formulated during his visit to Syria. The plan was rather moderate: Lebanon's confessional system was maintained, and the Christian-Maronite supremacy was reduced but not abolished. But the text of the new charter reflected the new reality in Lebanon only in a partial way. The significant novel element was a Syrian political hegemony buttressed by a military presence.[9] Syria's intervention created new dynamics which carried the Lebanese crisis and the Syrian intervention far beyond the original intentions of its authors.

It was in response to this new situation that the dramatic *volte-face* of the Lebanese civil war took place. The Christian-Maronite leadership recognized the realities of the new situation and rather than oppose the Syrians decided to accept their reform plan and to cooperate with them. Their decision was governed by the realization that no better alternative was available to them as long as no external power (such as the U.S. or Israel) would oppose Syria's military presence in Lebanon. Opposition to Syria's policy came from the camp on whose side it had presumably intervened, and particularly from Kamal Jumblatt, the leader of the Lebanese Left. There was further opposition from other Arab governments and from Lebanese leftist leaders and the PLO, who rejected the notion of Syrian hegemony and opposed the moderate nature of the reform plan. Muslim and leftist groups wanted no less than an immediate transformation of the Lebanese political system. Syria's rivals and critics in the Arab world—Egypt, Iraq, and Libya—opposed both Syrian mastery in Lebanon and the direction of Syria's policy. They possessed sufficient influence in Lebanon in order to stir or encourage active opposition to Syria's reform plan.

In the late winter and early spring of 1976, this opposition threatened to abort Syria's reform plan and indeed Syria's policy in Lebanon. The cease-fire broke down, Lieutenant al-Khatib's Lebanese Arab Army seceded from the Lebanese army, and Brigadier al-Ahdab staged a mysterious coup d'etat. The continued fighting presented Syria with some very difficult challenges. The Christian militias were unable to hold their own, so in order to put an end to the fighting Syria actually had to intervene directly on their behalf. The political *volte-face* of January and February had been difficult in itself. Supporting this new stance by the use of force against traditional allies and clients was all the more difficult. And yet failure to use force meant more than failure to achieve the original goals of the intervention. By then the regime's prestige and the need to justify the decision to intervene were also at stake.

The result was that in April Syria decided to employ its own regular forces in Lebanon, though still in a marginal way. The decision to employ Syrian forces and its execution followed a pattern which came to characterize the political style of Hafez al-Assad. The decision-making process regarding a difficult problem was slow and lengthy. Once the decision was made its execution was preceded by political groundwork. Implementation was deliberate. This time the political groundwork was not directed at the U.S. as much as it was concerned with preparing Syrian and Arab public opinion. The main effort in this direction was a Syrian government communique issued on April 1 (the main points of the communique were reiterated by President Assad in a speech he delivered on April 12).[10] The communique offered a detailed version of Syria's involvement in the Lebanese crisis, denounced the parties whose actions perpetuated the crisis and warned them of the awesome responsibility for their deeds. It was at once a threat to take a more direct and decisive action and a justification of Syria's past and future record in Lebanon.

Additional Syrian forces entered Lebanon in mid-March and early April, but they were unable to effect either a cease-fire or any progress toward a political solution. Syria's candidate, Elias Sarkis, was elected president on May 9 and was to replace President Frangieh in September, but at that stage it represented an isolated and therefore not a very significant success. Clearly, if Syria sought to achieve concrete results in Lebanon a more decisive action was required. In May a decision to stage a full dress invasion of Lebanon was made with the aim of forcing Syria's opponents to accept her version of a political settlement. Again, implementation was preceded by lengthy political preparations. On June 1 the invasion was staged, but within a few days its failure became apparent.[11] Syria halted the invasion but continued to exercise pressure on its rivals in Lebanon. The outcome was a stalemate which prevailed in Lebanon throughout the summer of 1976. During this period several interim results of Syria's intervention in Lebanon came into a sharper focus.

Results of Intervention

In the preceding paragraphs an attempt was made to follow the escalatory dynamics of Syria's intervention in the Lebanese civil war from the Syrian regime's point of view. The evolution of these dynamics was characteristic of interventionist politics in two important ways. The investments and commitments made in the process of intervention created new vested interests that were not necessarily tied to the original aims of the intervention. Also, while the authors of the intervention were genuinely convinced of the soundness of their judgment and of the purity of their motives, they failed to transmit this conviction to domestic and external critics.

Domestically, Syria's intervention in Lebanon precipitated the first period of sustained political difficulties that the Assad regime had to encounter. The seriousness of these difficulties, indicated at the time by various press reports, was manifested by President Assad's speech of July 20, 1976.[12] It was a lengthy, detailed, and unusually concrete and revealing apologia for his regime's Lebanese policy. The president's attempts to mollify both Ba'ath and non-Ba'ath critics shed much light on his regime's outlook on the Lebanese problem as well as on the major complaints to which he responded.

The direction and course of Syria's intervention in Lebanon aroused opposition in Syria even from the start. Opposition seems to have come first from military and civilian members of the Ba'ath who resented Syria's apparent switch of allegiances. They found the need to engage in combat against Palestinian, Muslim, and leftist elements objectionable. Non- and anti-Ba'ath Syrians tended to ascribe the regime's conduct to sectarian motives.[13] Many of them perceive the Ba'ath regime as an

'Alawi-dominated regime and saw its decision to support an essentially Christian camp against an essentially Muslim one as the natural extension of Syria's domestic politics. The failure to achieve and show concrete results and particularly the failure of the June offensive damaged the regime's image and bred internecine friction. The costs of Syria's Lebanese operations and the dislocations caused by the influx of large numbers of refugees from Lebanon were additional sources of problems and complaints.

Syria's role in Lebanon placed her in the midst of an intense inter-Arab controversy. Objection to her policy came, naturally, from her protagonists in Lebanon but also from Libya, Egypt, and Iraq. Libya was opposed to the direction of Syria's policy, but Egypt and Iraq had broader aims as well. It was all too apparent to Egypt that Syria's regional schemes and ambitions were in part directed at her and were designed to benefit Syria at Egypt's expense. Also the memories of Syria's denunciation of the Sinai Agreement and her attempt to isolate Egypt in its wake were still fresh. The unpopular path which Syria came to follow in Lebanon and the increasing difficulties it met provided Egypt with an excellent opportunity to mount a political counteroffensive. Iraq, too, was worried about the regional context of Syria's success in Lebanon which, coupled with the progress of the Syrian-Jordanian alliance, was likely to bolster the position of the Syrian Ba'ath in its struggle against the rival regime in Iraq. In order to undermine that position, Iraq supported anti-Syrian forces in Lebanon, amplified its propaganda campaign against Syria, and encouraged the opposition inside Syria to President Assad's Lebanese policy. Syria thus found itself against a broad Arab front with Jordan the only explicit supporter of its conduct in Lebanon.[14]

This issue precipitated also a period of tension in Syrian-Soviet relations which began in the spring of 1976 and lasted into 1977. The process of Syria's drift away from an almost complete dependence on the Soviet Union in the conduct of its foreign policy began in 1974. As has been suggested above, Syria's decision to intervene in the Lebanese civil war in January 1976, was influenced by this process. During the late winter and spring of 1976, the Soviet Union became increasingly critical of the general direction of Syria's policy and of the course it chose to follow in Lebanon. The Soviets were aware of Syria's plan to invade Lebanon early in June, and Prime Minister Kosygin in his June 1 visit to Damascus intended to caution the Syrians against the move. But he was confronted with a fait accompli carried out on the eve of his arrival, so that the disagreement was aggravated by an insult. Assad's motivation was quite evident: he intended to keep the decision-making process in Syria clear of Soviet interference. The price, though, was an overt and exacerbated conflict with the Soviet Union.

From Stalemate to Second Offensive, June–October 1976

Following the failure of the June offensive, Syria ceased her military drive in Lebanon and agreed to the dispatching of an inter-Arab military force as a face-saving formula. But Syria did continue to apply pressure on her opponents in Lebanon. This pressure was instrumental in tilting the balance toward the pro-status quo camp but was not sufficient in order to decide the issue and Ba'ath a Syrian solution. The result was a stalemate which lasted through the summer of 1976. By that time Lebanon was actually divided into four parts: the eastern part of the state which became a virtual Syrian protectorate; an autonomous Christian area based on parts of Mount Lebanon, the northern littoral, and Beirut with a political center in Jounieh; and other parts of the country (Tripoli, parts of Beirut, Mount Lebanon, and the southern littoral) which were under Muslim, Palestinian, and leftist control. In south Lebanon a political and administrative vacuum prevailed. A central government as a political entity and its military and administrative agencies were practically nonexistent.

Syria's plan, as it unfolded during the summer, sought to alter this situation. On September 23 Elias Sarkis, the president-elect, was to replace President Frangieh. Around him Syria tried to rebuild the power and authority of the central government and the Lebanese state. A pro-Syrian force, the Vanguards of Lebanon's Arab Army, was formed in the Bekaa Valley as a nucleus for a revived Lebanese army. A group of political factions and personalities who were pro-Syrian or supported Syria's policy in Lebanon, were being organized into a kind of central camp, steering a middle course between the two broad original coalitions which fought the civil war. The central camp was to provide a new president with a political basis from which he would be able to proceed with his efforts to accomplish the major tasks confronting him: bringing the fighting to an end, effecting a national reconciliation and a political settlement, and rehabilitating the Lebanese state and the Lebanese economy. Following the implementation of such a program, Syria's paramount position in Lebanon could be maintained by drawing on several assets: Syria's influence over the president and his embryonic army and bureaucracy; Syria's military presence in various parts of Lebanon and massive presence in the eastern part of the country; and the support of the pro-

Syrian central camp and Syria's position as the arbiter between the warring parties to the Lebanese conflict.

Implicit in this outlook was the precarious and provisional nature of Syria's alliance with the essentially Christian militias and parties who constituted the backbone of the pro–status quo coalition. Syria was forced into this alliance by the circumstances which were created in January and February 1976, and was acutely aware of the damage it caused to the image which the Ba'ath regime sought to project. Nor did the apparent long-term plans of Syria's Lebanese allies accord with her own plans. During the summer while the Muslim-leftist-Palestinian coalition continued its active opposition to Syria's policy, these differences remained latent but both sides were aware of their potential significance.

The intensive political activity which took place during the summer of 1976 affords also an illuminating glimpse into the inner workings of the Syrian Ba'ath regime. An essential characteristic of the Assad regime since its inception has been a sharp but unacknowledged dichotomy between its formal structure and the actual distribution of power and functioning procedures within it. The president and the small coterie which surrounds him control and activate the army, government, party organizations, and the state bureaucracy through an informal network whose existence is known but hardly perceptible. The Lebanese civil war did much to expose this network and to illuminate the decision-making process within the Ba'ath regime. Not only was it a lengthy and critical crisis which required the president's confidants to engage in a sustained political effort and to attend to the minutest details, but the need to operate in the more open political system exposed them to closer scrutiny. Thus it was natural for the Syrian minister of foreign affairs to come to Lebanon to negotiate and mediate or for the chief of staff to review military operations. As it happened, both were close associates of President Assad, and their formal positions were in tune with their ranking in the Ba'ath regime informal hierarchy. But when the head of Syrian Air Force Intelligence or the commander of the Military Police came on political missions to Lebanon, it was clear that they were not serving in their official capacities but rather as trusted members of the president's entourage or network.[15]

Syria's Conflict with the PLO and the Greater Syria Concept

Syria's growing involvement in Lebanon resulted also in the further development of two themes which had been inherent in its regional policy in 1974 and 1975. These are: Syria's claim to a role as great as that of the PLO in the Palestinian movement, and Syria's assertion of the goal of a Greater Syria as a legitimate objective of Syrian policy.

To the PLO's establishment, Syria was a close ally but also a source of danger. Syria and the Ba'ath party were intimately involved in Palestinian affairs and possessed their own Palestinian organization, al-Sa'iqa (a large and important component of the PLO). Syria viewed and presented itself as a custodian of the Palestinian cause whose claim to this effect sometimes conflicted with that of the PLO. When Syria proposed in the spring of 1975 a union of military and political commands, for example, the PLO politely but firmly declined.

The Lebanese civil war developed this tension into a full blown conflict. The PLO's leadership believed that a Syrian hegemony in Lebanon would result in Palestinian subordination to Damascus. The salient role played in the execution of Syria's policy in Lebanon by the leader of al-Sa'iqa, Zuheir Mohsin, and the repercussions of these developments on the domestic politics of the PLO further aggravated the anxiety of the organization's leadership. It therefore sought to obstruct Syria's efforts in Lebanon, and as the major military force in the anti-Syrian camp it did most of the fighting against the invading Syrian army. Syria, in turn, sought to undermine the PLO's moral and political basis. In the course of 1976, it employed two chief arguments against the PLO: (1) that it strayed away from its original aim and course, and in President Assad's words "is fighting today for the purposes of others and against the interests and aims of the Arab Palestinian people"; and (2) that the PLO did not have the sole right to determine what the true interests of the Palestinian people and cause were. Syria's right to do so was as strong. Again, in Assad's words "the problem is sacred for us. The problem is our problem and not one of individuals, particularly when these individuals behave in a way harmful to the problem."[16]

Implicit in this argument was the claim that Syria, because of its position as the heartland of Arabism and because of its record in the struggle for the Palestinian cause, had a say in this matter that was at least equal to that of the PLO. This theme had already appeared earlier in the occasional Syrian references to the notion of Greater or geographic Syria and to Palestine as the major part of southern Syria. The roots of these concepts go back to the years right after World War I when King Faisal reigned in Damascus at the head of an embryonic Syrian state which claimed sovereignty over the whole area of geographic Syria. Since the 1920s the idea has been revised at times by political parties (the SSNP:

Syrian Social Nationalist Party) and by ambitious Hashemite princes and politicians.

In the early 1970s when a comparatively coherent state finally emerged and began to develop ambitions for hegemony over its weaker Arab neighbors, the concept of Greater Syria was revived as a legitimizing notion rather than as a concrete plan of action. But in 1976, as a result of the turn that the Lebanese civil war has taken, the Assad regime discovered and began to emphasize two other useful aspects of the Greater Syria concept. It could justify both Syria's military intervention and presence in Lebanon and its claim to a special status with regard to the Palestinian issue. And indeed in the summer of 1976 and particularly in September, as Elias Sarkis was about to assume the presidency, various Syrian spokesmen (none of them official) began to expound the idea of a federation embracing Syria, Lebanon, Jordan, and the West Bank that would be centered in Damascus. Thus, on September 22, Shawqi Khayr Allah, a former member of the SSNP then employed by the Syrian media, came out with a "program of popular action" seeking to establish "a federation of the countries of the Arab East together with Syria and Jordan. . . . It is the right of the Palestinians and our right and duty that the Palestinians return to their land and that their return be based on an understanding that Palestine is Southern Syria."[17] Earlier in the month, the Lebanese newspaper *al-Sayyad,* quoting Lebanese leaders who had returned from a visit to Damascus, emphasized an advantage accruing to Lebanon from the implementation of such a plan—"the Palestinian concentration in Lebanon will decrease . . . after the federation, including the West Bank, is established."[18]

THE ROAD TO RIYADH

The various political strategies employed by Syria during the summer of 1976 did not bring a political solution in Lebanon any closer. To break the deadlock Syria decided on a second military offensive which it staged at the end of September. This time it was well planned and executed and met with no real resistance. Within a few days the Syrian forces were in a position to subdue the opposition by force and impose a settlement. But rather than do that the Syrian leadership chose to stop short of complete victory and accepted Saudi Arabia's invitation to come to the Riyadh conference.

There were several good reasons for accepting the Saudi invitation. For one thing it was not a mere invitation—refusal to attend would have resulted in heavy financial and political penalties. Syria realized also that by coming to the conference from a position of military strength it could accomplish most of its policy goals in Lebanon. Conversely, a total military victory in Lebanon was against the grain of Syria's Lebanese policy. It would have meant growing dependence on the Christian militias in Lebanon and continued bitter conflict with the Muslim-leftist-Palestinian coalition as well as with the major Arab states. A violent suppression of the PLO in Lebanon was likely to aggravate the regime's domestic problems. Nor were these issues divorced from the broader context of Syrian policy. The Riyadh conference sought to settle the Lebanese conflict in a way that would revive the Arab coalition which went to the October War. The resurrected coalition could then attempt to persuade a new American administration, soon to be elected, to force Israel to make new and major concessions to the Arabs. The Syrian leadership was interested in the reactivation of this coalition and realized that a settlement in Lebanon was an essential precondition.

As it happened, the settlement arrived at in Riyadh and sanctioned in Cairo was favorable to Syria. Syria had to give up its campaign against the PLO's leadership and to accept some limitations on its activity in Lebanon. But these concessions were clearly outweighted by several impressive gains. An Arab consensus came to recognize Syria's paramount position in Lebanon. Its military presence in Lebanon was legitimized by the creation of a largely fictitious Arab Deterrent Force, the bulk of which was Syrian. The expenses of this force, furthermore, were to be paid by oil-producing Arab states. Part of the settlement which was formulated in Riyadh was implemented swiftly and effectively. A cease-fire was enforced and maintained throughout most of Lebanon; the Arab Deterrent Force was formed, composed, indeed, mostly of Syrian units; and a new Lebanese cabinet was formed and the Sarkis administration began the process of rehabilitation and normalization. In these respects the Lebanese civil war came to an end, or to a temporary halt. Other matters remained unresolved and continued to preoccupy Syria's policymakers.

SYRIA'S ROLE IN LEBANON

The months which have elapsed since the end of the Lebanese civil war afford only a limited perspective on Syria's role in that war. The goals of

Syrian policy remained those of summer 1976: to maintain the cease-fire and to promote a long-term political solution that would preserve Syrian supremacy but would do so without requiring the presence and active intervention of large Syrian forces. In pursuing these goals several important successes were registered: the cease-fire, order, and stability were maintained (until the summer of 1978, at any rate, except in the south); the opposition to Syria was neutralized or chose to act in subtler ways; and the Lebanese press was brought under control. Syria was less successful in other respects: little was achieved by way of resolving the fundamental issues which had led to the civil war: the rival camps were not disarmed and a massive, costly, and visible Syrian presence is required to maintain a fragile truce; Lebanon is virtually divided into several areas, only a part of which is actually controlled by Syria; Syria's efforts to build the Sarkis administration and its army have made little progress, and what little progress there was threatened to evaporate in June and July 1978, as Syrian forces shelled Christian strongholds in Beirut and Sarkis threatened to resign; south Lebanon remains an area of political vacuum; and the Christian villages remain tied to Israel through "the good fence," and the danger of renewed warfare in that area remained acute. Nothing was achieved by way of settling the relationship between the Palestinian organizations and the Lebanese state.

Some of the cardinal issues raised by Syria's participation in the Lebanese civil war lost their intensity and acuteness with the passage of time and the emergence of other issues. Syria's position in the system of inter-Arab relations has changed twice since October 1976. The Arab world is no longer preoccupied with the Lebanese problem but rather with the opening of the Israeli-Egyptian dialog. Syria's quarrel with the PLO has been replaced by cooperation in an effort to restrain and control the dialog. Syria's relations with the Soviet Union were mended early in 1977 and had improved considerably by the end of that year.

But Syria's leaders are still coping with the underlying problems of the Lebanese crisis. Their inability to solve these problems is to be explained, at least in part, by some of the misconceptions and miscalculations that were involved in the various phases of Syria's intervention in Lebanon. One concerned the extent of Syria's freedom of action. As a result of American and Israeli acquiescence and of the powerlessness of her Arab rivals, Syria developed in 1976 a capability to intervene militarily in Lebanon and to exercise power in that country. But in actual fact Syria's freedom of action remained constrained by the watchfulness of other external factors, particularly the U.S., Israel, and a number of Arab states. Equally important has been the limited degree to which

Syria's military and political action has affected the domestic political process in Lebanon. Syria has made some important inroads into Muslim and leftist groups in Lebanon. It has not been as successful with the more powerful Christian and Palestinian camps. Nor can it force any of these three major components of the political map in Lebanon into making far-reaching concessions on fundamental issues. After the opening of the Egyptian-Israeli dialog in November 1977, Syria's freedom of maneuver vis-à-vis the major factions in Lebanon became rather limited. In common opposition to Egyptian policy Syria closed ranks with the Palestinian organizations and as a result drew closer to their position in Lebanon as well. This reinforced an earlier tendency to break away from the often awkward cooperation with the Christian militias. While Syrian cooperation with the Frangieh family remained smooth, Syria's relations with the Phalangist and Chamounist militias became strained. The armed conflicts and Syrian shelling of Christian suburbs of Beirut which resulted from this development interfered with Assad's efforts to project the image of an "honest broker" in Lebanon and by causing fresh Syrian casualties further aggravated the impact that the Lebanese crisis had already had on Syria's domestic politics.

Syria's own internal politics also affected her actions in Lebanon. When Syria intervened in Lebanon it did so on the assumption that a coherent state governed by an effective regime can solve the problems of a disintegrating neighboring state. This view, however, overlooked the fact that Syria shared with Lebanon the problems of a fragmented polity and that Syria's own coherence was recent, relative, and fragile. During 1976 and 1977, it transpired clearly that the Ba'ath regime could not afford to conduct the policy which suited its perceived interests in Lebanon. Rather, its involvement in the Lebanese civil war and the policies it chose to pursue seem to have been the most important immediate reason for the severest domestic crisis that the Assad regime had to face. The economic strains, the internecine squabbling, and the exacerbation of confessional tensions have all been felt in 1976. Yet, despite the regime's sustained efforts to contain them, the processes set in motion by Syria's intervention and continued presence in Lebanon continued to plague the Ba'ath regime in 1977 and 1978. At one point, spokesmen for the regime addressed the issue directly and explicitly. Thus on May 21, 1977, the editor of the government's newspaper al-Thawra, Ali Suleiman, warned against subversion and domestic dangers. The enemy, he charged, was employing a dual strategy: trying to keep Syria preoccupied with external problems while eroding it from within. Syria's enemies, he explained, acted in indirect ways "to inject into our country part of what had happened in Lebanon."

Syria's dilemma in Lebanon can thus be described in the following terms. Syria's newly acquired position in Lebanon is something the Ba'ath leaders would like to maintain and develop. Important interests and a large and controversial investment are at stake, and the prospect of an undisputed Syria hegemony is enticing. Yet, the regime's prestige, image, and stability are exposed to serious risks due to the precariousness of Syria's position. A swift consolidation of this position is not in sight. In these circumstances the Syrian Ba'ath regime seems to have formulated a long-term strategy. It envisages a lengthy Syrian stay in Lebanon based eventually not so much on an Arab consensus as on a bilateral arrangement between Syria and the Lebanese government. Syria should press for no radical or rapid changes and should rather rely on the gradual cumulative impact of its presence and subtle pressure. The success of this strategy and its eventual impact on the Lebanese political system are, of course, a matter of the future.

THE MILITARY DIMENSION

Lawrence L. Whetten

THE RECENT CIVIL WAR in Lebanon was one of the most complex military engagements in contemporary Middle Eastern history.[1] At the outbreak of hostilities there were numerous Christian, Muslim, and non-Arab sects and approximately twenty identifiable political groups.[2] As the fighting intensified, international interests and numerous foreign military units became involved, and the various indigenous groups formed highly fluid ad hoc coalitions or split into rival factions. A conservative estimate is that there were no less than thirty separate combat groupings actively engaged at the height of hostilities with some religious sects fighting against coreligionists. The complex task of identifying the components and reconstructing events is further complicated by the diversity of external aid provided the combatants and the relationship between local hostilities and the national interests of foreign powers. This chapter will attempt to explain the major tactical military operations during the two-year civil war.

THE BEGINNING

At the outset of hostilities, the military objectives of both sides had been to inflict as heavy casualties as possible.[3] By July 1975, however, both sides realized that to achieve decisive military advantage they must seize and control the opponent's territory or enclaves. These new objectives intensified and extended the fighting beyond Beirut. In September the Christian town and stronghold of President Frangieh, Zagharta, was besieged by leftist forces. The government committed regular army units to establish a buffer between the two sides.[4] The government was reluctant, however, to deploy the army into Beirut where fighting continued, because of the distinct possibility of precipitating irreparable fissures throughout the military establishment. Christians (who represented 64 percent of the officer corps) repeatedly demanded that a state of emergency be declared, which would allow the army freedom of movement throughout Beirut. Premier Rashid Karameh refused and, at the same time, rejected Christian demands that political talks be returned to the National Assembly (where the rightists held a majority) rather than be conducted in the twenty-member ad hoc National Dialogue Committee (which favored the leftists). Thus a stalemate developed even on the procedural approaches to negotiations, virtually shelving substantive considerations and relegating the cease-fires to the status of lulls in the fighting necessary to regroup, replenish, and redeploy. Fighting throughout the summer remained at sporadic, although locally intensive, levels.

Heavy fighting resumed in Beirut and Tripoli on October 8 and a new dimension was added. Up to this point, the Palestinians had largely remained neutral. Only individual rejectionist units had intervened. By October 15, however, the important refugee camp of Tel al-Za'atar in Beirut was shelled for alleged complicity in attacks against Christians, and the Palestinians retaliated against neighboring Christian sections. Palestinian guerrilla units became increasingly committed to the leftist cause. At the same time, the quantity, size, and kill potential of weapons on both sides sharply escalated.[5] The complexion of the war began to change, and the levels of violence increased. Defensive lines were rapidly being drawn throughout Beirut and the country, requiring even larger quantities of heavy weapons to neutralize them.[6] By year's end, casualties had reportedly reached 6,650 killed and 14,000 wounded.[7]

By mid-December 1975 the fourteenth cease-fire in eleven weeks collapsed in the wake of an increasing level of sectarian murders; the Phalangists blockaded and shelled the Palestinian camps in the eastern and northern suburbs of Beirut. Christian villages in the north were attacked in retaliation, and PLO leader Yasir Arafat threatened full-scale intervention.

Syria viewed this new escalation with alarm and first agreed to a Palestinian request for a demonstration of support. In mid-January 1,500–2,000 troops from the Syrian-controlled Palestinian Liberation Army (PLA) were withdrawn from veteran October War brigades and deployed across the border. They secured the portion of the Bekaa Valley from Jannine, Masnaa, Rayak, and Majdalun. This line gave them control of the two major roads leading into northern Lebanon and into Beirut.[8] By the release of the PLA units, Syria gave a clear indication of its informal support for the continued Palestinian presence in Lebanon under the Cairo accords. Reinforcements were now readily available if the Palestinian camps were again seriously threatened.[9]

NEGOTIATIONS IN DAMASCUS

As a follow-up move to the deployment of the PLA units, Syria put firm pressure on the Lebanese leaders to reach a settlement. On January 21, 1976, rightist and leftist leaders reached a compromise known as the Damascus Pact of February 1976. The political structure of the country was to be altered: the National Assembly was to be enlarged to include an equal number of Muslim and Christian representatives; the religious quota system for hiring in the governmental bureaucracy, that had favored Christians, was to be retained; the prime minister was no longer to be appointed by the president but would be elected by the national legislature, and the president would continue to be Christian. The accord also sanctioned the stationing of PLA troops in Lebanon for the purpose of enforcing the cease-fire accompanying the pact. It also provided that the Cairo Agreements would be strictly observed and Syria would have authority over how and where guerrilla forces would be deployed.[10] But the political reforms and the military limits imposed on the Palestinians satisfied neither side.

The aggregate of the political reforms represented significant concessions by the rightists, but the Palestinians' intervention had swung the balance of forces in favor of the leftists. In order to alleviate rightist apprehensions and to persuade them to accept political compromise, Syria was compelled to guarantee Palestinian respect for Lebanese sovereignty by controlling the disposition of guerrilla forces. Palestinian respect for Lebanese sovereignty meant, among other things, foregoing attacks against Israel from Lebanese territory. Since such activities were a central cause of the civil war, Syrian guarantees, if enforced, could constrain Palestinian operations and improve domestic stability. Doubts about the credibility of the Syrian pledge, however, fostered skepticism among rightists.

Moreover, Syrian restraint of the guerrillas was unpalatable to the leftists who feared that strict subordination of the guerrillas would deny them the military edge necessary to implement their political reforms. Major clashes, in some cases decisive victories, had occurred during the winter fighting at Akkar and Tripoli in the north, Jisr al-Basha, Dbayeh, Zahle in the east, and at Damour and Saadiyet in the south. The leftists now had a decisive military advantage.[11] With over 80 percent of the country under leftist control, there were strong pressures for the Muslims to opt for partition, rather than accept the Damascus Pact. Syria and other Arab states were strongly opposed to partitioning as an untenable solution (e.g., divided Beirut), an undesirable precedent for the settlement of other grievances throughout the Middle East, and an untimely manifestation for the Palestinians that Arabs could not live in a unified, secularized state. Confident and at the same time frustrated, the leftists attempted initiatives in several additional venues.

In March 1976, several thousand Muslim members of the army mutinied and joined the Lebanese Arab Army under Lieutenant Ahmed Al-Khatib. The army seized several garrisons and large amounts of weapons and equipment.[12] General Azziz al-Ahdab, commander of the Beirut Military District, fearing complete disintegration of the country, staged a coup on March 11 and declared himself military governor of Lebanon. He called for the resignation of President Frangieh and the Karameh Cabinet.[13] When many officers declared themselves for Frangieh, it was clear that the army had disintegrated into rival factions, which intensified the war, and Ahdab abandoned his efforts.[14]

THE LEFTIST SPRING OFFENSIVE

The leftists took the offensive again in March. Their intention was to oust the president, the strongest single Christian leader. Frangieh was widely regarded as an obstacle to a durable compromise. Yet when the leftists shelled the palace on March 25, the Syrians transferred an additional 1,000 troops to Lebanon, ostensibly to protect the president, who took refuge in the Christian stronghold of Jounieh.[15] A solution was found when the Syrians forced Frangieh to accept a constitutional amendment permitting his resignation before September and new elections in May. The Syrian-backed candidate, Elias Sarkis, was elected, and the prospects for a political settlement seemed to improve.

During the leftist Spring offensive, the rightists were forced out of the hotel district of Beirut, along the important beach front. Rightist bastions elsewhere began to shrink, and the center of gravity shifted to the southern mountains. Syria openly accused Kamal Jumblatt of sabotaging the Damascus Pact and threatened retaliation against a central leftist base at Aley.[16] After one year of fighting the casualties had mounted to 14,000 killed and nearly 30,000 wounded.[17]

SYRIA CHANGES SIDES

Syria invested its prestige heavily in the February Pact. As the leftist campaign mounted, it altered its support from the Palestinians to the rightists in order to avert the catastrophe of partition. Syrian-controlled troops occupied the entire portion of eastern Lebanon and clashed with leftists troops on the perimeter of Tripoli and the road junction town of Zahle.[18] Syria also conducted an embargo of land-transported supplies and imposed a partially effective sea blockade against Tripoli. (Tripoli is close to Syrian waters; sea traffic into Sidon and Tyre in the south was monitored by the Israelis.)

After the election of Sarkis, Syria launched a major security operation that initially fell well short of its objective.[19] The Syrians for the first time deployed their own forces: an armored column of 60 tanks and 2,000 men. The complexion of the war had again changed. The Syrian force split: one element moved south through Bekaa Valley and then west across the lower Shouf region toward Sidon; it was finally halted at the oil refinery of Zahrani near Sidon. Another moved west along the Damascus-Beirut highway toward Mount Lebanon overlooking the capital. A third detachment pushed north through the upper Bekaa Valley and strengthened units near Tripoli. Within several months the leftists and Palestinians had been forced back into their strongholds around key seaports and western Beirut. The most noteworthy result, however, was the recognition by Jumblatt of the need for mediation to avert a "showdown between the Syrian Army and the leftists and Palestinians."[20] The Syrian strategy had been to isolate and besiege the leftists and Palestinians, but too small a force was committed against opponents with extensive reserves.

The Syrian motives were widely questioned. Israel feared that Syria intended to dominate Lebanon politically and thus extend its military presence throughout the region of Greater Syria, lengthening by sixty miles Israel's northern front. Accordingly, Israel repeatedly warned Damascus through the United States that it could not tolerate the annexation of Lebanon nor the entry of Syrian troops into Fatahland (or south of the so-called "red line" at the Litani River). The Soviets were concerned lest these punitive operations were intended to emulate the Jordanian 1970 crushing of the Palestinians.[21] Sadat condemned the action as unilateral and called for a unified Arab peace-keeping force and reconciliation of Arab differences.[22]

Syria continued to ignore calls from other Arab states for a ceasefire, since, as later became apparent, its objectives were not so far-reaching. Damascus had concluded that it was not in its interests or those of the Arab world to allow a Palestinian-leftist coalition, dominated by the rejectionists, to come to power in Beirut. Such a development would be intolerable to Israel and might invite a pre-emptive war, for which Syria was not prepared. It might also compel the rightists to opt for partitioning. Finally, Syrian constraint of the rejectionists in Lebanon was a clear signal to Jordan and Israel that Syria would be concerned about the eventual establishment of a radical Palestinian regime on the West Bank, underscoring the common interest all three neighbors shared on this issue. At first the PLO accepted this rationale, but as pressure mounted against the camps, it shifted support to the beleaguered Palestinians.

While Syria conducted a countrywide rescue operation for the besieged rightists, the Phalangists attacked the Palestinian camps at Jisr al-Basha and Tel al-Za'atar, the last remaining Palestinian enclaves in the Christian half of Beirut, lending credence to reports of the imminent partitioning. The attacks could not begin until after the Syrians broke the leftists' siege of the Christian city and road junction of Zahle which had been hostage, precluding actions against the camps. A joint pincer maneuver developed at Zahle: when the Syrians advanced from the east, the rightists attacked from the west, forcing the leftists to disperse and freeing rightist forces inside Zahle for operations against the camps. Similar tactics were used near Tripoli, forcing the leftists back into the city.[23] These actions suggest not joint planning, but coordination of key operations.

The Syrian move to isolate Fatahland and surround Sidon ran into difficulty. In their dash forward, the Syrian forces were confined to the roads and moved without adequate infantry support. The psychological effect of tanks soon wore down among the veteran street fighters, and the Syrians lost more tanks and personnel than expected. Local commanders shifted tactics and employed artillery and tanks as fire support for infantry assaults, substantially reducing their losses. Indeed, Syria soon agreed to provide weapons and fire support for rightist infantry, thus remaining on the fringe of the fighting. But without adequate rightist militia in southern Lebanon, Syrian forces withdrew from the outskirts of Sidon, only to force their way back into Jezzine a month later.[24]

The situation in Beirut deteriorated rapidly during the summer, as embassies and foreign nationals began to evacuate. In late June the 1,000-man advance party of the Arab peace-keeping force lacked the military weight and political authority to enforce its mandate against reluctant belligerents.[25] In August Tel al-Za'atar finally fell with considerable loss of life, and the rightists renewed their offensive in the north. By September, however, the PLO submitted to Syrian and Saudi pressure and reached a compromise with President-elect Sarkis in Chtoura in eastern Lebanon. The provisions essentially embodied those of the February 1976 Damascus Pact. The rejectionists, however, refused to accept its terms, and Syria felt compelled to launch yet another punitive offensive with 15,000 men.[26]

From the vicinity of Zahle one Syrian column struck west into the mountains controlling the Beirut highway toward Aley, the last leftist stronghold before the besieged enclave in West Beirut. A second column reinforced operations against Tripoli, and a third detachment retook Jezzine, twelve miles from Sidon, and then Rum. Finally, on October 14 Arba, four miles from the port, was occupied and the peace-keeping force withdrew.[27] Sidon and Tyre were at Syrian mercy.

During this penultimate phase of the civil war, still another international facet emerged. With Israeli encouragement, rightists moved into or reinforced villages in southern Lebanon and served as a buffer in the border region. The Israelis provided weapons, equipment, training, logistics, and artillery fire support (see below). They also implemented a new "open fences" policy: rightists were provided food, welfare services, jobs, and markets inside Israel. The Israeli government publicly warned that it would not tolerate a return of the Palestinians into southern Lebanon. Accordingly, rightists with Israeli fire support attacked the leftist-held town of Marjayoun, which controls the access road to Fatahland.[28] The rightists gradually consolidated their control over about three-fourths of the border villages.

By mid-October the leftist-Palestinian position was clearly untenable. They were out-numbered five-to-one and severely out-gunned. The blockade had had a crippling effect, and they had lost virtually all of their previous territorial gains. Syrian elements now controlled two-thirds of the country and the rightists about one-sixth more, while the leftists-Palestinians were confined largely to three urban areas and inhospitable southern mountains. The Syrian Army had learned important lessons. In combined arms operations, the Syrians emphasized their advantages in firepower and protected their weaknesses. The pattern of heavy, systematic fire from defiladed positions was not intended to achieve dramatic breakthroughs but to convince the leftists that further resistance was hopeless and to indicate that the alternative was a final military solution. During the latter phases of the war, the Palestinians had absorbed a disproportionately high degree of the fighting for the entire leftist coalition, yet the rejectionists now had become the main obstacle to a compromise.

NEGOTIATIONS IN RIYADH

Under increasingly heavy pressure from Saudi Arabia and Kuwait, Presidents Assad and Sadat agreed to meet in Riyadh to resolve their differences over Lebanon. Sadat was concerned about the long-term implications of Syria becoming mired down in a Lebanese "Vietnam" and the subsequent distraction of the Arabs from the more urgent issue of reconvening the Geneva peace talks with Israel. When reassured of the modesty of Assad's aims, Sadat agreed to an accord virtually on Syrian terms. The provisions of the October Riyadh Accord are essentially the same as those of the Damascus Pact, imposing strict regulations on Palestinian forces in Lebanon. In some ways, however, the Riyadh terms were even harsher. Enforcement responsibilities were assigned to the 30,000-man Arab peace-keeping forces, composed mainly of Syrians and subordinated to Lebanese President Sarkis, a Christian. Arafat was then invited to Riyadh where he accepted Syria's terms; the summit conference endorsed the accord and a cease-fire was proclaimed.[29]

Implementation of the cease-fire, however, proved difficult. In a war that had cost over 65,000 lives and had witnessed the breakdown of 60 separate cease-fires, personal emotions remained high.[30] (In comparison, there were 21,000 killed on all sides during the first Arab-Israeli War and only 39,800 in all Arab-Israeli wars, despite much larger numbers of troops involved, using far more advanced weapons systems.)[31] The leaders of the various Lebanese factions had not been invited to Riyadh, and they regarded the accord as a settlement of Palestinian-Syrian differences rather than intra-Lebanese disputes. Yet the Lebanese were exhausted, and without the direct support of foreign military forces the resumption of heavy fighting was impossible. These factors made the implementation of the accord turn on Palestinian compliance with its terms and Syrian ability and willingness to enforce them.

From Syria's viewpoint there were four central problems whose resolution was essential to maintain the cease-fire: (1) separation of belligerent forces; (2) disposition of Palestinian guerrilla forces; (3) disarmament of all factions; and (4) preclusion of activities that might invite Israeli reprisals against Lebanon or might perpetuate continued Israeli support for the rightists. It was imperative to separate and then disarm the combatants. On November 15, Syrian forces moved unopposed into rightist and leftist-held sectors of Beirut and on November 21 occupied the other major cities without serious incident.[32] Disarming the factions proved far more difficult. Both sides refused to surrender their heavy weapons, and the Palestinians, in light of the scale of the fighting for Tel al-Za'atar, insisted that the definition of heavy weapons in the 1969 Cairo accords be significantly upgraded.

When the Arab League endorsed the cease-fire it established a committee, composed of Syria, Egypt, Kuwait, and Saudi Arabia, with Sarkis as chairman, to supervise compliance with its provisions, yet clashes and bombings continued sporadically. The Arab League Cease-fire Supervision Committee set a deadline of January 13 for the withdrawal of the PLA units (which was met) and for the collection and storage of all heavy weapons at prearranged sites under Arab Deterrent Force's (ADF) custodianship. This formula was subsequently approved on March 27 by the Arab League but was not honored in practice by the belligerents. Tension and fighting increased during January with leftists attacks on the key stronghold of Khiyyam, north of the Israeli town of Metulla, and clashes occurred between Syrian and PFLP-GC (General Command) forces.

RESTRAINTS ON THE PALESTINIANS

On February 12, 1977, the committee agreed to impose even more stringent controls on the Palestinians, supplementing the Cairo, Damascus, and Riyadh accords. The terms provided that: (1) all heavy weapons were prohibited inside the fifteen refugee camps; (2) the Palestinian factions were to be held financially responsible for any damages suffered by the Lebanese as a result of Israeli reprisals; (3) members of Palestinian Armed Struggle, a force based on the ratio of 5 men per 1000 refugees, armed only with automatic rifles and subordinated to the ADF, were to provide internal camp security; (4) a ceiling of 200,000 on the number of Palestinians permitted in Lebanon was imposed, 100,000 fewer than were presently in the country; (5) all Palestinian radio stations were banned;

(6) all Palestinian publications were subjected to Lebanese law; (7) Palestinian participation in Lebanese politics was prohibited; and (8) all heavy weapons storage sites and guerrilla forces were confined to an area later specified as three new camps to be built by Saudi Arabia between Tyre, Nabatiyeh, and Sidon, but controlled by the ADF. Arafat and Sarkis signed the new agreement in Damascus.[33]

These were clearly the most severe restraints yet imposed on the Palestinians. When the various accords are viewed separately, each represents an unquestionable indication that not just the Lebanese Right but the majority of the Arab League members were prepared systematically to escalate the restrictions against the Palestinians. Although the terms were harsh, some of their provisions were only gradually enforced and others were relaxed. Many guerrilla groups agreed to relocate to the south with their weapons if the Syrians withdrew their armored battalions surrounding the Beirut camps, which Damascus did on February 15.[34] In April the Lebanese government began refusing entry to all Palestinians with passports from other countries, reducing through attrition the number of Palestinian refugees. Sarkis then ordered 4,000 Palestinian refugees from Tel al-Za'atar, who had relocated in the former Christian town of Damour, to evacuate in order to allow 8,000 Christian refugees to resettle. Paradoxically, while the moderate Arab states were imposing stricter controls on guerrilla activities, they also demonstrated greater consensus for support of PLO demands to participate in the Geneva peace negotiations and guarantee that Palestinian national rights would be a central agenda issue.

In response to the enforcement requirements of the new accord and to strong U.S. pressure, Syria agreed on February 15 to withdraw its forces from the Nabatiyeh-Aichiyeh-Marjayoun line, roughly 9–10 miles from the Israeli border. As the guerrillas began to move south, however, the rightists, who had little faith in the Damascus Pacts and the Riyadh Accords, launched a pre-emptive coordinated offensive aimed at filling the vacuum and extending their control to the entire length of the sixty-mile border, of course, with strong Israeli encouragement. They struck in three directions: against the Palestinian stronghold of Bint Jubeil, six miles from the Israeli border and under siege since November 1976; along the southern edge of the Arkoub region in the northeast; and along the Litani River between Uym and Nabatiyeh. The offensive accelerated the redeployment southward of guerrilla forces, as weak counterthrusts were made at the Christian village of Debel, ten miles from Israel. More importantly, the offensive exacerbated tension between the various Palestinian factions. Initially, al-Fatah and al-Sa'iqa (who had fought each other during the height of the civil war) sided against the rejectionists. By June the rejectionists had split, and severe clashes erupted between the PFLP-GC, who supported the Syrian measures to stalemate the Lebanese crisis, and the PFLP, who opposed constraints against Palestinian operations.[35] A final repercussion of the offensive was that it convinced the PLO that it would have to replace the withdrawn PLA units with a new regular army. Guerrillas were inadequately trained for conventional warfare and coordinated arms operations using heavy weapons. The new organization, called Ajnadin after an ancient Islamic battle, received its first officer graduates on May 31.[36]

Intra-Palestinian clashes in March, the assassination of leftist leader Kamal Jumblatt, and the murder in reprisal of an estimated 200 Christians increased tensions. But Israeli support for rightist offensives and the fall of Taybeh and four other villages prompted the Syrians to reverse sides. Syrian artillery batteries now moved back toward the "red line" to provide fire support for the Palestinians whose camps they were formally threatening and whose activities they were supposedly constraining. This was yet another demonstration of Syrian political dexterity in trying to achieve and maintain a military stalemate in Lebanon among various armed forces with widely divergent objectives. Syria warned that the rightist-Israeli "alliance" was upsetting the balance, and with close Syrian artillery support, the Palestinians recaptured Taybeh and other villages and Khiyyam changed hands several times.[37] Arab pressure for restraint mounted.

ISRAEL INTERVENES

In May the right-wing Lebanese National Front repudiated the Cairo accords and declared that the Palestinian presence in Lebanon was illegal and a burden that must be more equitably shared by other Arab states. The call went unheeded as the Palestinians increased pressure on the rightists. Israel responded by deploying ground units directly against the Palestinians inside Lebanon.[38] Both Syrian and Israeli actions were sufficiently constrained that only minimal casualties were inflicted. Even so, both outside powers had indicated their respective interests in the border area and their willingness to escalate their respective commitments if necessary.

As the intensity of the fighting and internal clashes increased, the level of destruction grew without significant exchanges of territory or advantages. U.S. and Arab pressure for restraint mounted. On July 25 Arafat and Sarkis agreed to abide by and enforce the provisions on all the previous accords governing Palestinian activities. Furthermore, both Palestinian and rightist units were to withdraw nine miles from the border. The ADF was authorized to establish monitoring posts around all Palestinian camps and to enter the camps if weapons levels exceeded prescribed ceilings. All Palestinian offices outside the camps were to be closed for security purposes, and the evacuated border area was to be demilitarized and policed by the reconstituted Lebanese army.[39]

Despite these agreements, fighting resumed in August,[40] and in September the rightist National Front threatened to withdraw support from Sarkis unless the restraints on the Palestinians were enforced.[41] On September 16 Israel dramatized its determination to prevent the return of the Palestinians to the border area by sending an infantry battalion supported by armor and artillery into the renewed battle for Khiyyam. The bombardment reached 1,000 artillery rounds per day, yet the Israelis were unable to take the complex set of bunkers with only a battalion. Faced with the decision of either increasing its involvement or pulling out and confronted with strong U.S. pressure, Israel withdrew its forces across the border and the tenth cease-fire in one year was accepted in October. The Palestinians agreed to withdraw its 5,000-man force to a line nine miles from the border, the rightists agreed to demobilize in place, and the "demilitarized" zone was to be patrolled by the Lebanese army, consisting of three 350-men battalions—two mixed and one purely Christian. The Palestinians were permitted to leave a token force of 250 men in place, but no significant reductions in fighting occurred. Indeed, on November 6 the Palestinians launched a series of rocket attacks against the Israeli coastal resort town of Nahariyeh, killing three civilians. Israel responded with the heaviest artillery barrage yet and, when the attacks continued, launched the heaviest ever air strikes. Over 100 were killed and 170 wounded, and the village of Hezzieh was completely destroyed. Israeli Chief-of-Staff Gur commented about the raids: "We had to explain to the Syrians and the PLO that this new policy [rocket attacks] was quite dangerous."[42]

THE IMPORTANCE OF EXTERNAL SUPPORT

As a result of the inability of the ADF to disarm the rival factions, Lebanon remains a virtually partitioned country, with the two sides as far

from cooperation as before the war. The Palestinians are gradually concentrating in the south. But this modest population shift, however, has
not yet contributed to a solution of the main problem, namely preventing those Palestinian actions against Israel that might either invite Israeli
retaliation against Lebanon or strengthen the ties between Israel and the
rightists. Only more determined efforts by external powers can enforce
compliance with the constraints established in the Riyadh Accords.

The pattern of external assistance provided the warring factions
presented an even more checkered picture of alternating sources of supply that is germane to an assessment of the political implications of the
war. The plethora of types and caliber of weapons soon became a constraint of military efficiency. Initially, the rightists received financial
backing from the conservative Arab states, anxious to contain the rise of
rejectionist influence. This discrete infusion was halted, however, after
the rightist attack on the Palestinian camps and the reported mistreat-
ment of leftist prisoners.[43] The destruction of Tel al-Za'atar and the alleged murder of prisoners further alienated these sources of funds.

During the initial phases these funds were used to procure arms directly from state agencies in Czechoslovakia and Bulgaria. These nations
provided a wide range of supplies and light weapons up to full shipload
allotments. Apparently, the objections of the various regional Communist parties and the Palestinians closed this source of arms and
materials.[44] The largest arms markets, however, were apparently the private manufacturers in western Europe, especially, France, Belgium, and
Spain, and the international arms merchants based mainly in Cyprus.[45]
The collapse in March 1976 of the Lebanese army provided a new source
of arms but also escalated heavy weapons procurement. Bringing the cy-
cle nearly full circle from the initial support extended by the conservative
Arab states, Israel became the most reliable source of weapons, equipment, and logistical support for the rightists during the later stages of the
war. Israel supplied significant quantities of weapons across its northern
border and via third-country carriers to the northern Christian port of
Jounieh.[46] At the same time, Israel exercised an active blockade against
the ports of Tyre and Sidon. A simultaneous Syrian blockade of Tripoli
was only partially effective. For example, as late as August 1976, some
ten freighters and tankers were sighted on a single day awaiting off-
loading. The Israelis' main targets were the small local gunrunning
craft.[47] The problems associated with the diversification of weapons was
partially compensated for by the readily available new sources and a
gradually widening range of arms.

External support for the leftists and the Palestinians was equally heterogeneous. Initially, the Syrians kept open the "Arafat Trail" on the road over the northern shoulder of Mount Hermon into Fatahland. This came to be regarded by all concerned as virtually an extraterritorial conduit between Syria and the Palestinians, despite the fact that it traversed Lebanese territory. Over this route Syria supplied the bulk of the military requirements for both the Palestinians and the leftists.[48] Kuwait was the next largest donor during this period, supplying funds for foreign procurements.

As the war progressed and arms deliveries became increasingly uncertain, Fatah became reluctant to share its resources with the rejectionists. Accordingly, the latter groups sought and received support from the radical Arab states, mainly Libya and Iraq. The seaports rapidly became the main funnels for funds and weapons. Indeed, Iraq reportedly sent both arms and manpower via Alexandria. (It is not known, however, whether the men were Iraqi "volunteers" or Palestinians from the Iraqi-controlled Arab Liberation Front.) When the Syrians restricted the traffic along the overland route in spring 1976, the leftists inevitably concentrated their procurement activities on Cyprus. Limassol and Larnaca became principal shipping heads for resupply operations, including a vast range of military equipment.[49] The specific origin of the equipment remains unclear, but the continued extensive use of Warsaw Pact weapons and munitions strongly suggests the suppliers were East Europeans.

Since neither side had an indigenous ability to produce arms or munitions, the total war-waging capability had to be procured from foreign sources. No official public estimates have yet been made of the scale of the purchases or their dollar values. Such high casualties, however, indicate that the magnitude of arms transfer was immense, and accordingly, demonstrate the dependency of the factions on the prevailing international climate. The Arab peace-keeping force was charged with the responsibility for controlling the flow of military supplies to the belligerents, but such utter dependency generated corresponding ingenuity in preserving and augmenting existing stocks, especially in the heavy weapons category.[50]

The war is likely to be classified as a war fought by the wrong people for the wrong reasons. No indigenous faction had an advantage in weaponry, all were equally dependent upon foreign sources. Military expediencies required the enlistment of foreign military forces to advance the respective belligerents' goals. The rejectionists sought military victory for the leftists, the PLO became increasingly concerned about extradition with honor and the retention of its surrogate homeland, and Syria could not avoid the necessity for a stalemate, requiring periodic changing of sides. Syrian dexterity probably blocked the radicalization or formal partitioning of Lebanon, its priority objectives in the war, but it did not resolve the interfactional conflicts; indeed, it intensified the international dependency of all groups. While the war satisfied none of the factions, all emerged exhausted.

The continuing Syrian military presence and the indispensability of the international linkage as the prerequisite for the resumption of hostilities augurs well for the continuation of the stalemate, if the radicals can be disciplined. If not, and the level of Israeli and rightist reprisals continue, little will have been achieved politically and the principal result of the war will have been merely the underscoring of Lebanon's dependence on other nations for its continued existence as a unified state.

THE ISRAELI INVASION OF SOUTHERN LEBANON

Israel's incursion into Lebanon in mid-March 1978 dramatized Lebanon's present inability to maintain her sovereignty and unity. Within Israel it was generally felt that terrorist raids near Tel Aviv warranted strong reprisals, but most Israelis expected incisive commando raids or the customary heavy air attacks. The Israeli government, however, decided to launch an operation that would deny the PLO its war option, that is, to preclude further shelling of Israel from Lebanese territory. Israel had already effectively persuaded Egypt, Jordan, and Syria to prohibit PLO military attacks from their territory, but had failed to secure the same sanctions in Lebanon in 1975 because of the weakness of the Beirut government. The Israeli government, therefore, was determined to operate directly against the PLO in Fatahland.

The military command had two choices: either to advance frontally across the border to a depth of roughly six miles, or to strike north to Tyre and then swing east below the Litani River to cut off the Palestinians and then systematically reduce them. The latter option appeared the more costly in casualties, and the former plan was implemented. The operation required a protracted three-day buildup that was readily observed by the Palestinians, who withdrew men and equipment, leaving only a strong rearguard. When the U.S. introduced a Security Council resolution calling for withdrawal, Israel decided to shift objectives and occupy all of Fatahland up to the Litani, a maneuver that hit numerous operational snags. Palestinian resistance was stronger than expected, resulting in only thirty Israeli deaths, but forcing the Israelis to inflict much higher property damage than anticipated. While the Palestinians were hurt temporarily, thousands of volunteers came from the diaspora and Iraq, and millions of dollars were privately donated to the PLO. At the same time, Israel was forced to use long-range artillery and onerous weapons, such as white phosphorous and cluster munitions against Palestinians defending population centers, and to destroy systematically many border villages.

The heavy civilian casualties that resulted from Israel's attacks alienated European, American, and some segments of Israeli opinion. The extent of the destruction, for example, was reported in Israel only by foreign media, indicating the government's nervousness on the issue. The introduction of UN forces with a mandate to pacify the region between the Litani and the Israeli border, with force if necessary, had two immediate effects: Israel gradually turned over control of southern Lebanon to the UN commanders and withdrew toward the border; while the PLO was forced once again to face the military consequences of terrorism. The struggle that ensued appeared to deepen the rifts within the movement and to trigger the arrest of the Abu Daoud faction. As the fighting subsided, Israel had managed to add the UN troops to its own strike force and its alliance with the Christian villagers and Saad Haddad's 700-man military force, and, in this way, had increased her protection against the concentration of large numbers of Palestinian troops in southern Lebanon.[51]

ISRAEL

Lewis W. Snider, P. Edward Haley,
Abraham R. Wagner, and Nicki J. Cohen

Until the late 1960s Israeli leaders could regard Lebanon as playing only a limited military and political part in the Arab-Israeli conflict. Dominated by conservative politicians, many of whom were Muslim as well as Christian, Lebanon gave only rhetorical and diplomatic support to the Arab confrontation states and Palestinians. Lebanon stayed out of the wars of 1947, 1956, and 1967, as well as 1973. Pulled toward the West by its disproportionately influential Christian and particularly Maronite communities, Lebanon was at the same time pushed toward the Arab and Palestinian causes by its own Muslim and progressive groups, including large numbers of increasingly militant Palestinians. All too aware of Israel's military power and fearful of the internal consequences of any major change in foreign policy, the established Lebanese political leadership skillfully achieved an immobility in foreign affairs that helped to preserve a fragile democracy without completely satisfying any of the parties, inside or outside Lebanon's borders.

Appearances were deceiving. What seemed to be a remarkable talent for flexibility and give-and-take on foreign and domestic policy actually concealed the failure of Lebanon's political system to resolve her internal and external problems. When in 1967 the despair of Egypt and Syria over their crushing defeat by Israel was added to the growing militancy of the Palestinians, and the Arab cause gained more and more support inside Lebanon, the country began to pay dearly for the long years of immobilism.

At Cairo in May 1969 the Lebanese government felt compelled to permit the PLO to use Lebanese territory to launch attacks against Israel. As noted by Barakat and Cooley, the Cairo Agreement gave control of the Palestinian population in Lebanon to the Palestinian resistance move-

The authors wish to express their thanks to Jim Price for research assistance and William Brownlee for helpful substantive comments and suggestions.

ment. Under the terms of the Cairo Agreement, Lebanon was the only country to permit assault squads to conduct raids across its frontier with Israel.[1] No doubt the Lebanese government accepted the Cairo Agreement in order to placate Muslim and progressive opinion at home and, in this way, to prevent a rupture between Christians and Muslims in the tiny country. They also hoped to maintain good relations with the major Arab governments on whose tolerance and forbearance depended Lebanon's sovereignty and independence. No doubt they also hoped to escape Israeli reprisal. All three hopes were vain. Politics in Lebanon grew more tense, the Arab governments gave no sure help, and Israel struck heavily again and again at both Lebanon and the Palestinians there, in an attempt to compel the Lebanese government to repudiate the Cairo Agreement. The situation inside Lebanon grew more explosive after 1970, when thousands of Palestinians escaped to Lebanon from Jordan, quickly overfilling the refugee camps around Beirut, with their squalid living conditions. Treated as second-class citizens, the Palestinians in these camps bitterly resented both the Israelis and many of the well-to-do Lebanese as well.[2]

When the Palestinians attacked from Lebanon, Israel struck back harder, catching the Lebanese government in a cross fire. Conservatives in Lebanon demanded that the government curb the guerrillas. Lebanese progressives and many Muslims demanded that, on the contrary, the government and army defend Lebanon and protect the Palestinians. Unable to satisfy either of these demands, the Christian-dominated government watched its position and competence crumble. By 1975 the Lebanese government was paralyzed and the army was unable to restrain the Palestinians. The country was wide open to foreign intervention; indeed major groups inside Lebanon courted outside supporters. Of all those outsiders who meddled in the Lebanese crisis, Israel and Syria had the most at stake and committed the greatest human and material resources to realize their objectives.

Sustained fighting broke out in Lebanon in the summer of 1975, and it went against the Maronite Christians and the Phalange.[3] Israel's response was to strengthen its ties with the Christian minority. Israel gave covert military aid to the Christians and, through the "good fence" policy along the Lebanon-Israel border, provided jobs and medical assistance to residents of southern Lebanon.[4] Israel had several reasons for supporting the Maronites at the beginning of the conflict. While the Christians had dominated the Lebanese government, the border with Israel had been quiet and Lebanon had been a fairly stable country. In addition, the primary obstacle to the achievement of Syrian aims in Lebanon and the driving force behind opposition to the PLO was Camille Chamoun. President Sarkis, the Phalange led by Pierre Gemayel, and former president Suleiman Frangieh favored a continued Syrian presence within well-defined limits. Although Chamoun's militia numbered only some 4,000 compared to a Phalange militia of 10,000, Chamoun remained the most important Maronite leader and the only Lebanese figure willing to mobilize a general rightist resistance to Syria. Without external support his movement lacked the resources to challenge Syria. Israel became the main source of that support.

Initially Israel opposed Syrian involvement in Lebanon because of Syria's support for the Lebanese Muslim/leftist-Palestinian coalition. From January 1976 Syria appeared to be working for a political settlement that only slightly improved the position of the Muslims and did not compromise Israel's security interests. By March 1976 the Syrians had clearly begun to shift their support toward the Christian rightists in an effort to end the fighting in Lebanon and reestablish political stability. A gradual, limited overlap of Syrian and Israeli objectives in Lebanon began to emerge: both wished to end the civil war, prevent Lebanon from falling under the dominance of Lebanese leftists and their Palestinian allies, and preserve as much of the Christian political and economic positions in Lebanon as was possible. In response, Israel began to signal both Syria and the United States that although she recognized the overlap of objectives, Syrian dominance throughout Lebanon would be viewed as a threat to Israel's security. Israel issued repeated warnings to the Assad government that prolonged Syrian intervention, let alone control of southern Lebanon, would bring greater Israeli involvement and perhaps direct reprisals against Syrian targets.

While they were willing to recognize a limited coincidence of objectives with Syria, both the Begin government and its Labor predecessors made clear where those objectives diverged. This was particularly evident in the artificial separation of south Lebanon from the rest of the country. Only the Christian war effort in the south was supported by direct, massive Israeli intervention on the ground in the spring of 1978. The war in the south eventually became divorced from the rest of the country, taking on a dynamic of its own even though it had grown out of the same social, political, economic, and military problems that faced Lebanon as a whole.

ISRAELI INTERVENTION I: December 1975–July 1977

Israel launched a major raid into southern Lebanon in December 1975, as an explicit warning to both the PLO and Lebanese government that fur-

ther terrorist activity would be met with a strong Israeli response. This
was the first phase of Israeli intervention into Lebanon, and it was characterized by three elements worth noting:

1. Israel supported Christian units inside Lebanon covertly with
supplies of arms and overtly in southern Lebanon through heavy artillery and air support.
2. Israel and Syria tacitly agreed on the nature and extent of Syrian
involvement, expressed by Israel in terms of the "thin red line" (the Litani
River by most interpretations) beyond which Syrian movement would
not be tolerated.
3. Israel initiated the "good fence" policy along the Israeli-Lebanese
frontier, under which Lebanese civilians were encouraged to cross the
frontier on a daily basis after jobs in neighboring Israeli settlements,
medical attention, and other social amenities.

Although Syria and Israel each had different reasons for supporting
the Christian forces, their aid enabled the Christian militias to try to seize
or destroy the remaining Palestinian positions in southern Lebanon. By
February Syria was determined to stabilize Lebanon. The Syrians decided to rescue the declining Christian position in order to make use of
the Christian militias in the effort to stop the fighting and reach a political settlement satisfactory to all sides. Because of the threat of Israeli
invasion Syria could not extend her influence into southern Lebanon. Realizing their chance, Christian forces exploited Syrian and Israeli policy
for their own purposes and attempted to complete the destruction of the
Palestinian forces in that part of the country. Caught between two fires,
Palestinian officials agreed on February 26, 1977, to withdraw from the
Israeli border provided the Syrians halted their shelling of Palestinian
refugee camps around Beirut.

Large scale fighting erupted on April 2 when Christian rightist militiamen supported by Israeli artillery launched a major offensive aimed at
capturing the entire region along the border with Israel. Palestinian and
leftist forces counterattacked on April 4 with Syrian consent and possibly Syrian artillery support as well. Three days later Palestinian leftist
forces recaptured the village of Khiyyam. As the rightist offensive began
losing ground the Palestinians suspended their operations in southern
Lebanon instead of going on the offensive themselves. This suspension
was accompanied by a Syrian warning on April 10 that Damascus would
not tolerate the escalation of tensions in southern Lebanon.[5] Syria wished

to curb the immediate Palestinian threat to Israel in order to prevent Israel and the Christians from destroying Palestinian positions in the south. The warning from Damascus was a signal to Israel to reciprocate Syrian restraint by resisting the temptation to aid the Christians in their faltering offensive. Syria, the signal suggested, would not allow the Palestinians to annihilate the rightist militias.

If that was the signal it elicited a negative reply. Fighting intensified on April 11 and 12, and Israeli Foreign Minister Yigal Allon warned that Israel "shall not tolerate activity against Lebanese villages that are so close to our borders" and that such activity could trigger an all-out Middle East War.[6] Israel, in other words, might allow the Palestinians to try to hold on to some of their positions in the south if these were four to six miles away from the border and did not lead to the decisive defeat of the rightists, which Israel would prevent by direct intervention on the ground. Fighting continued between Christian and Palestinian factions in the south, and Lebanon began to fall into Syrian and Israeli spheres of influence. Syria and Israel had fashioned policies that were mirror images of each other. Israel was actively involved in the south and covertly aided the beleaguered Christians in the north; Syria remained actively involved in the fighting around Beirut and covertly aided the PLO in the south.

The Palestinian buildup in the south and the collisions with the Christians and Israel followed Syria's defeat of the Palestinians in the north. By July 1977, however the uneasy partnership between Syria and the rightists had become strained and Palestinian-Syrian relations were on the mend. In July Syria and the PLO agreed to pacify southern Lebanon. The main agreement called for the withdrawal of all combatants from the south, the establishment of demilitarized zones, and the stationing of Lebanese troops in the area. The plan was based on the 1969 Cairo Agreement. The Christian leadership, in the meantime, had denounced the Cairo Agreement as void and had declared that the presence of any Palestinians in Lebanon was illegal.[7] With compromise impossible, a new outbreak of fighting became certain, and it brought a new round of Israeli intervention.

ISRAELI INTERVENTION II: August 1977–March 1978

Shortly after he became Prime Minister in May 1977, Menahem Begin openly acknowledged Israel's role in Lebanon, both in the north and in the south. Israeli ground forces were actively participating in the fighting in southern Lebanon, he said, and they would defend the Christians from "annihilation" and stamp out the bases for terrorist activities. Begin likened the plight of the Lebanese Christians to those Jews killed during the Second World War by the Nazis. At his urging, the Israeli Cabinet repeatedly voted to support the Christian forces in times of crisis, utilizing military support where necessary and maintaining political support for the Christians vis-à-vis the rest of the world.

Long the leader of Israel's political opposition, Begin had for some two decades chided the Labor governments for not taking stronger action against the PLO and "cutting off the arm" that was killing innocent Israeli civilians. Now, as Israel's leader, Begin had little choice but to take such actions himself when confronted with terrorist acts. One effect of Begin's activist policy was a pledge to create an autonomous defense capacity for the Christians in southern Lebanon. The openness of Begin's policy had the effect of undercutting the authority of President Sarkis in his own country and of spiking a Syrian plan to pacify the south by replacing the Palestinians with Lebanese forces loyal to Sarkis.

Israeli support operations, which had been thinly veiled at best, were now publicized widely. Coordination between Israeli Defense Force (IDF) units and Christian forces operating in the south received widespread media attention. Joint patrols, training programs, and support operations increased the scope of Israeli involvement dramatically. A United States proposal for a UN military force in Lebanon received lukewarm support from Israel. Skeptical of the ability of any UN force to maintain order in the absence of a commitment of the parties to refrain from violence, Israel held little hope that such a force could in fact curb PLO activities, or protect the outnumbered Christian militias from PLO or Lebanese Muslim forces.

Israel's actions in southern Lebanon of themselves might have prompted the Palestinians to increase their attacks on Israeli territory. Two other developments increased the pressure on the PLO and made a dramatic step of this kind unavoidable. They were Begin's support for additional Israeli settlements on the West Bank and the Carter Administration's call for a conference at Geneva to settle the Arab-Israeli conflict, at which conference the PLO and Palestinian interests might be given short shrift. On August 15 Palestinian military sources in Beirut announced that the PLO would step up its military operations within Israel in response to Israel's apparent moves toward annexation of occupied territory.[8]

On September 2 Israeli troops reportedly crossed into southern Lebanon and seized sixteen persons.[9] Throughout September Israel maintained infantry and armored units in Lebanon in support of the rightist forces. An American-mediated cease fire was finally imposed September 26, and Israeli troops and armor reportedly returned to their own side of the border. The IDF also stepped up its bombing of terrorist bases in southern Lebanon in retaliation for PLO attacks on the Israeli town of Nahariyah and other settlements. The resultant damage and its portrayal in the media brought even greater pressure from the U.S. and other world powers to curtail such retaliatory raids.

Despite constant Israeli pressure on Palestinian positions in the south, arms continued to flow to them, with the greatest concentration of weapons moving to the PLO in the area of Tyre. At one point, Palestinian guerrillas were caught smuggling arms through the Israeli port of Haifa to positions north of the frontier. The Lebanese National Movement and the PLO joined forces in January 1978, clearly outnumbering the Maronite Christians of Camille Chamoun and his followers. These combined forces moved increasingly underground, while they continued their terrorist activities against Israeli targets. These targets included the Israeli town of Metulla, which was shelled regularly along with other settlements in the Hula Valley of Israel.

ISRAELI INTERVENTION III: March 1978–July 1978

Becoming more involved in southern Lebanon, Israel actively sought the use of Lebanese villages as staging areas and bases from which to attack terrorist sites. At the same time the PLO increased terrorist activity against Israel causing the IDF to increase its troop concentrations near the frontier. There is some evidence to suggest that Saiqa terrorists became active in the area of southern Lebanon in addition to PLO regulars, and some have even suggested that PLO units were partially manned by Syrian regulars. The military situation thus looked increasingly dangerous to the Maronite Christians, and they turned more and more to Israel for military support of all kinds, as well as for economic aid and a continuation of the "good fence" policy. It was in this context that Palestinian terrorists commandeered an Israeli bus on March 11, 1978, and drove it into a wild gun battle with Israeli security forces. This horrifying attack caused the loss of thirty-seven lives in Israel and injured eighty-two, and was more a symptom of the ongoing conflict than an injury to Israel's security. The Begin government, nonetheless, found in the attack the justification for a major escalation of its involvement in Lebanon.

There was considerable uncertainty in the days after the attack on the bus about the form and extent of the Israeli response, although it was widely assumed that the Israeli government would react strongly. Attacks on southern Lebanon as well as the Beirut area were anticipated. Arabs, fearing a massive Israeli response, began to flee southern Lebanon for the north, causing yet greater pressure on a war-torn Beirut. Both the United States and Egypt cautioned the Israeli leaders against overreacting to the incident; both recognized that such warnings were unlikely to be heeded.

Egypt's attitude concerned the Israelis, although it was clear to Begin and his key advisors that Sadat would not be likely to interfere with an Israeli reaction in this case. Palestinian terrorists in Cyprus had recently assassinated the Editor of *al-Ahram*, Yusef al-Sebai, a close friend of Sadat, and the Egyptian President was not about to risk the fate of his peace initiative in an attempt to curb an Israeli strike against the PLO bases in Lebanon. Israel quite likely informed Egypt of its intention to react strongly in advance of the invasion of southern Lebanon.

Stone of Wisdom

Before dawn on March 14, 1978, the IDF launched its awaited response to the bus attack. It was Israel's largest incursion ever into southern Lebanon. The IDF attacked suspected terrorist bases and created what was termed a "Stage I security belt." Israeli forces occupied a band of territory along the frontier some seven miles in width. There is some evidence to suggest that this operation, termed "Stone of Wisdom," was coordinated with Christian forces, and that the overall objective of the operation was to turn over control of the security belt to the Christian militia. Whether or not it was part of the initial plan, the IDF then commenced a second stage of the operation by moving toward the Litani River and to the outskirts of Tyre. Within this considerably expanded zone the IDF used heavy air and artillery bombardment to rid the area of PLO strongholds and positions.

Israel's principal reason for invading southern Lebanon was to secure the Israeli-Lebanese border area from further terrorism. The Palestinian terrorist attack on an Israeli tour bus March 11, however, apparently provided an opportunity and justification for an operation already in preparation. In retrospect the "Litani Campaign" appears to have been the opening move in a new round of bargaining between Israel and Syria, along with the United States and the PLO, for suitable arrangements in the south to insure safety along the Israeli-Lebanese frontier. It was also an Israeli effort to re-establish a tacit understanding with Damascus on the limits to which Israel would tolerate Syrian activity south of the Litani.

The Deteriorating Christian Position in the South

Prior to the Palestinian attack of March 11, Israel had sought to reverse the deteriorating position of the Christian forces in Lebanon, a deterioration which Israel perceived to have been actively abetted by Syria. In February Israel was reportedly seeking the use of Lebanese villages in order to establish road and telephone links with Israel and to move the border fence to the other side of the village, Meis al-Jabal, situated about a mile and a half from the Israeli border.[10] On March 2 a joint Palestinian-leftist force overran the Christian village of Marun al-Ra's. The village is located one mile north of the Israeli border. The Christian defenders suffered heavy losses, and the attackers captured some Israeli-supplied weapons and vehicles.[11] On March 7, Israeli military concentrations along the Lebanese border were reportedly reinforced with tanks and troop transports. Israeli aircraft were reported to be undertaking continuous reconnaissance flights over the areas of Tyre and Bint Jubail where the Palestinian and leftist forces were located.[12] On March 9, two days before the terrorist attack on the Israeli tour bus, a delegation from the Christian enclave in southern Lebanon informed Israeli officials of the critical situation prevailing in the enclave villages as a result of the capture of Marun al-Ra's. The villagers claimed that al-Sa'iqa which is under Syrian control had used leaflets to warn villages in the area not to accept aid from Israel and that, in any case, Israel could not be relied upon since its hands were tied by the attempts to work out a peace agreement with the Arabs.[13]

Israel, in short, was faced with a credibility problem. The Christian Lebanese militia commander, Major Sa'ad Haddad, described it when he said: "The question now [after the fall of Marun al-Ra's] is whether or not Israel really will come to the aid of the Christian villages when the Syrians attack again."[14] Israel would be unable to count on the Christian militias and villages to act as a security buffer against Palestinian penetration if it appeared that she would not aid the Christians in an emergency. Moreover the reports of Syrian-controlled al-Saiqa participation was a challenge to Israel's warnings against the presence of "foreign troops" south of the Litani. It is difficult to know for certain if the attack on Marun al-Ra's was indeed evidence of an expanded Syrian presence in the south. What is important is that Israel's Christian allies thought so, which meant that Israel could not ignore the situation indefinitely.

Armies the size of the Israeli force that invaded Lebanon—fifteen to twenty thousand troops in a combined air, sea, and ground assault—do not move on three days of planning. Israeli sources were quoted after the invasion to say that a move into Lebanon to establish a security belt had been under study for two years. The plan had been revived in February when reinforcements, including a large group from Syria, had arrived for the Palestinians.[15] Moreover, the size and ferocity of the invasion force indicate that the Israeli action was meant to accomplish more than retaliation for a terrorist attack. Retaliation would have been carried out by a quick, heavy air strike, as had often been done in the past. No Israeli official could claim that driving the Palestinians out of southern Lebanon could physically prevent a repetition of the kind of seaborne raid that occurred on March 11. Those raiders had come not from southern Lebanon but from Damour, just a few miles south of Beirut.

Operation Stone of Wisdom was, on one level, an attempt by Israel to establish a *modus vivendi* on its border with Lebanon similar to those worked out with Syria and Jordan along their frontiers with the Jewish state. In Israeli eyes the prohibition of terrorist attacks on Israel from Lebanon may also have been a prerequisite for successful bilateral or multilateral negotiations with the Arab states. As Israel's Chief of Staff Mordechai Gur observed in an interview on March 17:

> It has become clear that failure to solve the Israeli-Arab conflict in an absolutely clear manner in all spheres would lead to problems in time of peace. During our talks in Egypt, at least in my presentation of the security problems of the State of Israel, we put heavy stress on that point. Here we had an example. While negotiations with Egypt were going on, and everyone was hoping it [sic] would reach a successful conclusion, we were faced with a security problem on another front, and the State of Israel acted according to all its legitimate rights.[16]

Israel alone cannot control terrorist activity along its frontiers with Syria and Jordan. Israel's policy of holding host governments responsible for guerrilla attacks originating from their territory eventually persuaded Jordan and Syria to become silent partners in controlling terrorists along their frontiers with Israel. As mentioned earlier, Israel's policy of holding the Lebanese government responsible for Palestinian attacks originating from Lebanese soil had proven unworkable and had contributed to the tensions that triggered the civil war. In 1978 there was no effective indigenous governmental authority in Lebanon with whom Israel could form a silent partnership to control terrorism. The remaining alternative candidates were United Nations forces, the Lebanese Christian militias, and the Syrians. The principal problem with Syria was that Damascus was the only actor in the Lebanese crisis capable of imposing the effective control on Palestinian guerrilla activities that Israel sought. That role, however, would require a Syrian military presence south of the Litani, a development which Israel opposed. From the Israeli point of view, relying on Syria to control terrorism in southern Lebanon risked undermining one of Israel's principal objectives in Lebanon—the minimizing of Syrian presence there.

Israeli policy-makers have never had much faith in the ability or the determination of UN forces to police and contain Palestinian infiltrators. The Christians in southern Lebanon could be counted on to counter Palestinian penetration effectively. However, as the fall of Marun al-Ra's suggested, the Christians could not neutralize a determined Palestinian buildup in the south without direct Israeli military intervention. Thus some control had to be imposed on the Palestinian guerrillas north of the Christian enclave along Israel's border. Syria was in the best position to exercise that control; by the threat implicit in the larger-scale invasion, Israel meant to compel Syria to exercise it. In the bargain, by the systematic and calculated bombardment of civilians in the south, Israel would empty that area of many of those sympathetic to the Palestinians. In Maoist terms, Israel would strangle the guerrilla-fish by pumping out the water.

Israel attacked and destroyed the villages used by the guerrillas without regard to the presence of civilians. This caused very heavy loss of life. Two thousand Arab civilians died during the fighting, according to news reports. In contrast, only two hundred Palestinian commandos were killed and four hundred wounded. Israel's losses were sixteen killed and forty-two wounded.[17] Moreover, the IDF conducted full-scale warfare through the whole territory south of the Litani River. This, too, caused losses, and resulted in the flight of 200,000 civilians who escaped, carrying what belongings they could. These new refugees found rough shelter at best. The reports from journalists in Arab Lebanon and with the IDF are chilling and provide conclusive evidence of the character of the Israeli invasion.[18] In an eye-witness report from Tyre, Dean Brelis, a correspondent for *Time*, noted that what had been a city of 45,000 was virtually emptied by Israeli air and sea bombardment. "The port remained undamaged. What had been hit and hit hard was the civilian dwellings. Was this deliberate counter-terror on the part of the Israelis? It certainly looked that way."[19]

Once again the Israelis had inflicted far more suffering than they had endured. The disproportion in hardship and death bore every sign of calculation. Israel intended to punish the commandos and the civilians close to them, to destroy their bases, and to eliminate the Palestinians' preparations and arrangements for attacking Israel.[20] Israel was not ready to stay its hand even though the punishment would fall heaviest not on the commandos but on civilians and would drive hundreds of thousands from their homes. The reasons for this emerged clearly in an interview of Israel's Chief of Staff, Lieutenant General Mordechai Gur, on the Jerusalem Domestic Television Service program "Weekly Newsreel," in Hebrew on March 24, 1978. General Gur was interviewed by 'Amiram Nir:

> *Nir:* Was the relatively large number, maybe hundreds, of Lebanese citizens killed in the course of the action and villages which were sacrified really necessary?
> *Gur:* The questions faced us: How justified was it for us to take casualties by using less fire on those villages, and what was the most correct way to hit the terrorists. We decided that, on all grounds, it would be better to use the method of directing fire and afterwards moving in to mop up. As a result of that, these villages were badly hit.
> *Nir:* I would nevertheless like to pause here on the moral aspect. Is the technical-military justification for hitting villages and the civilians living in them strong enough to justify a different moral level concerning the philosophy of security?
> *Gur:* Let us go back a little. . . . The northern border and its settlements suffered so much for very many years—innocent civilians, both women and children and adults, were forced to live for fairly long periods of time in shelters, to travel in convoys, to be afraid of practically every bang of a cup or a door lest it turn out to be that of a bomb or a katyusha. That means that today we acted after very many years of unceasing suffering . . . while on the other side there were villages which, willingly or unwillingly, but for years, hosted the terrorists and knew what they were doing. . . .
> I must remind you now that, as a result of terrorist activity in the Jordan Valley, the entire Jordan Valley was emptied of inhabitants. Our people did not evacuate, but they held on for 2 and ½ years, 3 years, under endless shellings and shooting and ambushes. This means that the question of suffering applies to both sides. The power of resistance of our inhabi-

tants was stronger. When it came to the test we took into account the historic accumulation of our population's suffering, and we had to decide whether the time had come to change that base of the terrorists and hit it or not. . . .

I regret very much the fact that civilians were hit on the other side, and I am not just saying this, I am really sorry. But in this fight between us and the Arabs, I think that it must be understood that it is impossible to place a population in the front line. . . . I hope that, in the settlement now being mulled over, this population, ours in the north of the country and theirs in southern Lebanon, will really get completely out of the fighting arena.[21]

There is nothing unprecedented about this kind of warfare in the twentieth century. What disturbed the United States government and, indeed, many Israelis was that Israel apparently could not discover other ways to guarantee its security. In their eyes Israeli security had come to depend on causing massive dislocations in Arab lands and very heavy loss of life, together with the extension of control over Arab territory.

Withdrawal of the IDF from Lebanon

Israel was at best lukewarm to the replacement of IDF units in Lebanon by UN forces. Apart from doubts about the ability and determination of such forces to prevent Palestinian infiltration into the south, the presence of UN troops would serve as a buffer against any future Israeli re-entry into Lebanon if the border area were once again threatened. Therefore Israel preferred that units of the Lebanese army and the Christian militias exercise a peacekeeping role in the south. That option, however, was unworkable for two reasons. First, no Lebanese army was a cohesive organization. It had long since disintegrated. Efforts to rebuild it since an uneasy peace had been imposed in October 1976 had been delayed by continued disagreement among Lebanon's political leaders. Second, the Christian militias were unwilling to cooperate with other Lebanese forces, fearing they would be sympathetic to Syria and would supplant Christian authority in the south. Therefore, Israel held out for an arrangement that would keep the Palestinian bases north of the Litani. This decision is reflected in Israel's second foray from the initial 10 km "security belt" to the Litani River on March 19, allegedly in response to the rapidity with which the UN Security Council, at the urging of the United States, adopted Resolution 425, creating the United Nations Interim Force in Lebanon (UNIFIL). Given Israel's doubts about UNIFIL's ability to prevent a return to Palestinian guerrillas to the south it was deemed prudent to move the eventual area to be occupied by these forces farther north than the original 10 km belt.[22]

The reaction of the United States to Israel's invasion clearly showed that Israel could not remain in southern Lebanon indefinitely. While Washington was not openly critical in the beginning, the White House immediately sought an early Israeli withdrawal from Lebanon. The sense of urgency accompanying the American proposal for sending United Nations troops to replace IDF units also suggested that American support was definitely qualified.

The initial American response was summed up by a State Department official. When asked what the U.S. planned to do, he responded, "It all depends how far they [the Israelis] go."[23] The White House regarded the invasion as a diversion from the primary problem of overcoming the impasse in the peace talks and therefore pressed Israel for a rapid withdrawal from Lebanon.[24]

The limits to which Israel could count on American support for the Lebanon operation were underscored by official allegations that Israel had violated agreements with the United States concerning the use of American-supplied military equipment in southern Lebanon. Of particular concern to the White House and members of Congress was the use of anti-personnel weapons such as cluster bombs against civilian targets. Under the terms of the Arms Export Control Act, Israel might have been ruled ineligible for continued military assistance which was running at about one billion dollars a year at the time. However, because Israeli officials gave assurances that IDF units would be withdrawn from Lebanon and because of efforts "to restore momentum to the vital peace negotiations," Secretary of State Cyrus Vance decided against recommending any further U.S. action against Israel. Implicit in a letter from Vance to House Speaker Thomas P. O'Neill, Jr., reporting the violation was a clear warning that if Israeli troops were not withdrawn from Lebanon soon, Israel might be ruled ineligible for further military assistance.[25]

Open criticism of Israel's policies and negotiating positions was voiced by such staunch Israeli supporters in the American Jewish community as Senators Abraham Ribicoff (D-Conn) and Jacob Javits (R-NY). While the criticism by no means advocated a lessening of American support for Israel, it clearly indicated that particular Israeli actions needed to be scrutinized rather than automatically supported.[26]

While pressures from the United States were important, Syria's reaction to the invasion was also crucial in determining the conditions of Israel's evacuation and the extent to which Israel could claim success in

ridding the border area of guerrilla concentrations. Israel stressed repeatedly that Operation Stone of Wisdom was directed only at the Palestinian guerrilla positions in southern Lebanon and not against Syrian
troops. However, Israel also informed Syria through the United States
that any Syrian military response would be considered an act of war.
The Syrians would have been engaging Israel without Egyptian military
support on the Sinai front. From a strategic standpoint, then, the Israeli
operation in Lebanon demonstrated to Syria, Jordan, and Iraq that talk
about a war on the eastern front was senseless. If anything Israel was
stronger than ever.

Israel also sought Syria's tacit cooperation in restricting guerrilla
activities in Lebanon. Syrian control of the Palestinians was probably
more important once the presence of a UN force in the south became imminent. Syrian cooperation would enhance UNIFIL's ability to stop Palestinian re-entry into the south. Even without committing its own forces,
Syria could permit the continued supply of ammunition and light weapons to guerrilla forces. The Palestinians would then be able to wage a
protracted guerrilla war against Israeli forces in Lebanon. One important
factor was that al-Sa'iqa, the Syrian arm of the PLO, had been the most
active and the most effective force opposing Israel's sweeps of southern
Lebanon.

Syria's potential for helping to create a Vietnam-like quagmire for
Israel in the south was implicit in a warning by Hafez al-Assad that resistance would escalate unless Israel ceased its advance and withdrew its
troops. While remaining vague about the commitment of Syrian forces,
Assad announced that Syrian land and air space would be open to any
Arab country that wished to supply Palestinian forces.[27] Assad also as-
sented to an Iraqi request to be allowed to ship arms and ammunition
through Syria to the PLO in Lebanon. Any arrangement indicating a
measure of cooperation between the mutually antagonistic governments
in Damascus and Baghdad could foreshadow a tougher, more powerful
Arab reaction to the Litani campaign. Israel could easily win an all-out
war if it came to that, but victory could be achieved only at the expense
of severe additional Israeli casualties. A protracted campaign against
guerrilla forces who operated among a friendly population would also
cost Israel dearly. Unless Syria agreed tacitly to cooperate in suppressing
guerrilla activities in Lebanon, Israel's invasion would not have enhanced her security. These conditions help to explain Israel's acceptance
of UN forces in southern Lebanon and the rapidity with which the first
stage of the IDF withdrawal from their north-most positions began.

It was the combined external pressures and Syrian acquiescence to

Israel's basic demand for control of terrorism that led to Israel's fairly rapid, phased withdrawal from Lebanon. Tacit Arab cooperation was expressed in PLO willingness to cooperate with UN peacekeeping forces. On March 24 the Lebanese government and the Syrian-dominated Arab Deterrent Force announced a total ban on military assistance for Palestinian guerrillas in southern Lebanon. The announcement stated that with UN troops entering Israeli-occupied Lebanon it was necessary to ensure that there was no interference with "current efforts designed to bring about a speedy Israeli withdrawal."[28] The ban on all military aid came three days after a unilateral Israeli ceasefire in the operation against Palestinian bases.

Benefits and Losses

Operation Stone of Wisdom helped Israel to eliminate Palestinian guerrilla bases in southern Lebanon and to reach a tacit agreement with Syria on policing Palestinian forces in Lebanon. The Palestinians were pushed into a strip of land north of the Litani River, a few miles south of Syria's forward positions. Between the Palestinians and the border Israel has installed a dual buffer composed of UN peacekeeping forces and the Christian enclave. Moreover, the operation can hardly be said to have seriously jeopardized negotiations for a comprehensive peace settlement or a bilateral treaty with Egypt. Indeed, while Israel was occupying southern Lebanon, Israel's Defence Minister, Ezer Weizman, was welcomed in Cairo by Sadat for talks aimed at renewing the stalled peace negotiations.

The operation was not without risks and costs. The invasion and the strengthening of Israel's commitment to the ultra-nationalist Christian forces prolonged the strife in Lebanon and may have sown the seeds for further conflict. Lebanon has become more explosive in the wake of the Israeli invasion. Israel's commitment to Christian forces in the south who refuse to accept the authority of the Lebanese government has indefinitely postponed the final pacification of Lebanon, which could bring Israel the security she seeks. The harassment of Syrian peacekeeping forces by Christian militias in Beirut and the demands of the Maronite chieftains such as Camille Chamoun for Syria's withdrawal from Lebanon present further problems. Israel demonstrated throughout the summer of 1978 that she would not tolerate complete Syrian suppression of the Christian forces. Yet the presence of a UN buffer in the south seriously complicates any large-scale Israeli efforts on the ground to intervene militarily on behalf of the Phalangists and other Christian forces in Beirut. If the Christian militias are not brought under control and Syria is forced to withdraw from Lebanon, fighting would undoubtedly resume; only then Israel would be bereft of an effective silent partner to control Palestinian terrorism in Lebanon. Thus while Israel was able to withdraw its forces from Lebanon, its commitment to an intransigent Christian minority means that, like Syria, Israel has not entirely escaped the quagmire that is Lebanon. Instead Israel has become a partner with Syria in an unpredictable process that could lead to peace, a far wider war, or more of the same dangerous cliff-hanging in one of the world's most volatile regions.

INTERPRETATION

Israeli objectives in Lebanon may be inferred from her behavior there since 1975. Israel's first concern has been to protect herself against attacks from Lebanon by Palestinian guerrillas. For many years it was possible to rely on the Lebanese government to prevent the attacks. As the Lebanese government faltered, it is perhaps understandable that Israel first tried to compel Lebanon to prevent the attacks. Instead of strengthening the government, Israel's heavy-handed raids and reprisals hastened the downfall of organized political life in Lebanon by compromising the armed forces, polarizing Lebanese politics, and adding to the numbers of homeless refugees. When the government of Lebanon collapsed in 1975 Israel changed its methods but kept the same objective. In the chaos that engulfed Lebanon Israel would counter the Palestinians by arming and assisting the Christians covertly, at first, and then openly with large-scale air and ground operations that culminated in the invasion of southern Lebanon in March 1978 and the outright occupation of a security belt north of the frontier.

When Syria intervened politically and then militarily in Lebanon Israel moved to limit Syrian involvement in the Lebanese civil conflict and to deny Syria the use and control of all of Lebanon. By threatening reprisal in public and communicating with Syria through the United States in private Israel compelled Syria to stay north of the Litani River. Just as the Christians were useful to Israel because they fought the Palestinians, the Syrians were useful because they sought to stabilize the political and military situation in the rest of the country. In any case Israel's ability to prevent Syria from exercising its will in northern and central Lebanon was quite limited. With the security belt north of the frontier firmly in Israel's hands or at least effectively denied the Palestinians and Syrians through a combination of UN and Christian forces, Israel could afford to tolerate a stabilizing Syrian role in the rest of Lebanon. No doubt Israel seeks the restoration of a sovereign Lebanon free of Syrian occupation and Soviet or Palestinian influence, but the vital security interests have already been realized. In addition, by invading Lebanon at a delicate moment in the Israeli-Egyptian negotiations after Sadat's visit to Jerusalem, Israel demonstrated that not even the prospect of peace with Egypt will prevent her from denying the use of Lebanon for attacks on Israel, whether by the Palestinians or Syrians or both in combination with a more aggressive Lebanese government. In all of this the connection with the Christians in Lebanon is of considerable importance to Israel. By helping to rescue and sustain the Christians, Israel alters the political future of Lebanon, strikes at the Palestinians, and builds obstacles to the use of Lebanon's territory, manpower, and resources against Israel.

Israel's military and policy responses to the Lebanese crisis and to the shifting fortunes of the Maronite Christian community have changed Israel's political position in the Arab world. By becoming an active participant in an Arab conflict Israel has become an active participant in Arab politics, notwithstanding the near absence of direct contacts with other Arab governments. Israel's collaboration with an Arab ally (an Arab ally which does not consider itself Arab) has reduced Israel's security problems on its northeastern frontier. The connection with an Arab minority also led Israel to develop new non-military policy instruments for dealing with Arab populations and leaders. Few had been needed while no Arab state would recognize the legitimacy of Israel's existence.

Israel has not, at least overtly, attempted to interject herself into other Arab bloc problems, although there is at least one other precedent. In the fall of 1970 Israel massed her armored forces on the Golan Heights to deter Syria from intervening on behalf of the Palestinians in the Jordanian civil war. Israel opposes the radicalization and disintegration of Lebanon and enjoys a limited overlap of interests with Syria. Her opposition to extremist Arab movements and to Soviet-supported groups creates a certain convergence of interests with the Saudi regime and Jordan's King Hussein as well.

While Israel exercised a remarkable freedom of action in Lebanon, there were restraints on her behavior. One group of these restraints comes from the United States government. Following the 1975 raid into Lebanon, the Ford Administration insisted on closer consultation with Israel in advance of any political and military moves, and the Americans have repeatedly opposed the large scale use of ground forces to respond to terrorist attacks. Other limits set by the United States prevent the use of certain American-supplied weapons except in the event of all-out war.[29] United States law restricts to legitimate self-defense the use of precision-guided munitions, such as the TOW anti-tank missile, and "smart bombs," cluster bombs, or air-to-air missiles such as the Sidewinder. A sharp disagreement arose between the United States and Israel over the use of cluster bombs during the invasion of Lebanon in March 1978.[30] In addition, the United States opposes any large-scale Israeli military operations against Syria and seeks to limit the area covered by Israeli aerial reconnaissance. The effects of the restraining influence of the United States on Israel's actions in Lebanon are reflected in an interview with Israeli Defense Minister Ezer Weizman a week after Israel's invasion. Responding to a question concerning official American reaction to Stone of Wisdom, Weizman noted: "Our announcement in advance that we had no intention of staying in southern Lebanon permanently and our unilateral declaration of a cease-fire were conducive toward making the U.S. position more calm and understanding."[31]

More subtle restraints on Israel's freedom of action in Lebanon are imposed by the momentum toward a peace agreement with Egypt and the American commitment to a comprehensive Middle Eastern peace settlement. For example, during the foray into southern Lebanon Chief of Staff Lieut. General Mordechai Gur expressed his hope that the campaign would not affect the negotiations between Israel and Egypt. Peace between Israel and Egypt, and the rest of the Arab world, Gur said, "is something which is too important and great to be affected by a specific event—even if it is an unpleasant event like what happened the past week, beginning with the attack in Israel and the attacks against the terrorists in southern Lebanon.[32] He added that Israel's relations with the outside powers, particularly the United States, were "a projection of the continued maintenance of the political momentum between Israel and Egypt" toward a final settlement. "If the world becomes aware that this momentum is continuing," Gur concluded, "it can better tolerate the events of the past week and view them in the proper perspective. We shall see in the next few days whether this will indeed, take place."[33]

Implicit in these remarks was the possibility of some give in Israel's negotiating position in the peace talks in exchange for U.S. and Egyptian tolerance of Israel's effort to sweep the Palestinians and their Lebanese supporters out of southern Lebanon. Israel was probably constrained from extending the level of material and military support it desired to the Christian rightist forces in Beirut in August and September 1978 as intensive fighting erupted between them and Syrian members of the Arab peacekeeping forces. Israel was thus torn between providing unequivocal support for its embattled ally and jeopardizing its relations with the United States and Egypt, particularly in the wake of the agreements concluded at Camp David.

Finally, Israel is necessarily responsive to the reactions of the major Arab confrontation states to its own actions with respect to Lebanon as Israel attempts to demonstrate strength and involvement without igniting a major Arab-Israeli war or severely jeopardizing negotiations for a final Middle Eastern peace settlement. Israeli sensitivity is reflected in a statement by Weizman that the prevention of Syrian participation in the fighting was one of the crucial considerations in planning Operation Stone of Wisdom and that the military operations were basically dictated by this consideration. "Therefore we did not cross the Litani except for two ambushes laid north of it along the coastal road. We carried out such an operation, on such a scale, without having the Middle East burst or explode, and this was the decisive part in our early planning."[34]

To a major extent, Israel has been successful in its policy, gaining at least tacit Egyptian and Jordanian approval of major actions in Lebanon prior to their implementation. Negotiations usually centered on conditions under which Israel initiated retaliatory attacks on Palestinian guerrilla positions in "Fatahland." The conditions included the scope and intensity of Israeli operations (i.e., air strikes or naval bombardment instead of attacks by ground forces) and the geographic limits beyond which Israeli actions would be viewed as too provocative. Many contacts were indirect via intermediaries such as the United States, Romania, or Lt. General Ensio Siilasvuo, Chief Coordinator for U.N. Peace Missions in the Middle East. Direct contacts took place between high level Egyptian, Jordanian and Israeli officials in Morocco and between Jordanian and Israeli officials in remote areas south of the Dead Sea.[35]

One manifestation of Egyptian approval of major Israeli actions against the Palestinians in Lebanon occurred November 9, 1977. Israel launched a large-scale air attack on Palestinian positions in southern Lebanon allegedly in response to Palestinian shelling of the border area. It was the most massive attack in two years, killing more than 87 people and injuring more than 100 others.[36] On the same day in Cairo Egypt's President Anwar Sadat announced that he was "ready to go to the Knesset itself" to negotiate peace. He further announced the acceptability of "any procedural conditions Israel wants" in order to begin the talks. Even if the two events had been sheer coincidence the mild response from Cairo and Amman to the Israeli raids suggested the latters' tacit acceplance of limited Israeli actions against Palestinian provocations. The timing of Sadat's announcement and his mild reaction to Israel's air raids the same day was a signal to both Israel and the Palestinians that Sadat was not going to allow the continuing conflict in south Lebanon to ruin any opportunities to work out an agreement with Israel to settle the Arab-Israeli conflict.

The degree to which Israel has succeeded in securing at least tacit Egyptian and Jordanian agreement for certain types of actions extends beyond the gradual forging of contacts between Israel and these two countries. One possible effect of such approval from Arab regimes friendly to the United States is to minimize or even reduce American restrictions on Israel's actions in Lebanon. That is to say, the securing of such approval—tacit or explicit—for certain types and levels of actions makes it more difficult for the United States to restrict Israel to operations *below* those levels tacitly approved by Egypt or Jordan or more restricted in scope, direction or intensity.

CONCLUSION

Since 1976, Israel has been an important actor in Lebanese internal politics through its support of Chamoun and other rightists. This support has maintained a level of turmoil sufficiently great to impede leftist or Palestinian control and to limit Syrian influence to certain sub-groups of the population. Syria has been forced to depend upon its own forces, whether openly or nominally Palestinian (PLA or al-Saiqa) to maintain the level of its control. Here the advantages to Israel of requiring Syria to divert some 30,000 of its forces to virtually occupy Lebanon are clear.

If Chamoun and other anti-Syrian elements were eliminated, Syria would be able to exert greater control than it currently enjoys with little more than a skeleton force in-country. The Phalange and the PPS-Palestinian alliance would be relatively weak, and would continue to require at least some Syrian support, serving as a guarantee of continued loyalty to Damascus.

The longer-term implications of the Syrian strategy are directly relevant to the larger military picture of the Arab-Israeli conflict. Syrian control over Lebanon at its present or a more effective level through an alliance with the Phalangists in the Muslim sector, would pave the way for a substantially reduced Syrian military presence on the ground. Syria will then move toward the implementation of its earlier plan to establish a pro-Syrian Lebanese Army. Although this army will be relatively ineffectual as a military force, it could, once armed and trained by the Syrians, given terrain factors in southern Lebanon, divert and tie down a far greater level of Israeli military manpower than in the past. Certainly, its influence would be viewed as much more disruptive to Israeli interests than ever before, especially since Lebanon had no real interest in war before and Syria did.

Israel's best hope of countering such a Syrian strategy is to broaden the Israeli base among the Lebanese Christians beyond Chamoun, looking to second generation Christian leaders. Ultimately, however, the only support Gemayel, Chamoun, and the rest of the Christian right could depend upon in a confrontation with Syria is direct Israeli military intervention. Such an intervention would, perhaps, serve Israel's short-term security interests but would further erode Lebanon's prospects for survival as an independent unified country. A large-scale Israeli intervention either against terrorists or in favor of the Christians against Syria would also obstruct and perhaps prevent the conclusion of a general settlement. The tacit partnership between Israel and Syria in Lebanon has become extremely important. It prevents terrorism and another breakdown of order in Lebanon and, in this way, sustains hope for bilateral and multilateral negotiations. The web of contacts between Israel and Syria also serves as an early warning device. Its disappearance will surely signal another round of fighting in the Middle East.

SAUDI ARABIA

M. Graeme Bannerman

Two occurrences in the mid-1970s have significantly altered the implementation of Saudi foreign policy—the rapid increase in oil prices and the death of King Faisal. The Arab oil embargo and OPEC price hikes of 1973–1974 combined to focus world attention on Saudi Arabia's economic muscle. Subsequently, Riyadh has found it increasingly difficult to play the quiet, behind-the-scenes role outside the international spotlight that it previously preferred. Each Saudi economic and political move became the object of international interest, and Saudi support was assiduously cultivated throughout the non-Communist world.

The death of King Faisal in 1975 removed the steady hand which had guided Saudi foreign policy for decades. It would be difficult to conceive of anyone inheriting the late king's mantle to wield the kind of dominating influence over the kingdom's foreign relations that Faisal did. Faisal was a leader who, by his respected position and dominant personality, could convince even the most skeptical subject to follow his lead. The new Saudi leadership has continued to pursue Faisal's policies but not with the overwhelming influence which allowed him to bring along the doubters.

The Lebanese civil war began almost simultaneously with the post-Faisal era, engulfing Arab politics and exacerbating inter-Arab differences. The civil war became an overriding concern of the new Saudi leadership and its first major foreign policy challenge. It was a crucible in which the new leadership was tested. In order to appreciate the Saudi performance during the Lebanese War, the fundamentals of Saudi foreign policy as established by Faisal must be understood.

THE FUNDAMENTALS OF SAUDI FOREIGN POLICY

King Faisal laid the foundation upon which subsequent Saudi foreign policy was built. This policy has three pillars—the advancement of Is-

113

lam, the cultivation of Arabism, and the preservation of the monarchy.

As symbolized by their guardianship of the Islamic holy cities, the Saudis consider the protection and spread of Islam a primary objective. Faisal was a devout Muslim who attempted to live by the precepts of Islam and to encourage others to do likewise. Many world leaders have used religion as a political tool, but for Faisal Islam was his way of life. This precept, in fact, is as old as the monarchy itself. The genesis of the Saudi state was in the eighteenth century Islamic revivalist movement founded by Muhammad ibn Abd al-Wahhab. Islamic fundamentalism was the cement which held the early Saudi state together by transcending traditional tribal rivalries and providing the impetus for expansion. Commitment to a strict adherence to God's teachings in relations with others was a pervasive element in this doctrine.

Faisal was nurtured on his Islamic heritage and accepted it as a guide to political relations with Muslim and non-Muslim alike.[1] The Islamic peoples were his people, and he felt an obligation toward as well as a closeness to other Muslims. This affinity with his fellow Muslims was reflected in practical political decisions such as the granting of aid—the vast majority of Saudi foreign assistance has been given to Muslim states. The Saudis also were the primary impetus behind joint Islamic action in a variety of international fora. The fervor of Faisal's Islamic views was further illustrated in his strong objection to Israeli occupation of East Jerusalem following the 1967 war.

Faisal's emphasis on Islam continued to be a driving force in Saudi Arabia's foreign policy under his successors. A primary reason, for instance, that the Saudis did not support Sadat's initiative in November 1977, when he went to Jerusalem was that he offended their Islamic sensitivities. By praying in al-Aksa mosque, one of the holiest Islamic shrines, on one of the holiest days while the Israelis still occupied the city, Sadat offended many Saudis, including King Khalid. As a result, despite considerable encouragement from those who believed that such support would have been in the Saudis' own interests, Riyadh refused to be openly associated with the Sadat initiative.

The centrality of Islam in Saudi foreign policy has greatly affected its relations with non-Muslim states as well. Western states with a predominantly Christian heritage have been accepted by the Saudis while the Soviets with their godless Communism have not. Westerners were viewed as "people of the book," those who believed in the same God but had not received the complete prophesy, but the atheistic beliefs of Communist states were rejected outright. Communism was viewed as a major threat to the Muslim way of life. As a consequence, the Saudis have resisted both Soviet advances in the Middle East and the growth of indigenous forces which professed a Communist philosophy. The Saudis have supported—both politically and financially—those elements in the Arab world which resisted the spread of Communism.

As a corollary to their anti-Communism, the Saudis, under Faisal, viewed Zionism as part of an anti-Islamic conspiracy. The linkage between Zionism and Communism, tenuous at best, was to the Saudis very real and reflected in their foreign policy. A distinction was drawn between Zionism, the political movement, and Judaism, although sometimes not very carefully. Intellectually, Jews, like Christians, were accepted as people of the book, but the Saudis resented Jewish assistance to political Zionism in Israel.

The second pillar of Saudi foreign policy as developed by Faisal is Arabism. Arabia, in Faisal's view, was the cradle of Arab civilization as well as Islam, and the two, at times, were almost indistinguishable.[2] In Faisal's words: "We do not need to import foreign traditions. We have a history and a glorious past. We led the Arabs and the World. . . . With what did we lead with—the Word of the one God and the Shariah of His Prophet."[3] Because of this special relationship with Islam and the Arab heritage, the Saudis perceive that they have a unique role in the Arab world. They not only were the source of Arabness but were the preservers of its purity. Faisal felt an obligation to preserve Arab unity by bridging differences between his Arab brothers. To the Saudis, this unity remains a prerequisite for the Arabs to reassert their rightful leadership role in world affairs.

Arabism as understood by Faisal differed considerably from that of his Arab neighbors to the north and west. For Faisal, Arabism was rooted in Islam and in the traditions of the deserts of the peninsula. The virulent urban ideologically oriented Arabism, as espoused by the Ba'athis, Nasserists, and others remained an anathema to him. The appeals of the proponents of these philosophies often appeared to be using the veil of Arabism to introduce alien secular political concepts and to promote social revolution. As a consequence, he led the Saudis during the 1950s and 1960s in combating what appeared to him to be a misuse of Arabism.

The third pillar is preserving the position of the Saudi ruling elite. Faisal was fundamentally conservative, desiring the preservation of the status quo or supporting an orderly evolution. This attitude was exhibited throughout Saudi foreign relations and was reflected by the general rule that the Saudis support the regime in power. They oppose radical change but have counseled relatively progressive actions by friendly governments. This advice, however, was usually given to prevent a radical change or to establish a regime more nearly in tune with the precepts of Islam.

Faisal and his relatives exhibited a healthy desire to preserve their autonomy and their standing. Nevertheless, large segments of society were brought into the power structure through marriage and personal loyalties. In addition to the 3,000 or so royal princes, two closely allied families, the al-Shaykh, the relatives of the Wahhabi founder, and the Sudayri were very close to the Saudi. Further, the great tribal families were generally tied into the ruling elite. As a consequence, through a complicated network of personal relationships, an inordinately large segment of society had direct links with the leaders of the state. In turn, the decision-makers felt a need to look after the interests of a broad spectrum of society. Therefore, efforts to preserve the ruling elite, in fact, were viewed by the Saudi princes as designed to defend Saudi society and values.

Saudi Arabia has rarely had a strategically integrated foreign policy; instead, it had often conflicting foreign policies. Foreign policy naturally reflects a state decision-making process, and the Saudi case is no exception. For the Saudis this process is based on consensus within the royal family and within the government. Obtaining a consensus on controversial issues is difficult under the best of circumstances. Nevertheless, because of his ability to manipulate and dominate the family, Faisal was able to give direction and cohesion to Saudi foreign policy. Even under Faisal, however, various princes assumed a major responsibility for specific areas of policy. Prince Sultan, for instance, has taken particular interest in the Yemens. Other princes have taken the lead in other areas. Under Faisal the ultimate determinor of policy always was the king, and his personal imprint on foreign policy was manifest.

With the passing of Faisal, his successor, King Khalid, has not had the same consuming interest in foreign affairs that Faisal exhibited for most of his life, and foreign policy does not bear the king's personal imprint to the same degree. As a result, policy decisions have been more difficult to attain as the inner leadership group struggled to reach a consensus before proceeding on controversial issues. Moreover, a number of the more difficult issues became enmeshed in Saudi bureaucratic politics. Various royal and nonroyal cabinet members would line up one or the other side, thus complicating the decision-making process even more and making policy coordination all the more difficult. Thus Saudi policy at times seemed contradictory and at odds with itself.

THE LEBANESE CRISIS

For the Saudis the Lebanese crisis was of such a complex and self-contradictory nature that they never could quite formulate a policy which was designed to resolve the fundamental Lebanese and Palestinian problems. The immediacy of particular incidents and the unending series of crises absorbed all Saudi attention. One should note that the Saudis were not alone in this dilemma for few, if any, of the outside participants had a long-range, far-sighted policy with regard to Lebanon. To the Saudis the Lebanese appeared as though they possessed a strange death wish. They not only brought destruction upon themselves but they also seriously jeopardized Arab unity and Middle East peace. In addition, chaos in Lebanon provided a fertile arena for more radical elements to work their evil. Among those who appeared to the Saudis to be uncomfortably active in Lebanon were the Soviets, Iraqis, and Libyans. Finally, the Lebanese crisis distracted the Arab states from their primary purpose of confronting Israel while at the same time offering Israel an opportunity to interfere in the internal affairs of an Arab state. Therefore, the Saudi primary concerns with the Lebanese crisis were the regional and international ramifications and not so much the impact on Lebanon.

Saudi interest in Lebanon itself, although secondary, was genuine. They had a long tradition of friendship with many Lebanese leaders. Saeb Salem, Kamal Jumblatt, Pierre Gemayel, among others, had had ties with the Saudis for many years. This friendship transcended political differences. For instance, at the height of the Lebanese War when Kamal Jumblatt was leading the Lebanese Nationalists, whose pronouncements were not only revolutionary but at times anti-Saudi, the Druze leader was still welcomed in Riyadh. This resulted partially from a Saudi desire not to lose contact and influence with any element in the traditional Lebanese political spectrum, but equally important were the warm personal ties Saudi princes had with Jumblatt and many of the Lebanese leaders. Of all the Lebanese, Saeb Salem appeared to have the deepest and most important relationship with the Saudis. He, among the myriad of Lebanese politicians, combined both the close personal ties with similar political views—a conservative, western-oriented Sunni Muslim.

There are four distinct phases of the Saudi involvement in the Lebanese situation. The first encompasses the period from the onset of the Lebanese conflict to the second Sinai disengagement agreement. The second phase of Saudi concern begins with Sinai II and ends with the horrendous Saturday in December 1975, when Christian thugs massacred several hundred Muslims for no reason other than their religion. The third period ended in June 1976, with the Riyadh meeting of the Syrian and Egyptian prime ministers. The final period concluded in the Saudis being the midwife to the Assad-Sadat reconciliation in October 1976, and the termination of the civil war.

On the Sidelines

The first phase of Saudi concern with Lebanon, March 1975–September 1, 1975, was characterized by little direct Saudi interest in the events in Lebanon. Certainly, the Saudis were disgusted by the Ain al-Rammaneh massacre and shocked at Frangieh's clumsy attempt to undercut the influence of traditional Muslim leadership by appointing the puppet military government. No doubt they were relieved to see the traditional Lebanese leaders establish themselves with the Karameh government in early July. Lebanon, however, was not seriously affecting either the key Saudi domestic or international concerns.

At home the Saudis were attempting to cope with the new order following the March 25 assassination of King Faisal. While the transition had gone smoothly with Khalid becoming king, Fahd becoming crown prince, and Abdullah the number three man in the administration, internal relationships had yet to be worked out. Many western observers predicted that Khalid would merely be a figurehead while Fahd would be the real power; tradition and family rivalries militated against this, however. Faisal had established a system whereby the king was the final mediator in family disputes. Khalid was not inclined to give up this responsibility. Moreover, Khalid apparently felt a great obligation to fill the void left by Faisal's death. Several months, therefore, passed before Fahd and Khalid determined precisely which responsibilities were in each other's purview. Further down the hierarchy other princes maneuvered for influence. Prince Sultan seemed somewhat disappointed with the relative decline of his position, and many traditional princes were concerned that one branch of the family, the "Sudayri Seven," had achieved a dominant position in the family council. Much time and effort, which could have been spent on Lebanon, was taken in working out family relationships.

With regard to Saudi foreign policy, Prince Fahd led the push for a more assertive Saudi policy. The key Saudi concern at that time was the maintenance of Syrian and Egyptian cooperation so that peace negotiations under U.S. auspices could continue. Sinai I and Golan I had been signed, but subsequent U.S. efforts foundered. The tension of difficult negotiations was creating strains between Damascus and Cairo. These strains played upon traditional Syrian-Egyptian suspicions. Assad believed that Sadat might reach a bilateral accommodation with Israel, leaving the Syrians alone to face the Israeli Defense Forces. From Cairo, Assad appeared unduly involved with Palestinian concerns and not sufficiently determined to regain Arab lands. Arafat and Assad appeared to the Egyptians to be in alliance against Cairo and determined to thwart all moves toward peace.

Arafat had gained great respectability and acceptance in the Rabat Summit in November 1974. At that time, all the Arab states had recognized the PLO as the legitimate and only representative of the Palestinians. What this in fact meant was the Arab recognition of Arafat's right, instead of the Jordanians, to negotiate for the West Bank. Arafat used his newly accepted responsibility to insinuate the PLO into the inter-Arab power balance. By the spring of 1975, he was throwing his weight behind Assad in attempting to prevent a second disengagement. The Egyptians greatly resented what they viewed as Arafat's obstructionism.

From the Saudi perspective a second round of disengagements, which was being pressed by the U.S., offered the possibility of regaining Arab lands. Arab unity was necessary for a second agreement to have meaning; therefore, the thrust of Saudi policy was to reconcile Sadat with Assad and, to a lesser extent, Arafat. If the three could agree on a policy, the Saudis believed that the Arabs, with the help of Secretary of State Kissinger, could regain considerably more of the occupied territory. Overcoming the differences between Sadat and Arafat was not easy. Reportedly, even at Faisal's funeral, the Saudis lobbied with both Arafat and Sadat to put aside their differences. This apparently was to no avail, for Sadat allegedly warned Salah Khalaf that Egypt would not be intimidated by PLO machinations.

While the Saudis apparently were also unhappy with the Palestinian position, they adopted a considerably different attitude from that of the Egyptians. They maintained contacts with Arafat and other relative moderates within the PLO. The understanding among the Saudis was that if totally alienated, either Arafat and others of his ilk would be replaced by more radical elements, or, the more probable prospect, Arafat would become more extreme himself. In either case the Saudis preferred to maintain the link with the hope of moderating PLO policy in the future.

The growing Palestinian role in Lebanon served further to alienate the Saudis as well as the Egyptians. The Saudis were concerned that Palestinian policy in Lebanon was shortsighted and could lead to tragedy for the Arabs. The Palestinian fedayeen in February, March, and April had taken very unhelpful actions which, it was widely believed, could either draw Israel into Lebanon or help contribute to civil war. In 1975 these actions included daily distribution of weapons to the Lebanese public; construction of armed concrete bunkers in Beirut refugee camps opposite Lebanese army barracks; participation in the late February antigovernment clashes in Sidon and the use of heavy weapons against the Lebanese army barracks there; shelling of Israel from Lebanese territory resulting in Israeli retaliatory shelling of Lebanese army positions; and the constant build-up of Palestinians arms depots with large deliveries of weapons from a variety of sources including Libya and Iraq.

With the Palestinians seemingly determined to be uncooperative in Lebanon as well in a broader Middle Eastern context, the new Saudi leadership in April 1975, concentrated its efforts on reconciling Assad and Sadat. A major step in that direction was the holding of a trilateral summit in Riyadh. The events in Lebanon were not discussed at any length, and the statement issued following the meeting did not mention either Lebanon or the PLO.[4]

Although Assad and Sadat agreed on the basic parameters for moving toward a Middle East peace, the Saudis surely realized that the summit had not ended mutual Egyptian-Syrian suspicions; they undoubtedly hoped that it had fostered a little trust between the two presidents. What none of the participants understood was that the basis for bitter disagreement between Assad and Sadat following Sinai II had been laid. The leaders agreed that "any action on a particular front should be part of the overall action along the entire Arab front with Israel."[5] Assad believed that Sinai II broke this pact. On the other hand, the leaders also "confirmed their determination not to allow the situation of no war and no peace to continue." For Sadat this was what he was doing in Sinai II. He believed that his negotiations for Sinai II were in total agreement with this joint statement. Assad did not.

When the Riyadh summit ended, the initial and successful spurt of Saudi international activism under the new leadership slowed. It appeared that the Saudis had been able to foster a limited reconciliation between Syria and Egypt. Moreover, Fahd had gained limited success on other fronts. For instance, through the efforts of Ahmad Zaki al-Yamani, the Saudi Oil Minister, Iraq-Kuwaiti border tensions had been reduced. These successes undoubtedly reinforced the regime's commitment to a more activist Saudi role in inter-Arab affairs.

The more activist Saudi policy, however, could not be employed in

Lebanon as effectively as elsewhere. In the first place, the situation in Lebanon was increasingly muddled. Many of the participants, in the Saudi view, had right on their side, but each also appeared guilty of an increasing number of grievous acts. While the Lebanese rightists supported the status quo, cooperated with the world democracies, and were staunchly anti-Communist, they tended to be anti-Muslim and therefore repugnant to the Saudis. The traditional Muslim leaders were inept, did not properly control their followers, and were generally not overly devout. Nevertheless, these Muslims supported moderate views including cooperation with democracies, anti-Communism, and a willingness to reach an accommodation with Christian Lebanese in the context of a reasonable modification of the existing system. The more radical younger leftist elements were also Muslims. The young Muslims had legitimate complaints about the Lebanese system and were tacitly supported by a growing percentage of the Sunni Muslim community. Their radical pronouncements, association with Communists, and disrespect for the establishment, however, were quite troublesome to the leaders in Riyadh. Finally, the Palestinians of all political persuasions were worrisome. The Saudis were greatly sympathetic to the plight of the Palestinians and remained totally committed to their return to a homeland. In the Lebanese context the Saudis opposed any attempt by the rightists to force the Palestinians out of Lebanon, but at the same time they criticized Palestinian intervention in Lebanese internal affairs.

The only reasonable course of Saudi action was to encourage moderation by all. Encouragement generally meant financial grants to many with more generous amounts going to moderate leaders. In this way the Saudis assured themselves a hearing. They hoped their advice would be heeded. At the very least they provided a means for the factions to communicate with one another. A more activist role would have resulted in direct criticism of the Saudis and diminished their ability to influence the participants.

The immediacy of the Lebanese crisis subsided on July 1, when Rashid Karameh formed a new government. In contrast to the May 23 military cabinet,[6] which was a crude move by Frangieh designed to upset the political system and impose his views, the Karameh government was an attempt by the traditional leadership to set aside differences. Both Chamoun and Karameh were included while more radical elements, Pierre Gemayel and Kamal Jumblatt for example, were excluded. The cabinet, moreover, maintained the traditional confessional balance and was the last to be dominated by powerful representatives of the traditional Lebanese leadership.[7]

The Saudis shared the common hope that the Lebanese, while stumbling very close to the edge of a very dangerous precipice, had managed to pull themselves back just in the nick of time. Nevertheless, few doubted that if Karameh failed to re-establish equilibrium within the political system, there was a better-than-ever risk of a civil war worse than that of 1958, with a growing likelihood of direct Syrian and Israeli intervention. Karameh seems to have gotten off to the right start. Radio Beirut reported that the prime minister and Yasir Arafat had agreed on a plan to restore order. The plan included the arrest by Fatah as well as Internal Security Forces of undisciplined elements. A cease-fire was to go into effect, barricades were to be removed, and all armed men were to be taken off the street. Finally, the two agreed to have the Lebanese-Palestinian Coordinating Committee supervise the cease-fire.[8] What few, including the Saudis, realized was that despite the gestures toward reconciliation the situation in Lebanon had become so unravelled that a major crisis was inevitable unless the central government received immediate and massive outside assistance. This did not occur.

The Lebanese Crisis Becomes an Arab Crisis

Lebanon's agony did not become a major preoccupation of the Saudis or the other Arabs until the fall of 1975. At that time, many of the Saudis' worst fears began to be acted out in the streets of Beirut and on the Lebanese hillsides. From September 1975 until November 1976, other Arab concerns were secondary to the crisis in Lebanon. Step-by-step diplomacy and Israeli withdrawal became side issues. Lebanon became the primary playing field for inter-Arab and Arab-Israeli struggles.

Inter-Arab differences were greatly exacerbated by the second Sinai disengagement agreement of September. Hafez al-Assad was particularly incensed by the agreement, feeling he had been betrayed and deserted by the Egyptian president. The Syrians feared that the Egyptians had taken themselves out of the confrontation with Israel, leaving Damascus to face the Israelis alone. In return, the Syrian press stung Sadat with bitter criticism. For the Egyptians, these attacks were unfair and misplaced. Sadat had jeopardized Egyptian national interests during the negotiations by insisting that the U.S. continue to press for a second Golan Agreement. Sadat had threatened not to conclude a second agreement with the Israelis until he had received such an assurance from Kissinger.[9] Sadat believed that he had more than fulfilled his obligation to the Syrians and, therefore, responded personally and ferociously to the Syrian attacks.

The all-consuming Sadat-Assad rivalry was a disaster for Lebanon, which became a battlefield where Syrian and Egyptian surrogates attempted to thwart each other's policies. In addition to Cairo and Damascus, other Arabs used the Lebanese crisis as a forum to strike out at their Arab opponents. The Lebanese and Palestinians, with their myriad of factions and a general willingness to accept patronage from anyone willing to pay, provided fertile ground for Arab mischiefmaking. The situation in Lebanon deteriorated markedly after September 1, 1975, as battle lines between Christian and Muslim areas of Beirut began to take on a more permanent nature.

The collapse in Lebanon and the break-up of any semblance of Arab unity following the Sinai II agreement were very disconcerting to the Saudis. The thrust of Saudi foreign policy was directed to restoring the Syrian, Egyptian, and Saudi consensus which had vanished. In a practical sense this led to greater concern with the events in Lebanon, where the Arab nation appeared to be hemorrhaging. Syrian attempts to make political gains in Lebanon to offset their perceived setback because of Sinai II could create additional inter-Arab strife. The Saudis, therefore, opposed any Syrian move which might be interpreted as jeopardizing Lebanon's sovereignty.

Saudi concerns were undoubtedly fanned by the spate of media reports of Syrian intentions of taking advantage of Lebanon's crisis.[10] The Syrians allegedly had several plans which included the formation of a unified military command between Syria and Lebanon which would calm the situation and greatly enhance Damascus's control in Lebanon. Another Syrian plan which was the object of much discussion was the linkage of Syria, Jordan, and Lebanon in a federal union in which the Palestinians would have a role. The object of this idea was to form a northern front which would be militarily stronger and would give the Syrians a voice at least as influential as that of Egypt in Arab military affairs. Finally, the ancient Lebanese belief that Damascus coveted if not all Lebanon, at least the north and the Bekaa, was again raised. Syrians allegedly were waiting for the opportunity to partition Lebanon and to annex these districts. While the Saudis took these assertions with a healthy measure of skepticism, there were sufficient elements of truth to cause considerable concern. Much Saudi effort was expended in counseling restraint in Damascus.

While the Saudis opposed the more ambitious Syrian plans in Lebanon, the many Syrian concerns over Lebanon were shared by the Saudis. The Saudis, like the Syrians, opposed a radical transformation of Lebanese society and the establishment of a leftist Arab state or a pro-Iraqi state. Palestinian freedom of activity in Lebanon should be permitted, but Lebanese sovereignty must be respected. The Palestinians were viewed as making a tragic error by becoming involved in the Lebanese conflict. The Saudis were also concerned that the fighting could lead to a general Arab-Israeli war.

From the start, the Saudis favored joint Arab action to solve the Lebanese situation rather than unilateral action by individual Arab states. Therefore, in early October Kuwait, with Saudi blessing, called for an Arab League meeting to discuss Lebanon. The "Arabization" of the Lebanese crisis, as the Arab League move was widely viewed, was opposed by Hafez al-Assad, many Palestinians, and some Lebanese. In a statement issued October 14, Syria announced that it would not attend the conference. According to the statement, the Damascus government considered it preferable that the Arab foreign ministers meet to discuss the second Egyptian-Israeli interim agreement "because it forms the background to Lebanese developments."[11] Not stated in the announcement was an obvious Syrian concern that the meeting in Cairo would underline the centrality of Egypt to all Arab issues and would recognize a legitimate role for Sadat in Lebanese affairs. From Damascus's perspective, Lebanon belonged in the Syrian sphere of influence. The failure of the Kuwaiti initiative convinced the Saudis that subsequent attempts to reconcile Damascus and Cairo should not be through the Arab League, but under Riyadh's auspices or in conjunction with Kuwait. By avoiding the Arab League, the Syrians would not be embarrassed by having to meet in Cairo.

The Saudi ability to influence directly the Lebanon situation was limited. They financed a wide variety of groups and individuals who tended to be traditional leaders, both Muslim and Christian. They supported the feeble efforts of the Frangieh-Karameh government to reconcile differences and generally to give the Muslims a greater share in the governing process. Saudi advice and even the threat of the termination of Saudi financial aid was never the deciding factor in Lebanese and Palestinian decision-making. Saudi counseling was one consideration, however, and money and advice could be a restraining factor, but they did not give control. If Saudi influence was to have an impact in Lebanon, it had to be in the inter-Arab arena rather than on the ground in Lebanon.

Syria Intervenes

The nature of the Lebanese civil war was altered in early December. On a bloody Saturday, Christian elements in East Beirut, reacting to the murder of one of their own, massacred more than 200 Muslims, Lebanese and Palestinians, for no other reason than the religion stamped on their identity cards.[12] While Muslim-Christian hostility had been an element from the earliest stages of the fighting, political party, feudal loyalty, and attitude toward the Palestinians were equally important. Following the December massacres, religion, while not the only consideration, became a dominant issue.

For the Saudis as for most of the Arabs, the aggressive and barbaric attitude displayed by the Christians led to reappraisal of their position in Lebanon. Until that time the Saudis had been relatively even-handed toward Christian and Muslim alike. Some pressure in the royal family had been mounted to support more actively Muslim interests; nevertheless, those favoring a balanced approach had prevailed. They argued that Muslim interests were not easily defined and the Christians were anti-Communist. Moreover, Saudi support for anti-Christian elements would make the Saudis appear antedeluvian in outlook and tarnish an image of moderation which they were cultivating in the West.

Those among Saudi policymakers favoring a balanced approach to Lebanon's religious factions were further weakened when the Christians overran the Muslim and Palestinian districts of Maslakh and Karantina near the Beirut port in early January. The international media was filled with gruesome pictures of Christian Lebanese beating and torturing helpless Muslim men, women, and children. Rabid Arab opponents of the Christians paid for the publication of pictorial essays depicting Christian barbarism.[13] In addition, it became an open secret that the Christian militias were in contact with the Israelis, who remained the primary enemy in all Arab equations, and to deal with them was considered an inexcusable crime.[14]

As a result of these events, the Saudis changed their policy not only toward Lebanon but also toward Syria. The Saudis terminated assistance to the Christians in Lebanon. With regard to the Syrians, the Saudis became convinced that only Syria possessed the ability to bring events in Lebanon under control and to stop the senseless brutality. Unquestionably, the growing tragedy in Lebanon was an important item of discussion when King Khalid visited Damascus in late December. The content of the discussions is not known. Subsequent actions, however, appear to indicate that Hafez al-Assad won the king's consent in deploying to Lebanon Palestine Liberation Army (PLA) units which were loyal to Damascus. The Saudis apparently believed that this would be a temporary move and was not designed to give the Syrians a permanent presence in Lebanon.

Saudi support for a limited Syrian role in Lebanon marked a reversal of a long-standing Saudi belief in the noninterference of one Arab state in the internal affairs of another. The situation in Lebanon was unique and pleaded for outside intervention. Moreover, no one realized that the Syrian move marked the beginning of increasing Syrian involvement in Lebanon that would lead to years of direct Syrian military occupation of most of that country.

The changing attitude of the Saudis toward the Lebanese was one factor contributing to the increasing feeling of isolation of the Christian Lebanese. With the conservative Arab states turning their backs on them, the Christians' underlying belief that they were really different from the surrounding Arab community came to the fore. The Christians had no choice but to look for military and diplomatic support outside the Arab world. In effect, the lack of conservative Arab backing encouraged them to seek assistance from the Israelis and to call for the "internationalization" of the Lebanese crisis. This latter move was a marked change from their approach the preceding October when the Christians strongly favored an Arab League summit as the means of saving the Lebanese situation. By January 1976, however, the Christians viewed the Arab League as a hostile forum.

Christian calls for the internationalization of the Lebanese crisis were opposed by the Saudis, who viewed the Lebanon crisis as an Arab crisis and did not want outside elements interfering. They rejected all consideration of taking the issue to the United Nations. Moreover, Riyadh never supported France's offer of troops or the legitimacy of a role for France in Lebanon.

In January 1976, the entry of Syrian-backed PLA forces in Lebanon had sobering effects on the Christians and forced Frangieh to accept a compromise formula which gave the Muslims greater participation in the Lebanese political process.[15] At the same time, however, Syrian relations with the leftist Lebanese and their Palestinian allies soured. These elements did not consider minor tinkering with the current Lebanese political system an acceptable solution. Moreover, the PLO rejected the Syrian-sponsored plan because it would greatly restrict Palestinian freedom of action. By mid-February the Palestinians and Lebanese leftists had forged an anti-Syrian coalition. Elements of this alignment used Arab disunity to gain support from those states who opposed the Syrian role in Lebanon.

Arafat, Khaled al-Hassan, and others of the moderate wing of the PLO appealed to the Saudis. They argued that the Syrians were attempting to dominate the Palestinians as well as Lebanon. Further, they asserted that should Syria continue its present course in Lebanon, moderate Palestinian leaders, such as themselves, would lose ground to more radical groups such as the Popular Democratic Front for the Liberation of Palestine (PDFLP) and George Habbash's Popular Front for the Liberation of Palestine (PFLP). These radical elements had already made some inroads. These arguments never swayed the Saudis from their understanding that the Syrians were the only available Arab force capable of containing the Lebanese situation; nevertheless, the arguments played upon Saudi concerns that Syrian intervention may be of long duration. In any case, despite sometime intemperate Palestinian acts, the Saudis continued to provide financial assistance to the moderates.

The Syrian surrogates in Lebanon, the PLA and al-Sa'iqa, even augmented with Syrian regulars, could not control or contain the combination of leftist Lebanese and Palestinian forces. These forces were gaining increasing support from outside Lebanon. Libya, Iraq, and Egypt were supplying arms and money. In addition, throughout the spring anti-Syrian Palestinians arrived including "volunteers" from Iraq and the Egyptian-trained and dominated Ayn Jalout brigade of the PLA. With the growing strength of his opponents in Lebanon, Hafez al-Assad determined in March openly to introduce regular Syria troops. This began the gradual Syrian build-up in Lebanon.

For the Saudis, inter-Arab relations could not have been worse. The future of the Damascus regime was of great concern. Syria, however, seemed to be slowly sinking into the Lebanon imbroglio. While Damascus had little choice but to increase its involvement, the potential consequences were grave. The Israelis were threatening to strike at the Syrians, which would lead to an Israeli-Syrian war and possibly to a general Middle East war. Damascus's involvement in Lebanon was causing internal unrest at home. The loss of soldiers, the apparent alliance with the Christians against the Lebanese Muslim and Palestinians, and the economic hardships caused by the influx of refugees from Lebanon provided much ammunition for Assad's opponents. The Syrian regime was diplomatically isolated in the Arab world, save for Jordan. At the same time, Egypt, the key Arab state, which under Sadat had turned away from the Soviets and toward the West creating the best opportunity for an Arab-Israeli settlement in twenty years, remained irreconcilably opposed to Assad. Sadat's anti-Assad feelings drove the Egyptians into a tactical alliance in Lebanon with the most radical Arab regimes—Iraq and Libya. Egypt's alliance with these states and general anti-Syrian attitude greatly concerned the Saudis.

Despite their differences with both the Egyptians and the Syrians, the Saudis apparently realized that the key factor to ending the disaster in Lebanon as well as to improving the terrible state of inter-Arab affairs was to bridge the gap between Damascus and Cairo. By doing this and forging a moderate Arab alliance of Riyadh, Cairo, and Damascus, the Lebanon crisis could be contained, Syrian isolation could be broken, and the necessary prerequisites for an Arab-Israeli settlement could be attained. Therefore, Saudi efforts continued to be primarily directed toward mediating the differences between Assad and Sadat.

During April and early May, through a series of diplomatic contacts the Saudis, in conjunction with the Kuwaitis, attempted to arrange a meeting in Riyadh of the prime ministers of Egypt, Syria, Saudi Arabia, and Kuwait. The meeting, however, was aborted at the last moment because neither Cairo nor Damascus was willing to compromise on key issues. The Syrians were still demanding that Sadat disavow Sinai II as a prerequisite for any reconciliation. Failing that, the Sinai agreement had to be the principal topic of discussion and not Lebanon. The Egyptians, who under Saudi urging were willing to diminish propaganda attacks on Damascus and Amman, would not abandon Sinai II or admit they had abandoned the Arab cause by concluding it. Lebanon had to be the only topic of discussion. The Egyptians were not prepared to let the Syrians squirm out of the Lebanon quagmire without suffering. Another factor which may have been instrumental in aborting the May Riyadh meeting were Libyan efforts to dissuade Assad from attending. Libya was attempting to form a grouping of Arab states which opposed a negotiated peace settlement. Muammar al-Qadhafi used Libya's financial resources to entice the Syrians to join the rejectionists rather than side with the Saudis. Without the Syrians, the rejectionists were whistling in the wind, for none was a confrontation state. The Libyan leader appears to have successfully lobbied against Syrian participation at the Riyadh prime ministers' meeting.[16]

The failure to hold the Riyadh meeting was a Libyan victory in the quiet Libyan-Saudi competition. Each was attempting to forge a coalition of Arab states which could shape the direction of future Arab policy: the Libyan-supported coalition would reject a negotiated settlement, while the Saudis favored one. The pivotal state was Syria and the issue at hand was Lebanon. Although not apparent at the time, Libya actually had little chance in competition for Syrian favor. The Saudis had more resources and could directly affect Syria's future. When Syria needed financial assistance the Libyans offered a great deal but the Saudis were more reliable. Moreover, Saudi Arabia could make up deficits in the Syrian oil supply and transport it through the Transarabian Pipeline. The

Libyans had also the added liability of being allied with Syria's most un-compromising opponent, Iraq. Where the Libyans were forced to negoti-ate between Damascus and Baghdad, the Saudis could weigh in on the Syrian side. In addition, Libya and Iraq were the principal suppliers of Syria's adversaries in Lebanon. Press reports indicated that Qadhafi was paying more than a million dollars a day to anti-Syrian elements.

Despite the rebuff of the failed May meeting, the Saudis continued to work for an Egyptian-Syrian reconciliation. Both the Syrians and the Egyptians seemed willing to talk. The Syrians needed assistance, and the prospect of a Libyan alternative to the Saudis had dimmed. While Da-mascus had shown the world that it was determined to press on with its policy in Lebanon, the costs were great. The Iraqis were threatening along its eastern frontier, discontent was on the increase at home, and the state was in financial straits. Under these pressures, the Syrians shifted away from the position that Lebanon was solely in their sphere of influence and recognized the desirability of involving the Arab League, and Arab League force was designated to move into the Beirut area.[17] These shifts in Syrian policy facilitated Saudi efforts at arranging a Syrian-Egyptian meeting. Just a month after the abrogated May meeting, the Saudis and Kuwaitis managed to arrange a quadripartite prime min-ister's conference in Riyadh between June 22 and 24. The results of the meeting were modest. Syrian and Egyptian antipathy remained great. Their differences over Sinai II and Lebanon were still substantial. The Saudis subsequently realized that a Syrian-Egyptian rapprochement could occur only in the context of a summit meeting between Sadat and Assad. Nevertheless, communications were established and some minor steps to improve atmospherics were taken. The Syrians toned down their attacks on Sinai II, and the Egyptians acknowledged a continued major role for the Syrians in Lebanon.

The real winners were the Saudis. The process of reconciliation be-tween Egypt and Syria seemed to have begun. Although the course would be tortuous and several deep valleys remained to be crossed, the first step had been taken. In addition, the Syrians had been weaned away from any potential antisettlement block of Arab states. The greatest testi-mony to the Saudi success was in the criticism by Saudi rivals. Libyan Foreign Minister Abdel Salem Jalloud attributed his failure to solve the Lebanon crisis to "the hindrance by some Arab states [Saudi Arabia]." He also accused the Saudis "of a campaign to force the surrender of the Arabs [i.e., to negotiate a settlement]."[18] The Soviet Union viewed the Riyadh meeting as primarily directed against Moscow and its allies. Mos-cow Radio said that the Riyadh meeting, ostensibly called to coordinate

Arab policy, was in fact, designed to put political and economic pressure on Syria.[19]

THE RIYADH SUMMIT

The feeling of accomplishment following the June Riyadh prime ministers' meeting was shortlived. The Lebanese crisis over the summer of 1976 took a serious turn for the worse. The Syrians, having secured at least a thin veil of an Arab mandate, determined to press their advantage on the ground in Lebanon. A final push to Beirut and a scattering of the Palestinian and leftist forces presented the only means for Damascus to salvage its army's image after the Palestinians had stopped them cold during June in the mountains east of Beirut and in the streets of Sidon.

Even before the Syrian push to the sea, Saudi helplessness on the ground in Lebanon was brought home by the two great Christian "victories" of the entire war. The first was the conquest of the Koura—the fertile plain southeast of Tripoli. The Christian attack was in response to an abortive Palestinian leftist attempt to open another front. The ill-planned Palestinian venture quickly turned into a rout of the Palestinians and a Christian advance to the outskirts of Tripoli. This was the single largest piece of territory captured by the Christians. The second Christian success was the conclusion of the six week siege of Tel al-Za'atar. More than any other event the surrender of Tel al-Za'atar symbolized to the Arab world Syrian cooperation with the Christians and raised the possibility of the Syrian destruction of the independent Palestinian movement.

The Egyptians, for their part, stepped up assistance to the Palestinians. They also initiated a brutal media attack on Damascus. Moreover, the Egyptians did nothing to dissuade the Iraqis from moving troops to the Syrian border. This move was designed to force the Syrians to withdraw units from Lebanon to protect their eastern flank.[20] These efforts, however, were to no avail. When in the late summer the Syrians decided to advance, no one was able to stop them. Egyptian impotence was particularly frustrating; under Nasser, Cairo had assets in nearly every Arab country, and now in Beirut they no longer even controlled a newspaper. Sadat had to sit by helplessly and watch the Syrian advance.

The summer of 1976 was also a sobering experience for the Saudis. Since the death of Faisal the new leadership had been largely successful with its more active role in inter-Arab affairs. Certainly the necessity of aborting the May prime ministers' meeting had been a disappointment but in less than a month they had been able to hold such a meeting. In the summer of 1976, Saudi policy appeared to be a failure. Egypt and Syria were as far apart as ever. Saudi backing for the Syrians in Lebanon did not appear to be ending the conflict but only making it worse. Despite consistent support, Sadat stung the Saudis in his annual speech marking the anniversary of the revolution when he criticized sister Arab states for their inadequate and niggardly financial assistance. This came less than a week after Saudi Arabia, Kuwait, Qatar, and the UAE established the Gulf Organization for Development in Egypt with an initial capitalization of two billion dollars. The bitter realities of the summer of 1976 illustrated for the Saudis the limits of their ability.

Despite the disappointment, frustration, and feeling of helplessness, the Saudis pressed on in their search for a solution to the Lebanon crisis through mending the Syrian-Egyptian rift. The Saudi policy continued to be to support the Syrians in Lebanon, while cautioning restraint. Nevertheless, Riyadh illustrated occasional displeasure with Syria. For instance, the Syrian attacks on the Palestinians resulted in the Saudi withdrawal of their 5,000 soldiers from Syria. (These forces had been there since just after the 1973 war.) While the Saudis had intended to withdraw them for some time, the timing was widely viewed as a warning to Damascus.

The Saudis retained the firm belief that peace in Lebanon rested with a Syrian-Egyptian rapprochement more than in Lebanon itself. The key to this reconciliation was the acceptance by Assad that Sadat had not sold the Arabs out with the Sinai II agreement and the realization by Sadat that there was little he could do to challenge Syria's overwhelming tactical supremacy in Lebanon. By early October both conditions were attained. The Syrian attitude changed. Assad had won the war with the Syrian army, but to help Elias Sarkis regain peace Assad needed the assistance of both Egypt and Saudi Arabia. There was considerable doubt in Damascus whether Saudi financial assistance would be forthcoming if the Syrians continued to occupy Lebanon without the blessing of the other Arabs or at least their acquiescence. The cost for Saudi support, Assad well knew, was dropping Sinai II as an issue of contention with Cairo. By October Assad was prepared to do this.[21]

The Saudis and Kuwaitis quickly took advantage of the changing attitude in Damascus. Sadat had publicly stated in August that he would attend an Arab summit; he, therefore, was committed.[22] In mid-October a six-party summit—Syria, Egypt, Kuwait, Saudi Arabia, Sarkis, and Arafat—was arranged to discuss Lebanon. No mention was made of

Sinai II. The conference got off to a good start when Assad called on Sadat at his quarters. This gesture set the tone for the summit. After two days of deliberations, a declaration was issued.[23] There was something for everyone in the agreement: the summit endorsed the Syrian presence in Lebanon and gave Syrian forces a mantle of legitimacy by making them part of an Arab peacekeeping force; Syria no longer had to bear the full cost of maintaining its troops in Lebanon; Sarkis could tell Lebanese leaders that Syria was not a foreign occupier but rather a force approved by the Arab League; the PLO obtained an Arab League guarantee for their continued existence; and Sinai II no longer was an issue on which the Egyptians would be criticized.

The Riyadh summit was a great victory for the Saudis. It was the culmination of eighteen months of diplomatic efforts. The fighting in Lebanon ended and a Syrian-Egyptian-Saudi axis formed. The moderate coalition became the dominant force in inter-Arab politics and, while it held, made a negotiated Middle East settlement not only acceptable but the preferred goal for most Arab states. More importantly, the assertive foreign policy of the Saudis had proven effective. The Saudis learned both the extent of their ability to influence the policies of the other Arab states and the limits on that ability. The Lebanese civil war and the complicated Arab crisis which grew out of it was the crucible in which the post-Faisal Saudi leadership was tempered.

EGYPT

Mohammed Mughisuddin

Not until September 1975 did Egypt begin to manifest some concern about the situation in Lebanon. The event that seemed to have triggered an Egyptian response to the then six-month-old civil war was Syria's increasingly active role in the crisis—a role that the Egyptian government perceived to be against the country's national interests. Because the new Egyptian foreign policy sought a negotiated settlement of the Arab-Israeli conflict and a rapprochement with the so-called conservative governments in the region, Cairo lost much of its traditional influence among the Arab nationalists outside the country. In Lebanon the Nasserites were particularly incensed with Sadat for his apparent lack of enthusiasm for their political and social aspirations and goals. Because of its declining influence among the Nasserites and other Muslim groups in Lebanon, Egypt perceived Syria's rapidly increasing role in Lebanon as a further threat to its dwindling sphere of influence. Egypt's inability to take prompt action and affect substantial changes in the Lebanese civil war was a clear indication that Cairo had lost much of its credibility and charisma in regional affairs. This was a radical change from the Lebanese situation in 1958 when Nasser, riding high at the crest of a wave of popularity following the creation of the United Arab Republic that joined Syria and Egypt in a federal union, openly opposed the Chamounist forces that were being backed by the United States.

Although the 1958 conflict in Lebanon was much less intense and less complex than the current civil war, Egypt's involvement in the former was much more significant than its involvement in the latter. There are several reasons for this substantial change in Egyptian policy. The most important factor in this change is Sadat's willingness to reach a negotiated settlement with Israel. This willingness on the part of Sadat has caused a serious rift between Syria and Egypt. Furthermore, Sadat's policy has alienated most of the Palestinians who are allied with the Nasserites, the socialists, and leftist Muslims in Lebanon. Hence, even if Egypt had the material means (which it did) and local allies (which it did not), it

133

could not repeat its 1958 performance without making substantial changes in its regional alliances and foreign policy goals.

A CHANGING FOREIGN POLICY ENVIRONMENT

External constraints play a far more critical role than domestic factors in the formulation and implementation of Egyptian foreign policy. This is so because of Cairo's heavy reliance on foreign powers for economic, technical, military, and political help to solve the country's domestic and foreign policy problems. Prior to the advent of the Sadat era, Egypt, during Nasser's presidency, assumed the role of vanguard of social and political changes in the region. The Nasser regime and its regional and extra-regional allies were identified with revolution, and they expounded the notion of revolutionary changes in the Middle East. Revolutionary rhetoric, more than the practical steps taken by governments to alleviate social and economic conditions, were responsible for creating a politico-ideological bipolarity that split the Arab world into the so-called "traditional or moderate" and "progressive or revolutionary" regimes. Under this division all monarchical regimes in the Middle East were identified with traditionalism and all republican regimes with revolutionism. While neither all monarchies were conservative or traditional in all aspects of their domestic and foreign policies nor all republican regimes revolutionary in all aspects of their policies, this seemingly neat division of the Arab world nevertheless appealed to most foreign and Middle East scholars and politicians who, consequently, analyzed and measured foreign policies of the Arab states within the famework of an assumed ideological split in the region. Thus the overthrow of the Hashemite monarchy in Iraq (1958), the expulsion of the Imam in Yemen (1962), the coup against the Sanussi monarchy in Libya (1969), and the various coup attempts in Jordan and Morocco were greeted with a great deal of enthusiasm and support by the powerful "Voice of the Arabs" (Cairo) broadcast facilities and by the republican regimes of the region. The Egyptian government dogmatically assumed that the addition of new republican regimes in the area would make it easier to achieve the country's foreign policy goals. Egypt's relations with republican Iraq, Yemen, and Libya, would, however, prove this assumption erroneous.

Prior to the 1973 oil price hike and the consequent enrichment of the oil-producing states of the Middle East that would provide large-scale assistance to Egypt, Cairo's primary external sources of military and financial aid were the Soviet Union and the East European states. Although Saudi Arabia, Kuwait, and Libya had been providing financial assistance to Egypt (and to Syria, and to a lesser extent to Jordan and the Palestine Liberation Organization (PLO) since the end of the June 1967 war), this aid was not considered sufficient to meet the country's rapidly growing defense and economic needs. Thus prior to the expulsion of the Soviet technicians from Egypt in 1972, Egypt's foreign policy manifested a great deal of sympathy and understanding towards Soviet interests and foreign policy goals in the Middle East and North Africa.

Since the expulsion, however, the country's reliance on the Soviet Union has gradually decreased to an insignificant level. After the resumption of U.S.-Egyptian diplomatic relations in 1974, the United States has steadily increased its financial support to the Sadat regime and currently gives Egypt approximately one billion dollars annually in loans and grants. Regional actors such as Saudi Arabia, Iran, the United Arab Emirates, Kuwait, Qatar, and Bahrain have contributed hundreds of millions of additional dollars to the Egyptian economy since the end of the October 1973 war. Because of its notably generous contributions to the Egyptian economy and its firm commitment to re-equip the Egyptian armed forces with Western material, Saudi Arabia has become the single most important external factor in the formulation of Egyptian foreign policy.

In addition to Saudi Arabia, the United States has become a highly significant factor in the Middle East diplomatic and power equation. Thus it should be candidly assumed that in the formulation of the country's foreign policy, the Egyptian decision-makers take into serious consideration the views and interests of Saudi Arabia, the United States, and other external supporters of the Sadat regime.

CHANGING FOREIGN POLICY ORIENTATION

Since the advent of the Sadat era, Egypt's international posture has substantially changed. While still maintaining a posture of leadership in the Arab world, Egypt does not manifest much interest and enthusiasm in the concept of the "organic Arab unity" as expounded by Nasser. For Sadat and several other Arab leaders, Arab unity has assumed a new meaning that accepts the existence of the various political systems in the region and emphasizes functional and practical cooperation between the regional states. Sadat is interested in following a policy aimed at assuring a working relationship between Egypt and all other Arab states regardless of their social systems.

Sadat's aim of achieving a rapprochement with all Arab states has not been, however, successful because of the existence of traditional rivalries among the Arab states and divergence of their perceived national interests. Thus in 1978 Sadat found himself in serious disagreement with five Arab states—Algeria, Iraq, Libya, Syria, and the People's Democratic Republic of Yemen—the so-called "rejectionist" or "steadfast" states and with the Palestine Liberation Organization. These five states and the PLO accuse Sadat of violation of the Khartoum, Algiers, and Rabat declarations that forbade the Arab states from recognizing Israel and entering into direct negotiations with it. The main adversaries in this intra-Arab conflict are Egypt and Syria whose current disagreement stems primarily from the Sinai II accord signed by Egypt and Israel in September 1975. Syria accused Cairo of taking a unilateral action in rejecting the use of military force in the resolution of the Arab-Israeli conflict. Article I of the Sinai II agreement,[1] Damascus believes, removed Egypt from the Arab-Israeli conflict and left Syria to bear the brunt of Israeli military pressure on the Golan.

The Syrian sentiments were echoed by the Palestine Liberation Organization which strongly attacked the Egyptian-Israeli agreement and described it "as a capitulative agreement which ignored the rights of the Arabs to their occupied land by agreement to abandon the state of war with Israel without receiving anything in return."[2] Denouncing the Sinai II agreement, the Executive Committee and the Central Council of the PLO in a joint statement issued on September 10, 1975, said that the agreement between Egypt and Israel was a "separate partial agreement that ignores the Palestinian cause, which is the essence of the national cause. It ignores the nationality of the Arab struggle against the Zionist enemy, besides parting with the national soil and the national sovereignty of the Arab Republic of Egypt itself."[3]

For a brief period in mid-1976, the Syrians and Egyptians were constrained to reconcile their differences under pressure from Saudi Arabia and Kuwait, who sought to prevent Syria from joining the rejectionist/steadfast camp and to increase the peace-keeping role of other Arab states, besides Syria, in the Lebanese civil war. This reconciliation, however, was short lived, and the two adversaries—Egypt and Syria—soon reverted to accusing each other of betrayal of the Arab cause.

EGYPT AND SINAI II

After the signing of the Sinai II agreement, Lebanon became an arena for
the manifestation of the Syrian-Egyptian disagreement and hostility toward each other. Syrian Foreign Minister Abdel Halim Khaddam in a
statement near Beirut on September 25, 1975, linked the Lebanese crisis
directly to the signing of the Sinai II accord. On its part, Egypt criticized
Syrian interference in the internal affairs of Lebanon and warned the
Lebanese leaders against permitting Syria to engage in anti-Egyptian
propaganda in the country.[4]

While the Sinai II accord had apparently consolidated Syrian-
Palestinian relations and weakened Palestinian-Egyptian ties, the mas-
sive introduction of the Syrian troops as an anti-Palestinian force in
Lebanon in June 1976, caused a temporary reversal of PLO relations with
Syria and Egypt. Sadat was quick in exploiting the Syrian-Palestinian rift
over the role of the Syrian troops in Lebanon. He firmly supported the
Palestinians and strongly criticized Syria for its anti-Palestinian policy in
Lebanon. Sadat manifested his support to the Palestinians by allowing
them to reopen the "Voice of Palestine" radio station in Cairo that had
been closed by Egypt following the PLO criticism of Sadat over the Sinai
II agreement.

Although the reopening of the radio station was an indication of
Egypt's moral support for the PLO, Egyptian efforts were directed more
towards weakening the Palestinian-Syrian alliance than providing the
PLO with substantial and meaningful assistance in their effort at survival
in Lebanon. The limited Egyptian success in this respect was primarily
due to the tactical differences that surfaced in Lebanon between the PLO
and the Syrian government and not because of any significant agreement
between the PLO and Egypt. Currently, the PLO and Syria are strategic
allies; they have had serious tactical differences in Lebanon, but their
views on the Arab-Israeli conflict are congruent. In the case of Egypt, its
current foreign policy goals are incongruent with the goals and aspirations of Syria and the PLO. Thus despite the PLO-Syrian differences in
Lebanon, the Egyptian government failed to remove the PLO from the
Syrian orbit and effect a rapprochement with the PLO.

Ideologically, Egypt's current domestic and foreign policies are in
congruence with those of Saudi Arabia, the United Arab Emirates, Su-
dan, and other "moderate" regimes in the Middle East and North Africa.
The substantial change introduced by Sadat in the Egyptian domestic

and foreign policies has cost the country the goodwill and support of the Nasserites, the Palestinians, and other "revolutionary" groups in the Middle East. This lack of ideological support for Egypt among the Lebanese factions and the strategic differences between Egypt and the PLO left Sadat without many policy options in the Lebanese civil war.

Egyptian Foreign Policy Goals in Lebanon

Egyptian participation (or lack of it) in the Lebanese crisis of 1975–78 should be viewed and analyzed within the frame of reference provided by its goals and objectives in that conflict. Specifically these have been:

1. To prevent the crisis from escalating into an Arab-Israeli war that would draw Egypt into an armed conflict with Israel.
2. To prevent the radicalization of Lebanon—i.e., to prevent the leftist forces from taking over the country's government. This also is a Syrian goal in Lebanon.
3. To endeavor to maintain contacts with the Palestine Liberation Organization, especially when Syrian-Egyptian relations are tense. Egypt tried to assume the role of protector of the Palestinians in Lebanon.
4. To prevent Syria's hegemonic control of Lebanon by encouraging the creation of an international peacekeeping force in Lebanon.
5. To try to maintain a semblance of cordial relations with the Lebanese Muslim groups opposed to Syria's military intervention in the country.

While these are Egypt's general foreign policy goals in Lebanon, Cairo's direct role in the Lebanese crisis has varied from issuing statements supportive of the Palestinians and the territorial integrity and political independence of Lebanon, to sending small quantities of arms to the Palestinians and facilitating the transit of the Iraqi "volunteers" going to Lebanon to fight against the Syrian and rightist forces there. Lebanon became an issue over which Egypt and Syria (and other Arab states) intensified their disagreements, particularly over the question of peace and conditions of peace with Israel.

Egypt and the Palestinians

During the period under review, Egypt placed high priority on the question of peace with Israel. On the eve of the war in Lebanon, in the hope of achieving a peaceful agreement with Israel, Egypt had entered into two accords with Tel Aviv—the Sinai I and Sinai II agreements under which Israel withdrew its forces from certain sections of the Sinai peninsula. Under the Sinai II accord Egypt and Israel agreed that the "conflict between them and in the Middle East shall not be resolved by military force but by peaceful means."[5] In its drive for peace, Cairo has sought the support, or at least acquiescence, of the major Arab actors in the regional subsystem. In the case of the Sinai II agreement, however, Egypt was unsuccessful in acquiring the blessings of the PLO and Syria because both actors believed that the provisions of the agreement would remove Egypt from playing an active role in the struggle for the recovery of the Arab lands conquered by Israel in the June 1967 war.

In its initial reaction to the Sinai II agreement, the PLO criticized the United States but made no direct reference to Egypt or Sadat because the Palestinian organization has not yet found a strong protector to replace Egypt in the intra-Arab conflict in Lebanon. Prior to the publication of the Sinai II agreement, the PLO was engaged in efforts to strengthen its ties with both Syria and Iraq and to achieve a national unity among the Palestinians. In August 1975, the PLO made new contacts with Iraq to assure Baghdad's support for the mainstream Palestinians. This was the PLO's first contact after Iraq openly supported the Palestinian rejectionist front that opposed the moderate faction of the PLO. Simultaneously, the PLO increased its cooperation with Syria in its campaign to have Israel's U.N. membership suspended. Both actions by the PLO were tantamount to a direct challenge to Sadat's policies and leadership of the Arab world. These activities served as harbinger of increased tension between the PLO and Egypt.

A few days after the signing of the Sinai II agreement, however, the PLO Executive Committee officially condemned the agreement because "it radically contradicts the will and insults the dignity of the Arab masses, as well as their national sovereignty. . . ." The statement pointed out that Sinai II ignored the Palestinian issue, which "is the essence of the national cause. . . ." The statement urged the Egyptian people "to bear their responsibilities in full in facing this agreement, which is treason, condemning it, defeating it, and eliminating all its anti-national effects."[6] This statement broke the tenuous links that the PLO had maintained with the Egyptian regime and which the resistance had previously been careful not to sever. Henceforth, PLO-Egyptian relations began to deteriorate rapidly.

The September 15, 1975 Palestinian attack on the Egyptian embassy in Madrid was a reflection of the severe tension between the Palestinian and the Egyptian government which instituted a series of anti-Palestinian measures in the country, such as the closing down of the Voice of Palestine Radio in Cairo and closing the headquarters of the Palestinian writers and journalists union. The government also threatened to expel the 15,000 Palestinian students in Egypt.

Although the intensity of the Palestinian-Egyptian conflict had increased after the Sinai II agreement, disagreement on the question of peace with Israel was not a new phenomenon in their erratic relationship.[7] After the October War, the Palestinian-Egyptian relationship plummeted to a new low when Cairo accepted King Hussein as the spokesman of the Palestinians living on the East Bank of the Jordan and indicated Egypt's willingness to allow Amman to temporarily represent the West Bank Palestinians if that could help alleviate Israeli apprehensions and encourage them to relinquish control over the West Bank. While the Palestinian-Egyptian relationship was still in a state of flux, the Lebanese Phalangists, whose apprehension of Egypt's political role in the Arab world had reached maximum proportions in the 1958 Lebanese civil war, made an attempt to achieve a rapprochement with Egypt. In February 1974, at the invitation of the secretary-general of the Arab Socialist Union (ASU), Pierre Gemayel at the head of a Phalangist delegation visited Cairo and met with several party and government officials in an effort to reach an understanding with them. During these meetings, the Phalangist leader was assured that "Egyptian socialism was not for export."[8] Although no substantive results were achieved by Gemayel's visit, the mere fact that it took place at a time of incipient tension between the Palestinians and the Phalangists in Lebanon, and between the PLO and Egypt must have given serious cause to the Palestinian leadership to be wary of the Egyptian government in their assessment of the impending struggle for changing the balance of power in Lebanon.

While Sadat was still engaged in Secretary of State Kissinger's shuttle diplomacy in the hope of recovering the Sinai oil wells and the main mountain passes from Israeli occupation, he also was making every effort to manifest a semblance of Arab unity in the face of Israeli inflexibility and Arab criticism of his approach to peace. However, by March 1975, only a month before the beginning of the Lebanese civil war, Syria was openly critical of Sadat's policies and was urging the resistance to commence operations inside Israel as the only means of reactivating the blocked peace process. Although the PLO was in full agreement with the Syrian assessment of the Middle East situation, Yasir Arafat did not then wish to cause a rupture with Egypt whose support for the resistance was considered by him as an essential element in PLO strategy. Other PLO leaders, however, disagreed with Arafat; they wanted to maintain distance from Egypt and attack its policies. (For example, both Abu Iyad and Nayyaf Hawatmeh were opposed to Arafat's conciliatory stance toward Egypt.) Notwithstanding the conciliatory efforts of Sadat and Arafat, the Egyptian-Palestinian ties began to weaken under the pressure exerted by the Palestinian hardliners supported by Syria. As the PLO had rejected Secretary of State Kissinger's step-by-step diplomacy which the Palestinians believed was aimed at destroying Arab unity, Sadat found it necessary to turn down a PLO request to send a delegation to Cairo to inform him of the organization's views. Being fully aware of the lack of consensus in the PLO's Executive Committee, Sadat tried to exploit the situation in his favor by insisting on a meeting with the entire Executive Committee and not just a group of representatives from it. The PLO rejected the condition and consequently withdrew its two representatives from Cairo.

Two external factors, however, prevented the PLO-Egyptian relations from worsening: the failure of the Kissinger mission in Israel, where he had gone to urge the government to show flexibility in its Arab policies, and the timely intercessory efforts by Saudi Arabia in urging Sadat to modify his stand regarding a meeting with the PLO Executive Committee. Soon after Kissinger's announcement on March 22, 1975, that he had failed to extract concessions from the Israeli government, Sadat and Arafat achieved reconciliation for which the latter was fully supported by Assad. Similarly, a rapprochement between Assad and Sadat was achieved with the help of King Khalid who invited the two Arab leaders to Riyadh for an "open and frank discussion of their disagreements." Having failed to achieve further progress in the peace process through the efforts of Kissinger, Sadat found it necessary to reconcile his differences with the main Arab critic of his policies.

The Lebanese civil war began at a time when Egypt, Syria, and the PLO were apparently in accord with each other. There was, however, one factor that remained a source of potential conflict among the three: Sadat's continued reliance on the United States for a peaceful settlement of the Arab-Israeli conflict. Kissinger's failure, Sadat believed, was a temporary setback in the peace process that must not be allowed to be thwarted by Israeli "intransigence." Thus Egypt's relations with Syria and the PLO began to suffer soon after Kissinger resumed his shuttle diplomacy designed to achieve a new disengagement agreement between Egypt and Israel.

During the initial days of the Lebanese civil war, Egypt refrained from making any public statement that would give alarm to any faction in the country. Syria and the PLO, however, expressed the view that outside powers (U.S. and Israel) were responsible for the existence of a conflict situation deliberately created to weaken the Palestinian resistance and Syria on the eve of a possible renewal of hostilities with Israel. Egypt began to express its "deep" concern about the Lebanese crisis only after it had failed to persuade Syria to accept Egyptian leadership in the peace process with Israel. Having failed to reconcile their differences with Syria, the Egyptian policy-makers began to perceive a threat to their national interests in Lebanon by Syria's unilateral intervention in the Lebanese civil war. Cairo feared that Syria's hegemony in Lebanon would diminish Egyptian influence and create a strong anti-Egyptian sentiment in Lebanon. In September 1975, Sadat sent two messages to President Frangieh and Prime Minister Karameh in which he reaffirmed his belief in and support for: (1) unity of the Lebanese people and their cooperation with the Palestinians; (2) Lebanese sovereignty, independence, and territorial integrity and his rejection of foreign interference in the country. He offered Egyptian aid in terminating the crisis.

By the middle of October, the differences between Egypt and Syria had become acute, and the two parties increased their accusations and counteraccusations about their respective roles in the Arab world and the Lebanese crisis. At this point in time, Egypt's efforts were directed toward reducing Syria's role in Lebanon by encouraging other Arab states to take a more active part in the crisis. Encouraged by Egypt, Saudi Arabia, and others, the League of Arab States called a meeting of foreign ministers of member states in Cairo on October 15, 1975. Since the meeting was boycotted by Libya and two major actors in the Lebanese crisis—the PLO and Syria—the foreign ministers could not deal with substantive issues. They did, however, recommend a financial assistance plan for Lebanon.

A few days after the Arab League conference, President Sadat accused certain unnamed parties of responsibility for chaos in Lebanon. Urging all disputants to try to reach a peaceful solution of the Lebanese crisis, Sadat warned them that if the civil war did not soon end "the catastrophe in the country would be greater than the 1948 catastrophe in Palestine." Sadat enjoined all outside powers to keep hands off Lebanon.[9] Although Sadat did not name Syria or Libya as being responsible for the Lebanese crisis, their lack of cooperation with the League of Arab States in resolving the dispute made them an obvious target of criticism.

While Sadat endeavored to maintain a posture of Egyptian leadership in the Arab world by making statements on Lebanon and other issues of immediate concern to the Middle East, domestic opposition to his foreign and domestic policies was becoming more vocal. In May 1975, the proscribed Communist party of Egypt officially announced its re-formation, and in December it joined the Nasserites in assisting the antigovernment forces at the Mahalla Koubra industrial region and the Helwan industrial complex. The same forces jointly expressed their opposition to the Sinai II agreement.

The introduction of the Syrian-trained Palestinian Yarmouk Brigade into Lebanon in January 1976, caused Sadat to issue several declarations condemning the Syrian intervention and supporting the Lebanese National Movement and the PLO. Premier Mamdouh Salem also issued a statement in which he expressed Egypt's firm opposition to Syria's intervention that he said was designed to partition the country. The premier reaffirmed Egypt's support for the progressive nationalist forces and the PLO and called for joint Arab action to help the Lebanese find a political solution to their domestic conflict. During this period, Egypt also condemned the Phalangist attacks on and the capture of Dbayeh refugee camp and the blockade of the Tel al-Za'atar camp by the Christian forces.

Syria on its part endeavored to link the escalation of fighting in Lebanon to the Sinai II agreement. In an official statement issued on April 12, 1976, the Syrian government implied that the fighting was deliberately escalated by outside powers (Egypt and U.S.) who wished to draw attention away from the "unpopular" Sinai II agreement between Egypt and Israel.[10] If the Egyptian official statements on Lebanon were muted, the Egyptian media made up for it. Commenting on the Lebanese crisis, Radio Cairo's domestic service in Arabic stated that the Syrian military measures in Lebanon were aimed at tightening the ring around the PLO and preventing any supplies from reaching it. The commentary concluded that the Syrian plans were primarily aimed at bringing pressure to bear on the Palestinian resistance, especially on the PLO, "in order to force it to accept the Syrian line on a solution to the Lebanese problem. . . . The suspicion regarding Syrian plans for Lebanon have been confirmed, particularly following the recent Jordanian-Syrian rapprochement. . . . This has prompted some elements of the resistance to say that the situation of the Palestinians in Lebanon now, in view of the Syrian Ba'athist moves and policies, is similar to the situation they faced in Amman in 1970."[11]

As the Syrian pressure on the PLO and the leftist Lebanese forces increased, Egypt began to re-establish contact with the Palestinian leadership in the country. On April 12, 1976, the Middle East News Agency (MENA) reported from Vienna that Sadat had received an urgent message from Arafat on the serious situation arising from the Syrian pressure on the PLO in Lebanon. Arafat reportedly informed Sadat that attempts were being made to "liquidate the PLO and to set up Zuheir Mohsin, commander of the Syrian al-Sa'iqa (shock troops), as leader of the resistance."[12] On the same day MENA reported that Egypt would not "allow any action conducive to the liquidation of the Palestinian resistance, and that Egypt fully supports the Lebanese progressive elements led by Kamal Jumblatt."[13]

The repeated rejection by Frangieh of Sadat's proposal for a joint Arab peace-keeping force in Lebanon so incensed the Egyptian leader that he condemned the "corrupt rightwing" leaders for their insensitivities to the real needs of the country. Sadat said that Frangieh tried to block the introduction of the joint Arab force on the basis of legality "as if there remains any ruling legality in Lebanon." Lebanon was burning, Sadat said, "while Frangieh, its president, talks about legality. Lebanon is being lost while corrupt leaders in it raise marginal issues."[14]

Egypt's most influential Arabic newspaper, al-Ahram, published an article on April 23 by its chief editor, Ali Hamdi al-Jammal, in which he accused Syria of endeavoring to liquidate the PLO and replacing it with the pro-Syrian al-Sa'iqa with a view of reaching an agreement with Israel on the Golan front which would be acceptable to the resistance, "which in this case would not represent the Palestinians as much as it would represent Syrian Ba'ath Party."[15] Al-Ahram further accused Syria of collaboration with the United States in respect to Syria's anti-PLO actions in Lebanon. Al-Jammal said that "all Western papers have unanimously agreed that the Syrian-U.S. understanding includes the point that Syria will liquidate all of the national forces in Lebanon, which include the PLO and the Fatah organization, liquidating the Fatah organization in particular."[16]

The growing rift between the PLO and the Syrian government was a welcome sign for Sadat who availed himself of the opportunity to express his country's "continued concern" for the welfare of the resistance in Lebanon. As a goodwill gesture toward the PLO, Sadat reopened the Voice of Palestine in Cairo for attacks on Syrian policies.

While the Palestinian refugee camps, such as Tel al Za'atar, were being mercilessly demolished by the rightist forces, Sadat once again criticized Syria's role in Lebanon and urged Damascus to accept the Arab League resolution on the withdrawal of the Syrian forces and replacement of them by joint Arab forces.

CONCLUSION

Unlike the Lebanese crisis of 1958 in which Egypt was deeply involved in providing financial and material support to the Lebanese Muslims and other antigovernment forces in the country, in the current Lebanese crisis Egypt's role has been limited to verbal support and provision of small amounts of arms to the Palestinians only at a time when their relations with Syria were strained. There are several reasons for this change in the Egyptian policy, the most important being Sadat's firm belief that Egypt should not interfere in the domestic affairs of other Arab states. Sadat is endeavoring to get the Egyptians to focus their energies and efforts on the internal development of the country. He realizes that Egypt lost substantial human and material resources for the sake of "exporting socialist revolution" to other Arab and Middle East states which not only rejected such efforts but also were successful in thwarting them. Without abandoning Egyptian leadership of the Arab world, Sadat has adopted a policy of noninterference in the internal affairs of other Arab states.

Another factor that constrained Sadat to limit Egypt's role in Lebanon was the absence of clear divisions and delineation of the Lebanese factions participating in the civil war. The current situation in Lebanon is significantly more complex than the situation that existed in 1958. Although Egypt was deeply concerned about Syria's military involvement in Lebanon, Sadat was reluctant to put too much pressure on Assad lest he abandon Syria's flexibility in resolving the Arab-Israeli conflict. Furthermore, Sadat's domestic and foreign policies have cost Egypt the support of most of its traditional clients in Lebanon, hence the Egyptian reluctance to compete energetically with Syrian influence in Lebanon.

While Egypt is fully committed to the proposition that the conflict between Egypt and Israel and "in the Middle East shall not be resolved by military force but by peaceful means," it is inconceivable that Cairo would make radical changes in the policy course it has maintained since the beginning of the Lebanese crisis in February 1975. As long as Egypt and Syria entertain serious disagreements on the method of achieving peace in the Middle East, their respective policies in Lebanon also will continue to reflect their disagreements. As in the past, so in the future, both Egypt and Syria will continue to try to use the Palestinians as pawns in the intra-Arab struggle for leadership and influence in the Arab world.

Considering the tangible and intangible resources available to Egypt for pursuing its foreign policy goals, the Egyptian "actions" and "inactions" in the Lebanese civil war were consistent with Cairo's foreign policy aims and domestic considerations. A major aim of the Egyptian foreign policy was to prevent the radicalization of Lebanon and a take-over of the country by leftist forces. This explains Cairo's tolerance of Syria's intervention, which was also aimed at weakening the leftist forces in the country.

Egypt, however, was also concerned about the growing role of Syria with which Cairo was competing for influence in the Arab world. Egypt also sought to prevent the imposition of Syrian hegemony on Lebanon— not necessarily for the sake of preserving the territorial integrity and political independence of a small neighboring state but for the sake of preserving a semblance of Egyptian influence in the country. While Syria, with the help of Saudi Arabia and other conservative governments in the Middle East, eliminated the threat of immediate takeover of the Lebanese government by a leftist coalition and prevented a de jure parti-tion of the country, Cairo failed to maintain its ties with traditional allies in Lebanon. Egypt could not have both the old allies and the new policy. She chose to maintain her new course in foreign affairs and to accept the attendant costs and risks.

THE HASHEMITE KINGDOM OF JORDAN

Paul A. Jureidini and Ronald D. McLaurin

ALTHOUGH Jordan is an important neighbor of Lebanon and was closely aligned with the Lebanese Republic for years, the Hashemite Kingdom played no more than a peripheral role in the Lebanese civil-regional-international conflict of 1975–76. The reasons for this very limited role originate in Jordanian policy priorities and shifting regional alignments, as well as in the changed status of Lebanon itself.

JORDANIAN POLICY

Policy Objectives

Jordan's policy goals at the general level parallel those of other states— the preservation of national independence and territorial integrity and regime maintenance. Territorial integrity is more than a policy objective in Jordan: it is a policy issue arousing serious international controversy, because the so-called West Bank—that part of the country lying west of the Jordan River—has been under Israeli occupation since June 1967, and by the unanimous agreement of all Arab governments belongs to the Palestinians, although Hussein and Sadat have proposed a federal connection between the West Bank and the rest of Jordan.

Objectives more specific to Jordan include avoiding regional isolation, retaining a pivotal role in certain regional conflicts, remaining a channel of Arab-Western interaction, and, of course, developing Jordan's socioeconomic base.

Avoidance of Regional Isolation

Jordan's poverty in virtually all natural resources and relatively limited manpower base[1] have meant the kingdom must place a high pri-

147

ority on maintaining cooperative relations with sources of political, economic, or military support. Such support—since the country is hardly a major international actor—can only come from within the region and from the great powers. Consequently, although Amman has not hesitated to align and realign itself according to shifting perceptions of interest, the leadership not only seeks at all times to avoid isolation, but since at least October 1973, has sought to maintain close ties with as many Arab governments and movements as possible, whatever their disagreements with one another.

Maintenance of Pivotal Role in Conflicts

As a result of the limited resource base, Jordan holds no major inherent value to regional and external powers. This is an advantage to the extent it reduces the *casus belli* for a potential adversary, but, like regional isolation, it also reduces the benefits to potential allies of supporting Jordan in case of a confrontation between the kingdom and an enemy. Thus the palace has sought to hold and give substantial visibility to Jordan's key role in selected regional conflicts and contingencies.

The most carefully engineered Jordanian role has been that country's behaving as Saudi Arabia's shield against Israel, on the one hand, and Syria, on the other. In this regard, Jordan's traditionally moderate role, and indeed the monarchy itself, have served as *bona fides* to Saudi Arabia, overcoming the historic rivalry between the Saudi and Hashemite houses.[2] Similarly, Israel has viewed Jordan as a buffer between the Zionist state and regimes it considered its implacable foes, Iraq and Syria. Even after Jordan's reorientation toward an entente with Syria, Amman's moderate stance has been valued. The threat to the Jordanian regime in 1970 was viewed with such alarm in Israel that the latter was prepared to undertake military action to safeguard the Hashemite throne.[3]

A Window to the West

King Hussein, always close to the West, has tried to maintain Jordan's traditional role as the Arab window on the West. Except for very brief periods of strained relations—which were often as much a function of tactical manipulation as they were of real differences—Jordan's ties to the United States have been particularly close. Amman's determination

to serve as the crossroads of West and Middle East has been a further re-
inforcement to the policy of "moderation" (as it is called in the West).

Regional Conflicts and Alignments

Recognizing his country's limited resource base, King Hussein has
attempted to circumnavigate many of the regional conflicts and rivalries
(all the time retaining a visible role in others, as we have indicated), remaining neutral in most when his country's vital interests are not involved, while still supporting the "moderate" line. Neutrality in the
"Arab cold war"[4] is a viable approach for Jordan as a result of the breakdown of rigid ideological dichotomies in which the Middle East was mis-
leadingly conceptualized by leaders within and outside the region during
the 1950s and 1960s. These artificial distinctions were breaking down by
1970, when the civil war that erupted in Jordan led to the kingdom's virtually total isolation.

Following the Jordanian civil war[5] in 1970, and the anathematizing
of the Hashemite regime, a slow and scarcely discernible improvement in
Syrian-Jordanian relations occurred.[6] Syria, as well as other regimes with
historically poor relations with Europe and America, experienced a new
interest in and attention to the West. Jordan became in many respects the
Syrian window on the West. The emergence of the Jordanian interest in
serving as intermediary between regimes of any ideological persuasion
and the West is probably a direct result of the post-1970 period of isolation.

In spite of Jordan's recent adroitness in avoiding confrontations
through other states' rivalries, Amman has not hesitated to pursue political alliances related to major Jordanian foreign policy objectives. Nor
has the government hesitated to undertake direct military action against
superior forces as such alliances or policies required. During the civil war
in 1970, Royal Jordanian Air Force (RJAF) and Jordan Arab Army (JAA)
ground forces attacked Syrian troops that had moved into the kingdom
in support of Palestinian forces.[7] Three years later, Jordan's elite 40th Armored Brigade took part in the October 1973 war against Israel, seeing
action on the Golan front.[8]

Domestic Policy Constraints

We shall consider two principal types of domestic factors constituting constraints on foreign policy in Jordan. In many countries, even

within the Middle East, interest groups and their concepts of interest form the *parameters* of policy. Historically, however, the palace has had substantial freedom of action in foreign policy formulation, in part due to the almost mystical attachment of the Jordanian populace to its king,[9] and in part to their recognition that Middle East international relations are exceedingly complex. Thus interest groups are less critical factors in Jordanian policy than in the policies of the other major Middle East states. However, Jordan is like all countries in the nature of interest group articulation: groups coalesce and dissolve around specific issues or issue areas. Thus we shall first identify the principal interest groups and then consider the issue areas in terms of which these groups express themselves.

The primary division in Jordanian society is that between the East Bank "Jordanians" and the West Bank "Palestinians." Although this is a false dichotomy—the ethnic composition of both groups is in fact remarkably similar[10]—it accurately reflects a perceived distinction that underlies national political, economic, and social policies. This psychological division between "Palestinian" and "Jordanian," however, has important foreign policy implications and affects social and economic conditions within Jordan.[11] There are several secondary and tertiary conflicting interest groups, but the overlapping of all of them is considerable across several issue areas, so that policy disagreements in Jordan are fewer than, for example, in Syria[12] or Lebanon.[13]

Among the more important groups influencing the palace are those representing the urban areas of the north, on the one hand, and those of the rural—still largely Bedouin—south, on the other. This conflict has more impact on development strategies and the budget allocation controversy than on foreign policy, but the Bedouins have long been the strongest supporters of the Hashemite monarchy while the Palestinians (i.e., West Bank-origin Jordanian subjects as well as the refugees) and urbanized are more numerous in the north.[14]

In addition, there are schisms between politicians and the armed forces, and between young and old in both political and military elites. In a country in which loyalty is a major criterion of advancement, along with performance, and where seniority becomes a measure of loyalty, a certain degree of generational conflict must be expected.[15]

Other groups that should be considered, though they are subsumed under the East Bank label already discussed, are the ultranationalists,[16] the chief Jordanian tribal groups,[17] and the major families,[18] a handful of which have dominated the political elite since Transjordan was established. These groups played no particular role in the Lebanon crisis, however.

The most salient Jordanian issue connected with the Lebanese conflict is Arab-Israeli settlement and the role of Jordan in such a settlement. Virtually all members of Jordanian society, including those living or born in the West Bank, would prefer an end to a conflict that diverts resources from the socioeconomic development of the country. On the desirability of a settlement, then, there is little discord. The differences arise over the shape such a settlement should take—specifically, whether or not to seek (demand) the return of the West Bank to Jordanian control.

Unlike most situations in which a nation's territory is occupied by a foreign neighbor, ultranationalists tend to *oppose* Jordanian control over the West Bank. Although there are compelling demographic reasons for this view, most East Bankers seem to look upon the West Bank as an actual political burden with only potential economic benefits. The opponents of a Jordanian West Bank include many prominent leaders close to the palace.

Supporting a return to Jordanian sovereignty over the West Bank is the most powerful decisionmaker in Jordan—the king himself. Hussein has a strong personal attachment to the territory, and his acknowledgement of the PLO's right to act as sole legitimate representative of the Palestinian people should not be confused with the king's personal wishes to see the return of the West Bank to Jordanian control.[19]

Beyond but related to the king's personal feelings, Hussein must insist on Israeli withdrawal from Jerusalem and the West Bank as a *sine qua non* of any settlement. Jerusalem is important because the Hashemites have a special religious role with respect to the Muslim character of the city; the West Bank, because it is Palestinian territory, and insistence on its return is necessary to maintain good relations with the rest of the Arab world.

A second major foreign policy issue related to Lebanon is Jordan's recent alignment with Syria. Relations between the two countries began to improve soon after the accession to power within Syria of Hafez al-Assad in November 1970.[20] In spite of the constant and at times vocal opposition of some Jordanian leaders and much of the military—who felt that Syria could not be trusted and that Jordan should pursue more diligently its ties to Saudi Arabia—Hussein and Assad, and certain of their key advisors (among whom familial as well as political ties exist), have concentrated considerable personal effort into the development of the bilateral relationship.

The king sees that Jordan has a wide range of common interests with Syria: both are deeply involved in the Palestinian problem; both view the Iraqi regime with distrust; and both confront Israel and need each other's support in any military engagement with Israel. Jordan is the weakest of the major states in the area and can accomplish few of its objectives in isolation. Alignment with Syria strengthens Jordan and increases her influence in the region.

The other major issues of concern in Jordan today are over priorities —most notably, developmental priorities between regions and budget priorities between economic and security requirements. Such issues, whatever their importance for Jordanian politics and foreign policy as a whole, did not affect policy regarding the Lebanon conflict.

Great Power Relations

The cornerstone of Jordanian foreign policy remains a strong alignment with the United States. Partially idiosyncratic politics—King Hussein has historically identified strongly with the United States and Americans—the alignment is also an expression of the palace's assessment of which powers can most substantially support the realization of Jordanian policy goals. It is to the United States that Amman has looked for primary economic and military assistance, for support against other Arab regimes, and for pressure on Israel.[21]

Reliance on the United States, however, has not been exclusive. Relations with the Soviet Union have improved over the past few years, reflecting the superpower detente. When U.S.-Jordanian strains have emerged, the new Soviet ties have been used—with some success—to exert pressure on Washington.[22] Similarly, the kingdom recognizes and maintains diplomatic relations with the People's Republic of China. However, this new great power opening represents Amman's effort both to enhance its diplomatic flexibility and to keep in step with the Arab and Third World political tempo.

Relations with the European powers, by contrast, are real, historic, and important. The West as a whole has been very helpful to the underdeveloped Jordanian economy, and several European powers provide economic support. Jordan places a high priority on the improvement of its relations with the Club of Rome countries but has had only intermittent success in expanding these relations.[23]

Relations with Regional Powers

Since breaking out of the isolation in which Amman found itself following the 1970–71 civil war, Jordan has been able to develop and maintain full and reasonably active diplomatic relations with all Arab states, including now even Iraq and Libya. The recent history of Egyptian-Jordanian interaction has been characterized by sharp disconti- nuities. Since the 1967 war, however, Jordan, for its part has directed largely cooperative behavior toward Cairo, while Egypt, even under Sa- dat, has only recently reciprocated on a consistent basis.

The proposal by Hussein of a United Arab Kingdom plan to re- establish Jordanian control over the West Bank, following on the civil war of 1970–71, led to brief but vitriolic Egyptian polemic against Jor- dan. Since 1973, Egyptian-Jordanian relations have steadied, reflecting Syria's emergence as a key Levant actor and Egypt's dependence on out- side support. It is possible that Egyptian-Jordanian interaction will increase once again should serious negotiations toward an Arab-Israeli settlement occur within or outside the Camp David framework.

Jordanian relations with Syria and Iraq have also been relatively unstable. The current period of cooperation between Amman and Da- mascus eclipses all previous periods in continued terms of intensity and consistency. Although the two countries' relations did not improve dra- matically until 1973 on the basis of formal interactions—largely due to the official Syrian reaction to the outcome of the civil war in Jordan—in fact the quality of their relationship grew markedly throughout 1971, when informal political, economic, and communications cooperation contrasted sharply with the official confrontation between the two Arab neighbors.[24] Once the 1971 problems were behind, the two governments ushered in the new era of cooperation. Beginning slowly in 1972, rela- tions became particularly close following the October 1973 war. Indeed, we have elsewhere described these relations as the foundation of an en- tente that serves as the cornerstone of both countries' defense and foreign policies in the region.[25] Apart from close political coordination and coop- eration, the military strategy of both governments assumes a remarkable degree of joint planning and operation, based on mutual interests,[26] al- though Syria is clearly the more powerful of the two states.

Jordan has been very cautious in its interaction with Iraq. In a rela- tionship of mutual distrust, Amman has sought to avoid direct confron- tation with Baghdad: much of the conflict has been informal and sym- bolic. Iraq has been less restrained, but from Iraq, too, conflict has been limited except in 1958, as a result of the coup in Baghdad, and 1970 at the height of the Jordanian civil war. The dominant feature in the bilateral relations of Jordan and Iraq is not their tenor but rather their declining significance.

Notwithstanding the history of dynastic rivalry between Hashemite and Saudi, bilateral relations between the Saudi Arabian Kingdom and the Hashemite Kingdom of Jordan have been almost wholly cooperative, the Jordanians frequently representing Saudi views where the latter have not been direct actors. Jordan has been a recipient of Saudi largesse. The views and the political orientation of both governments are in fact remarkably similar. Both are important actors in the Persian Gulf area, where Jordan has established some defense responsibilities in relation to the Gulf sheikhdoms;[27] both look to the United States as their principal extraregional supporter; both distrust the Soviet Union and believe radical regimes in the area threaten regional stability and domestic public order.[28] Throughout the period of Jordan's isolation following the civil war, King Faisal expended considerable efforts to improve Jordan's ties with the Arab world.[29]

The popular mythology is that Jordan and Israel have established and maintained a *de facto* cooperative relationship. This view greatly misconstrues the nature of their interaction. The intensity of any de facto or tacit cooperation between the two countries is more than offset by the intensity of their conflictive interaction. Jordan and Lebanon are Israel's weakest Arab neighbors, the two countries that early recognized they had little chance to restore pre-1947 Palestine. It has been necessary for each to establish its own form of *modus vivendi* with Israel, and Jordan's comparatively moderate stance, the open bridges policy it has followed since 1967, its willingness to negotiate a settlement, and internal problems with the Palestinians have caused the kingdom to be viewed as cooperating with Israel. While it can be stated that Israeli leaders have been prepared to resort to force to protect Jordan,[30] it should be remembered as well that as recently as 1975 a number of key Israelis suggested that the Palestinians should eventually take over Jordan.[31] And Hussein's pragmatism notwithstanding, it should not be forgotten that Jordan has been a major belligerent in three general Arab-Israeli wars and is cooperating on military strategy with the enemy Israel considers most intransigent, Syria.[32]

IMPACT OF JORDANIAN POLICY ON THE LEBANESE CONFLICT

In order to understand the Jordanian approach to the Lebanese conflict the recent evolution of relations between the two countries must be reviewed. This history comprises four distinct periods, 1950 to 1958, 1958 to 1967, 1967 to 1970, and 1971 to the present.

1950–58

Both Lebanon and Jordan were among the so-called "conservative" Arab states supported by the United States and cooperating closely to isolate the "radical" forces, led by Egypt and Syria. Foreign policy in both countries derived largely from the personalities and inclinations of their leaders—the young King Hussein of Jordan, and Lebanese President Camille Chamoun. Both men were oriented toward Western ideology and values, both were strongly sympathetic to the United Kingdom and United States, and both were pragmatic.

1958–67

The violence of 1956, 1957, and 1958 changed the leadership of the Middle East markedly. In the context of this study, the presidential change from Chamoun to Fuad Shebab resulted in Lebanon's moving toward a neutral position in the struggles between Jordan and Egypt, on the one hand, and Jordan and Syria, on the other. Indeed, Lebanese relations with both these Jordanian antagonists (and erstwhile Lebanese foes) were consciously improved to try to avoid greater domestic problems. Jordan did not, however, isolate itself from Lebanon. On the contrary, like other countries the monarchy provided various forms of support to those individuals and groups in Lebanon thought to hold correct views— in Jordan's case, to Chamoun, Kamel As'ad, and several Christian and Shi'a groups.

1967–70

After 1967 the dominant tone of Lebanese-Jordanian relations continued to move away from cooperation. While Jordan attempted to reestablish and maintain control over all its East Bank territory, eventually including those areas in which Palestinians were settled, the Lebanese government chose to yield to increasing Palestinian autonomy. When the Jordanian civil war erupted over this issue, Lebanon did not oppose the attempt to isolate Jordan; indeed, Lebanese Middle East Airlines stopped flying to the kingdom, and the Jordanian military attache was declared *persona non grata.*[33]

More important than diverging public policy in Lebanese-Jordanian relations was the diminution in Lebanon's importance to Jordan. The decline in Lebanon's importance to the United States, the development of the port of Aqaba, and the death of Nasser, whose hegemonic ideas threatened the monarchy, all contributed to the decline in Lebanon's value. Moreover, the emergence of pragmatic Hafez al-Assad as the uncontested Syrian leader and the entente between the previous antagonists provided Jordan with far more regional influence over its destiny than continued alignment with increasingly unstable Lebanon.

After 1970

The relationship between Suleiman Frangieh and King Hussein was never equal to that between Frangieh's predecessors and the palace. The king saw little in Frangieh's background, values, or approach to commend him. As we have indicated, Jordanian-Lebanese relations were rapidly becoming marginal; Frangieh's election only accelerated the process.

Obviously, no one among the Jordanian elite wished for Palestinian take-over in Lebanon. To the extent such a change was the alternative to Frangieh, as the constitutional president, the palace certainly favored the constitutional alternative. But to the extent Frangieh's and Lebanese attitudes might contribute to the strengthening of Palestinian influence, Jordan felt its own approach was preferable in spite of the cost.

Jordanian Action and Policy

As we have indicated, Jordan's role in the Lebanese conflict was largely peripheral. It must be considered on three levels—action on the battlefield in Lebanon, action outside the region, and action in Jordan. None is really critical to an understanding of the conflict or its outcome; all are necessary to an assessment of Jordan's objectives and success.

Lebanon

Jordan's allies in Lebanon—principally, Chamoun and Kamel As'ad —have traditionally been selected Christian and Shi'a elements, and Jordanian financial and other material support for these groups has not been uncommon. Such outside support is time honored in Lebanese society as a standard political practice. Almost all major leaders, parties, and other groups have close ties to external sponsors or supporters. It is in this context that Jordanian support must be understood.

During the "civil" strife period of the Lebanese conflict (i.e., in the spring and summer of 1975) Jordan continued to provide support to its traditional allies. This support included financial subsidies and the reported transfer of military hardware.[34] Developments in Lebanon were of some concern to Amman, as they were to Damascus,[35] because instability could lead to Israeli intervention on some then unforeseeable pretext, and because increasing Palestinian freedom of action in Lebanon might undermine the chances of negotiating a peaceful settlement of the Arab-Israeli conflict.

The Lebanese fighting resumed in the second phase as a regional-international conflict. Although the role of foreign powers became more substantial when the second phase erupted in September of 1975, Jordan's role did not undergo any immediate change. Both Amman and Damascus viewed the Lebanese conflict as a threat to settlement aspirations, and Syria perceived it as an impediment to the evolution of the Syrian-Jordanian-Lebanese-Palestinian entente that became the Syrian strategy after Sinai II.

As perceived by the Jordanians, the alternatives in Lebanon included (1) implementation of a new system of governance according the Palestinians and their leftist, largely Sunni Lebanese allies a greater measure of influence within the Lebanese political system; (2) restoring the older confessional system along the anachronistic lines existing theretofore; or (3) resorting to some system imposed by outside (but regional) powers. The first alternative was undesirable to both the Jordanians and the Syrians because enhanced Palestinian power seemed to threaten the entente that was to serve as their negotiating power with Israel. This option became intolerable as the alliance led by Kamal Jumblatt decided nothing short of dominance in the system was acceptable. Amman and Damascus saw a "radical" Lebanon as a real possibility, and one that augured ill for their own interests.

The second alternative might have been preferable to both regimes if it were viable; but history seemed to have demonstrated that the existing balance of forces within the Lebanese polity could no longer accept the old system and the old distribution of power. Yet, despite the covert or indirect involvement in the conflict of a bewildering array of foreign interests, the only conceivable forces of direct intervention were those of Syria or Israel.

Consequently, Jordan served as an intermediary between Syria's and Jordan's traditional Lebanese allies, explaining the needs and perspectives of each to the other and the mutual interests of both to both. When Syria began to take a more forceful role in Lebanon, Jordan continued its role as a channel of communication, Lebanese and Syrian leaders traveling frequently to Amman. The changes made in the National Covenant in the fall and winter placed the traditional forces in power once again but included modifications to provide for system change. Both Amman and Damascus were pleased with this accord, and Syria's determination to use all necessary military force followed directly on the decision of the leftist alliance to undermine it.[36]

International Action

A second and no less critical foreign activity in support of Jordan's Lebanon policy was to present the palace's views frequently and at length to interested third parties—most importantly, the United States. The significance of this level of action lay in the later stages of the conflict when Syrian military forces intervened in Lebanon. The Jordanians expended considerable efforts to clarify the Syrian role to Washington, reassuring concerned American officials that no threat to Israel was intended and that such strict limits on the nature of the Syrian activities as might be required to indicate recognition of and responsiveness to Israeli fears in this regard would be respected.

Domestic Action

Within the kingdom Jordan's actions were of two types. The more publicized was the treatment accorded refugees from the civil war. Large numbers of Lebanese fled their country looking for sanctuary from the increasingly sanguinary conflict; they were housed, employed, and well treated, even though substantial cost—and a rapid inflation—resulted from this generous treatment.

The second thrust of policy in Jordan was indirect military support of Syria. In the summer of 1976 widely reported Iraqi redeployments toward its western border with Syria suggested possible military action. By that time thousands of Syria's best troops were in Lebanon, others remaining in the Golan. Those available to meet the Iraqi threat were very limited, though some redeployments took place. Jordan also redeployed its troops to support Syrian forces facing Iraq.[37] In accordance with the Jordanian policy of maintaining good relations with all of the Arab world, Amman gave little publicity to its redeployments, but the troop movements could not have gone without notice in Baghdad—or Damascus.

The limited Jordanian actions in the Lebanese conflict clearly supported national foreign policy objectives. The emergence of a Jumblatt-led "revolutionary-Palestinian alliance" at the helm of Lebanon could have initiated a move back toward the regional isolation of Jordan, although it is unlikely such an isolation could have been as severe as that of 1970 to 1973, given Amman's close ties to Saudi Arabia and Syria. In this regard, Jordan was able to support its allies in and outside Lebanon, reinforcing cooperation and the assistance those allies provide. Finally, the kingdom was able to serve—albeit in a very limited fashion—as Syria's window on the West in terms of clarifying Damascus's objectives and needs.

The Results of the Lebanese Conflict for Jordan

The Lebanese tragedy resulted in little change in Jordan's regional role, especially since Jordan was not a direct actor in the conflict. On balance, the wisdom of the kingdom's entente with Syria was reaffirmed, and Syria's eventual emergence as (limited) victor may be viewed as implicitly strengthening Jordan. In addition, the outcome of the war further reduced the independence of the PLO, making possible and desirable a rapprochement between that organization and Jordan while at the same time eliminating any residual political threat the PLO could exercise against Jordan.

The entente with Syria also supported the possibility and promise of a reconciliation between Jordan and the PLO, and indeed rumors about and attempts at such a movement abounded. Yet, even when discussions between Jordanian representatives and those of the PLO led to some measure of agreement, other factions—especially other PLO factions—blocked complete accord and succeeded in overturning or preventing the implementation of the initial agreement. At this writing, the rapprochement still has not been effected.

Results of the Jordanian Role on the Lebanese Conflict

Jordan's limited role had no appreciable impact on the fighting in Lebanon. The quantity and types of arms reputed to have been transferred were not critical, nor was the financial assistance provided. Indeed, the most significant action may well have been Jordan's redeployments, since the likelihood of an Iraqi attack on Syria—already scant without the Jordanian move—was by virtue of the redeployments negligible.[38]

The close alignment of Jordan and Syria undoubtedly provided Syria with some tangible, though largely incidental and minor, benefits in addition to enhanced security vis-à-vis Iraq. In the course of their frequent discussions of the complex Lebanese problem and the countries' objectives, interests, policies, and actions with respect to the continuing turmoil in Lebanon, a great deal of information was exchanged which served the purposes of both Jordan and Syria.

THE CONTINUING CONFLICT

The Israeli invasion of Lebanon in early 1978 vindicated, in Jordanian eyes, the palace's earlier policies toward the Palestinian presence and role in the kingdom. Jordanian leaders felt history had proven that a weak central government and strong Palestinian role that might lead to a prolonged civil war and a greater perceived threat to Israel would result in Israeli intervention. Moreover, they believed that once such a precedent was established it might become increasingly easy to intervene. The short-term interests of the Palestinian movement, it was felt, frequently conflicted with broader and longer-term interests of the Arab world as well, of course, as those of individual Arab governments. Specifically, in view of these conflicts of interest, the Israeli intervention also raised further questions in the Jordanian mind about the wisdom of the decisions taken at Rabat in 1974.

The internationalized conflict in Lebanon continued beyond 1977, particularly in southern Lebanon. Even if this on-going fighting were to spread, the Jordanian role will continue to be extremely limited. Only if the localized conflict goes beyond Lebanese borders or is used as an excuse to ignite another Arab-Israeli war will Jordan become more involved, and then only as the defender of the southern flank around the Golan. Hussein will continue to support the Assad policy in Lebanon, unless Syria is forced to participate fully and actively in the rejectionist front. In the latter case, Amman can be expected to distance itself from Syrian policy and to realign more closely with Sadat.

THE ARAB-ISRAELI CONFLICT

Fred J. Khouri

THE ARAB-ISRAELI CONFLICT—and especially the long-festering, unresolved issue of the Palestinians—helped to ignite the Lebanese civil war in April 1975, to intensify the fighting, and to exacerbate relations between the contending parties in Lebanon, thus making it more difficult to end the war and to bring lasting peace and reconciliation between the various religious and ideological factions in Lebanon. The Lebanese civil war, in turn, added major complications to the Arab-Israeli problem and hindered efforts being made by the United States to bring about an Arab-Israeli peace settlement. In brief, there were many interactions between the Lebanese and Arab-Israeli conflicts which were damaging not only to Lebanon but also to the cause of peace in the Middle East.

PRIOR TO THE LEBANESE WAR

While through the years attempts to come to grips with the Arab-Israeli question had been made sporadically—and usually in response to an erupting crisis in the Middle East—and while some very limited progress had been achieved after the October 1973 war in dealing with it, formidable obstacles to reaching a final, overall peace settlement remained.

After the June 1967 Arab-Israeli war, the UN Security Council adopted on November 22, 1967, Resolution 242 which, for the first time, sought to provide specific guidelines and a framework for what were generally considered essential principles for a fair and lasting peace settlement. This resolution provided, among other things, for the withdrawal of Israeli armed forces from occupied territories; termination of the state of belligerency and respect for "the sovereignty, territorial integrity, and political independence of every state in the area and their right to live in peace within secure and recognized boundaries"; and "just settlement of the refugee problem." While Israel, Egypt, Jordan, and Lebanon accepted Resolution 242, but only on the basis of their own interpretations of the withdrawal provision,[1] Syria and other Arab states rejected it on the grounds that it dealt with the Palestinians only as refugees and that there could be no real and lasting peace in the Middle East until Palestinian national rights had been adequately provided for. Virtually all Palestinian leaders and other militant Arabs opposed Resolution 242 because they refused to accept the existence of a "Zionist State of Israel" under any circumstances, and they persisted in their advocacy of a single, secular, democratic state for all of the former Palestine Mandate area.

However, by the early 1970s the views of Syria and some Palestinians had begun to change. On March 8, 1972, President Hafez al-Assad of Syria for the first time publicly accepted Resolution 242 on the conditions that Israel withdraw from all areas seized in 1967 and that Palestinian "rights" were recognized as an essential element in any peace settlement.[2] Moreover, the military and political power of the Palestinian resistance movement had been seriously weakened because in 1970–71 its forces had been defeated and completely driven out of Jordan by King Hussein's army and because Palestinian units in Syria had been placed under firm Syrian control. This outcome left the Palestinians largely free to organize and operate only in and from Lebanon. Some moderate Palestinian leaders, therefore, began to place more stress on public relations and political actions and less on guerrilla activities and to consider the possibility of adapting themselves, quietly and cautiously, to the growing trend in the Arab world toward a political settlement with Israel.[3] This less militant and intransigent approach by some Palestinian leaders —even though it was still hesitant and not always consistent and most Palestinians remained unyielding—enabled the Palestinians to win more sympathy and political support for their cause in many parts of the world, including Western Europe and, to a lesser extent, even the United States. The UN General Assembly began to pass resolutions which held that "respect for the rights of the Palestinians is an indispensable element in the establishment of a just and lasting peace" in the Middle East; and American officials began to state publicly that peace was not possible without "addressing" the "legitimate interests" of the Palestinians.[4]

Despite the increasing willingness of at least the more moderate Arab leaders to accept a final settlement with Israel based on UN resolutions and despite peacemaking efforts by the UN, the United States, and the Big Powers, no real progress toward negotiating a peace settlement was actually made.[5] The failure to achieve progress in the early 1970's spurred renewed Palestinian militancy and intensified both commando

activities against Israel from Lebanese territory and also Israeli retaliatory and punitive attacks on Lebanon. The upsurge in militancy further
aggravated relations not only between Israel and the Arabs, but also
between right-wing Christians and the Palestinians and their Lebanese
supporters. In addition, this failure led to a decision by the increasingly
impatient Egyptians and Syrians to initiate a war in October 1973, in the
hope of compelling Israel and the major powers to realize that the Arabs
would not accept the indefinite continuation of the status quo and also of
strengthening the Arab bargaining power vis-à-vis Israel by uniting the
Arabs, employing the oil weapon, and regaining some of their captured
lands.

Because the superpowers came close to a military confrontation
during the October War, they now realized how dangerous the continuation of the Arab-Israeli dispute would be to their interests and how vital
it was to resolve it. Thus they cooperated in pushing the passage of Security Council Resolution 338 which called for a halt in the fighting and for
immediate negotiations for the implementation of Resolution 242.

Having strengthened their bargaining position and restored some of
their lost pride and prestige by the war, most Arab states—including all
of the confrontation states and Saudi Arabia, which had become one of
the most influential of the Arab countries—were now more politically
and psychologically prepared than ever before to negotiate a final settlement with Israel. Following the war and especially following the disengagement agreements negotiated by Secretary of State Henry Kissinger
between Israel and Egypt, and Israel and Syria in early 1974, some of the
more moderate leaders of the Palestine Liberation Organization (PLO),
especially those associated with al-Fatah led by Yasir Arafat and the
Syrian-controlled al-Sa'iqa, now realized how slim their chances were of
attaining their goal of a single, secular, democratic state of Palestine.
They also feared that the United States might succeed in bringing about a
final Arab-Israeli peace settlement which would completely ignore Palestinian rights and would restore control over the West Bank to Jordan,
thus depriving them of any hope of ever attaining their own state in even
a part of Palestine. Consequently, these leaders concluded that despite
the violent opposition of their more militant and uncompromising opponents within the resistance movement it would be more realistic to scale
down their maximum demands and goals; to accept an invitation to attend a resumed Geneva conference provided that their national rights
were recognized as a major issue; and to agree to set up a Palestinian
state in those occupied territories evacuated by Israel as part of any final
peace agreement.[6] The more militant Palestinians, led by the Popular

Front for the Liberation of Palestine, vehemently objected to any acceptance of or any settlement with Israel. They formed the rejectionist front and, with the support of Iraq and Libya, worked to frustrate efforts at compromise with Israel. Thus as the more moderate Arabs and Palestinians moved closer to accepting Israel and to making major concessions for peace, the differences and hostility between the moderate and militant Arabs and Palestinians intensified, adversely affecting the situation not only within the Arab world, but also within Lebanon, where inter-Arab rivalries and conflicts were often reflected.

Although Israel was winning the October 1973 war militarily when it was finally brought to a halt by superpower pressures, she ended up suffering a major political and diplomatic defeat and finding herself even more isolated in the world and more dependent on the United States than ever before. Israeli leaders sought to delay serious peace negotiations not only because the various factions within the government coalition could not agree on specific terms for the territorial and other issues, but also because they wished to use the delay to improve their bargaining position by attaining even greater military superiority over the Arabs, by establishing more settlements in the occupied territories, and by waiting for the newly achieved Arab unity to fall apart and for the Arab oil weapon to lose much of its power.[7]

After the 1973 war, the great preponderance of the states in the world, including those in Western Europe, were more convinced than ever that the terms of Resolution 242 alone no longer provided a broad enough basis for peace because they had not concluded that the Palestinian national issue was basic to the overall Arab-Israeli conflict and had, therefore, to be adequately dealt with and provided for before there could be any realistic possibility for lasting peace in the Middle East.[8] In October 1974, even Jordan joined with all other Arab states at the Rabat Conference in proclaiming that the PLO was the only legitimate representative of the Palestinian people and the only organization able to negotiate the future of the West Bank and the Gaza Strip. The UN General Assembly continued to pass resolutions which backed the right of national self-determination for the Palestinians; and in the autumn of 1974 the General Assembly invited Arafat to make a statement before it and gave to the PLO observer status at the UN. These major political and public relations gains made by the PLO not only worried and embittered the Israelis, who had been trying to ignore and bypass the Palestinian issue in peace negotiations, but also greatly enhanced the positions of Arafat and the PLO within the world community, in Lebanon, and elsewhere in the Middle East. These developments further widened the gap between moderate and extremist Palestinian groups and leaders inside and outside of Lebanon.

Thus at the time the Lebanese War broke out in April 1975, the Arab-Israeli conflict remained unresolved despite Kissinger's persistent efforts to deal with it by a step-by-step approach, despite the fact that the overwhelming preponderance of UN members were now in general agreement as to the basic framework for a final settlement, and despite a growing readiness in the confrontation states to accept that framework. Israel was still stalling for time,[9] and the gap between the Arab and Palestinian moderates and rejectionists had widened throughout the Arab world and within Lebanon. Moreover, efforts launched by Kissinger in March 1975, to achieve a second withdrawal accord between Egypt and Israel created new distrust and dissension between Syria and the Palestinians on the one hand, and Egypt on the other. In the eyes of the Syrians and Palestinians, as well as many other Arabs, it appeared that Kissinger was deliberately trying to bypass the Palestinian and Golan Heights issues and to split the Arab world, and that Egypt was trying to gain back some more of her land, even if it meant disregarding the interests of the Syrians and Palestinians. Thus on the eve of the Lebanese War, a serious gap also began to develop even between some moderate Arab leaders.

By early April 1975, the absence of any movement toward resolving the overall Arab-Israeli dispute and Kissinger's persistence in ignoring the Palestinian problem and in concentrating on reaching another Sinai accord greatly worried both the right-wing Christians and the Palestinians in Lebanon. Many rightists, realizing that their best hope of eliminating their own Palestinian problem was through the attainment of a comprehensive Middle East peace settlement which provided for an independent Palestinian state, were deeply concerned that American efforts to arrive at only limited territorial agreements could leave them stuck indefinitely with the Palestinians and the resistance movement. They therefore concluded that the time had come for a showdown with the Palestinian commando organizations in order, one way or another, to destroy Palestinian military and political power in Lebanon and to compel the emigration of as many of the Palestinians as possible from their country.[10] For years these same Christians had not concealed their friendly feelings toward the Israelis, who were considered to be, like themselves, a product of the West and a threatened minority in a Muslim-dominated Middle East; and, if forced to the wall, they were prepared to look to the Israelis for political and military aid in their struggle against the Palestinians.[11] As for the Palestinians, they also feared that the Americans, Egyptians, and other Arabs would press for an Arab-Israeli settlement which disregarded Palestinian rights. Lebanon provided them with their last effective base of operations not only against Israel but also, through public relations and political activities, even against those Arab governments who might, in their opinion, be prepared to betray the Palestinian cause. Since they were also convinced that the Lebanese rightists and the Maronite-led army were out to destroy their movement, they were now more determined than ever to hold on to their bases and positions in Lebanon.[12]

In brief, the failure to bring about an overall Arab-Israeli peace settlement and Kissinger's limited step-by-step diplomacy heightened the concern of and the hostility between Lebanese rightists and the Palestinians and their supporters and, thereby, helped—together with various internal social, economic, psychological, ideological, and other forces and factors —to create conditions that could only lead to a violent confrontation.[13]

Not only did the unresolved Arab-Israeli conflict—and especially the Palestinian issue—help precipitate the civil war, but it also worked to exacerbate the war after it had broken out and to delay and obstruct efforts to end it. Thus during the civil war Israel provided weapons and, on occasion, even direct military support to right-wing forces because of her desire to emasculate the Palestinian Resistance Movement in Lebanon and to remove it as an active element in any future peace negotiations. Israel also sought to divide and distract the Arabs in order to lessen the Arab threat to her and to weaken Arab bargaining power; to delay American efforts to convene a Geneva conference; and to gain more time to enable her to strengthen her bargaining position vis-à-vis the Arabs before having to enter serious peace negotiations.[14] In short, Israel felt that, in so far as the Arab-Israeli arena was concerned, it was to her advantage to keep the civil war going, to help the rightists inflict a major defeat on the Palestinian forces and their Lebanese supporters, and to encourage and exploit Arab differences—such as between Syria and Egypt, and Syria and Iraq—in Lebanon, as well as elsewhere. At one stage of the war, substantial military aid from Israel and other outside sources, as well as some Syrian military actions against Palestinian positions, enabled the largely Maronite forces to take the offensive in an attempt to destroy the Palestinian commando groups and to take full control over the country.[15]

Whereas virtually from the beginning the smaller, more radical and militant commando units had been wholly and clearly involved in the fighting alongside Lebanese leftist forces led by the Druze leader, Kamal Jumblatt, the major Palestinian political and military organizations, such as al-Fatah, decided to enter the conflict more fully and openly than before only after they had become convinced that there was great danger that Maronite forces would drive them out of Lebanon as King Hussein had driven them out of Jordan.[16] But their complete entrance into the war had grave consequences. It cost them heavy losses in manpower and military equipment; lessened their ability to make attacks on Israel; heightened Arab disunity; intensified the fighting and made it more difficult to stop; added further complications to the Arab-Israeli problem; and further diverted Arab, American, and UN attention to the widening and increasingly more destructive Lebanese conflict and away from the Arab-Israeli conflict, thereby delaying the Arab-Israeli peacemaking process initiated by the United States.

The second Sinai disengagement agreement concluded on September 1, 1975, further inflamed the Lebanese civil war and delayed its termination.[17] Because the formal agreement provided for some territorial gains for Egypt without any reference to the other Arab-Israeli fronts and to the Palestinian issue,[18] it greatly increased inter-Arab divisions and distrust. Moreover, the new Sinai accord intensified the fear of the Palestinians and Maronites that the United States would ultimately succeed in bringing about an Arab-Israeli settlement which did not call for a Palestinian homeland. Consequently, the Maronites became even more determined not to halt combat until Palestinian power in Lebanon had been annihilated: the Palestinians were also now more determined than ever to fight to the end to save the last significant base of operations left to them which enabled them to remain a viable movement and provided them with some bargaining power not only in any future dealings with Israel and the United States, but also in their relations with Arab states.[19] Thus the second disengagement agreement worked to prolong the civil war—and this prolongation, in turn, worked to impede efforts to come to grips with the overall Arab-Israeli conflict.

Although following the Lebanese civil war some of the more moderate PLO leaders had become increasingly convinced of the need to be more flexible and to go along with the peace negotiating process if the Palestinians were to have a realistic opportunity of attaining even part of their desired objectives,[20] they were still unprepared to go as far as the United States demanded of them in so far as publicly and formally accepting Security Council Resolution 242. As a result, by the latter part of 1977 President Jimmy Carter and other high American officials began to claim both that the PLO had been so intractable that it had, at least for the immediate future, forfeited its right to participate in any peace negotiations and also that they did not favor the setting up of an independent Palestinian state. President Sadat was so angered by PLO attacks on him and his new peace drive that he warned that if the PLO did not alter its hostile stand, he would bypass it and seek out Palestinian leaders in the occupied areas to negotiate on behalf of the Palestinians.

The Palestinians were so resentful and apprehensive as a result of these statements that even moderate Palestinian leaders now concluded that there was need for some spectacular guerrilla operation against Israel which might help convince the United States and Israel that the PLO and Palestinian national rights could not be ignored with impunity in any peacemaking process. The operation decided upon involved the landing of commandos in Israel by sea and the seizure of hostages to exchange for Palestinian prisoners held in Israel. On March 11 commandos landed and seized a bus. In the shooting which followed, thirty-seven Israelis were killed. As indicated earlier, Israel used this bloody event as justification for launching a major attack on south Lebanon. Israel's invasion hurt the Palestinians in significant ways. Not only did the Palestinians lose heavily in military manpower and equipment, but their fortifications and bases in the south were destroyed and they were driven out of an area which had provided them with virtually their only important, independent base for artillery and land operations against Israel. Moreover, the Palestinian armed groups ended up being more dependent on and subject to the control of Syria than ever before and a growing number of Lebanese Muslims, especially those from the south, began to give increasing blame to the Palestinians for their plight.

Nevertheless, the Palestinians felt that they had, in the process, made some gains. Having fought well against the Israeli army, Palestinian morale, self-confidence, and unity had grown. Israel's overreaction helped to lessen the extent of outside condemnation of the bus attack and to tarnish still further Israel's image in the world community. In addition, the PLO gained more international recognition since the UN Secretary General and the commander of UNIFIL deemed it necessary to negotiate with the PLO as one of the parties involved in the conflict in southern Lebanon. This increased international recognition, as well as the weakened military position the PLO found itself in following Israel's invasion, encouraged the more moderate PLO leaders to formally agree to cooperate with UNIFIL and Lebanese government efforts to reassert its authority in the south; to give up, at least for the time being, their use of southern Lebanon as a base for direct military attacks on Israel; and to give greater stress once again to political and diplomatic, rather than to military, activities in order to see if in coming months progress could be made through American efforts to bring about a Middle East peace settlement which would adequately provide for Palestinian national rights and PLO involvement.[21]

If UNIFIL and the Lebanese government are able to take full, effective, and long-lasting control over all parts of south Lebanon, then they could help prevent the renewal of fighting across the Israeli-Lebanese border and between the Palestinian-Muslim and Christian factions in the area. However, even then some incidents could still take place by long-range artillery and land-to-land missiles fired by the Palestinians north of the Litani and by the Israelis south of the border. In addition, Palestinian and Israeli attacks could be made by air and sea over and around the southern zone. After all, on March 11 the fedayeen who made the bus attack had come by sea; and on June 9, 1978, Israeli commandos and paratroopers had landed by ship and helicopter and destroyed a Palestinian coastal base at Dhar al-Burj, about nine miles north of the Litani River.

If UNIFIL and the Lebanese government fail to take control over the entire Christian-dominated border zone, then armed Palestinians and Muslims will probably try to return to this area and it will again be torn by strife and conflict. Endangered UNIFIL units might then be withdrawn from the south, leaving the situation there more explosive than ever.

Moreover, if after some months Palestinian leaders believed that there had not been enough movement in the peacemaking process and especially if the Palestinians were being ignored, then even the moderates will once again decide, as they had done before March 11, to turn to some dramatic military operation in an attempt to prove their contentions: if they cannot achieve even limited goals by peaceful means then they have nothing to lose by resorting to force; peace cannot be achieved without the PLO and the recognition of Palestinian national rights. Such a turn of events would seriously and adversely affect efforts to resolve both the Lebanese and the Arab-Israeli problems and would increase instability and strife and ultimately lead to more conflicts involving Israel, Lebanon, and other Arab states, as well as the Palestinians.

In any case, until they had somehow received adequate assurances of being able to achieve at least their more limited goals as set by UN resolutions, the Palestinians would continue to consider it vital to hold on, regardless of the cost, to whatever bases left to them in Lebanon following the civil war, Israel's invasion of south Lebanon, and the introduction of UNIFIL into the area. Even if the PLO remained out of the American-led peace process for whatever reason, it could still retain enough influence in Lebanon and elsewhere in the Arab world, as well as in the Third World and the Communist bloc, either to frustrate efforts to arrive at an overall Arab-Israeli peace settlement and/or to prevent the successful implementation of any bilateral or multilateral peace agreements which overlooked the PLO and Palestinian rights.

Nevertheless, undue Palestinian militancy and intransigence in dealing with both the Lebanese and Arab-Israeli conflicts could, by reducing essential outside support for their cause and by adding to the already formidable obstacles to an Arab-Israeli peace, do more to impair than to enhance Palestinian ability to attain even limited goals and objectives.

Lebanon

For many years following the 1948 Palestine war, the Lebanese government, largely dominated by conservative and pro-Western Christian and Muslim elements, succeeded in keeping Lebanon at the fringes of the Arab-Israeli conflict. However, after the Palestinian Resistance Movement had been expelled from Jordan in 1970–71 and had begun to operate politically and militarily from Lebanon and after Israel began to mount large-scale retaliatory and punitive assaults on Lebanon and to intervene in the south, Lebanon became increasingly involved in the Arab-Israeli problem despite strenuous efforts by rightist leaders to prevent it. As indicated earlier, this new development helped to precipitate the Lebanese civil war. During the war, right-wing Christians tried to seize complete control of Lebanon in order to drive Palestinian power and influence out of their country and to remove Lebanon from the Arab-Israeli confrontation. But the rightists failed to achieve their goals. On the contrary, not only did the Palestinian Resistance Movement survive, but Lebanon became more enmeshed in the Arab-Israeli conflict than ever before. In fact, with large numbers of Syrian troops stationed in Lebanon, with the continued presence of Palestinian commando groups and bases, and with continued instability and strife in southern Lebanon, there was reason to fear that the situation in the south would ultimately spark another large-scale Arab-Israeli conflict and that Lebanon would become involved militarily in it.

President Sadat's peace drive not only impeded efforts to implement cease-fire agreements for the south,[22] but also further divided the contending sides in Lebanon and heightened tensions between them. The Palestinians and left-wing Lebanese vehemently denounced Sadat's actions and held large-scale demonstrations against them. The rightists generally supported Sadat, although they were concerned that he might seek a separate arrangement with Israel which would leave Lebanon's Palestinian problem unresolved. Because it had to take into account newly acquired Syrian power and influence in Lebanon and the strong conflicting views among its own people and because it also sought to maintain its fragile neutrality within the widely split Arab world, the Lebanese government refused to attend both the Sadat-sponsored peace talks in Cairo and also the anti-Sadat summit meeting held in Libya.

All Lebanese factions opposed, although for different reasons, Prime Minister Begin's proposal which would provide for only a limited autonomy for the Palestinians now living in the West Bank and which precluded the establishment of a Palestinian state and the return of those Palestinians living in Lebanon and other Arab countries. In early January 1978, President Elias Sarkis stated that Lebanon would reject any Middle East peace agreement which left Lebanon saddled with a large number of Palestinians, and he called for a settlement which would clearly provide for the "legitimate rights" of the Palestinians on their own land.[23] Some right-wing Christian leaders warned that there could be no national reconciliation as long as the Palestinians remained in their country and that if no real progress was made in the Egyptian-Israeli talks, Lebanon could again become the stage for inter-Arab and Arab-Israeli violence and disputes.[24]

The Israeli invasion and temporary occupation of south Lebanon clearly demonstrated how integrally involved Lebanon had become with the Arab-Israeli question. As a result of the invasion, large numbers of Lebanese had been killed and wounded and made, at least temporarily, homeless; many villages had been destroyed or damaged; and distrust and hostility between the Palestinians and their Muslim allies and the right-wing Christians had been further intensified. Thus this new conflict had brought still more suffering as well as more uncertainties and internal and external complications to Lebanon.

Nevertheless, if UNIFIL is able to fully and effectively carry out its mission, Lebanon could derive important benefits. UNIFIL could, for example, facilitate the reassertion of Lebanese governmental authority in the south; prevent further instability and strife in the border area; strengthen the government's ability to deal with other major internal problems; and help prevent the south from becoming the source of another Arab-Israeli conflict and lessen the chances of Lebanon becoming directly involved in the event of another Arab-Israeli war. But even with UNIFIL operating well along the border, some incidents—by air, sea, and artillery—could still take place and hundreds of thousands of Palestinians and thousands of dedicated and well-armed commandos would still remain in Lebanon. Consequently, as long as the Arab-Israeli problem remains unresolved, Lebanon cannot avoid being involved in it. Besides, if UNIFIL were to fail to carry out its mandate and especially if it were to be removed from the area, the situation in the south would deteriorate once again and could sooner or later help precipitate not only another Arab-Israeli conflict, but also another Lebanese civil war. Bitter fighting which developed in the middle of June between the private armies of the Phalangist party and former President Suleiman Frangieh further complicated and hindered the Lebanese government's ability to deal with the troubled situation in the south, as well as elsewhere in the country.

Some Maronite leaders continued to press for a separate Christian state or entity.[25] While such a separate state might be spared attacks from Israel, it would not be able to remove itself from the Arab-Israeli dispute. In fact, since it would be virtually allied and supported militarily by Israel, Arab governments would consider it as a satellite of their enemy. Therefore, such a state could not avoid being directly and actively entangled in the Arab-Israeli problem and being militarily involved in the event of another Arab-Israeli war.

In short, Lebanon found herself after the civil war much less able than before to avoid being entangled in the Arab-Israeli conflict, to make her own independent decisions, or to promote her own policies and objectives in the Arab-Israeli arena.

Egypt, Jordan, and Other Key Arab States

By increasing the divisions and mistrust within the Arab world and by causing a major part of Syria's army to be tied down in Lebanon, the Lebanese civil war had weakened the Arabs militarily and politically, thereby making it more difficult for Egypt to achieve her own objectives. President Sadat's trip to Jerusalem further heightened the animosity between Egypt, on the one hand, and Syria, several other Arab states, and the Palestinians and their Lebanese allies, on the other hand. It also tended, at least for a time, to isolate Egypt within the Arab Middle East, significantly reducing Egypt's bargaining power in her negotiations with Israel. Thus while the consequences of the Lebanese conflict might have played a part in bringing about Sadat's peace initiative, the final outcome did more to lessen than to improve the chances for its success.

After the conclusion of the second Sinai accord, Jordan developed close political and military ties with Syria and these survived the Lebanese civil war largely intact. Because of the increased Arab disarray, Syrian military preoccupation in Lebanon, and further worsening of relations between Syria and Iraq (whose combined and coordinated armed forces would be vital for the defense of Jordan and the eastern front with Israel), the civil war had diminished Jordan's ability to attain her own goals in the Arab-Israeli arena.[26]

Saudi Arabia enhanced her prestige and influence in the Arab world and among the Palestinians by being primarily instrumental in bringing the Lebanese civil war to an end and president Assad and Sadat together again. As a result, Saudi Arabia, whose leaders were convinced that their interests would be advanced by fostering peace and stability in the Middle East, was in a stronger position than before to move Egypt, Syria, and the Palestinians toward negotiating a final settlement with Israel with American assistance. Sadat's peace initiative surprised and vexed the Saudis, who had not been consulted beforehand. However, the great dependency of all the confrontation states and the Palestinians on Saudi financial and political might and the close ties and influence of Saudi Arabia with the United States ensured that the Saudi role in the Arab-Israeli arena would remain a major one whether Sadat's peace drive succeeded or failed.

As a consequence of the Lebanese conflict, the military and political power of those radical, rejectionist Palestinian organizations backed by Iraq and Libya was diminished, while Syrian control over Lebanon and the resistance movement was increased. These developments reduced both the influence of Iraq and Libya in Lebanon and also their ability to obstruct Arab-Israeli peace negotiations. This situation could change, nevertheless, were the moderate Arabs and Palestinians to lose hope of ever being able to achieve even their more limited goals by peaceful means, because in that event the hardline views of Iraq and Libya could spread to other parts of the Arab world and ultimately prevail.

THE PROSPECTS FOR PEACE OR WAR

Since the Palestinians and Arabs had come out of the war weaker and more divided, many Arab and Palestinian leaders were now more convinced than before that their military option provided little hope for success. Consequently, the confrontation states and the moderate Palestinians appeared readier than ever to seek a peaceful resolution of their differences with Israel based on UN resolutions. The civil war made the conservative Arab leaders in Saudi Arabia and elsewhere more concerned than ever about the dangers to them of continued instability and strife arising from both the Lebanese and Arab-Israeli conflicts. These leaders therefore felt that it would be to their advantage to increase their support for American peace efforts.

However, the additional mistrust and divisions which developed within the Arab world as a result of the civil war added further obstacles to peace because Arab disunity, as well as Israeli inflexibility on some critical issues, worked to frustrate American attempts to move the parties involved to a Geneva conference. American officials made it clear that a substantial degree of unity among at least the confrontation states was one major prerequisite for arriving at an overall Arab-Israeli settlement.

Moreover, continued disorder and strife in south Lebanon and the persistence of Palestinian commando activities against Israel and Israeli forays into southern Lebanon had kept tensions in that area so high that the Israelis, on the one hand, and the Arabs and Palestinians, on the other, were less psychologically prepared to deal with and accept the existence of each other. These developments added to the emotional and political barriers to peace.

Just as the civil war had weakened the political and military bargaining power of the Arabs and Palestinians, thus increasing their readiness to make concessions and to negotiate a peace settlement, the war, by improving Israel's bargaining position, did not encourage greater flexibility on the part of Jerusalem. Israel's invasion of south Lebanon and the inability of UNIFIL—at least up to this writing—to take control of the border area because of the opposition of Israel and her right-wing allies added to the existing uncertainties and instabilities in Lebanon and, thereby, further complicated the situation in the Middle East. In addition, since the Lebanese conflict had caused a virtual halt in American peace efforts over a period of many months, the delay, in the meantime, enabled a more hard-line government under Menachem Begin to come to power in Israel, and this further hindered American peace efforts.

By promoting further discord and instability in the Arab world in general and in Lebanon in particular and by adding further to Arab-Israeli mistrust and hostility, the Lebanese civil war helped to produce conditions which could actually be more conducive to war than to peace. The explosive state of affairs in south Lebanon which the war left in its wake provided—at least until UNIFIL was sent to the area—the greatest potential for the renewal of large-scale Arab-Israeli combat. If UNIFIL is able to effectively carry out its mandate, it could help prevent further strife and conflict in south Lebanon; provide a more favorable climate for dealing with both the Lebanese and the Arab-Israeli problems; and even make it easier for larger numbers of Israelis to put their trust in UN peace-keeping activities, rather than mere territorial expansion, for ensuring their future security needs. However, if UNIFIL were to fail in its mission, then the south will once again become the stage for more strife and conflict, and most Israelis will continue to insist that they cannot depend on the UN and that they must hold on to the occupied territories for reasons of security. There would then be not only less chance for resolving the Lebanese and Arab-Israeli problems but also the increased danger that sooner or later a military conflict could develop, intentionally or unintentionally, between Israel and Syria. The danger would vastly intensify if Egyptian-Israeli negotiations and American peace efforts were to fail because the Israelis and the Palestinians might then decide it would be to their advantage to escalate the conflict in or from southern Lebanon.

Moreover, if UNIFIL were to be withdrawn while UN peacekeeping units continue to man the buffer zones between Syria and Israel on the Golan Heights, and Egypt and Israel in the Sinai, south Lebanon could provide the most practical and likely arena for any major Arab-Israeli military combat to take place. This would be the case especially if Israel were to initiate the conflict because, while it would not be militarily feasible for the Arabs to attack Israel from Lebanon, Israel would find major advantages in invading Syria through Lebanese territory. In short, if UNIFIL were to be ineffective or its mandate were to be ended and if the Arab-Israeli problem were to remain unresolved, then southern Lebanon could provide both the precipitating agent or pretext and also the locale for the outbreak of another Arab-Israeli war.

CONCLUSION

Recent developments have made it increasingly clear that the Arab-Israeli and Lebanese problems have become so interrelated that any progress made in dealing with one of them would make it easier to make some headway with the other. By the same token, any worsening of conditions in one area would inevitably have harmful consequences on the other. It is obvious, therefore, that these problems cannot be effectively dealt with in complete isolation from each other.

While major combat in all parts of Lebanon outside of the south ended in October 1976, peace in that country remained fragile because the most important issues, both internal and external, which had caused the civil war had not been resolved. In fact, there seemed to be little hope that there could be full reconciliation and lasting peace and stability in Lebanon and that the internal impasse there could be broken until the Arab-Israeli problem—and especially the Palestinian phase of it—had been adequately resolved in all of its main aspects. Since the Palestinians could not be driven out of Lebanon by force and they would not leave voluntarily under existing circumstances, only the achievement of an overall Arab-Israeli peace settlement which provided for a Palestinian state or homeland would make it finally possible for the refugee camps in Lebanon to close down and large numbers of Palestinians to leave Lebanon. Only then would the Palestinians no longer need to retain those military forces and commando bases which enabled them to maintain a virtual state within a state. If the overall Arab-Israeli question were not resolved, not only would Lebanon remain fragmented, unstable, and subject to the danger of more strife and civil war, but she could become an active participant in another Arab-Israeli war. Consequently, Lebanon's stake in a Middle East peace settlement had become far greater than ever before. In fact, her very survival as a united and sovereign nation could very well depend on it.

As already noted, following the end of the civil war, Israel and some rightists and Palestinian elements prevented the Lebanese government from restoring its authority in south Lebanon, and failing to control it themselves, they worked to keep the area unsettled and insecure. While President Sadat sought, through his historic peace initiative, to dispel "mistrust, fear, and hostility" between Arabs and Israelis in order to break through the "psychological barriers" to peace,[27] his move added a new element of uncertainty to the situation in the south and contributed to the failure to implement those agreements calling for a cease-fire and a pullback of Palestinian units from the border areas. Besides threatening the stability and sovereignty of Lebanon and hindering efforts at reconciliation and reconstruction in that country, continued fighting in the south prevented the easing of the attitudes of the Palestinians and Israelis toward each other and created conditions which threatened to spark more Arab-Israeli and internal Lebanese conflicts. Much of the dangerous tension arising from this explosive situation could be relieved if the Lebanese army and UNIFIL were to assume full control over the entire southern sector, if Palestinian commandos were to remain north of the Litani River, if rightist armed units there were to be disarmed, and if Israel were to stop intervening in that area. But unfortunately, as of late June 1978, it was still uncertain as to whether the right-wing militiamen, backed by Israel, would peacefully allow UNIFIL to move into the Christian-controlled zone and, even if it were able to move into the zone, how fully and for how long the rightists, the Israelis, and the Palestinians would cooperate with UNIFIL to enable it to completely carry out its mission to restore peace and stability in and to facilitate the restoration of Lebanese government authority over all parts of the south.

Any attempt by some Maronite leaders to intensify their efforts to partition Lebanon and to develop closer military and political ties with Israel would ultimately prove to be much more harmful than helpful to Lebanon, the Arab world, and even Israel. Such moves would only add to existing tensions and instability in Lebanon and throughout the Middle East and further hamper efforts to bring reconciliation and peace within Lebanon and between the Arabs and Israelis.[28]

President Sadat's peace drive appeared to open new opportunities and raised expectations and hopes to high levels. But Egyptian-Israeli talks soon revealed that Israel's position had not softened under Begin's leadership. In fact, the actual positions of the two sides remained so far apart that they could not be easily and quickly reconciled. Nevertheless, Egyptian-Israeli contacts did bring about some important psychological and political changes which might endure. There had begun to emerge among the peoples in Israel, Egypt, and the United States, as well as elsewhere in the world, a vision of peace which, even if it could not be quickly realized, could create new pressures on the leaders in the Middle East and the United States to strive harder than ever before to break through the barriers of fear and mistrust in order to resolve fully, fairly, and finally the explosive Arab-Israeli problem. As of this writing, the obstacles to a Middle East settlement remained so formidable, however, that despite serious American efforts a complete, permanent collapse of Egyptian-Israeli negotiations could ultimately take place, thereby leaving tensions between Israel and the Arabs, as well as between the contending factions in Lebanon, higher than ever and seriously undermining the forces for peace in Lebanon and the Middle East. In that event, only if the United States acted with great courage, determination, and understanding could there be any chance that more bloody conflicts in Lebanon and the Middle East could be avoided and that the vital peace process could be revived.

INTER-ARAB RELATIONS

Lewis W. Snider

THE IMPACT of inter-Arab relations on the conflict in Lebanon is both obvious and important, for the deterioration of Lebanon's position in the inter-Arab arena helped plunge the country into civil war in 1975.[1] Less apparent is the short and longer-term impact of the Lebanese conflict on inter-Arab relations. The intensity, duration, and outcome of the conflict, and the gains and losses sustained by the various participants, affected the Arab states' abilities to deal with one another and with Israel. The purpose of this chapter is to analyze the effects of the Lebanese civil war and inter-Arab relations on one another.

INTER-ARAB POLITICS

Lebanon's relations with its Arab neighbors have traditionally been conditioned by two factors which are an extension of the National Covenant: (1) the formal, if not actual preponderance of the Christian element in the population; and (2) Lebanon's essentially Arab character as a nation. These two factors helped give Lebanon an established foreign policy of neutrality in inter-Arab conflicts, a passive role in the Arab-Israeli conflict, and an open door for an understanding with the West as a hedge against the threat of absorption into a larger Arab entity.

Lebanon's special character as defined by the National Covenant has been given formal recognition by the Arab states. At the founding conference of the Arab League in Alexandria in 1944, a special resolution was inserted into the protocol pledging the members' unanimous "respect for the independence and sovereignty of Lebanon within its present frontiers."[2]

Arab acceptance of Lebanon's passive role in pan-Arab affairs can also be seen in the nature of the United Arab Command established at the

Cairo summit meeting in 1964. While then-President Charles Helou agreed to the establishment of the command, it was only after the other countries agreed that no Egyptian, Jordanian, or Syrian troops would enter Lebanon without the formal request of the Lebanese government. Furthermore, it was agreed that Lebanon would not engage in offensive operations but would defend itself if attacked.[3] Similarly, in keeping with Lebanon's special status in inter-Arab politics, the Arab governments agreed at the summit conference in Khartoum in August 1967, to support Palestinian guerrilla operations against Israel from Egypt, Syria, and Jordan but not from Lebanon.[4]

The Changing Arab Position on Lebanon's Special Character

Two years after the Khartoum conference, however, a new consensus among the Arab states concerning Lebanon's role in the Arab-Israeli conflict had begun to take shape. Lebanon was now expected to extend its physical facilities to the Palestinian guerrillas and to allow them to carry out operations against Israel from Lebanese soil. The new consensus was defined in the "secret" Cairo accord of November 3, 1969.

The Cairo accord recognized the Palestinian resistance organizations, sponsored and financed by rival Arab states, as a part of the Arab world. As such, the sanction of their activity in Lebanon represented a political move by the guerrillas and their sponsors to assert the Palestinians' right to use any Arab land adjacent to Israel as a staging area for operations against the Jewish state. The key clause in this regard is: "The two delegations emphasize that the Palestinian armed struggle is in the interest of Lebanon as well as of the Palestinian revolution and all Arabs."[5] In return, the guerrillas agreed to work within the context of Lebanese sovereignty and territorial integrity. The details of implementing the accords were to be worked out between representatives of the Palestinian organizations and the Lebanese government.

What is important is that the two sides accepted the accord not so much because either party desired such an agreement, but because the outside Arab states, acting in concert, compelled acceptance. Equally important is that no matter how delicately phrased the terms, the Cairo accord was definitely an infringement upon Lebanon's sovereignty. Indeed, it allowed the guerrillas privileges and freedom of movement that the other Arab states would not tolerate within their own borders.

The Cairo accords served to enhance the legitimacy of the Palestinian nationalist movement in Lebanon which alarmed the largely Christian Right. The expulsion of the fedayeen from Jordan in 1970–71 only served to accelerate the expansion of the Palestinian presence in Lebanon. The Palestinians sought to learn from their costly defeat in Jordan and apply the lessons in Lebanon. One of those lessons was that they should never isolate themselves from the population and the "progressive" forces in the host country, nor pose as an alternative to those forces.[6] Adhering to this guideline, however, only served to further aggravate Lebanon's uneasy sectarian politics. The Palestinian movement in Lebanon demonstrated an ability to accommodate a wide range of ideological interests and displayed a degree of volunteerism and participation by the rank and file seldom seen in the Middle East. The movement's ability to accommodate diversity, yet work effectively toward a common goal had the effect if not the intention of presenting itself as an alternative political order to those Lebanese groups who sought to reform the country's rather rigid confessional spoils system. Thus it was logical but not inevitable that the Palestinians were seen by the right, particularly the Christian right, as posing an alternative to "their" Lebanon which they revered and controlled.

Arab Realignments and Their Impact on Lebanese Politics

Given the affinity of Lebanese political groups for external patrons and the tendency of these groups to espouse the conflicts and causes of their sponsors, the realignments in inter-Arab relations affected a corresponding realignment of forces, particularly on the left, within Lebanon. Prior to the June War, the Ba'athists, Nasserites, the Arab Nationalist Movement, the Communists, and others inside Lebanon were feuding over the same issues as were their external supporters and allies in the inter-Arab arena. Just as the outcome of the June War rendered these ideological issues in the Arab world moot, so too did they diminish in significance among the various leftist groups within Lebanon. Moreover, as the conflict with Israel became the main concern, a common ground on which leftists and more conservative Muslims could meet undoubtedly widened. A variety of ideological movements in Lebanon—ranging from the Muslim Brethren to the Syrian Nationalists to the Ba'athists and Nasserites to the Arab Nationalist Movement and various Communist groupings—had found a place in the Palestinian movement. Thus it was that the new Arab consensus was reflected in a new cohesiveness among the Muslims and Lebanese leftists—a cohesiveness which was perceived as very threatening by the Lebanese Christians who viewed the Cairo accords as a betrayal of Lebanese sovereignty.

The October War, Sinai II, and the Lebanese Crisis

The second Sinai disengagement, initialled September 1, 1975, dashed any hopes for a comprehensive approach to the Arab-Israeli conflict in the foreseeable future. One result was an escalation of the fighting in Lebanon. The escalation was due largely to the responses of the Christians and like-minded Muslims and the Palestinians to various peace efforts that were begun shortly after the end of the October War.

Until April 1975, there was still some hope in the Arab world that Egypt and Syria could conclude a comprehensive settlement with Israel. When no coordinated Arab effort had materialized, Egypt began, with Saudi support, to move towards another separate Egyptian-Israeli agreement. These efforts had generated considerable feelings of insecurity in both Lebanese camps, and this contributed to the outbreak of fighting that month.

The Palestinians feared that any comprehensive settlement of the Arab-Israeli conflict would be reached at the expense of their movement. Palestinian-Egyptian friction had already developed the previous February over Egypt's moves toward another interim agreement with Israel. The Palestinian organizations had already begun to strengthen their military positions in Lebanon following the armed clashes between the Lebanese army and the guerrilla forces in May 1973. They also began to coordinate their activities more closely with Lebanese radical parties and splinter groups than ever before. As the momentum toward a peace settlement increased, the Palestinians' insecurities became acute. Consequently, by early 1974 the Palestinian organizations sought to consolidate their position in Lebanon by stretching the terms of the 1969 Cairo Agreement to cover the Lebanese radical parties and organizations. This meant that these Lebanese groups including the Nasserites and the Ba'athists, would receive arms and form their own militias under the aegis of the Palestinian movement.[7] The PLO also approached the Syrian government with a proposal to coordinate policy in order to spike Egyptian cooperation with Henry Kissinger's step-by-step diplomacy.

The Christian Lebanese and the Muslims who shared their particularist views had also drawn hope from the October War and its aftermath. They had counted on a fairly quick settlement of the Palestinian problem at the conference table at Geneva.[8] Meanwhile, the Christian rightists were alarmed by the increasingly close collaboration between Palestinian

organizations and the Lebanese Left. The Christians were especially troubled by the formation of the leftist militias behind the Palestinian shield.
Further tension undoubtedly developed in early March 1975, when Syrian President Assad answered the PLO's proposal of policy coordination
with an offer to form a joint Syrian-Palestinian command (more on this
below). The timing of this offer is important. In March, when negotiations between Egypt and Israel broke down, Syria had reason to fear
Israeli retaliation because of Syrian opposition to another unilateral
agreement between Egypt and Israel. There were reports of massive Israeli buildups on the Syrian and Lebanese borders.[9] But to the Christian
rightists, a joint Syrian-Palestinian command must have appeared as a
tripartite threat composed of (1) the Lebanese leftists, (2) their Palestinian allies, linked to (3) the most militant and revolutionary (in Christian
eyes, at any rate) Levantine state. The hopes of the Lebanese right for a
Geneva settlement were finally dashed altogether in March 1975, as
Egyptians, Israelis, and Americans scaled down their expectations and
tried to reach another partial interim accord culminating in the second
Sinai disengagement in September.

The cumulative anxieties, insecurities, antagonisms, and tensions
between the Palestinian organizations and the largely Christian right are
reflected in the composition of forces in the first stage of the fighting in
the Lebanese War. Between April and June 1975, the bulk of the fighting
was not between Lebanese Muslim leftists and largely Christian rightists,
but between the Palestinian guerrillas and one of the Christian rightist
militias, the ultranationalist Phalangist forces.[10] The combat did not
evolve into a *civil* war (i.e., Lebanese right against Lebanese left) until
after June 1975.[11]

Sinai II and the Eastern Front

When hostilities have broken out in the past between rival Arab
camps other Arab states have moved to try to end the fighting. This sort
of response did not materialize in Lebanon in the spring or summer of
1975. Why?

An explanation can be found in the consequences of the second
Sinai disengagement agreement and the continuing Arab consensus that
Lebanon must remain an active frontline state in the struggle against
Israel. Briefly, the principal Arab states were already divided between
rejectionists and moderates (those who would be willing to try for a settlement with Israel). The latter included Egypt, Jordan, Syria, some
"moderate" Palestinian factions, Saudi Arabia, and Kuwait. The former

consisted of Iraq, Libya, Algeria, and most of the Palestinian organizations. Egypt's separate agreement with Israel intensified inter-Arab divisions and compounded them by breaking ranks with the other moderate confrontation states.

Basically, what was needed to stop the fighting in Lebanon was the curbing of the Palestinian guerrilla activities in Lebanon, thus assuaging Christian-rightist and ultranationalist anxieties. Syria was the principal patron, arms supplier, and quartermaster to the Palestinian forces in Lebanon. Had Syria and Jordan not been at odds with Egypt over the latter's movement toward another separate agreement with Israel, there would have been a better chance for Syria, Egypt, Jordan, and Saudi Arabia (in its role as a principal banker to al-Fatah as well as to Egypt and Syria), to have acted in concert and intervened to stop the fighting, and to have curbed Palestinian activities by insisting upon strict adherence to the 1969 Cairo Agreement. Syria, however, could not go against the Palestinians for two reasons.

First, to equivocate in its support for the Palestinians would have invited attacks from the rejectionists plus Egypt and possibly Saudi Arabia as well. Egypt would have seized the opportunity after Sinai II to ingratiate itself with the Palestinians and would have competed with Syria's other adversaries—principally Iraq—for sponsorship of the Palestinian movement. Iraq had been attempting to topple the Syrian regime. Baghdad had initiated contacts with Jordan and moved to reconcile its differences with Iran and Egypt. Iraq had also been courting the Palestinians, frequently condemning Syria's "soft" stand on a peace settlement with Israel. Iraqi success in gaining influence and control over the Palestinians could have posed a serious threat to Syria.

The nature of the Iraqi threat to Syria transcends Israel and the Palestinians. It involves the most enduring element of Syrian-Iraqi relations which is competition for leadership of the Fertile Crescent.[12] This competition dates back to the immediate post war-post independence period. Unlike the Nile Valley which is dominated by Egypt or the Arabian Peninsula dominated by Saudi Arabia, there is no clearly dominant power in the Fertile Crescent to whose policies the other countries in the region must adjust. The absence of one clearly dominating power in the region has encouraged a power struggle between Iraq and Syria in which Syria, with its smaller population and resource base, is at a disadvantage. An increase in Iraqi influence over Jordan and the Palestinian movement would have left Syria extremely isolated and more susceptible to domination by Iraq.

A second reason was more important in terms of the consequences for Lebanon. The move toward another Egyptian-Israeli agreement in March meant that Egypt had been effectively taken out of the lineup of confrontation states. Syria alone had no credible, effective military option against Israel. The elimination of Egypt in effect neutralized Syria's demands for Israeli withdrawal from the Golan Heights and participation of the Palestinians in a future peace settlement. Without a credible military option Syria was in no position to press these demands. In the absence of a credible military threat Israel would agree only to "cosmetic" adjustments of the armistice lines which would not disturb the military settlements it had established in the Golan Heights. To deter a possible Israeli offensive against Damascus, Syria attempted to form a new coalition against Israel that became known as the Eastern Front.

The Eastern Front as it developed between March and September 1975, refers to a line of confrontation states on Israel's northern and eastern borders comprising Syria, Jordan, Lebanon, and including the PLO entrenched in southern Lebanon.[13]

The front had its antecedents in a proposal made by PLO chairman Yasir Arafat to the Syrian government in December 1974. This was an offer to coordinate PLO and Syrian policy to counter Egypt's determination to adhere to Kissinger's step-by-step approach to a settlement with Israel. Arafat's proposal was attractive to Syria for at least four reasons. First, it would provide Syria with more influence over Jordan and Lebanon and any Palestinian state that might be established in the future. Second, it would provide a counterweight to the influence of the rival Ba'athist regime in Iraq over the Palestinians. Third, a Syrian-led unified command would undoubtedly enforce greater unity among Palestinian factions, making the guerrillas a more credible military factor to be reckoned with and make the issue of Palestinian participation in any future negotiations inescapable. It would also strengthen the Palestinians' position in southern Lebanon, thereby enabling them to escalate their harassment of Israeli settlements along the borders. Fourth, the proposal offered Syria the opportunity for additional control of the Palestinian resistance movement. This could be accomplished indirectly by working through al-Sa'iqa (a Palestinian guerrilla organization composed of Syrian regulars as well as Palestinians and totally under Syrian control), in order to achieve Syrian domination over Yasir Arafat and al-Fatah.

On March 3, 1975, a little over a month before the first round of fighting erupted in Lebanon, President Hafez al-Assad proposed the creation of a Syrian-Palestinian unified command.[14] But a unified command would be ineffective without Jordan and Lebanon. Israel could easily outflank the Syrian army in the Golan Heights region by attacking through northern Jordan. On March 4, 1975, Syria resumed normal relations with Jordan under a far-reaching trade agreement signed in Damascus. On March 5, two days after Assad's proposal of a unified command to the PLO, the Arab News Agency in Beirut reported that there was a secret agreement accompanying the accord. Under that agreement, Syria and Jordan would allegedly coordinate their policies toward Israel and the PLO.[15] Reports also circulated in June that Syria and Jordan had concluded an agreement including military coordination under joint military command during President Assad's visit to Jordan.[16] There were additional reports of joint military command in August following a visit by the Syrian prime minister to Jordan.[17]

The possibility of a joint Syrian-Jordanian-PLO command was credible in a military sense, but it began partly as a device to put political pressure on Egypt, Israel, and the United States and to compel them not to ignore Syrian, Jordanian, and Palestinian interests in any interim agreements. Only after Sinai II was concluded does it appear that Syria transformed its proposal for a joint military command into an actual defensive military strategy for the entire Eastern Front. Implementing this strategy, however, created a compelling need for the exertion of Syrian influence in Lebanon.

The emerging strategic value of Lebanon in Syrian defense planning stemmed largely from the proposed unified command with the PLO and the guerrilla concentration in southern Lebanon. Some sort of effective military force friendly to Syria was required in southern Lebanon in order to help protect Syria's western flank from an Israeli attack. Syria could not count on the Lebanese army with its predominantly Maronite (anti-Syrian) officer corps to fill this role. The only viable alternative was the guerrilla forces. The fedayeen had been using southern Lebanon to attack Israeli settlements and to maintain direct links with Syria. By May 1975, guerrilla attacks on Israel had increased noticeably and so had Israeli retaliatory raids in southern Lebanon. Reports circulated that Israel was actually preparing to seize southern Lebanon in order to outflank the Syrian army from the west by advancing through the Bekaa Valley and over the western slopes of Mount Hermon overlooking the Golan Heights.[18] There is no way to make certain that the reports accurately reflected Israeli planning. Nevertheless, the prospect of such an attack further demonstrated to Syria the urgent need to incorporate Lebanon in its defense planning.

Syria's actions in Lebanon appear to be an extension of Syrian hegemony once the authority of the Lebanese government had broken down. The principal aim was to end the fighting in order to retain the possibility of implementing the Eastern Front strategy. Israel's intervention in the form of active support for Christian forces in the south and the threat of military invasion if Syrian troops should enter Lebanon, thwarted Syria's strategy, particularly the possibility that Syrian units, disguised as Palestinians, might deploy in southern Lebanon. Israel's invasion of Lebanon in March 1978, foreclosed that possibility, for the invasion and Israel's subsequent withdrawal created two buffer zones between Israel and Syrian and Palestinian forces: one zone under UN observation (UN Interim Forces in Lebanon, UNIFIL), the other under the control of Israeli-trained and equipped Christian-Druze and anti-Palestinian Muslims located between UNIFIL positions and Israel's border.

For Jordan the Eastern Front was the only realistic chance King Hussein had to end Jordan's isolation in the Arab world without having to compromise too heavily with the Palestinians and risk undermining his own regime. It also meant an increase in Jordanian security against attack from Israel should the latter launch flanking attacks on Syria through Jordan. The front was also Amman's best chance of being included by Israel and the United States in any further steps toward a peace settlement. If Jordan refused to participate in the front, Amman risked being relegated to the political sidelines in any eventual negotiation over the final status of the West Bank and the Palestinians. Without the support of at least Syria among the Arab hardliners, Jordan could not hope to speak for the Palestinians or participate in negotiations concerning the West Bank, even given American and Israeli distaste for dealing directly with PLO representatives. Because Syria would try to draw Jordan away from them, Iraq, Libya, Saudi Arabia, and Egypt opposed Syria's efforts to implement the Eastern Front strategy but for contradictory reasons. However, these five powers had one thing in common: their principal worry was not the future of an independent Lebanon or of the Palestinian cause, but the potential consequences of a victory by the mainly Christian status quo forces or the largely Muslim-Palestinian-leftist camp. The Iraqi and Libyan rejectionists sought to weaken Syria's willingness to try for a settlement with Israel, hence their support for the extremist leftist splinter groups in Lebanon. These forces would not entertain any proposals for a compromise with Israel nor would they be expected to cooperate with Syria in any conciliatory moves toward Israel. Saudi Arabia, that champion and defender of Islamic purity, initially threw its support to the Christian rightists out of concern over leftist and Communist influence in Lebanon. This position was not necessarily governed by any anti-Syrian intentions. Riyadh was, after all, bankrolling Syria's rearmament after the 1973 war. By November 1975, however, the Saudis began to have second thoughts as the Christians began to talk seriously of partitioning the country.

Egypt sought to diminish Syrian influence largely because Cairo perceived the Syrians as being an obstacle to further peace agreements. Syrian success in Lebanon—either in establishing its hegemony or in effecting settlement that would not come unstuck—would seriously challenge the image Egypt had sought to cultivate in Washington as *the* key to a Middle East peace. If Syria should emerge as the country to deal with in the Eastern Arab world in any further negotiations, Egypt's ability to obtain American support for its policies could be eroded. When Syria's direct intervention in Lebanon to achieve a cease-fire and a political settlement there drew a favorable response from the United States, Egypt's President Anwar Sadat had more reason to be concerned. The prospect of Syria drifting away from the Soviet Union toward even limited collaboration with the United States meant that the benefits of Egypt's break with Moscow and realignment with Washington could be reduced if the U.S. sought to expand its newly achieved political foothold in the Middle East in response to Syria's changing policy. Furthermore, Syrian political aggrandizement would pose a serious challenge to Egyptian efforts to re-establish Cairo's leadership position in the Arab world. Among other things, Syrian success would detract from an impression that Cairo was seeking to foster in the Arab world—that Egypt was the Arab country in the position to get the most favorable terms for the Arabs in any comprehensive Middle East settlement.[19] The successful maintenance of these images depended partly upon Egypt's ability to "deliver" the Palestinians in any final peace settlement. Egypt could not claim this ability if Syria could demonstrate credible hegemony over the Palestinians in Lebanon. Thus Egypt, too, supplied arms to the Phalangist forces in order to head off a victory by the Muslim-leftist-Palestinian forces who, at the time, were supported by Syria. The only way to forestall Syrian aggrandizement in the inter-Arab arena was to block any military victory by Syria's protégés in Lebanon.[20]

Considering the array of opposition, Syria had reason to be suspicious when, after a lull of some eight weeks or more, the Lebanese conflict suddenly erupted into a new round of intense combat. The resumption of fighting in late August and early September stemmed mainly from a variety of domestic factors.[21] There is not sufficient evidence from unclassified sources to allow one to determine the extent to which Israeli, Arab, and international (mainly U.S.) forces which were pushing for a Middle Eastern settlement were involved in the resumption of the fighting. But in a sense that is irrelevant. The Syrians believed that the outbreak of the fighting was linked to the second Sinai accord initialled September 1 and the Syrian-Palestinian opposition to it. Syria believed that the September hostilities served three Israeli (and American) objectives, the attainment of which could also benefit Egypt. They were: (1) to divert Syrian and Palestinian energies and attention from the Sinai II agreement; (2) to accelerate Palestinian and Phalangist hostilities to the point where the Christian-led Lebanese army would intervene and reduce the Palestinian presence in southern Lebanon; and (3) to neutralize the Syrian-Palestinian alliance thereby frustrating Syria's Eastern Front strategy by exacerbating sectarian tensions to the point where partition of the country could be justified.[22]

The Syrians believed they had ample reason to suspect such a scheme was engineered by Israel with the aid of the United States. Apart from reports of Israeli troop concentration on Lebanon's southern border in early October, President Assad is reported to have received information during his visit to the Soviet Union that the renewed fighting in Lebanon was a prelude to an Israeli attack on Syria.[23] Presumably the purpose of the attack was to reduce the Palestinians and Syria to military irrelevance, thereby eliminating the need for Israel to make further territorial concessions in return for a peace settlement. The renewed fighting in Lebanon, therefore, was perceived by Syria as a serious security threat and a threat to the Eastern Front strategy as well.

These perceptions explain Syria's resistance to "Arabization" of the Lebanese crisis, for this would afford Egypt the opportunity, through the medium of the Arab League, to minimize Syrian influence in Lebanon. Syria had even more to fear from Iraq. More active Syrian intervention in Lebanon was prompted by an Iraqi initiative to undermine Lebanese Prime Minister Rashid Karameh, considered to be pro-Syrian by the Baghdad government. The Iraqis had been exerting pressure on President Frangieh to replace Karameh with their own candidate, Takieddine Solh. The latter was considered close to Baghdad and to President Frangieh whom he assisted as an advisor.[24] This in turn helps to explain why the neighboring Arab states did not coalesce and move to end the fighting as they had in other instances. No consensus and no concerted action could occur without the cooperation of Syria and the PLO. Syria and the PLO boycotted a two-day meeting of the Arab League on the Lebanese crisis in mid-October, thereby ensuring that the other League members could take no effective action.

These perceived threats also help to explain Syrian resistance to "internationalization" of the war as that would provide an opening for the United States (and through the U.S. Israel) to influence the crisis. Syria was able to maintain its position as the sole outside mediator in the conflict and resist pressure to Arabize or internationalize it partly because the Lebanese resisted their habit of identifying with conflicting external forces. In this case rival Lebanese factions were reluctant to appeal to various Arab countries or to the Arab League for assistance or mediation. The reason was that while each group had special ties to some Arab governments they all had reason to fear the intervention or mediation of other Arab states.

In retrospect the second Sinai agreement and Syria's efforts to make the Eastern Front a viable defense strategy cannot be seen to have caused the fighting in Lebanon. Syria's attempt to place the Eastern Front on a solid footing, however, defined the context in which the conflict was waged. In a sense it also defined in large measure its duration and its outcome. To the extent that Syria achieved its objectives in Lebanon that outcome illuminated a changing distribution of power in the Arab world which was only dimly perceived before the war in Lebanon occurred.

Unlike the other Arab countries mentioned earlier, Syria had a stake in preserving the independence, territorial integrity, and sovereignty of Lebanon if for no other reason than to maintain its viability as a confrontation state, and so establish the Eastern Front. This was imperative if Syria was to succeed in establishing a defense perimeter from Ras al-Nakoura to the Gulf of Aqaba (see note 13). Damascus had to neutralize the disruptive influence of any faction—rightist or leftist—whose actions would (1) increase the intensity of the fighting thereby further draining Syrian and Palestinian energies; (2) accelerate any trend toward partition of the country; or (3) create a pretext for Israeli intervention in the conflict. Fulfilling this requirement implied the achievement of a military stalemate among the combatants. Only then would the contending factions be amenable to negotiating a settlement of their differences under Syrian aegis.

Therefore, Syria's initial support of the leftists while trying to mediate the conflict was motivated by the need to (1) reduce the power of the Christian rightist forces to a level roughly equivalent to that of the Muslim leftists, thereby making the Christians amenable to reform of the Lebanese political system; and (2) induce all factions to accept the necessity of Syria's mediation and so strengthen Syria's position in Lebanon and guarantee Lebanon's place in the Eastern Front.[25]

Syria pressed vigorously in January 1976, for a cease-fire at the very time the alliance of progressive forces (the Lebanese left and the Palestinians) appeared to be making significant military gains and the rightists losing ground steadily. The first tangible sign of Syrian success occurred in late January with the announcement that a cease-fire that was agreed to by "all parties" and involved "an all-embracing political settlement."[26] The cease-fire was to be supervised by a joint Syrian-Lebanese-Palestinian Higher Military Committee. The agreement referred to political reforms reportedly agreed to by all sides. These included: (1) equal representation by Muslim deputies in the Parliament; (2) abolition of the sectarian structure of government posts below the top-level positions; (3) election of the prime minister by the Chamber of Deputies; and (4) improvement in the electoral laws.[27] The instruments to be used to enforce the agreement were the Syrian-backed al-Sa'iqa units and troops from the Palestinian Liberation Army (PLA). At the same time the press and radio in Damascus ceased their denunciations of the rightists, emphasizing instead Syria's desire to work for the good "of all our Lebanese brothers."

Had the Syrian initiative succeeded, Syria would have reaped the prestige—both in the Arab world and the West—of having made peace in Lebanon, while laying the foundation for its Eastern Front coalition. As it happened, however, Syrian success was short lived. As the Christian rightist position weakened, the power of the left increased and with it the leftists' unwillingness to compromise. The rightists' response was to talk more of partition while creating their own separate governmental institutions in the territories remaining under their control.

Much of the fighting that occurred between February and June, when Syria sent a full armored regiment to Lebanon to aid the Christian forces, can be said to have been over the substance and implementation of the Syrian-imposed settlement and the progressive forces' refusal to accept a military stalemate. In March Syria cut off arms supplies to the leftists after a meeting with Kamal Jumblatt, leader of the leftist-Muslim forces, when the latter continued to oppose Assad's efforts to reach a settlement before the Christian rightists were decisively defeated.[28] Jumblatt's insistence on the military defeat of the rightist forces and his desire to set up a secular people's republic in Lebanon created an important turning point in Syria's position toward the leftists and the Palestinians. The implications of this shift for the conflict and inter-Arab relations will be discussed below.

IMPACT OF THE WAR

So far this chapter has focused on the nexus of regional and indigenous forces in order to shed some light on how regional politics shaped the conflict. The impact of the war in inter-Arab relations is no less significant but more elusive to pinpoint for two reasons. First, in assessing the gains and losses of various parties, one must bear in mind that even those forces who seemed to emerge from the conflict stronger than when it began sustained serious defeats along the way. Second, it is often difficult to determine the extent to which the changing relationships that may have been clearly observable at the near-termination of the conflict in January 1977, were the by-products of the conflict or merely illuminated by it. An overview of the major changes in inter-Arab relations that emerged during the fighting or after its near termination is presented below. It is followed by an assessment of the gains and losses sustained by the major regional actors in the Lebanese war. The biggest loser, obviously, was Lebanon.

Generally, the war in Lebanon intensified previous divisions among the Arab states while changing some important relationships and the distribution of power among some of them. The old bloc alignments of "conservative" vs. "revolutionary," pro-Soviet vs. pro-West, "confrontation states" vs. "rear echelon" governments were obliterated. Just as the confrontation-rear echelon cleavage had supplanted the more "revolutionary"-"conservative" blocs after the 1967 war, so too was it displaced by a new definition of issues in inter-Arab politics. The new cleavages could be defined by how conciliatory each Arab state—front line or rear echelon, progressive or conservative—was willing to be to achieve a settlement with Israel, while taking whatever measures it could to defend itself from Israel's clear-cut strategic superiority. This new defining characteristic became more evident because of the conflict in Lebanon. These changing inter-Arab alignments and the war in Lebanon combined to produce some strange political bedfellows. Formerly "radical" Syria and "conservative" Jordan had formed a new entente that replaced the post-1967 Cairo-Amman axis. "Leftist" Syria was backing the conservative "isolationist" forces in Lebanon against the leftist "progressive" alliance. Instead of being the most militant champion of Palestinian "rights," Syria was trying to reduce the power of the movement. The PLO had become disaffected with "militant" Syria and had begun to mend its fences with "moderate" Egypt, who had "betrayed" the Palestinian cause by signing the second Sinai disengagement agreement. By October 1976, Arab unity was at the lowest ebb it had been in more than a decade. The deepest cleavage remained the disagreement among the Arab states concerning a settlement with Israel. The breakdown of the coalition of confrontation states over Egypt's separate agreement with Israel was exacerbated and prolonged by further deterioration of Egyptian-Syrian relations and further impeded the development of a common position on further negotiations with Israel.

Eventually, the dynamics of the war in Lebanon contributed to a reconciliation among the "moderates." This occurred at a meeting of the leaders of Syria, Egypt, Lebanon, Kuwait, and the PLO at Saudi Arabian insistence in Riyadh in October 1976. The meeting was called to end the fighting in Lebanon in order to revive the coalition of "moderates" which fought in the October war. Settling the conflict in Lebanon was an essential precondition to reactivating that coalition. The meetings in Riyadh and the continuing crisis in Lebanon produced a reconciliation between Assad and Sadat. What emerged was a new Saudi-mediated coalition comprising Saudi Arabia, Egypt, Syria, and Jordan (as Syria's ally). This coalition managed to function until November 1977, when Anwar Sadat made his historic trip to Jerusalem. Egyptian-Syrian relations were normalized after the Cairo summit conference in late October. The reconciliation between Cairo and Damascus was underscored by reports in January 1977, that Egypt would send a number of high-ranking army officers to Lebanon to assist in the training of the new Lebanese army.[29] This was a remarkable turn of events considering that Syria had been extremely jealous of its military presence in Lebanon. Further evidence is suggested by reports that when Iraq tried to send military personnel, disguised as tourists, into Lebanon via Egypt in October, the Egyptians lodged a strong protest with Baghdad and took immediate measures to close that route.[30] This is in marked contrast to the previous summer when Egypt reportedly allowed some Iraqi forces to transit its territory on their way to Lebanon. With this reconciliation and the winding down of the war in Lebanon the moderates were able to turn their attention to bargaining strategies and procedural questions in preparation for the resumption of the Geneva Conference to work out a settlement of the Arab-Israeli conflict. This new coalition was, through Syria, able to exert more control over the Palestinians. As a result, the rejectionist front was more isolated. The revival of the coalition of moderates undoubtedly would have taken place much sooner had the fighting in Lebanon not occurred.

The war definitely worsened Iraqi-Syrian relations. Iraqi support of the Palestinians and their Lebanese leftist allies enabled the coalition of progressive forces to continue to resist Syrian efforts to curb their power.[31] Iraqi threats to send troops into Syria if the Syrian army became substantially involved in Lebanon can only have hobbled Syrian efforts to end the crisis.[32] When Iraq redeployed forces toward the Syrian border following the intervention by the Syrian army in June 1976, Syrian and Jordanian forces responded in kind. In addition, by autumn 1976, Iraq reportedly managed to infiltrate, with Turkish assistance, a large number of its troops into Lebanon. Perhaps this was why Iraq was the only country to oppose the Cairo summit proposal that the bulk of the suggested 30,000 Arab Deterrent Force be made up mainly from Syrian forces already in Lebanon.[33] It is ironic but illustrative of the extent of Arab disarray growing out of the Lebanese crisis that the first and only military activation of the Eastern Front was not for defense against Israel but against another Arab state, Iraq.[34] When Syria demanded higher transit fees on Iraqi oil transported through pipelines across Syria to Lebanon, Iraq shut off the oil. Syria had been taking these fees in oil. Thus Damascus became dependent upon Saudi Arabia to make up for this oil embargo and less susceptible to Iraqi-Libyan urging to join an expanded "rejectionist front."

The rejectionists sought to reverse their isolation in the Fertile Crescent in 1978 in the wake of Sadat's peace initiative to Israel. The aim was to draw Syria into their ranks by supporting Syria's position in Lebanon. The fighting that broke out between Syrian contingents of the Arab Deterrent Force (ADF) and a mixed bag of Lebanese soldiers and Christian militiamen in February 1978, was viewed by diplomatic observers in the area as an attempt to frustrate Syrian moves to reorient its policies to achieve more political and military self-reliance.[35] To these observers and particularly to the Syrians, the logical outside force to encourage a Lebanese challenge to Syrian authority there appeared to be Egypt in retaliation for Assad's continued refusal to support Egypt's peace initiative with Israel.

Syrian rapproachment with Libya, Algeria, the PLO and the Soviet Union appeared to be a tactical maneuver with the aim of enabling Damascus to stand alone against Israeli pressures in the absence of support from Egypt and in the event that Hussein should eventually follow Sadat to Jerusalem. Syria was rumored to be anxious to avoid too heavy financial—and political—indebtedness to the Soviet Union and Saudi Arabia by persuading other Arab states to pay for the new weapons it was seeking. In this regard Libya had begun to emerge as Syria's principal financial angel. The Syrian-dominated ADF crackdown on various Lebanese right-wing factions can be seen in the context of a policy switch toward accommodating a minimum number of Libyan demands.

The rejectionists may have made a move to undermine the Saudi-sponsored moderate coalition when Libya offered to finance the ADF—an offer that carried with it the tacit assumption that the forces will remain in Lebanon and that their mandate would be extended when it expired in March 1978.[36] The offer illuminated the vague outlines of possibly a new inter-Arab bloc struggle with the two main contenders being Saudi Arabia and Libya, the battlefield being Lebanon, and the stakes being Syria's membership in a "moderate" or a "radical" coalition. The instruments of the competition would be the Syrian-dominated Arab Deterrent Force and its continued financing, which Syria cannot afford to undertake. The outcome of this new bloc struggle—if, indeed, it does emerge—is hard to predict. For the short run, however, its main by-product is likely to be the further institutionalization of Syrian political and military presence in Lebanon.

The war in Lebanon and Syrian efforts to settle it illuminated the changed status of Lebanon which had heretofore gone unnoticed or unappreciated. For all practical purposes Lebanon was now a confrontation state, in spite of itself. The country's status in the inter-Arab arena was forthrightly acknowledged by none other than President Frangieh when he declared Lebanon to be an "Arab state."[37] For a Maronite leader of Frangieh's Lebanese ultranationalist persuasion, the description of Lebanon as an Arab state was acknowledgement that Lebanon's aloofness from active participation in Arab politics was no longer tenable. The degree to which even the rightists were willing to acknowledge what had been a fact for several years can be better appreciated by noting a change in the right wing position on the 1969 Cairo Agreement. When the "secret" agreement was first worked out the Lebanese conservatives, particularly the Christians, denounced it as an abridgement of Lebanon's "sovereignty" (read Lebanon's time-honored practice of remaining neutral in inter-Arab affairs). At the time the rightists saw the Cairo agreement as promoting the aggrandizement of the Palestinians and through them the influence of outside powers. In 1976 the accord was viewed as the principal device by which Palestinian presence in Lebanon could be diminished and regulated. None other than Interior Minister Camille Chamoun, considered one of the most hard-line of the right-wing Christian leaders, stated in February 1976, that Palestinian adherence to the 1969 Cairo Agreement would be "an essential condition" for the maintenance of peace in Lebanon.[38] In that regard the Arab consensus concerning Lebanon's place in inter-Arab relations was reaffirmed. The difference was that in 1976 there was also an Arab consensus on the implementation of the Cairo accords with the help of a 30,000-man Arab Deterrent Force dominated by the Syrian troops.

Another source of recognition of Lebanon's changed status is expressed in the most prominent change in inter-Arab relations, namely Israel's active intervention in an inter-Arab conflict. Prior to 1976 Israel had played no active role in inter-Arab brawling. At the most Jerusalem may have aggravated some quarrels among various Lebanese factions by large scale military reprisal raids in Lebanon, such as the Beirut airport raid in 1968. The most spectacular incident was the Beirut "Rent-a-car raid" in April 1973, during which an Israeli hit team assassinated high-level PLO officials in their own apartments. This incident led to the resignation of Premier Saeb Salem and armed clashes between the Palestinian guerrillas and the Lebanese army and air force in May. Otherwise, active Israeli intervention was limited to one instance in 1970 when Israeli forces were massed along the Golan Heights to deter Syria from military intervention in Jordan on behalf of the Palestinian guerrillas.

The Lebanese crisis, however, was the first inter-Arab conflict in which Israel pursued an activist policy, intervening directly on one side against the other in the conflict. It thereby helped shape its duration. Israel not only actively supported the Christian forces but repeatedly threatened to attack Syria should the latter intervene directly in the fighting. In November 1975, for example, Israeli diplomats were asserting that "fear of an invasion by Israel is the main reason keeping the Syrians from marching into Lebanon."[39] Prime Minister Yitzhak Rabin repeatedly stated Israel's position: "We shall not interfere as long as the fighting is an internal Lebanese matter. But if Syria were to intervene, it would create a new situation and face us with grave dangers."[40]

After Syria opened contacts with the Phalangists in December and indicated that it was working for a stalemate rather than a leftist victory, Israel's position began to change. Israel was reported to have cautiously welcomed the Syrian-sponsored political settlement in January, which only slightly altered the balance of forces in the Muslim's favor without compromising Israeli security interests.[41] As differences accumulated between Syria and the Palestinians and the leftists, Israel seemed less concerned about possible small-scale Syrian intervention than by the rising power of the alliance of progressive forces in Lebanon.[42] By April Israel had advanced the "red line" policy, a line beyond which Syria should not cross without expecting some sort of hostile Israeli response.

It is highly likely that had the Israeli government advanced the policy of the "red line" in October 1975, or even in January 1976, Syria might have intervened with sufficient forces to effectively enforce a cease-fire and halt the conflict so that the terms of the settlement, announced January 21, could be implemented. Similarly, Israel's refusal to permit Arab peace-keeping forces below the Litani River prolonged the fighting in southern Lebanon between Palestinian guerrillas and Israeli-supported Christian troops, and this in turn resulted in greater destruction and loss of life in that area.

For all practical purposes Israel has been an important actor in Lebanese politics since 1976 through its support for Camille Chamoun and other rightists. The support has maintained a level of turmoil sufficiently intense to impede leftist or Palestinian regrouping in southern Lebanon and to limit Syrian influences over these groups. Israel's active support of the Christian militias had the effect of keeping the pot boiling in southern Lebanon and keeping Syrian forces in the north disposed and occupied. This took the form mainly of encouraging and supporting Christian attacks on leftist-Muslim strongholds in south Lebanon, refusing to allow the ADF to pacify the area and finally by invading and occupying the region for two months (on this point see the chapters by John Cooley and Fred Khouri elsewhere in this volume), and threatening military intervention if Syria crushed Christian forces. During this time Israel armed and trained Christians, Druze, and anti-Palestinian Muslim militia forces to replace Israeli troops in the six-mile "security belt" created by the invasion. These tactics may have improved Israel's security, but they have impeded the re-establishment of Lebanese government authority in southern Lebanon. Ultimately, they impeded the re-establishment of Lebanese government authority throughout Lebanon.

The Israeli track record in Lebanon drives home a clear lesson. Inter-Arab relations, particularly inter-Arab conflict can no longer be conducted without heeding Israeli interests, military power, and propensity for further expansion. If nothing else, Israel's entry into the inter-Arab arena underscored the need for direct communications between Israel and the surrounding Arab states. This new factor in the international relations of the area could serve a conflict-dampening function. However, so far it has had the opposite impact.

Syria and the Palestinians

One of the first casualties of the fighting in Lebanon was the western flank of Syria's Eastern Front. The successful operation of the front required both a stable Lebanon and a reasonably cohesive Palestinian resistance movement allied with Syria. Syria could not achieve the former condition without sacrificing the latter. Not only were Syrian-Palestinian ties severely strained, but the fabric of the Palestinian resistance was further damaged as tension increased among the Syrian-controlled al-Sa'iqa, the PLO "mainstream," and the rejection front allied with the Lebanese leftists.

However, in the process of trying to establish the Eastern Front, Syria can be said to have scored impressive gains in Lebanon and in the inter-Arab and international arenas. By working for a military stalemate and dealing with both sides to achieve a political settlement, Syria demonstrated that it was the only Arab country capable of influencing events inside Lebanon. Tacit recognition of this new position was even conceded by Israel. When President Assad sent PLA troops into Lebanon to enforce the cease-fire, Israel was one of the first to reject charges by rightist leader Camille Chamoun that Syria had openly intervened in his country's conflict.[43] In this way Jerusalem tacitly conceded that Syria had a special interest in Lebanon and could exercise its power there without provoking a confrontation with Israel. Syria's interests in Lebanon were finally acknowledged by the other Arab states later in October 1976, when they accepted an Arab League peace-keeping force in Lebanon composed overwhelmingly of Syrian troops. The composition of this force not only helped to insure the continuation of Syrian hegemony, but helped to keep Iraqi and Egyptian influence at bay.

Second, Syria established itself as a key to peace in Lebanon. To the extent that the conflict in Lebanon retarded any movement toward a broader Arab-Israeli settlement, Syria also became more important in reaching a broader Middle East peace settlement. This new status was belatedly acknowledged by the United States. By January 1976, the U.S. seemed to agree with the assessment of columnist Joseph Kraft that Syria, not Egypt, seemed to be the key to peace in Lebanon.[44] Washington reportedly sent a message to the Christian leaders in Lebanon informing them that their "last and best" opportunity of salvaging their position lay in cooperating with Syria.[45] When Syria sent PLA units into Lebanon to maintain order in January 1976, it was reportedly American pressure that helped mute Israel's reaction to their presence in Lebanon.[46] When Syria finally sent large scale forces into Lebanon in early June, the U.S. described the intervention as "helpful."[47] In May L. Dean Brown, the American special envoy to Lebanon, claimed the U.S. had probably "made a mistake" in discouraging Syria from sending troops into Beirut in April as a peace-making force. "We, [the United States] reined in the Syrians too much to please the Israelis. . . . It resulted in a lot more killing."[48]

The main outlines of the Syrian-sponsored settlement and Syria's preeminent position in Lebanon were given formal acknowledgement at a meeting of six Arab leaders in Riyadh, October 16–18, at the insistence of Saudi Arabia. An inducement to Syria to allow at least a modicum of Arabization of the conflict was a Saudi offer to finance the costs of the Arab Deterrent Force that would be composed mainly of Syrian troops. This ended Syria's growing isolation in the Arab world, reduced the heavy drain on its treasury from supporting its forces in Lebanon, and recognized Syria's special position in Lebanon. The earlier Arab consensus was re-established concerning Lebanon as a confrontation state in that the Palestinians were compelled to comply with the 1969 Cairo Agreement. This time the terms were guaranteed by a 30,000-man peacekeeping force. There was also an unspoken consensus in Riyadh to curb Palestinian elements that were unwilling to go along with the peace plan.

As for the Palestinians, the termination of hostilities left the movement weaker and more divided than ever. Indeed, it could almost be said that the PLO managed to snatch defeat from the jaws of victory. Initially, the PLO emerged in January and February 1976, in the wake of the Syrian-sponsored cease-fire and political settlement, with its military position in Lebanon much improved and a stronger presence there than the movement had enjoyed before. Moreover, as the settlement relied on PLA forces to enforce the cease-fire, the PLO mainstream emerged stronger vis-à-vis the rejectionists. At this point, however, the consequence of the Palestinians' fear of "plots" to liquidate them and their hesitation to collaborate too closely with any one Arab government lest they lose their independence prompted Yasir Arafat to gamble the future of the movement on defying Syria and supporting Kamal Jumblatt's alliance of progressive forces in March.

The Lebanese conflict in retrospect illuminated the limited scope for cooperation between the Palestinians and Syria as well as the Palestinians' inability to trust any Arab government or to endorse any policy without reservations. These obstacles and limitations had undoubtedly existed under the surface of Syrian-Palestinian relations at least since the end of the October War, but circumstances had allowed them to remain dormant. The principal constraint was that all the confrontation states were willing to try for a settlement with Israel which, almost by definition, denied the claims of the Palestinian national movement. The war in Lebanon thrust that divergence of interests to the surface.

The transformation of the Eastern Front from a political pressure tactic to a viable military strategy required Syrian collaboration with the Palestinians' two arch enemies—the Lebanese Right and Jordan's King Hussein. Moreover, Syria was amenable to reaching a settlement with Israel if acceptable terms were proffered. Any significant movement in the direction of a Syrian-Israeli settlement would only have the disrupted Syrian coordination with the PLO. For example, in February 1976, rumors began to circulate concerning an American peace plan that involved Israeli withdrawal from at least part of the Golan Heights and the creation of a Palestinian state on the West Bank in exchange for Syrian and Jordanian nonbelligerency with Israel.[49] Syria was now viewed in Washington as serving as a restraining influence on Lebanese and Palestinian rejectionists who were a threat to a settlement on the Golan as well as to stability in Lebanon. These reports had been preceded by rumors which spoke of the need to control the Palestinians and to reduce the power of the rejectionists in Lebanon. These coincided with an attack by Syrian-controlled al-Sa'iqa forces on two pro-Iraqi Beirut newspapers. The attack was interpreted as a signal to the rejectionists—and their Iraqi and Libyan backers—of what might happen in the future if the rejectionists stepped out of line.[50]

The PLO had already become alarmed when Syria first opened contacts with the Phalangists in December 1975. The stalemate which Syria wished to foster in order to mediate a settlement meant that the rightists would be sufficiently strong to threaten the Palestinians' position in Lebanon in the future. That outcome did eventually materialize, but it occurred mainly because of Arafat's decision to defy Syria and throw Palestinian support to Jumblatt's alliance of progressive forces. To the extent that any Arab state can "control" or "deliver" the Palestinians in any future peace settlement, it is Syria, not Egypt. Indeed, Egypt's unilateral peace initiative in November 1977, helped facilitate a Syrian-PLO reconciliation that the Riyadh agreements could not have achieved.

Because of the war in Lebanon, the Eastern Front could not be implemented as a war strategy. However, the near-termination of the fighting in December 1976, and the emergence of Syria's pivotal position in Lebanon suggests that the Eastern Front may contribute to peace.[51] The utility of what is left of the Eastern Front strategy as one of the foundations of a general peace settlement in the Middle East will depend largely upon whether Israel, with United States urging, eventually agrees to withdraw from Arab territories and agrees to self-determination for Palestinians. Were this to materialize, a Syrian-Jordanian entente and control of the Palestinians would be crucial ingredients to a final settlement. Failure to reach a regional settlement or the conclusion of a separate agreement between Egypt and Israel could activate the front into a defensive military strategy. In this framework the Syrian-controlled Palestinians would function not as a guerrilla force harassing Israeli settlements but as regular units who would have a defensive role that would be coordinated by the joint Syrian-Jordanian military command.

For the Eastern Front to contribute to peace Syria must not only control the Palestinians, pacify Lebanon, and restructure its political system, but the fighting between the Palestinians and the Israeli-backed Christian forces in southern Lebanon must end as well. As mentioned earlier in this essay, Israel's intervention in the conflict can be understood partly in terms of its effort to frustrate the Eastern Front strategy. If that proposition is correct then Israel's continued support of the Christian extremists in the south and its refusal to tolerate Syrian forces south of the Litani River can be seen as a continued effort to keep the area in sufficient turmoil so that the Palestinians can not carry out the defensive tasks outlined above. Syrian forces sufficient to enforce order in southern Lebanon would be insufficient to threaten Israel. Moreover, Syrian troops are widely dispersed in Lebanon and thinned out along the Golan. As long as Syrian forces are occupying Lebanon they cannot be concentrated for an attack on Israel. Ironically, Syria intervened in Lebanon partly to secure the western flank of the Eastern Front against Israel. As it is Syria is probably less able to defend itself against an Israeli attack than before April 1975, notwithstanding additional quantities of Soviet military aid.

Jordan

Jordan's impact on the conflict was at best marginal. At the beginning of the hostilities when it was still largely a Phalangist-Palestinian conflict, Jordan provided arms and ammunition to the Phalangist forces. However, after the Phalangists reduced Karantina and Maslakh to ruins in an orgy of bloodshed, Christian operations took on too many anti-Muslim connotations and the military aid from Jordan was terminated. If Jordanian policy had any indirect impact on the conflict, it was in the form of King Hussein's persuading the Ford Administration and Congress that only Syrian military intervention could restore order in Lebanon. Hussein's appeal to the United States not to allow Israel to invade Lebanon in response to limited Syrian military intervention undoubtedly helped persuade Washington to give Damascus an amber light in Lebanon.

Yet although it was on the sidelines, Jordan's position in inter-Arab and perhaps international relations was stronger partly as a consequence of the fighting. First, Jordan's association with Syria, the most visible champion of Arab and Palestinian interests, raised King Hussein's standing in the Arab world and with his own subjects. The entente with Damascus ended Jordan's isolation in inter-Arab affairs that resulted from King Hussein's expulsion of the Palestinian guerrillas from Jordan in 1970. Most important, the end of isolation was achieved without having to readmit the Palestinian guerrillas to Jordanian territory.

Second, the Jordanian leadership was counting on Syria to tame the leftist fringes of the PLO and to silence left-wing Palestinians who reject the idea of a negotiated settlement with Israel. In this regard, the weakening of the PLO to the point where it could even be bypassed in future peace negotiations can only have benefited Jordan. The strengthening of Jordan vis-à-vis the PLO in the wake of the fighting in Lebanon is underscored by a statement by King Hussein in an interview with a French reporter in September 1977. When asked if he would not find it difficult to share power with Yasir Arafat in a Jordanian-Palestinian federated state, Hussein bluntly inquired: "Who says the Palestinians will elect Arafat or representatives of the PLO?" He went on to say that after Israeli withdrawal from the occupied Arab territories "peacetime elections can turn out quite differently."[52] The entente with Syria also meant Jordan was more insulated from pressures from Iraq.

Egypt and Saudi Arabia

A comparison of Saudi and Egyptian roles in the conflict suggests that the war in Lebanon clarified the changing positions of these two countries in inter-Arab relations that had been evolving since the October War. Since the end of that war, Egypt's policies, particularly toward Israel, seemed to remove Cairo further and further from the center of inter-Arab and pan-Arab concerns. In contrast to the Lebanese crises in 1958 and 1969, Egypt's estrangement from Syria left Cairo with little or no leverage on the conflict. True, there was the Egyptian-Palestinian reconciliation in May 1976. This was the first step back from an isolation in which Anwar Sadat had found himself after signing the second Sinai agreement with Israel. But this reconciliation was more in response to Syria's efforts to curb the Palestinians than to any genuine composure of Egyptian-PLO differences. Egypt reportedly agreed to release the Egyptian-based brigade (the Ain Jalout Brigade) of the Palestinian Liberation Army to counter the Syrian-controlled al-Sa'iqa forces and the Hitten Brigade of the PLA also under Syrian control. In return, the PLO agreed to tone down its criticism of the Sinai II agreement.[53]

The extent to which this reconciliation benefited Egypt's position in inter-Arab relations is probably nil. In the end the Palestinians were finally brought to heel, and the forces that contributed toward the gradual winding down of the conflict had little to do with Egypt or Egyptian initiatives. Egypt could not provide the PLO with massive military aid without strengthening the very forces to which Cairo was opposed—the left-wing elements of the PLO and the rejection front forces that were implacably opposed to a settlement with Israel. Thus unlike previous inter-Arab disputes in recent history, Egypt exerted little influence, either on the context of the conflict itself or on its settlement. To the extent that Egyptian actions may have dampened the conflict in Lebanon or influenced Syrian activities there, Sadat's call in March 1976, for a meeting of the Arab League to consider a pan-Arab solution to the conflict may have had some impact. It was Sadat's intention to press for the establishment of an Arab peace-keeping force in which Egypt would provide most of the troops if necessary. This threat to Arabize the conflict lent urgency to Syrian mediation efforts. If a cease-fire could be imposed and negotiations begun before the Arab League considered Sadat's proposal Egypt would once again be relegated to a peripheral role in the crisis.

Because Egypt had been relegated to the sidelines in the most serious Arab political crisis since the June war, Sadat's position at home emerged shakier than before April–September 1975. Even though Sinai II did not cause the renewed fighting in Lebanon that coincided with the signing of that agreement, Egypt was shown not to be the mover and shaker in inter-Arab politics that it had been in earlier crises. To a certain extent the amount of financial aid Egypt could obtain from the conservative oil-rich regimes in the Gulf depended in large measure on the role Egypt plays in the conflict with Israel and in shaping inter-Arab affairs. It can almost be stated axiomatically that when Sadat succeeds the Saudis and other oil-rich countries tend to be generous. When he fails or is inactive these countries are less forthcoming in their financial backing. Thus failure to play a dominant role in Lebanon undoubtedly undermined Sadat's ability to gain more support for his peace initiative to Israel from Saudi Arabia and Jordan.[54]

In contrast to Egypt, Saudi Arabia gained political influence in the inter-Arab political arena as a result of the conflict in Lebanon. It was at Saudi behest that the leaders of Syria, Egypt, the PLO, and Lebanon met together in Riyadh and worked out a settlement in Lebanon. Each of these contenders depended upon Saudi financial support. Syria and Egypt looked to Saudi influence in Washington to nudge the United States government toward more pressure on Israel to make the necessary concessions for a final settlement. No matter how badly Anwar Sadat might wish to make a separate peace with Israel—as shown by the results of the meeting at Camp David—he was not likely to do so at the risk of terminating the economic subventions from Riyadh that were helping to keep the shaky Egyptian economy from total collapse. Saudi Arabia was the one country that was on good terms with all the moderates including the moderates in the PLO. It was the one country that had enough influence with all the members of this coalition to give it sufficient cohesion to coordinate negotiating strategies for a peace settlement, or to coordinate military tasks in renewed preparations for war should negotiations fail to produce acceptable results. In this regard the outcome of the war in Lebanon indicated that Saudi Arabia was emerging as a critical behind-the-scenes third (along with Syria and Egypt) key to peace in the region.

CONCLUSION

The conflict in Lebanon was not the first time that country had become a stage on which regional conflicts and issues played major roles in what began as an indigenous drama. However, it was unlike previous crises such as those in 1958 and 1969, for by 1978 it appeared that Lebanon was not likely to regain a very large measure of control over its internal affairs free from outside (mainly Syrian and Israeli) influence. Nor did it appear likely to regain complete authority over its own territory, particularly after the Israeli invasion of south Lebanon, as the continuing triangular struggle among the Palestinians, the surrounding Arab states, and Israel continued to make Lebanon a battleground for regional conflicts. For the foreseeable future it does not appear that any indigenous conflict can occur in Lebanon without being overshadowed by outside forces and submerged in broader regional issues. The internecine fighting in the Christian camp between the Frangieh's private army and Pierre Gemayel's Phalangist forces underscores this prognosis as does the reaction in Lebanon to the Camp David accords.

What apparently began in June 1978, as an attempt by the Gemayel clan to achieve a position of undisputed leadership of the Christian community quickly became enmeshed in broader regional issues. The Phalangists' action was a challenge to Syria's position as it challenged the Syrian-supported Sarkis regime. To the extent that Phalangist success increased the prospects of a partitioned Lebanon, the Gemayels' bid for local supremacy was also a challenge to Syria's strategic position, hence the strong Syrian military response in July as Syrian peace-keeping forces laid siege to the Christian sector of Ashrifayyeh in Beirut. The Syrian leadership reportedly saw the Phalangist action as part of an Israeli-Christian plot. Syrian hesitation to launch an all-out attack on the Christian recalcitrants was thought to be caused by Syrian desire to forestall direct Israeli intervention on behalf of the Phalangists.

There also appears to be a strong connection between lack of progress toward a comprehensive Arab-Israeli settlement and the outbreak of fighting in Lebanon. As mentioned earlier, the shift away from trying to reach a general Arab-Israeli agreement in spring 1975, in favor of concluding a second bilateral Egyptian-Israeli agreement in Sinai intensified the fears of the Christian rightists that they would be left alone to deal with the Palestinians and their leftist allies in Lebanon. It also helped to convince the Syrians that they must take control in Lebanon. The Christians reacted by attacking the Palestinians. The Syrians' immediate response was to step up their diplomatic efforts to mediate a settlement and restore stability to the country. When diplomacy failed they also resorted to force.

A similar pattern appears to have marked the response in Lebanon and Syria to the Camp David agreements. While there had been sporadic fighting between Syrian and Christian forces since summer 1978, a deadly, prolonged battle erupted in September and October. The accords offered no foreseeable solution to the Palestinian problem as the Christian rightists defined it. In other words, there would be no Palestinian state on the West Bank to absorb the unwanted Palestinians in Lebanon. Israel would certainly be reluctant to intervene on a large scale lest its chance for reaching a separate agreement with Egypt be jeopardized and Israel's relations with Washington strained. Once again the Christians were confronted with the prospect of being left unaided to deal with the Palestinians. In 1978, however, the Christian forces were militarily superior to the Palestinians. They were prevented from further reducing Palestinian strength and expelling the Palestinians from Lebanon by the presence of Syrian forces. Therefore, Syria had to be harassed into withdrawing from Lebanon.

From Syria's vantage point Egypt's apparent decision to negotiate a separate agreement with Israel gave Jerusalem sufficient freedom of action for a military showdown without fear of Egyptian intervention. Armed clashes between Christian militiamen and Syrian forces in Lebanon after an Israel-Egyptian peace would almost certainly bring an Israeli military response and even a direct military confrontation between Syria

206 LEBANON IN CRISIS

and Israel. Syria had to act immediately. The antagonistic Christian forces had to be crushed before the Israeli-Egyptian peace negotiations were completed, before Israel had a free hand to intervene on the Christians' behalf.

Similarly, Lebanon's prospects for survival as an independent state in substance as well as in name will depend in a large measure upon the conflicts and alignments in the inter-Arab political arena and further developments in the Arabs' conflict with Israel. For example, by the summer of 1978, Lebanon's position was beginning to improve as a result of shifting alignments in the Arab world. The principal new element was the growing concern in Arab capitals over increasing Soviet penetration in Africa and South Yemen. The result was growing cooperation between Kuwait and Saudi Arabia and Iraq. No matter how much they disagreed with one another, all of the Arab states were eager to prevent any one of the Middle East major oil producers from falling under direct Soviet control. That meant support for revolutionary groups in the region was likely to be reduced substantially. Support for the Palestinians was becoming restricted to helping them obtain a national home. But as long as revolutionary activity was perceived by key regional actors (and financial angles) as foreshadowing Soviet penetration of the Arab East, the Palestinians were unlikely to receive much help if they carried on their struggle against Israel from other countries. It is worth noting that Palestinian statements in late May and early June expressed a willingness to meet the requirements of the Lebanese government to extend its jurisdiction over all Lebanese territory. These coincided with Iraq's move away from open support of revolutionary groups and Israel's withdrawal from southern Lebanon and its transfer of control to hostile, anti-Palestinian Christian and Muslim militias. Thus just as changing issues had once led to a changing Arab consensus over Lebanon's position in the Arab world and so contributed to the country's turmoil, it appeared as though threats from another direction would help establish a new Arab consensus that would allow Lebanon to survive and flourish once again *insha'allah*.

PART II

International Politics

THE SOVIET UNION

James F. Collins

IF SOVIET INFLUENCE has declined in the Middle East and especially in Egypt and Syria since the high-water years of the early 1970s, there is ample reason to expect the USSR to continue to play an active part in the Middle East and to attempt to make good her losses.[1] The Soviet Union has impressive advantages in carrying out these tasks: to great economic and military power must be added a geographical closeness to and ideological affinity for important nations and movements in the Arab world. At the same time, the USSR encounters a number of significant problems in getting its way in the Middle East, and these were much in evidence during the Lebanese civil war.[2] The conflict in Lebanon damaged the Soviet position in that country and in the Fertile Crescent, and weakened Soviet hopes to maintain the unity of Arab regimes favorable to the USSR, to focus all attention on the Arab-Israeli conflict, and to defeat U.S. step-by-step diplomacy and return to the Geneva negotiations. Soviet involvement in the Lebanese conflict reveals some important limits on superpower influence in the Middle East.

SOVIET POLICY BEFORE SINAI II

The USSR's approach to the early stages of civil strife in Lebanon was shaped by its attempt to cope with the negotiations between Egypt and Israel on a second disengagement agreement. Having acquiesced in U.S. mediation of the first two disengagement agreements between Israel and Egypt and Syria, Moscow had hoped, indeed demanded, that Arab-Israeli settlement efforts move to the Geneva Middle East Peace Conference.[3] The Egyptian-Israeli decision to negotiate a second agreement under U.S. auspices was, therefore, a severe blow to the USSR's effort to realize its claim to an equal share in determining both the negotiation and the substance of an Arab-Israeli peace settlement.[4] The decision also influenced future Soviet Middle Eastern policy.

The progress in Sinai reinforced Moscow's conviction that its future interests as well as its co-equal status with the U.S. in the area would depend on the Soviet Union's ability to consolidate relations with the "progressive" Arab states, those closely associated with the USSR. Other developments, meanwhile, particularly the steady downturn in Soviet-Egyptian relations and an increasingly active Saudi policy throughout the Middle East, lent greater urgency to an effort to strengthen the Soviet Union's position in the Arab world. As a result, by early 1975, the USSR was engaged in vigorous efforts to compensate for its declining influence over the Arab-Israeli peace process by strengthening ties with the "progressive" Arabs, particularly Syria and the PLO, and seeking to enlist their support for Soviet objectives.

On the one hand, the USSR's increasing need for the support of the "progressive" Arabs strengthened the Soviet inclination to work for revision of the political structure in Lebanon. Political and social change there, brought about by leftist-Muslim authority, could be expected to lead Lebanon away from its traditional pro-Western orientation and, the Soviets hoped, to associate Lebanon more closely with the Arab regimes sympathetic to the USSR. At the same time, the USSR's growing stake in the survival of an independent PLO argued strongly for promoting a political environment in Lebanon which would secure Palestinian autonomy. These considerations, along with Moscow's obvious ideological preference for the left, suggested the USSR abandon the more or less even-handed approach which it had taken toward earlier outbreaks of violence and give strong support to the leftist-Muslim cause.[5]

Other elements in the Lebanese situation and in Moscow's assessment of it urged the USSR toward caution. In Lebanon itself the outcome of the factional fighting was problematical, and the risks in Muslim-leftist efforts to impose their political demands by force were correspondingly large. A defeat for Moscow's clients would run the risk of emasculating Soviet influence there. Furthermore, given the anti-Palestinian aims of the Christian-rightist factions, a defeat could also lead to serious setbacks for the PLO. At the same time, the USSR probably believed that internationalization of the conflict was likely if the fighting tipped decisively in favor of either side, or if it escalated to the point where such a development seemed imminent.[6] Moscow, however, had significant reasons for wanting to avoid outside intervention. Intervention by Israel or Western powers, a possibility that the USSR could certainly not rule out if the leftist-Muslim side were winning, would inevitably confront the

USSR with an unpalatable choice between aiding its friends or seeing them defeated. A Christian-rightist victory or the threat of one, meanwhile, would certainly tempt Arabs sympathetic to the Muslim cause to intervene, thereby risking reaction by Israel or the West.

Plagued by contradictory interests which made the definition of a policy exceedingly difficult, the USSR followed an ambivalent approach to the conflict. On the one hand, Moscow publicly supported the leftist-Muslim faction. Soviet media portrayed demands by the "progressive and national-patriotic forces" sympathetically. "Lebanese reaction" and the Phalange, meanwhile, were regularly vilified as defenders of unjust and unreasonable privilege and as enemies of the Arab cause. On the more tangible level Soviet arms flowed to Kamal Jumblatt and his allies from Soviet-equipped Arab arsenals apparently without hindrance, suggesting at least tacit Soviet support for the transfers. On the other hand, even as it expressed support for the Muslim-leftist factions, Moscow also hinted at the need for reason and moderation by them in pressing their case. Moscow regularly bemoaned the human and monetary costs of the fighting. It also encouraged the parties to settle their differences through negotiations, suggesting that the USSR at least had reservations about leftist-Muslim attempts to settle accounts in the streets.

To summarize, the Sinai II agreement had mixed results for Soviet efforts to advance their interests in the Arab world. It clearly set back Moscow's effort to bring Arab-Israeli settlement talks back to the Geneva conference where Moscow had an assured role. Furthermore, President Sadat's drift toward the West was given a significant boost, and the USSR's influence in Egypt declined further. Soviet dependence on the "progressive" Arab community increased as a result. The violent reaction against Sinai II by Syria, the PLO, Iraq, and Libya significantly increased the congruence of interest between the USSR and its remaining friends. Furthermore, it opened new opportunities to exploit their hostility to Sadat's action. In this way the USSR hoped to prevent further successes for U.S.-sponsored step-by-step diplomacy and to gather backing for a return to Geneva.

FROM SINAI II TO THE JANUARY CEASE-FIRE

In the Lebanese context, meanwhile, the effects of the agreement on Soviet interests and policies was essentially negative but more complex.

The accord was followed by an outburst of violence which intensified throughout the fall and early winter. The escalation of the conflict, in turn, made Lebanon the primary concern among the majority of actors in the Middle East. Soviet hopes for a revival of Geneva negotiations were set back as a result. Much against its wishes, the USSR had to focus on Lebanon rather than on the Arab-Israeli conflict where their interests were more precisely defined. In Lebanon the contradictions in the USSR's attitude toward the growing conflict had, if anything, become more pronounced following Sinai II.

The Kremlin's interest in strengthening the opponents of step-by-step diplomacy certainly argued for greater efforts to promote a new political orientation in Beirut which promised to align Lebanon with pro-Soviet elements in the Arab world. But Sinai II also reinforced Soviet incentives to contain the conflict and prevent its internationalization. The widely held assumption that Egypt, in agreeing to Sinai II, had opted out of another war with Israel, at least for the time being, as well as Israel's relatively stronger military posture two years after the 1973 war, made an escalation of tension on Israel's frontiers extremely dangerous. The agreement also deepened the USSR's stake in preserving Syrian-PLO cooperation, since harmony between the two was essential to Soviet hopes for any coalition of "progressive" Arabs. And finally, given the increasing significance the Kremlin accorded to the PLO as an independent partner in the Arab world, the Sinai II agreement deepened the USSR's interest in preventing development of a struggle in Lebanon that could significantly weaken the PLO.[7]

Thus even after Sinai II the Soviets had a strong interest in preventing the conflict in Lebanon from spreading or intensifying. Unfortunately, however, the greater Soviet interest in the status of the conflict was unmatched by an increase in Soviet influence over events there. Indeed, the USSR's growing dependence on Syria and the PLO had only further raised the potential risks in opposing them or their allies in the leftist-Muslim coalition. As the crisis in Lebanon deepened during the fall, therefore, Moscow had even fewer policy options than previously that did not entail unacceptable costs to other interests. As a result, Moscow stuck largely by its previous policy, all the while bemoaning the greater level of hostilities, intensifying public calls for containing the conflict, and trying to define and protect its interests in the crisis.

In this context Moscow gave priority to preventing outside military involvement in the conflict. Soviet propaganda consistently emphasized Moscow's opposition to a role by outsiders with news coverage and commentary tailored to support and promote its policy, without raising neuralgic issues with interested or involved Arabs. The campaign, thus, repeatedly warned against Israeli intervention in Lebanon and frequently reported alleged plots by Tel Aviv to exploit the conflict as a pretense to strike at the Palestinians in south Lebanon. This line of comment seemed calculated both to dissuade Israel and to dramatize the danger to the PLO of any rash action that might induce an Israeli backlash.[8] On the Arab side, meanwhile, Moscow also encouraged restraint indirectly. Soviet propaganda stressed the positive benefits of avoiding involvement in the conflict, praising the PLO, in particular, for its wisdom and maturity in thwarting attempts to draw Palestinian forces into the fighting.

Even as it warned against military involvement by outsiders, the USSR publicly and privately encouraged efforts to end the fighting both by those directly involved and by Syria and the PLO. Prime Minister Karameh was regularly praised for trying to stop the bloodshed. Arafat, meanwhile, also received praise for supporting efforts to halt the conflict and encourage political compromise. It was Syrian mediation, however, on which the USSR clearly placed its main hope as the fighting wore on. There were fairly good indications that Assad had been encouraged to pursue his effort to bring peace in Lebanon during his visit to the USSR in October 1975. Meanwhile, throughout the late fall and early winter Moscow gave consistent public support to Syrian efforts to use their good offices among the squabbling Lebanese factions.

In the meantime, Moscow remained reticent in presenting its own views about the terms for a political settlement. One point, however, was emphasized: any settlement had to prevent the partition of Lebanon and that country had to survive as a "united state."[9] Otherwise, Soviet media generally avoided offering any prescription for a settlement, providing instead only implicit endorsement of leftist-Muslim demands for reform by giving them wide publicity.

THE JANUARY CEASE-FIRE

Having been disappointed regularly by the failure of efforts to stop the seemingly intractable Lebanese conflict throughout the fall, Moscow reacted cautiously to indications at the end of January 1976, that Syrian mediation was at last paying off. Its relief at the announcement by President Frangieh that a new cease-fire and "an all-embracing political settlement" had been reached was clear, however.

In Moscow's view there was now ample reason to end the conflict at the earliest possible time. The military situation in January seemed to be taking an increasingly disturbing turn. The Lebanese army was becoming more deeply involved in the fighting, and the danger of greater PLO military involvement was clearly mounting.[10] At the same time, leftist-Muslim successes in the fighting and their growing military advantage provided a sound military base from which to pursue negotiations. The Soviet Union also had every reason to be pleased with most aspects of the agreement which was to serve as the basis for negotiating a political compromise.

So far as Lebanon itself was concerned, the negotiating framework met the terms which the USSR had promoted as a reasonable basis for ending the conflict. Lebanon's territorial integrity was to be preserved, and a greater share of political power would fall to the elements in the country closest to the USSR. More importantly, the accord seemed to meet Soviet concerns about the Palestinians. The PLO's position in Lebanon was reaffirmed under the terms of the 1969 Cairo Agreement, and the signs of Syrian-PLO cooperation in negotiating the agreement in January were encouraging as a harbinger of strengthened ties between the two.

Like so many developments affecting Soviet interests throughout the civil war, however, the accord had its ominous side. Moscow had consistently encouraged both the PLO and Syria to avoid military involvement in the Lebanese conflict for the reasons noted earlier. The agreement worked out by Syria, however, provided instead for a substantial increase in the military role of both. Syrian-controlled PLA forces, which entered Lebanon in late January, had responsibilities for patrolling segments of the cease-fire lines, and PLO units were to be similarly employed in addition to maintaining peace in the Palestinian camps. A joint Syrian-PLO-Lebanese military command was to coordinate and control the military elements of the three sides. If Moscow had misgivings about this side of the accords, it kept silent about them and for the most part ignored the implications of the new development.[11] Nevertheless, it was the new Syrian military role and its expansion during the next six months that were to be most troublesome for the USSR in its attempt to shape an approach to Lebanon.

FOCUS ON SYRIA

In the winter and early spring of 1976, the Soviets again found themselves pulled in different directions. Moscow had to cope, on the one hand, with developments in Lebanon and in the area which deepened its desire to maintain the closest relations with Assad. On the other hand, Syrian behavior in Lebanon soon created serious rifts between Damascus and the Palestinians, and in Assad's relations with the Lebanese Left which increasingly threatened Soviet interests and began to cause Soviet doubts about Syrian intentions.

The USSR's favorable view of the January cease-fire and the prospect of a political compromise in Lebanon under Syrian auspices led Moscow to give the fullest backing to Assad's role there. Throughout the late winter the Soviets made their support clear through sustained public backing for Damascus's attempts to control the fighting and Assad's effort to prod the feuding factions toward a political agreement. In March and April, however, events began to complicate Moscow's ability to define its interests with such precision or arrive at a policy which was consistent.

Certain developments impelled the USSR toward even greater support for Assad and Syria. Soviet influence in Egypt, already seriously eroded by Moscow's criticism of Sinai II and its alignment with Sadat's critics, took a further nosedive in mid-March when President Sadat announced abrogation of the 1971 Soviet-Egyptian Treaty of Friendship and Cooperation in retaliation for Soviet refusal to provide military equipment and ease demands for repayment of Egypt's debt to the USSR.[12] Shortly thereafter, Soviet interests suffered another blow when Sadat made a second announcement that Soviet naval access to Egyptian ports would be terminated.[13] Sadat's action not only diminished Soviet influence in the Arab world but also sharply increased Moscow's stake in future close ties with Syria, its last remaining entree among the confrontation states in the Arab-Israeli conflict.[14] At the same time, however, the worsening Lebanese situation and Syria's ineffective efforts to control it simultaneously began to generate concern in Moscow about Assad's intentions and to suggest that too close association with Syria in that context could become costly in terms of other Soviet interests.

The situation in Lebanon was, in fact, growing worse. The Lebanese army began to break up along confessional lines in March, and the addition of its Muslim elements to the ranks of the Muslim-leftist forces emboldened Jumblatt and his supporters both on the battlefield and in the political arena. Punishing offensives against Christian positions were gradually making it clear that the military balance was shifting heavily in favor of the Muslim-leftist side. The attempted coup against President Frangieh, meanwhile, led to greater polarization in the political environment as the left now made Frangieh's removal a condition for further cooperation in political bargaining. Moscow expressed mixed feelings about these developments. It seemed to welcome the increasing security the left's new military advantage provided for its ability to protect leftist-Muslim interests. Even so, as the Soviet media also made clear, the USSR was concerned that full-scale civil war would erupt. Moscow gave wide publicity to affirmations by leftist leaders of their continuing support for a political solution to the crisis as a signal of Soviet hopes that war could be avoided.[15]

Whatever Moscow's worries about the Lebanese situation, it was almost certainly Syrian intentions that troubled the Kremlin most. Growing leftist-Muslim military power and its increasingly effective employment against the Christians had become a source of major worry to Assad. In an effort to limit the growth in leftist military strength he suspended military shipments to the Palestinians in late March in hopes of cutting the flow of arms to the Lebanese left. The only significant result of this step, however, was a rise in Syrian-Palestinian tensions and a further downturn in Syria's relations with Jumblatt. Militarily the move had little impact because the breakup of the Lebanese army offset its effect by putting additional equipment and personnel at the disposal of the Muslim side. Unwilling to accept an outcome that could place Lebanon in control of political forces closely linked with Syria's rivals in the Arab world, particularly Iraq, Assad finally moved Syrian regular forces into eastern Lebanon in an effort to stem the tide.[16]

The appearance of Syrian regulars in Lebanon marked a turning point in the USSR's attitude toward the Lebanese conflict in at least two respects. Syrian military involvement in the crisis henceforth became the focal point in shaping Syrian-Soviet relations, and Moscow now found Syrian-PLO relations at the center of its concern over Lebanon. Moscow had made clear its opposition to the employment of outside military forces in Lebanon, including Syrian forces, from the beginning of the conflict. It had accepted the increase in Palestinian and Syrian (via its Palestinian surrogates) military involvement in the crisis in January mainly because it could do little to prevent it but also because Moscow saw the development as the only hope for bringing an end to the fighting and securing a political outcome favorable to Soviet interests. Moscow had probably not altered its negative view of deeper involvement by outsiders, however, and the worsening of the crisis in the early spring apparently deepened Soviet misgivings about more outside involvement. Thus on the eve of Assad's April decision to send Syrian forces into Lebanon, the Soviets strongly reiterated their opposition to the introduction of outside military forces into Lebanon by reaffirming Soviet support for the "legitimate aspiration of the Lebanese people to be the masters of their own destiny."[17]

Although Moscow never articulated the reasons behind its opposition to a greater Syrian role in Lebanon, the Palestinian factor was probably central in its considerations. On the one hand, Moscow could scarcely calculate Israel's reaction to a Syrian move into Lebanon with any certainty. Israel's opposition to any and all Syrian forces in Lebanon was certainly well known. However, the chances were better than ever that an Israeli move would be aimed not at Syrian forces in the first instance, but rather at the Palestinians in southern Lebanon. Assad's action in April, therefore, at least in Moscow's eyes probably ran an unacceptable risk of setting in motion events that could lead to a significant setback for PLO political and military prestige if not the destruction of Palestinian military power.

Even if this danger were averted, however, Syrian actions gave Moscow ample cause to worry. The Palestinians were certain to see an increase in Syria's military presence in Lebanon as threatening, and at minimum Moscow probably calculated that a rise in friction between Damascus and the PLO would follow the introduction of Syrian troops. The Soviets must also have shared Palestinian doubts about Syrian intentions toward the Palestinians and there were ample grounds for having lingering suspicions that Assad coveted greater influence over the PLO. Moscow for its part, saw its own role as patron to the Palestinian cause as one of its strongest remaining sources of influence over events in the Middle East and certainly had no wish to see Arafat and his organization fall under the domination of Syria.

In the event, of course, Soviet misgivings about the dangers for Soviet interests in a direct Syrian military role in Lebanon proved to be well founded. Assad's stationing of forces in eastern Lebanon produced an immediate outcry from the leftist-Muslim factions and a demand from that quarter for their removal. The resulting downturn in Assad's relations with the Lebanese Left, meanwhile, was further exacerbated during the election campaign to select President Frangieh's successor. Jumblatt and his followers supported Raymond Edde against Elias Sarkis, who had Syrian and rightist backing, and the bitter election campaign combined with continued leftist-Muslim military operations created a seemingly irreparable breech between Syria and the Muslim-leftist coalition. Concurrently, the antagonism between Assad and the left helped persuade the majority of the USSR's "progressive" Arab clients to side with the Jumblatt forces. The PLO, already disturbed at the presence of Syrian regulars in Lebanon, moved toward greater involvement in the military struggle as allies of the left. Tensions between Assad and Arafat were mounting as a result. Meanwhile, Iraq, Libya, and Algeria, partly because of developments in Lebanon and partly for other considerations, were increasingly throwing their weight behind the Muslim-leftist-Palestinian cause, thereby isolating Syria and the USSR increasingly from the "progressive" Arab community.

The Kosygin Visit

The Soviet Union was clearly troubled at the currents flowing in the Arab world during the late spring of 1976. The seriousness with which Moscow viewed the turn of events in Lebanon and the fallout from them was reflected in the USSR's decision to send Prime Minister Alexei Kosygin to Iraq and Syria at the end of May.[18] On the eve of the visit the picture in the Middle East generally and in Lebanon, from Moscow's perspective, did indeed seem bleak. Soviet efforts to refocus Arab attention on the Arab-Israeli conflict and to revive Geneva negotiations had been all but ignored.[19] In any case they had certainly failed to alter the Arabs' overwhelming preoccupation with Lebanon. Moreover, the crisis had seriously undermined Moscow's ability to exploit Arab opposition to Sinai II for its own ends. The "progressive" northern front, far from being united around the USSR, was in a shambles, and tensions among Moscow's erstwhile allies had reached alarming proportions.

The Syrian break with Jumblatt and his Lebanese supporters was nearly complete. More disturbingly, Syrian-PLO differences were growing and tensions were rising. The endemic Syrian-Iraqi feud, fed partly by Lebanese developments and partly by a particularly sharp dispute over distribution of water resources, had reached disturbing levels with threatened or actual military movements reported on both sides. Syria's military involvement in Lebanon, meanwhile, had neither quelled the violence nor limited its extent, and Moscow was almost surely beginning to worry again about Assad's next steps.

There were, on the other hand, some elements in the regional situation which the USSR certainly welcomed. Despite the rancor among the members of the USSR's contentious Arab family, none had yet left home. Assad had ultimately turned down Saudi offers to mediate between Syria and Egypt at the end of May, and the proposed summit in Riyadh had not taken place. Nor had U.S. involvement during the spring negotiations to reach a compromise regarding election of a new president in Lebanon given Moscow reason to believe that Assad had abandoned his opposition to Western involvement in the crisis. Sadat's apparent attempt to improve relations with the PLO had also produced no significant change in that relationship. Meanwhile, Libya, despite repeated failures, continued to pursue efforts to mediate Syrian-Iraqi differences and to relieve tensions between Syria and the Palestinians. If the purpose of the Kosygin visit was to buttress these more positive trends and to assist in reducing tensions among Moscow's "progressive" Arab allies by undertaking a direct role in the effort, the results of his mission were bitterly disappointing. Assad's order to launch an offensive into the heart of Lebanon coincided with the Soviet premier's arrival in Damascus, and his action certainly cast a cloud over the talks that followed. Furthermore, Assad had almost certainly timed the move deliberately in order to create the impression of Soviet concurrence in his action. The Soviets must have been embarrassed by the event, particularly in view of Kosygin's assurances to the Iraqis only the day before that the USSR continued to oppose outside intervention in Lebanon and to support the Lebanese right to determine their own fate.[20] Whether Kosygin seriously tried to reverse Assad's decision is unknown. Nor was it clear that Moscow had yet decided to seek a reversal of Syria's move. In any event, at the conclusion of Kosygin's visit to Damascus the question of Soviet reaction to what amounted to direct Syrian defiance of Soviet policy remained in doubt.[21]

A Period of Waiting

The developments which followed Syria's military offensive and the outbreak of Syrian-Palestinian hostilities prompted a major turnabout in Soviet policy toward the Lebanese crisis. Within a week of Kosygin's return to Moscow, the USSR began to distance itself from Syria's military action and to establish a position midway between Assad and the Palestinians. The Soviets moved gradually and cautiously reflecting their uncertainty throughout June about where events were going. An authoritative TASS statement on June 9 clearly expressed Soviet displeasure with the outbreak of fighting between Syrian and Palestinian forces. It portrayed Syria's military move as counterproductive and expressed regret that the Palestinians were squandering their resources on the "sanguinary fratricidal war."[22] For the remainder of June, the Soviets kept their options open. There was some increase in public criticism of

Syrian actions in the Soviet media accompanied by a few gestures to the Palestinians.[23] However, the public record suggested that Moscow was intent on avoiding serious damage to relations with Assad in hopes peace would be achieved or Assad would see the error of his ways.

By early July, however, Moscow had increasing reason to wonder about Syrian intentions and to be concerned about the trend of events in Lebanon. Moscow's call for a cease-fire together with Arab efforts to mediate the Syrian-PLO conflict, most notably that by Prime Minister Abdel Salem Jalloud of Libya, had brought no lessening in the level of conflict. Furthermore, by the end of June the introduction of Syrian forces had effectively reversed the military balance in Lebanon, and Christian forces had taken the offensive. Assad, meanwhile, had reversed himself regarding contact with Egypt and had sent his foreign minister to the June 24 meeting in Riyadh, a development which almost certainly generated misgivings in the Kremlin. Moscow, therefore, invited Syrian Foreign Minister Abdel Halim Khaddam to Moscow, presumably intent on setting forth Soviet views and clarifying Syrian intentions. If the Soviet leaders hoped that the Khaddam visit would permit a meeting of minds with Assad on Lebanon, they were clearly disappointed. Indeed, the evidence suggests that the talks went badly and may have worsened the growing strain between Moscow and Damascus.

From the Khaddam visit on through the remainder of the summer, Soviet policy took on a fairly consistent, almost monotonous character. Moscow seemed to be all but resigned to a place on the sidelines, and its policy remained almost totally reactive. Policy pronouncements issued with varying degrees of authority reiterated the USSR's desire for a cease-fire but for the most part expressed skepticism that any end to the fighting would occur until some decisive turn in events altered the Lebanese picture significantly. From Moscow's perspective the only really hopeful sign during the summer seemed to emerge from the July 29 agreement worked out by Syrian Foreign Minister Khaddam and PLO Political Department Chief Fouad Kaddumi on steps to end the Lebanon crisis. There were reports that Moscow had taken a direct hand in shaping the agreement,[24] and it was certainly welcomed by the Soviet media despite the now almost routine doubts that it would succeed.

Soviet propaganda took on an increasingly pro-Palestinian bias, and criticism of Syria's military role in Lebanon grew more pointed. However, there seemed to be carefully calibrated limits on how far the USSR was willing to move in the direction of either side. In general, for example, Soviet media avoided taking positions on conditions for Syrian-PLO reconciliation and gave no publicity to the repeated demands from the Palestinians that the USSR suspend military and economic aid to Syria or that the USSR itself become more active in Lebanon. Criticism of Syria was mainly confined to the Lebanese context and Damascus' military role in Lebanon and to charges that Syrian actions were aiding "imperialism" and Israel.[25] On the Palestinian side, meanwhile, Moscow provided a continual stream of assurances of support for the PLO, Arafat, and the "national patriotic forces" in Lebanon.

Aside from rhetoric, however, there was little evidence that the USSR took more decisive steps to put teeth behind its efforts to influence events during the summer, although for the first time in several years there was no Soviet-Syrian arms agreement in 1976. At the same time there were repeated reports from Christian sources that the USSR was providing military aid directly to the PLO-leftist military, though these were not confirmed, and claims of aircraft deliveries were never borne out by their appearance over the battlefield.[26] Arms of Soviet origin did flow to the PLO-leftist forces through Libya, Iraq, and Egypt, and there was never indication that the USSR objected to the transfers.

SARKIS' INAUGURATION TO THE RIYADH SUMMIT

Moscow's last effort to exert some influence over the Lebanese War coincided with the round of diplomatic activity surrounding the inauguration of Elias Sarkis in September. The Soviets early in the month appeared to believe that the events in Lebanon had reached a turning point; that Sarkis's assumption of the presidency held the possibility of moving forward with negotiations to end the fighting; and that Syria's military power had given Assad an irreversible advantage over his opponents. In this context Moscow significantly modified its public position on the Lebanese crisis by reiterating condemnation of Syria's military intervention as a mistake; but indicating acceptance of the fact that a Syrian-PLO settlement might leave Syrian forces in Lebanon; and condemning for the first time "die-hard extremists and rejectionists among the Left" who refused negotiations with Syria on any terms.[27] The new Soviet public position was then followed by a round of diplomatic activity in Damascus, Beirut, and Moscow evidently in support of efforts to bring about an end to the Syrian-PLO military conflict and to patch together a compromise.[28] In the event the USSR's hopes for a compromise under its own influence were dashed by a new and punishing Syrian-rightist offensive against

Palestinian and leftist positions in early October which ended Moscow's diplomatic effort and its last opportunity to mediate the conflict.[29]

The Riyadh Summit

The USSR's inability to bring an end to the fighting between its clients was certainly bitterly disappointing, but its failure was made doubly frustrating when Saudi Arabia shortly afterward became the catalyst for agreement to stop the war. The Riyadh summit set back Soviet interests in the Arab world in at least two respects. In the Lebanese context the successful Saudi mediation spelled defeat for the one remaining Soviet objective that had not already been totally thwarted or seriously undermined by the course of the civil war, the exclusion of its Western and Arab adversaries from an influential political role in resolving the crisis. Moscow regularly criticized Western or conservative Arab mediation efforts as plots designed to divide the "anti-imperialist" Arabs, those sympathetic to the USSR, and to undermine their power in the area. At the same time Moscow did what it could to bring about a settlement either under auspices friendly to the USSR or, following the rift between Syria and the PLO, through its own efforts. Whatever relief the USSR felt at having the fighting ended was, therefore, tempered by its failure to have any real influence over the achievement of a truce.

If the way in which the cease-fire was achieved was disappointing, the outcome of the Riyadh meeting also had disquieting implications for the future of Soviet influence in the Arab world, particularly in Syria. The summit significantly enhanced Assad's position and authority. Syria's isolation in the Arab world was ended without a significant reduction of its dominance in Lebanon. From the Soviet perspective the result was a substantial decline in the USSR's demonstrably limited leverage over Damascus and a corresponding increase in Assad's freedom of maneuver in dealing with his superpower patron.

In regard to Lebanon, the Riyadh agreements, if anything, increased the USSR's dependence on Syria. The transitory congruence of interest between the USSR and Egypt during the fighting between Syria and the PLO had brought no real improvement in Soviet-Egyptian relations or increase in Soviet influence with Cairo. PLO military setbacks during the war, meanwhile, had converted that pillar of Soviet support in the Arab world into a weak reed. The Iraqi and Libyan refusal to accept the Riyadh agreement further set back Soviet hopes for "progressive" Arab unity by adding disagreement over Lebanon to the existing differences over approaches to the Arab-Israeli conflict which already divided Moscow's Arab friends. In Lebanon itself, meanwhile, whatever hopes the USSR may have entertained regarding leftist ascendancy following the war seemed no closer to realization, and Syria's new authority over the future of that state certainly cast doubts on future Soviet ability to exercise influence over Lebanon's future political orientation.

POSTSCRIPT

The contradictory and conflicting interests which largely immobilized Soviet efforts to cope effectively with the Lebanese civil war have been little affected by the significant changes in the Middle East since 1976. President Sadat's visit to Jerusalem and Egyptian-Israeli efforts to find the basis for a peace settlement, like the earlier Sinai II agreement, seem only to have intensified the USSR's dependence on and stake in maintaining close ties with its remaining "progressive" allies and in nurturing their unity. At the same time the unsolved Lebanese conflict retains serious potential for disrupting that unity as well as Soviet relations with the parties involved. If evidence was needed that the Soviet dilemma over Lebanon has yet to be resolved, it was graphically provided during the crisis in southern Lebanon in March 1978. Faced with sharply divided opinion in the Arab world about the UN Security Council resolution calling for Israeli withdrawal from Lebanese territory and the creation of a UN force to assist in returning the area to Lebanese control, Moscow abstained.

THE UNITED STATES

Robert W. Stookey

THE AMERICAN INTEREST

THE AMERICAN concern with Lebanon began with the dispatch of two
Protestant missionaries to Beirut in the second decade of the nineteenth
century and developed into a complex network of cultural, economic
and political relations. The early New England proselytizing impulse
evolved into secular education enterprise, leading to the founding of the
Syrian Protestant College, later the American University of Beirut, with
its associated medical school and hospital. By the 1950s the American
government acknowledged the university as a national asset by lending it
financial support.

Following the intercommunal strife of the 1860s, Lebanese began to
immigrate to the United States in significant numbers. The Lebanese-
American community is now several hundred thousand strong, and
while it is less cohesive and vocal than some other ethnic groups in the
United States, it contributes to a sympathetic public concern with Lebanese affairs.

In the 1940s Lebanon was integrated into the international oil industry with the construction of terminals at the ports of Tripoli and Sidon,
respectively, for the Iraq Petroleum Company and Arabian-American
Oil Company pipelines. Conveniently situated and offering a uniquely
hospitable environment for business enterprise, Beirut became the Middle Eastern headquarters for dozens of American international financial
and commercial firms. Lebanon became a financial and political crossroads for the region itself and a natural center for American information-

The author gratefully acknowledges his debt to the Honorable L. Dean Brown, President of the Middle East Institute, the Honorable Talcott W. Seelye, Deputy Assistant Secretary of State, and several other officers of the Department of State who contributed
generously of their expert knowledge for the preparation of this article.

gathering activities both official and private, as well as for the regional operations of specialized agencies and philanthropic institutions.

Lebanon entered upon its status as an independent state under representative institutions that gave the major sectors of the country's public an effective voice in national affairs and the opportunity to choose new leadership in regularly held elections. Gradually, it became clear that these processes masked feudal arrangements that tended to preserve and exacerbate social and economic inequities. Meanwhile, Lebanon commended itself to the United States as a meritorious exception to the authoritarianism prevalent elsewhere in the Middle East. As Lebanese governments furthermore adhered rather consistently to moderate, non-disputive external policies, the country appeared to deserve a solicitous American concern not otherwise justified by its small area and population, or its minor importance as an economic or military power.

THE 1958 AMERICAN INTERVENTION

In the summer of 1958, two decades before civil war erupted, the United States landed 15,000 Marines in Lebanon, preserved the established political and social order, and helped restore stability to that country. The 1958 intervention is relevant to this inquiry because one learns from it the extent to which American policy, attitudes, intentions, and capabilities had changed by 1975-77.

In March 1957, the U.S. Congress had authorized the president to resort to military intervention, if necessary, to protect nations in the Middle East from international Communism. With large sections of his country and capital in open rebellion, and convinced that the United Arab Republic sought to overthrow his government, Lebanese President Camille Chamoun invoked the Eisenhower Doctrine, as the Congressional resolution was known, and appealed urgently to the United States for help. Already worried by the deteriorating situation in Lebanon, the United States landed the Marines around Beirut on July 15, 1958, within a day of the overthrow of the Hashemite monarchy and Nuri al-Said in Iraq.

It would be unenlightening to dismiss the American action as simply a naive and heavy-handed over-reaction. The United States had adopted toward Abdul Nasser's 1952 revolution a cautiously sympathetic attitude. This posture was severely strained by the Egyptian-Soviet arms deal of 1955 but not so far as to deter the United States from opposing the 1956 tripartite attack against Egypt. The latter, nevertheless, continued to cultivate ever closer relations with the USSR and to mount effective campaigns against the Baghdad Pact and other assets America and its allies considered important to their security. The American government relied on the Eisenhower Doctrine to justify the intervention in Lebanon, but this suggests only the anti-Soviet thread in American policy, an emphasis that in any case surely was required in order to obtain popular and congressional support for the use of force. In addition to casting the Lebanese affair into the mold of its strategic competition with the USSR, the American government sought several other important objectives. With Syria joined in union with Egypt and with a revolutionary government in Iraq headed no one knew where, the administration was determined to keep at least Lebanon and Jordan outside Nasser's grasp, to deflate Soviet power in Arab eyes, by revealing the limits of Soviet ability to come to their aid, and to bring at least temporary stability to the eastern Mediterranean.

Although by no means fully informed on the domestic origins of the Lebanese insurgency, which had nothing to do with the cold war or Communism, Eisenhower was well aware that Chamoun had aspired to succeed himself as president, in circumvention of the Lebanese Constitution, and that his intentions in this respect remained ambiguous. Eisenhower was determined that American forces should not be used to gratify this ambition.[1] The personal intervention of U.S. Ambassador Robert Mc-Clintock helped to forestall forceful opposition to the American landings by the Lebanese army, with attendant bloodshed and probable further aggravation of the local situation. However, because he was accredited to Chamoun and his government, he was in no position to consult with the leaders of rebellious Lebanese factions in search of a compromise acceptable to all. On the other hand, Eisenhower's special representative, Robert Murphy, was under no such restrictions. His assessment of the situation, based on discussions with both loyal and dissident elements, led him to conclude that the UAR intervention was incidental to a basically domestic crisis of which an immediate solution lay in a return to the traditional Lebanese neutrality in international and inter-Arab affairs, restoration of the historical allocation of authority within the government, and respect for constitutional procedures in the choice of Chamoun's successor. He lent his moral weight, reinforced by the American military presence, to an accomodation along these lines advocated by the Lebanese "Third Force." The result—the accession of Fuad Shehab as president and the appointment of Rashid Karameh as prime minister—was criticized in some American business quarters as a reward of lawlessness and had an ironical aspect in that it coincided with a solution long advocated by President Nasser. The intervention and the political settlement restored the established institutions and practices of Lebanon's religious and communal politics. For a decade Lebanon was to know prosperity and relative tranquility. Even so, many of the grievances of the Muslim community went unsatisfied; they had fuelled the rebellion against Chamoun and would surface again in the 1970s in circumstances that would be much less favorable to easy settlement.

CHANGE IN THE LEBANESE EXTERNAL ENVIRONMENT

The Lebanese solution to the problem of authority in a plural society, as embodied in the National Pact, placed narrow restrictions on governmental powers without providing deterrents against appeal for foreign support by one or another of the constituent communities. The erosion after 1958 of the pact's viability as a framework for domestic politics is traced elsewhere in this volume. The regional environment was also changing in ways that made outside interference in Lebanon more and more likely. The American role in this process was indirect and unintentional, but not without significance.

After the 1967 War, Syria and Egypt kept Palestinian activities within their borders under tight control in order to avoid Israeli reprisals. It was Lebanese and Jordanian territory that served as bases for Palestinian incursions into Israel, and those two nations bore the brunt of Israeli retaliation. In 1969 the guerrillas' defiance of Lebanese government efforts to restrain their operations contributed to an outbreak of intercommunal strife between Lebanese Muslims and Maronites. Although domestic calm was restored by the traditional process of negotiation among religious leaders and political bosses, Lebanon felt obliged to accept the Cairo Accords, arrangements formulated under Arab League auspices that allowed the Palestine Liberation Organization (PLO) full freedom of action in a sector of southeastern Lebanon adjoining Israel and Syria.[2]

The Cairo Accords marked a stage in the acceptance by the Arab governments of the PLO as an entity possessing attributes of sovereignty, even if devoid of territory peculiarly its own. No Arab support for King Hussein, thus, was forthcoming in 1970, when Palestinian groups in Jordan formed what amounted to a rival government implicitly aimed at overthrowing the Hashemite monarchy. The United States had good reason to believe that the replacement of Hussein's regime by a militant one under Palestinian leadership would provoke an Israeli invasion of the East Bank and touch off a new round of war. American help was therefore promptly extended when Hussein resolved to assert his authority, in defiance of Arab opinion. His campaign succeeded in repulsing a Syrian invasion in support of the insurgents and in eliminating Palestinian military formations from Jordan. An ancillary consequence of the operation was a marked increase in the number of Palestinian militants in Lebanon, and in their weight as a factor in domestic Lebanese politics.

Having no territorial dispute with Israel, Lebanon was not considered a significant factor in the American effort to achieve peace between Israel and the Arab states after the October 1973 War. Secretary of State Kissinger envisaged the Egyptian and Syrian disengagement agreements with Israel as merely the first in a succession of steps leading to an eventual overall settlement. It was vital, in his judgment, that the process be kept in motion. A prolonged stalemate carried the risk of another Middle East war that could bring a conflict with the Soviet Union and the oil-rich Arab states and could endanger both the security and economic well-being of all the industrial nations, including the United States.[3]

The second Sinai agreement of September 1975 broke a deadlock already of a year and a half duration. However, it set Egypt, which emerged as the most accommodating of the Arab parties to the dispute, at odds with most other Arab states, especially with Syria, eclipsed Egyptian influence in Arab councils, and compromised the prospect of other steps toward peace. By this time the Lebanese civil war had been in progress for six months. Given the rivalry between Egypt and Syria for influence in Lebanon, it was to be expected that the two countries would move from mutual vituperation to active support of opposing factions in the struggle, thus internationalizing the crisis and reducing the incentive for the Lebanese to restore a modus vivendi among themselves.

AMERICAN AIMS AND CAPABILITIES

Official attitudes and actions by the United States with respect to the civil war developed in three general phases. From the outbreak of disturbances until late 1975 it was assumed that the crisis was, and would remain, essentially a domestic one; established American policies, conducted at intermediate official levels, were permitted to operate routinely. When it became clear that outside intervention was probable and of such a nature as to compromise American efforts toward a regional peace, the secretary of state and, at times, the president personally attempted to assist in achieving a Lebanese settlement. Although this enterprise at first appeared promising, it was frustrated by the resumption of hostilities in May 1976. The United States then acknowledged its own inability to bring an end to the conflict and concentrated its actions upon encouraging the initiatives of Arab mediators toward that end.

One group of American attitudes remained constant throughout the war. With respect, first, to the Lebanese conditions which had brought on the war, the analysts who informed American decision-makers were well aware that the distribution of political powers among the various sects, as established by the 1943 National Pact, no longer reflected accurately their relative size. They recognized the many Lebanese Muslims possessed legitimate political and economic grievances which could not be satisfied within the established Lebanese political order. It appeared axiomatic to them that change of some sort was requisite to the establishment in Lebanon of a government broadly accepted as just and legitimate by Muslims and Christians alike, possessing sufficient strength to regulate the actions of the Palestinian Arabs present in the country, and self-confident enough to adhere to Lebanon's traditional neutral stance on regional and international affairs. The United States had no preconceived notion as to whether change ought to take place within the existing confessional system or assume the form of a shift to a more secular polity. No religious or social element was singled out as an American client or as the repository of United States interests, and no direct material support, open or covert, was given to any of the Lebanese factions.

American officials were also sensitive, from the outset of the disturbances, to the possibility of foreign involvement. Because outside intervention implied a threat to regional peace, the United States tried consistently to dissuade other countries from military action in Lebanon. American policy makers considered that the partition of Lebanon along sectarian lines, as advocated by some Maronite leaders, would introduce a new disruptive factor in the Middle East, and the United States did not deviate from support for the preservation of Lebanon's territorial unity.

Out of concern for the human suffering attendant on the war, the United States encouraged the continued operation of the American University hospital, under exceedingly trying conditions, and sent substantial quantities of medical supplies and equipment for distribution wherever they could be effectively used without discrimination among the warring factions. A final constant preoccupation was the safety of American citizens, a traditional subject of concern to the American public, which holds the government strictly to account for the welfare of United States nationals abroad.

The United States had some potential assets on which to draw in pursuing its aims. It had a major naval force in the region, the Sixth Fleet, which was in fact utilized in evacuating American citizens. Use of military power to stop the fighting or to influence the outcome of the struggle was, however, not a feasible option for the American leadership. With the Vietnam experience still of recent memory, the idea of committing American soldiers to new adventures abroad was highly unpalatable to the public; leaders of Congress repeatedly and solemnly warned the administration against such an involvement in Lebanon or elsewhere. The secretary of state confessed frankly in March 1976, that there was nothing the United States could do "physically" in Lebanon, implying that it would have to rely on moral suasion.[4]

The United States was fortunately in a better position to impress its views on the key Arab states than before the 1973 War, when it had only limited access to Egyptian officials, no formal contact with Syria, and significant policy differences with the government of Saudi Arabia. When the Lebanese crisis arose, by contrast, America and Saudi Arabia were embarked on a broad program of mutual cooperation and Egypt was striving anxiously to develop its ties with America and the West. While Syrian and American views diverged on many issues, the emphasis of the moderate Ba'athists then in power in Syria on economic development and liberalization created some Syrian-American community of interest in regional stability, and a constructive dialog was in progress. These developments also touched United States relations with Israel. In addition, the 1975 "reappraisal" of American Middle East policy and the considerable pressure on Israel used to achieve the second Sinai agreement noticeably diminished Israel's disposition to heed American counsel.

In contrast to 1958 when the United States was at odds with Egypt, a flow of reliable information resulted from improved relations with Egypt, Syria, and Saudi Arabia. Information from these states and from other sources on the attitude and intentions of the numerous Lebanese and Palestinian factions reached American policy-makers undiluted, without being filtered through successive layers of bureaucracy. When Syrian intervention became a probability, the Lebanese civil war qualified, in Secretary of State Kissinger's view, as a major issue deserving his personal handling. He assigned to working-level officers in the State Department's Bureau of Intelligence and Research the task of preparing a comprehensive daily report on the situation, distribution of which was confined strictly to himself and a handful of his aides on Middle Eastern affairs.[5] Given Kissinger's extraordinary ability to assimilate masses of detailed information, he rapidly became familiar with the complexities of the Lebanese scene.

While the United States was well informed on the significant aspects of the Lebanese situation, there were definite limits to its ability to influence the course of events. Among these was an accidental lack of continuity in the direction of the American diplomatic mission in Lebanon. The accredited ambassador, G. McMurtrie Godley, left the country early in 1976 following a surgical operation, and in several months passed before it became clear that he would not be able to resume his duties. His successor, Francis E. Meloy, Jr., was not appointed until April 21. He had been in Lebanon scarcely a month and had not yet presented his credentials to President Frangieh, when tragically he was waylaid and murdered, on June 16. A permanent successor was named only well after the formal accession of President Sarkis and the organization of a new Lebanese government. On two occasions special envoys were designated to carry out specific diplomatic assignments: the Brown mediation effort of April–May 1976, and the Seelye mission in June and July.

Although the U.S. had no ambassador in Lebanon during these critical months, the continuous presence of an able ambassador would not necessarily have enhanced the American ability to influence the situation, given the progressive disintegration of governmental authority in Lebanon and the increasing difficulty of movement to and from the embassy chancery. As early as March 1976, President Frangieh found the presidential palace at Baabda untenable and moved to the vicinity of Jounieh, well to the north of Beirut. During the Brown mission it was feasible for the envoy to travel to outlying areas by helicopter, although to reach the airport it was necessary to pass various roadblocks, some manned by rag-tag, undisciplined youngsters.[6] By the first week in June the Beirut airport was shut down, and the embassy could maintain regular contact only with certain leftist leaders, including Kamal Jumblatt, Prime Minister Karameh, whose authority was virtually at an end, and a few old-line politicians such as Saeb Salem and Raymond Edde, who possessed no armed forces and consequently limited influence. After careful consideration the United States decided not to follow the British example of stationing an embassy officer at Jounieh. Although the expedient would have afforded continuous access to the Lebanese chief of state and other key Maronite leaders, it would at the same time have lent plausibility to accusations, repeatedly voiced by the Palestinians and echoed by the Syrians and even some Lebanese Christians, that the United States was collaborating with Israel and the more intransigent Maronites to partition Lebanon.

By mid-summer the American embassy was in the anomalous situation of operating in a district of Beirut where security, communications and public services were largely in the hands of authorities with whom the mission was forbidden to engage in formal discussion or otherwise recognize. The stricture stemmed from the "secret" understandings between Israel and the United States concluded in the context of the second Sinai agreement,[7] by which the United States agreed to hold no discussions of any sort with the Palestine Liberation Organization so long as it refused to acknowledge the Israeli state's right to exist. Whatever its propriety in the broader context, it deprived American diplomacy of any ability to influence one major factor in the Lebanese equation. With a constituency of 400,000,[8] the PLO could not be ignored in any Lebanese settlement in view of the political and material support it commanded from other Arab countries, its military capability, and its vital interest in free use of Lebanese territory. Secretary Kissinger, personally involved in this commitment to Israel, attached much importance to its strict observance, and while practical necessity forced relaxation of the prohibition to the extent of contact between the embassy security officer and Palestinian commandos regarding the safety of American nationals, no exchanges of a political nature occurred.[9]

The domestic political situation in the United States moreover required the responsible officials to move circumspectly with regard to Lebanon. A bitter contest for the 1976 presidential election had begun almost as soon as President Ford assumed office in 1974. The secretary of state, although shorn of the concurrent post of national security advisor, remained a highly controversial figure, not only because of objective disagreement with some of his policies but also because of his implication in certain aspects of Watergate and the secretive style of his diplomacy. Although relying heavily on Kissinger, the president found it tactically advisable to place some distance between himself and the secretary, and to demonstrate publicly that he was in effective, personal charge of the country's foreign affairs.

The requirements of the campaign occasionally resulted in minor discrepancies between statements emanating respectively from the White House and the State Department. Both the president and secretary of state nonetheless sought to avoid any bold or risky initiative that might misfire and increase the administration's vulnerability. Above all, the president and secretary of state sought to safeguard the accomplishments of step-by-step diplomacy and to produce an atmosphere in which further movement might be made toward regional peace. The outbreak of another Arab-Israel war would, it was feared, negate the progress already made, destroy the possibility of further constructive initiatives, perhaps precipitate a new global crisis, and compromise the president's prospects at the polls. This concern, together with the constraints already mentioned, guided American actions with respect to the Lebanese internal war. In the earlier stages the focus was on encouraging arrangements among the various Lebanese communities which would reduce the likelihood of outside involvement. When this failed, and intervention actually occurred from several quarters, the United States endeavored to forestall any miscalculations of such a nature as to broaden the struggle into regional war. Meanwhile, every effort was made to support other powers which were seeking to promote domestic peace in Lebanon and reconciliation among the Arab states implicated there.

THE MARONITES

One legacy of the American intervention of 1958 in Lebanon was the assumption, widely held among Lebanese of all sects, that the United States had a particular affinity and responsibility for the Maronite community. The operation did, in effect, support policies of a Maronite president, and during the occupation the American military engaged in some logistical cooperation with the Phalanges, which were then supporting Chamoun. Nevertheless, sponsorship of any single community in Lebanon was never an element of American policy. As the internal Lebanese situation deteriorated in 1975 the United States sought, by diplomatic means, to encourage all elements of Lebanese society to reach accommodation among themselves. The effort was complicated by the widespread supposition that America, as a great power, was able to manipulate events from behind the scene—indeed, was doing so—and by the absence among the Maronites of a common policy. Opinions among them ranged from support for a separate Christian state, through rigid adherence to the 1943 distribution of powers among the sects, to acceptance of some compromise with Muslim demands.

Suleiman Frangieh's election as president in 1970 was widely interpreted as a warning to the Palestinians that no challenge to Lebanese government authority would be tolerated, a posture to which the United States did not object. President Frangieh, furthermore, had no sympathy for the idea of partitioning the country. On the other hand, he opposed any substantial relinquishment of Christian prerogatives, which the United States considered essential to establish domestic harmony in Lebanon. Ambassador Godley kept a certain distance between himself and Frangieh, while ostentatiously cultivating Rashid Karameh, Raymond Edde, and other politicians who favored gradual political reform.[10] American pressure was made more explicit in November 1975, when Secretary Kissinger addressed a letter to Karameh expressing American support for his efforts to end the violence and institute a process of political accommodation leading to "a new basis of stability with security" for all Lebanese.[11] The message, publicized by the embassy, irked President Frangieh, who was on cool terms with his prime minister, but had no other measurable effect on the situation. The United States, nevertheless, stood by its guns, and as late as June 1976, the State Department specifically urged the Lebanese Christian community to restrain themselves in order that Lebanon's independence and sovereignty might be salvaged.

While disapproving the intransigent political posture of some Lebanese Christian factions, the United States did not attempt to deny them the means of defending themselves and prosecuting the war against their Palestinian and left-wing opponents. In July 1975, the State Department approved a private shipment of small arms reportedly destined for Lebanese Christian elements but rescinded the license after questions were raised in Congress regarding the transaction.[12] No serious attempt was made to obstruct the shipment of weapons to Christian militia from Israel, which emerged as a principal source.[13] As Israel and the Maronites faced common adversaries in the more radical Palestinian and Muslim elements, there was a certain logic in their cooperation. Israel sent substantial quantities of arms through Cyprus to the Lebanese Christians and even across Syrian territory during the time the Syrian government sought to prevent a decisive defeat of the Christians. Many of these weapons were Russian-made, from stocks captured by the Israelis in past wars with the Arabs, and the United States was consequently spared the delicate decision of approving or vetoing the transfer of American-supplied arms.

More disturbing to the United States was the danger that the strife might escalate into regional war as a result of direct Israeli military intervention in support of the Christians. The issue was dramatized on December 2, 1975, when Israel, ostensibly in retaliation for a bombing incident in Jerusalem in mid-November, conducted concerted air raids against Palestinian camps at Nabatiyeh, in southern Lebanon, but also at Nahr al-Bard, Badawi, and adjacent villages in the north near Tripoli, where Lebanese Muslims allied with Palestinian guerrillas were heavily engaged with President Frangieh's militia, the Liberation Army of Zagharta.

Acting under its "secret" understandings with Israel, the United States opposed a UN Security Council resolution condemning the raids.[14] Deeply concerned, however, President Ford sent a message to Israeli Prime Minister Rabin urging consultation in advance of such operations. Israel's response was the public assertion of its intention to retain its freedom of action.[15] Its apparent inability to deter Israel from acts of which the possible consequences were dangerously unpredictable only served to strengthen the opposition of the American government to armed intervention in Lebanon from whatever source.

THE BROWN MISSION

By March 1976, successive mediation attempts by France, the Vatican, the Arab League, and Syria, all encouraged by the United States, had failed to produce lasting results. Syria, whose interests were the most vitally involved in the outcome, had put forth the most persistent effort. The United States consulted closely with the Syrian government on its diplomatic effort, and Secretary Kissinger frequently expressed support of it in public and in private.

The anarchy nonetheless intensified. When King Hussein visited Washington at the end of March, after meeting with his ally, President Assad, he stressed the Syrian conviction that the leftists in Lebanon could be restrained only by armed intervention. Syria, he advised, contemplated sending in its own forces to prevent the emergence of a radical regime which would endanger regional peace and wished to know if the United States would restrain Israel from an excessive reaction to the operation.[16]

It was in these delicate circumstances that a distinguished diplomat experienced in Middle Eastern affairs, L. Dean Brown, was recalled from retirement to undertake an American attempt at mediation. His task was designed to support, rather than to preempt, an ambitious Syrian program for the establishment of a new cease-fire that would permit the Lebanese Parliament to meet; for the amendment of the Lebanese Constitution to authorize President Frangieh to resign in advance of his term's expiration date; and for the election of a new president whose government would introduce the reforms proposed earlier in the year. This framework, in fact, was made specific in an American message to Prime Minister Karameh delivered simultaneously with Ambassador Brown's arrival, endorsing the Syrian initiative as well as expressing American support for the moderate Lebanese factions.

During his five-week mission, Ambassador Brown consulted intensively with the leaders of the various Lebanese communities, holding out the prospect of an American-organized international consortium to assist in Lebanon's reconstruction after the restoration of domestic tranquility. Before his departure, the Parliament had met (on April 10) and adopted the constitutional amendment contemplated in the Syrian plan. After a new round of fighting, the legislators again convened, on May 8, and elected Elias Sarkis to succeed Frangieh as president. The leftist groups offered their cooperation to the president-elect on condition that he keep Syria out of Lebanese internal affairs and protect the Palestinian presence in the country.

These constructive moves were not, of course, solely the achievement of the American envoy's diplomacy; other mediators, both Arab and French, were also in the field. There is, nevertheless, no doubt that Brown's efforts contributed significantly to the result. In particular, he established a productive relationship with Kamal Jumblatt, the senior leader of the leftist coalition who was then at odds with the Syrians; Jumblatt acknowledged publicly that it was Brown's persuasion that led him to order a cease-fire on the eve of the May 8 parliamentary meeting.[17]

These promising results were unfortunately overtaken by the broadening of the Lebanese and Palestinian conflict into an inter-Arab one. President Frangieh, in the event, refused to resign, and Sarkis's inauguration was deferred until September. A cautious build-up of Syrian forces in Lebanon had begun even as Ambassador Brown began his mission. Egypt reacted by mending its relations with the PLO leadership and by sending the Ain Jalout Brigade of the Palestine Liberation Army to Lebanon, in effect aligning Egypt with the rejectionist front. Iraqi and Libyan support for the far-left elements in Lebanon was increased, and the war resumed at an enhanced level of violence.

SYRIAN INTERVENTION

Upon leaving Lebanon, Ambassador Brown openly praised President-elect Sarkis and stated his conviction that Syria had no intention, notwithstanding its armed intervention, of making Lebanon its satellite.[18] He stated his views still more forthrightly in a press interview later in the month, after completing his tour of official duty. The firm United States opposition to the Syrian military action had, he believed, been unwise. It had encouraged Syrian suspicions of American intentions in the Middle East[19] and, by decelerating the Syrian advance, resulted in unnecessary bloodshed. Even so, the Syrian action, in cooperation with Palestinian forces under firm PLO control, had assisted in establishing a neutral zone in Beirut, had provided a measure of security for the hard-pressed Maronites, and had helped to create conditions necessary for a return to constitutional government.[20] These opinions departed from established United States policy, and a State Department telegram of reproof was delivered to Brown at Amman, which he was visiting as a private citizen.

Although the United States did not approve the Syrian intervention, American and Syrian interests converged in Lebanon. Both governments feared the imminent emergence of a radical regime responsive to Iraqi and Libyan attitudes, which might well provoke hostilities with Israel, in which Syria would inevitably become involved. This would have destroyed any early prospect for general peace, an objective shared by America and Syria. The evolution of the civil war demonstrated that the Lebanese and the resident Palestinians, if left to themselves, would pursue the armed conflict until either the conservatives or the leftists suffered a crushing defeat. This would have eliminated the possibility of a viable national reconciliation. The alternative of partition, in the Syrian and the American view, would simply have aggravated regional instability. Both agreed that Syria alone was in a practical position to impose domestic order and territorial unity in Lebanon without dangerously internationalizing the dispute.

The United States, moreover, had reason to be solicitous of the Syrian president's position, for he was a key figure in any progress toward an Arab-Israeli settlement. Assad was deeply committed to the goal of a stable, centrist regime in a territorially intact Lebanon. The collapse of the political system in Lebanon would have disturbing implications for Syria's own, scarcely less plural, society. Failure of Assad's policies in Lebanon might compromise his position at home, while ensuring the rise of a Lebanese regime sympathetic to Syria's Arab adversaries. This rationale was found so compelling that, in spite of repeated authoritative denials, the conviction was nearly universal that the United States had encouraged the invasion, or at least acquiesced to it in advance.[21]

Once the Syrian intervention occurred, American policy shifted to deterring a counter-invasion by Israel, which had not been overly concerned by the entry of Palestinian forces but had publicly threatened re-

THE UNITED STATES   239

taliation if regular Syrian forces were sent into Lebanon. In the American view Syria sought to end the war, to prevent a decisive military victory by any single faction, and to bring about a political balance. American diplomats consulted intensively with both Syrians and Israelis, informing the latter of the American interpretation of the purpose of the successive Syrian military operations and cautioning the Syrians against actions likely to provoke forceful Israeli reaction.

The resulting restraint somewhat impaired the effectiveness of the Syrian peace-keeping effort. As Israel made clear, it would tolerate no Syrian troops south of a "red line" that emerged as the Litani River. The Syrians were unable to prevent occasional incursions by Palestinian guerrillas into Israel (for which Israel, with debatable logic, blamed Syria, as now responsible for order and discipline in Lebanon) and operational coordination between Lebanese Christian militias and Israeli forces.[22] In the highly volatile situation there was a real possibility that, in the absence of timely and reliable information, miscalculation might have tempted Israel or Syria to a rash act which would have touched off hostilities both preferred to avoid. The American communications channel made possible an indispensable flow of information between Syria and Israel.

THE ARAB SOLUTION

At a meeting in Paris on June 22 of Secretary Kissinger, the American ambassadors to Syria, Jordan, Egypt, and Saudi Arabia, and Ambassador Talcott W. Seelye, newly appointed to take temporary charge of the embassy at Beirut, the consensus was that there was no promising initiative the United States could take in the existing circumstances.[23] Furthermore, with Syrian forces moving on Beirut, and the capital's port area occupied by radical Palestinian factions beyond effective PLO control, the security of American residents, many located in Ras Beirut not far west of the port, appeared precarious. The decision was made to organize the evacuation of those Americans who wished to leave. The operation was a delicate one, as the PLO, seeking American pressure on Syria to permit reopening of the Beirut airport, thus restoring the PLO supply line, refused to ensure the safety of a surface convoy to Damascus and threatened to obstruct an evacuation by sea. The threat was not carried through, however, and some 200 Americans, and a larger number of other foreigners, were evacuated by Sixth Fleet vessels on July 26.[24] A calculated risk was taken by keeping the American embassy open with a minimum staff. While the mission could exert no political influence locally, it continued to perform a valuable information function and provided a symbol of American interest in Lebanon and in the cultural and humanitarian activities of the American University and Hospital.

The United States continued to support the efforts of other governments to bring about reconciliation and civic order in Lebanon. A quite circumspect endorsement was given to a French offer, which led nowhere, to provide a peace-keeping force. Clearly, only the Arab countries had it in their power to bring about a solution. For their influence to be made effective, an adequate consensus among them had to be mobilized around a common policy in Lebanon, a difficult diplomatic task in view of the prevailing disharmony. The Arab League had sought to mediate among the Lebanese and Palestinian groups, and its efforts had been publicly encouraged by the United States. The league, however, was so closely identified with Egyptian policy that after conclusion of the second Sinai agreement, and Egypt's resulting political isolation, its effectiveness was impaired.

Of the Arab states Saudi Arabia was in the strongest position to exert constructive influence, since it had a broad clientele in Lebanon itself, and was the principal financial backer of both Syria and Egypt, the principal outside adversaries in the conflict. In the earlier stages of the civil war, the Saudis provided subsidies to a wide range of elements in Lebanon, both Christian and Muslim, extending even to radical (but non-Communist) Palestinian guerrilla groups. In diplomatic exchanges the United States urged Saudi Arabia toward a more selective use of its resources, and the counsel may have had some effect. It appears to have been the prospect of a crushing defeat of the Palestinians in Lebanon, however, that prompted the Saudis to undertake the complex and successful program of diplomacy that produced the October 18 Riyadh Accords which made possible the winding down of the Lebanese conflict.

THE BALANCE SHEET

On the occasion of President Sarkis' inauguration on September 23, the State Department issued a statement summarizing American attitudes and aims in the Lebanese civil war.[25] The press corps at the department apparently dismissed the statement as platitudinous, and no major American newspaper printed the text. It nonetheless provides a useful check-list by which to measure the success of American policies in the struggle.

1. The United States sought, first, the preservation of Lebanese territorial integrity and national unity, fearing that partition would result in nonviable states vulnerable to outside interference and disruptive of stability in the region. In the event, Lebanon has remained nominally unified, in large part because of the presence of peace-keeping forces provided by Arab governments which strongly oppose fragmentation of the country. Separatist sentiment remains alive among some Christian groups and could assert itself if no path is found toward a genuine national reconciliation.

2. The adjustments in the Lebanese political, economic, and social system the United States considered necessary in order to form a "partnership of equals" perceived as just by all Lebanese have not yet been introduced. The reforms proposed in January–February 1976, explicitly endorsed by the United States, presumably represent the most likely form of change. As they preserve the confessional framework, they fail to meet the demands of the political left for a secular structure, while many Christians will not easily accept the reduction of their community's preponderant position.

3. The United States would like to see at the disposition of the Lebanese government a loyal security force able to restore confidence in its authority to maintain domestic order. Following some controversy over the selection of a commanding officer, the Sarkis government began the organizing of a new army, with equipment and technical support provided by the United States. Its first major task was assigned only in September 1977, when units were sent south to end the fighting between Christian and Palestinian guerrillas near the Israeli border. Following a general cease-fire agreement concluded in July 1977, on Syrian initiative with vigorous American diplomatic encouragement, it was contemplated that the new force, then at brigade strength, would be sent to southern Lebanon at the end of September to occupy positions held both by the allied Palestinian and Lebanese Muslim forces and their Israeli-backed Christian opponents. The force commander, however, dared not expose his untried multiconfessional force to the emotional stresses necessarily involved in the mission, whose feasibility in any case soon disappeared with the collapse of the cease-fire and resumption of Israeli incursions into Lebanon. The Lebanese soldiers, both Muslim and Christian, acted in full harmony and acquitted themselves well in clashes with the Syrian

garrison in February 1978. Whether the reorganized army would be paralyzed by conflicting loyalties in a situation of peace-keeping among purely domestic factions remains unclear. The civil war intensified intersectarian animosities, however, and the possibility remains that the new forces will be paralyzed by divided loyalties as in the past.

4. Domestic stability in Lebanon, in the American view, requires that the Palestinians in the country live in peace with their hosts and submit to Lebanese government authority. Weakened by its encounter with the Syrian army and the Christian militias, the Palestinian mainstream as represented by the PLO may abide by the 1969 Cairo Accords, or some negotiated substitute, and respect its obligations so long as it is urged to do so by its key backers among the Arab states. The rejectionist groupings, on the other hand, will likely continue to resist Lebanese authority and collaborate with indigenous revolutionary elements. Until they have a homeland of their own, the Palestinians will remain a complicating factor in Lebanese domestic politics.

5. The State Department's statement, issued at a juncture when intervention by various Arab states was fanning the flames of civil war, pointed out that the governments in the area and the Arab League were in a position to contribute to a political solution of the conflict. This judgment was confirmed by events of the ensuing months, which demonstrated that restraint and cooperation on the part of the Palestinians depended upon unity among the key Arab states. The Riyadh Accords were, of course, the result of Arab initiatives; these were nevertheless actively encouraged by the United States and produced results generally consistent with American objectives. The exclusion of King Hussein from the Riyadh arrangements, on the other hand, constituted a setback for the American aim of confirming the king as the principal spokesman for the Palestinians.

6. The press release emphasized the American humanitarian concern for the suffering and destruction caused by the war. It took credit for the medical programs conducted throughout the conflict and promised American assistance in reconstruction when a settlement was reached. The American University and Hospital survived the war; the former even received an advance of operating funds from the Lebanese government early in 1976 which permitted its virtually uninterrupted operation. In response to the United States invitation, President Sarkis sent an envoy to Washington in December 1976, to discuss ways in which America might assist in reconstruction.[26] Preoccupied with other issues, however, the interim government has been slow in coming to grips with eco-

nomic problems and has not taken full advantage of possible American assistance.

7. The State Department, finally, recorded its conviction that the fighting in Lebanon endangered peace in the Middle East and international stability. By diplomatic action the United States succeeded in preventing a miscalculation that might have precipitated an Israeli invasion of Lebanon and a broader crisis. This, perhaps, was the most notable achievement of American policy during the conflict.

Some American objectives were thus met by United States action or by the initiative of Arab states with American encouragement, while other major aims proved impossible to attain. Some Lebanese politicians, and some American commentators, have attributed the limited accomplishments of American policy to the abandonment of American responsibility, lack of foresight, failure to protect the friends of the United States, and dereliction in the duty to build constructive United States influence.[27] Implicit in such a critique is the assumption that American "leadership of the free world" is a sort of talisman that needs only to be seized in order to be efficacious: an assumption valid only insofar as leader and led are agreed on the path to be taken. This was not true in the Lebanese case. The United States saw that reform in the Lebanese confessional system was needed to avoid civil strife. It had, however, to deal with a legitimately constituted government whose head opposed such reform and which included dissatisfied elements willing to co-opt the Palestinians into the Lebanese political system in support of their aspirations.

A conceivable alternative might have been for the United States to have chosen some Lebanese faction as its client and to have thrown its full weight in its support. This would have involved clandestine and unconventional operations of a sort largely discredited among broad sectors of the American public and was thus not a realistic choice for a vulnerable president seeking election in his own right, or for a secretary of state whose every act had come under intensely hostile scrutiny. It is perhaps true that the Lebanese situation had deteriorated beyond retrieval before it engaged the concentrated attention of the top American leaders. By then, any moral force the United States may have possessed was largely irrelevant, and use of its military capability to restore and maintain peace was precluded as unacceptable to the American electorate. Finally, for reasons extraneous to the Lebanese conflict, the United States abstained from political contact with, and any opportunity to influence, the PLO, which as events showed, commanded the preponderant armed force within Lebanon.

EVOLVING AMERICAN PERCEPTIONS

During the years between 1958 and the 1975–77 Lebanese war, changes occurred both in the objective factors of Middle East politics and in the American perception of them. Great-power rivalry for influence and clients among the Arab states continued. Russia gradually acquired a military and naval capability in the Eastern Mediterranean comparable to that of the United States, which now had to consider the possibility of a Soviet reaction to any contemplated use of armed force. Despite the Kennedy Administration's sympathetic view of progressive political and social movements abroad, United States ties remained closest with the traditional Arab regimes, and America thus seemed to oppose progress in the region, as well as deeply-felt Arab aspirations. Undisguised American partiality toward Israel in the June 1967 war provoked the severance of official relations with over half the Arab states. In the wake of the war, the Johnson Administration conducted a searching review of American interests in the region and concluded that these, among them the supply of Middle Eastern oil to Western Europe, could be adequately protected by ensuring that Israel remained militarily powerful enough to defeat any likely combination of Arab forces. The United States could thus safely disregard demands by the Arabs that it recognize and support their interests where these impinged upon those of Israel.

This general attitude prevailed through the ensuing administration, until the October War demonstrated its inadequacies. President Nixon and Henry Kissinger, his national security advisor, judged that the Arab-Israel problem was essentially insoluble in the prevailing circumstances. They ensured a substantial increase in the flow of arms to Israel. In order to discourage Arab breaches of the fragile truce, they hoped to persuade the Soviet Union, in the developing atmosphere of detente, to restrain its Arab clients. They also sought to convince the Arabs that, while Russia could provide them weapons, their only hope of regaining their lost territories or securing other Israeli concessions rested in the United States. The situation was viewed differently in the State Department, where it was felt that the unstable Arab-Israeli stalemate could only lead to resumed warfare which might well develop into a superpower confrontation. UN mediation having failed, the United States could and should actively pursue the aim of a negotiated settlement. Whatever the merits of the two views, the successive plans advanced by Secretary Rogers were given only pro forma support, if not actually undercut, by the White House.

The president's policy was put to a severe test in 1970 when Syria's invasion of Jordan in support of Palestinian insurgents was frustrated with American assistance and the threat of Israeli intervention. While the American actions helped Hussein preserve his throne, the victorious Jordanian army drove thousands of Palestinian militants into Lebanon, whose government lacked the ability to impose its authority over them. The defects of the American posture were further dramatized by the October 1973 War, the Arab oil embargo, the spectacular rise in the cost of OPEC oil, and the demonstration of America's dependence on the Arab states for its energy supply.

When Kissinger became secretary of state, he was obliged to deal with Middle Eastern affairs on their own terms as well as a function of superpower relations. He was understandably reluctant to become involved in the search for an Arab-Israeli settlement. The October War and the oil embargo apparently convinced him that a settlement was essential to the security of American interests in the region and that the United States could act effectively to bring one about by working with Israel and a newly independent Egypt, backed by Saudi Arabia. Negotiation of the Egyptian and Syrian disengagement agreements represented a distinct turning point in the American approach to the Middle East. In order to achieve a truce and institute progress toward eventual peace, the United States had to act upon, instead of simply paying lip service to, the principle that Arab demands as generally defined in pertinent UN resolutions were legitimate. This, in turn, committed the United States to seek corresponding concessions from Israel.

The secretary's overriding objective throughout the Ford Administration was to sustain the momentum of a phased movement toward an overall settlement. This concern guided American attitudes toward the Lebanese civil war, a potential source of renewed regional strife. The opposition of the U.S. government to outside intervention was calculated to reduce the likelihood of large-scale Israeli involvement. Nevertheless, when Syrian intervention occurred, the circumspect American attitude reflected the tacit recognition that Syria was a stabilizing element in the Lebanese situation, and furthermore avoided an altercation with President Assad, whose cooperation was indispensable in any further progress toward regional peace. Similarly, the close American consultation with Syria and Israel to avert ill-calculated actions in Lebanon contributed to the development of patterns that may prove useful in future exchanges on broader issues. Interestingly, the American attitude toward the Syrian intervention contrasted with that of the Soviet Union, which strongly opposed it, presumably calculating that revolutionary Lebanese and Palestinian elements would otherwise gain the upper hand. The Syrian break with the Soviets in this regard encouraged confidence that Syria shared the American concern for regional stability and an eventual peace settlement.

THE ISRAELI INVASION OF LEBANON

By the time the Carter Administration took office, Kissinger's incremental approach apparently had reached a dead end. Secretary of State Cyrus Vance kept Kissinger's team of experts virtually intact, and consultations were begun looking toward a general regional conference at Geneva. After President Sadat's dramatic visit to Jerusalem in November 1977, and the beginning of direct Israeli-Egyptian discussions, the American role shifted to support of these endeavors and diplomatic effort to win the approval and cooperation of other Arab states, few of which approved of Sadat's unilateral initiative.

When the Israeli-Egyptian talks began to address the core issues of the dispute they encountered difficulties and were in suspense when Israel invaded Lebanon, partially in response to an incursion on March 11, 1978, by Palestinian commandos based in Lebanon. Eventually, Israel occupied most of the territory up to the Litani River and defeated the Palestinian forces in the area and put them to flight, along with most of the local Muslim population.

During the Nixon administration, the United States had promised Israel that it would no longer publicly condemn Israeli retaliation beyond its borders against terrorist acts by Palestinian guerrillas. Both out of respect for this commitment and to avoid further deterioration in the regional negotiating atmosphere, the United States deliberately chose not to criticize the March invasion.[28] The invasion, nevertheless, was particularly disturbing to American officials since it differed from previous reprisals, which had typically been quick strikes against specific targets, followed by prompt withdrawal. The U.S. feared that its silence might be understood by other nations to imply approval of Israeli occupation of the territory of yet another Arab country, one not directly responsible for Palestinian raids, and that this would impair the effectiveness of the United States as a mediator. Zionist (not Israeli government) economic studies in the past had pointed to the advantage of drawing Israel's northern border so as to embrace the Litani River, and the general complexion of the Begin government aroused apprehension that Israel might be tempted to annex the occupied territory.[29] It was feared moreover that Syria might feel compelled to use its peace-keeping force in Lebanon to repel the Israelis, at the risk of a new outbreak of general war. Finally, the operation could be expected further to intensify Syria's opposition to the peace initiative of President Sadat who, before Israel's move into Lebanon, had sharply condemned the March 11 Palestinian raid.[30]

Instead of protesting against Israel's operation, the United States concentrated its attention upon ensuring the earliest possible evacuation of its forces. On the day of the invasion, the State Department noted the "brutal" nature of the March 11 raid and the danger to Israeli security constituted by the Palestinian presence in southern Lebanon. At the same time it took pointed cognizance of a statement by Israeli Defense Minister Weizman that Israel did not intend to hold the seized territory. Prime Minister Begin meanwhile declared categorically that Israel would not withdraw in circumstances which would permit the Palestinians to return to southern Lebanon.

Since the reconstituted Lebanese army was as yet incapable of assuming control in the south, and since Israel remained opposed to the presence of Syrian forces there, even under nominal Lebanese command, the United States decided that introduction of a UN peace-keeping force was the only feasible means of ensuring Israeli evacuation. Accordingly, the American delegation introduced a resolution in the Security Council calling for immediate Israeli withdrawal and the stationing of a UN force in southern Lebanon until the Lebanese government could establish effective control.[31] By dint of intensive diplomatic effort, the United States persuaded Israel, Syria, and Lebanon, all of which were initially opposed, to accept this approach. The resolution was adopted on March 19, and the first contingents of a multinational force entered southern Lebanon on March 22. Israel completed her withdrawal from Lebanon on June 13, after turning over tanks and munitions to the Lebanese Christian militia in the area.

The invasion and the circumstances that brought it about inevitably placed new obstacles before the quest for peace in the Middle East. While acknowledging this, Secretary Vance expressed the determination of the United States to persevere in the effort to reach a settlement. The insertion of the UN force in southern Lebanon was a modest and provisional accomplishment. By facilitating Israeli withdrawal it at least made possible the resumption of progress toward an overall settlement, although progress was by no means certain. As the last Israeli units withdrew from Lebanon, the United States resumed its active role as mediator by asking the Israeli government to state unequivocally what would happen to the West Bank after the five-year period mentioned in the Begin plan for granting local autonomy to Arabs living there. Much depends on the answer.[32]

American initiatives bore fruit at Camp David in September 1978, when Egypt and Israel agreed on a framework for peace both between themselves and in regard to the region as a whole, including the West Bank and Gaza. As the summit ended, all three leaders—Presidents Carter and Sadat and Prime Minister Begin—promised to turn their attention to Lebanon and recognized the intimate connection between a general Middle Eastern settlement and the Lebanese conflict. They clearly hoped that their achievements at the summit would make it possible for all the parties to bring peace to Lebanon at last.

BRITAIN AND THE MIDDLE EAST

P. Edward Haley

A STUDIED if sympathetic abstinence marked the policy of the British government toward the war in Lebanon. While distressed by the heavy loss of life that accompanied months of undisciplined fighting between confessional and ideological rivals in Lebanon, the British government and people found in this no reason for their country to take important diplomatic let alone military steps toward that country or any of the nations in the region, and none were taken. Two decades earlier, fearing that civil authority would collapse in Lebanon and the contagion endanger an ally, Jordan, the United States and Britain landed troops and sustained the regimes in those two countries.[1] The British response in 1975–77 could not have been more different. Joint and decisive military action had given way to a sad silence while the slaughter dragged on, punctuated by several expressions of multilateral European concern.

The changed British response testified to the reduction of British power in the Middle East during the years since 1958.[2] By 1975 Britain no longer possessed the capability to intervene militarily in the eastern Mediterranean or anywhere in the Middle East. British Middle Eastern policy now concentrates not on alliances and intervention but on multilateral diplomacy in the United Nations and the European Economic Community, and on commerce and economic and military assistance in the region, particularly with Iran and the nations of the Arabian peninsula. During the Lebanese conflict from 1975–77 Britain, like every other non-Arab power, concluded that the Lebanese civil war was an Arab problem and that only Arab governments and movements could resolve it. After Israel invaded southern Lebanon in March 1978, the United Nations Security Council acted to establish a cease-fire and dispatch a peace-keeping force to that area. Britain took a leading role at the UN in both these decisions.

Britain's quiescence during the Lebanese War heightens the impression of her disengagement from the Middle East, particularly when compared to the joint Anglo-American landings twenty years earlier. One should not be misled. Taken together, Britain's close relations with the Gulf states, Saudi Arabia, and Iran, her active summit diplomacy, and the important flows of commerce and assistance to and from the region amount to a substantial involvement in the Middle East. Britain's role in the Middle East is that of a medium-sized power which, even if it cannot exercise control, may nonetheless exert political influence on events.

The purpose of this chapter is in part to analyze Britain's response to the Lebanese War. That is easily done, for she intentionally played a very small part in that conflict. A second purpose of the chapter is to determine the present nature and extent of Britain's involvement in the Middle East. Specifically, what are Britain's military capabilities in the region? What countries in the region trade with Britain and receive her military and economic aid and foreign investment? What amounts of trade, aid, and investment change hands? Are any or all of these increasing or decreasing?

A third purpose of the chapter is to examine Britain's role in Lebanon and the Middle East as an example of the international behavior of medium-sized powers, in order to try to anticipate the direction the Middle Eastern policies these nations will take in the future. As it happened, the Lebanese War did not harm the vital interests of Britain or of any country outside the Fertile Crescent. A wider war could have erupted, nonetheless, with attendant risks of the disruption of oil supplies and the collision of the super powers. For Britain, as for the other nations of Europe as well as Japan, the containment of the fighting in Lebanon and the protection of their vital interests were fortuitous. That all went well for Britain and the other medium-sized powers alters nothing about their inability to influence the course of events. This conjunction of vital interest and impotence defines the status of "middle powers" and suggests that the nations in this quandary will try to escape it. It also directs attention to the foreign policy instruments available to Britain and the other middle powers and invites a search for new ways in which they will use these instruments in the future to advance their interests in the Middle East. Are the policy instruments now in use capable of accomplishing the goals of Britain's foreign policy in the Middle East? If not, what kinds of instruments would be consistent with these goals? Alternatively, could existing instruments be used in new ways to achieve these goals? The answers to these questions not only identify Britain's policy instruments but provide interesting and sometimes startling glimpses of the policies likely to be pursued in the future in the Middle East by Britain and other middle powers, of which the most important is France, as they cope with the quandaries and opportunities they face in the Middle East.

BRITISH INVOLVEMENT

The public record shows Britain attempted no significant unilateral initiatives during the Lebanese War. Her leaders expressed their regret at the loss of life and their support for the territorial integrity of Lebanon. They discussed the conflict with the Americans and took part in the Euro-Arab dialog.[3] The Anglo-American discussions no doubt allowed the British to learn about the role the United States was playing between Syria and Israel but seem to have led to little else. Both the conversations with representatives of Arab governments and a need to keep pace with the new American administration of Jimmy Carter led the governments in the European Economic Community (EEC) to issue a statement that revealed a slight European shift in favor of the Palestinians, but little else. The statement recorded the nine members as supporting "the need for a homeland for the Palestinian people" and "appropriate" Palestinian participation in any negotiations on the Middle East.[4] Nothing in the Euro-Arab or EEC deliberations either affected the fighting in Lebanon or increased British influence in the region. The empty gestures of Giscard d'Estaing notwithstanding, no European government was able to influence the course of the war or the nature of the eventual settlements.[5]

At first glance this inability to alter events in their favor would seem consistent with a reduced European role in the Middle East, whether obligatory as in Britain's departures, or self-imposed, as in De-Gaulle's 1967 embargo on French arms sales to the Arab-Israeli combatants (only recently relaxed). This impression is misleading. It is true that Britain and the rest of the Europeans lacked the power and influence that could have halted or decisively affected the outcome of the civil war in Lebanon. But this is true of the Soviet Union and the United States as well. One must not make of the ability to act effectively in Lebanon a test that disguises Britain's recent activity in the Middle East. If the Soviets and Americans in the Middle East might be likened to brawny woodsmen wielding two-bladed axes at their work in the forest, the British and the other Europeans might be seen as cautious gardeners at work on flower beds with trowel and pruning shears. The woodsmen act on a grand scale and achieve effects immediately; the gardeners move in smaller orbits and gain their ends only gradually, but their accomplishments are often attractive and enduring. To understand Britain's contemporary role in the Middle East one must, therefore, ask what policy instruments Britain possesses in the region. One also must ask for what ends they might be used.

POLICY INSTRUMENTS

The analysis begins with a survey of British defense policy, a traditional means for achieving Britain's objectives in the region. The main bilateral policy instruments considered are economic aid and investment, trade, and military aid. The multilateral instrument discussed is the European Economic Community and its recent concessions to the Arab states and Israel. The analysis shows that Britain has lost the ability to influence events in the Middle East by the use or demonstration of military force. Trade, economic and military assistance, and membership in the EEC, on the other hand, give Britain policy instruments of considerable and increasing value in the Middle East. British trade and assistance to all the nations of the area are growing rapidly, and in the complicated Arab and Israeli connections with the EEC a new and extremely important means has been attained by which Britain and the other West European governments may make their needs and interests felt.

It is correct to stress the uncertainties that attend the relation between donor and recipient. Russian failure in Egypt and the American fiasco in Vietnam testify that neither billions in aid nor the presence of thousands of troops and advisers will either make the recipient obey or protect the donor's policy against reversal or collapse. Indigenous nationalism and political change and new external alignments can scar or ruin decades of effort, however solid or costly the facade of the relationship might have seemed. In addition, Egypt now uses Saudi money to purchase weapons from the West. She is a consumer and Britain and France are suppliers. In this sense, at least, Sadat must feel more dependent on the Saudis than on his European suppliers, who have strong industrial reasons of their own for making the sales, even at reduced prices. One must, at the same time, recognize that trade, significant military and economic assistance, and multilateral preferences create opportunities for the exercise of influence.[6]

These developments have occurred at a time when Britain's military presence in the Middle East has all but vanished. This may be more than coincidence. Egypt has allowed the re-entry of Britain and France for many reasons, but Sadat seems likely to have turned to them at this particular time precisely because they had quit the region militarily.[7] Regardless of the truth of this observation, one cannot understand Britain's contemporary role in the Lebanese civil war and in the Middle East without appreciating the evolution of British defense policy during the last decade.

Defense Policy

In 1965 after a major defense review, a new Labor government set a course for British defense policy. None of the three governments that followed have altered that course.[8] Labor and Conservative alike, all have accepted the concentration of Britain's defense effort in north-western Europe and the Northern Atlantic, the surrender of all major commitments outside Europe, and the reduction of the defense budget by at least as much as is taken from welfare services, whenever cuts are made in government spending to hasten economic recovery.[9] On the average for the years 1960–70 in constant prices Britain made no increase whatever in defense expenditure, while for the years 1971–76 British defense outlays grew an average of 1.4 percent each year.[10] Britain's per capita expenditures on defense have kept pace with Belgium and Denmark but not with Germany and France, although it is true she spends a larger proportion of her gross national product on defense than either of her allies to the east.[11]

Steady, heavy reductions in Britain's military forces were made in the ten years after 1965. British active strength in the armed forces, according to official, annual Defense Statements, fell from nearly 455,000 to 352,000 in 1975, a loss of nearly 25 percent. Severe cuts were made in all branches, but the air force seems to have been hardest hit, losing 35,500 service personnel, or 27 percent of its strength in eleven years. By comparison, the army dropped 49,000 or 22 percent, and the navy 23,000 or 23 percent.

With these cuts went any chance of maintaining a significant military presence in the eastern Mediterranean or the Persian Gulf. By 1975 the British government had decided not to station ships permanently in the Mediterranean.[12] Periodically, destroyers and frigates were to visit the Mediterranean and Persian Gulf; Britain would contribute to the NATO force on call for duty in the Mediterranean; a Marine commando group was based at Malta; and larger ships would visit the Mediterranean "from time to time": but that was the extent of Britain's naval forces in the region. During the emergency in Cyprus in 1974–75, Britain increased her forces there to three infantry battalions, two armored reconnaissance regiments, and the Marine Commando group from Malta, and added a squadron of Phantom fighter-bombers to the garrison's maritime patrol airplanes and helicopters. Britain continued to give arms, training, and limited combat support to the sultan of Oman in his war against the rebels in Dhofar, that country's southwestern province. In addition, elements of Britain's armed forces helped clear and open the Suez Canal.

As slight as they are, these small numbers of ships, planes, and men exaggerate British military strength in general and in the eastern Mediterranean and Middle East. On taking office again in March 1974, the Labor government began another major review of defense commitments and expenditures through 1983–84. Like the Conservatives before them, the Labor government called their predecessor's programs and commitments too costly and promised to reduce both severely. The government declared it would take £4,700 million from the Conservatives' planned expenditures during the next ten years. A British commitment to the defense of Europe and the United Kingdom would be maintained, but at a significantly lower level. Active strength in the armed services would be cut by 38,000, or 11 percent. In addition to terminating a permanent British naval presence in the Mediterranean, the government decided that the Commando Group on Malta would be disbanded in 1979, the Joint Airborne Task Force abandoned, the U.K. Mobile Force cut by more than two-thirds, and the principal British aircraft (Nimrods and Canberras) withdrawn from the Mediterranean. Outside the NATO area, while maintaining the nation's commitments on paper, the government pledged to withdraw the few British forces remaining in Malaysia, Singapore, Brunei, Gan, Mauritius, and the West Indies. No forces would be assigned to CENTO, and the Simonstown Agreement for a naval base in South Africa would be (and soon was) terminated.[13]

Defense expenditures were to be reduced as severely as manpower. In addition to four short-term cuts that had taken £300 million in 1974, the Labor government intended to reduce the planned expenditures by 12 percent, from an average of £4,300 a year to an average of £3,800 a year; they also meant to lower the proportion of Gross National Product spent on defense from 5.5 to 4.5 percent. Within a month a further cut of £110 million was made, and in July 1976, another of £100 million.[14] With the reductions Britain would spend less for defense at constant prices in 1978–79 than in 1970–71.

The cuts in defense expenditure came at a time when the Soviet Union had significantly increased its land, missile, and naval forces. Conclusive evidence of this was presented by the Labor government in the very same report that announced major cuts in Britain's defenses.[15] It is plain from this contradiction that Labor's plans for Britain's defense are not based primarily on the military threat facing the country. What their basis might be was revealed by the bitter criticisms aimed at the Labor government from within its own ranks as well as from the opposition following the announcement of the results of the Defense Review.[16] Conservative critics of the government sounded a familiar note: they agreed with the decision to concentrate on Northern Europe and the Eastern Atlantic but feared that such drastic cuts endangered Britain's security and sea communications and surrendered her "residual interests" elsewhere.[17] This is a version of the claim to superior efficiency favored by opposition parties on both sides of the Atlantic. If the conservatives were to be returned to office in the early 1980s and repeated their earlier performances, they would honor their claim by cutting defense less heavily than their opponents rather than by stabilizing let alone increasing forces and budget.

This interpretation had its supporters within the Labor government and party, but they were more than matched by Laborites advocating major reductions in defense spending that would, at a minimum, be in the same proportion as cuts to other departments. Others in the party, acting from strong political and pacifist convictions, sought even greater cuts, and subjected the government to intense public as well as private criticism. Any government statement on defense in the House of Commons, for example, naturally moves the Conservatives to suggest that Labor's defense cuts endanger the nation's security. What is unusual is that the same statement draws even more bitter and passionate condemnation from Labor members of the House, who demand even more drastic surgery. Those in government who favored making the less drastic but still very severe reductions in the same proportion in all departments argued that unless welfare—the "social wage"—were protected in this manner, the government would lose the cooperation of the trade unions in any future restraint of wages.[18] This position, however appealing on practical and political grounds, disguised the burden imposed on the armed services by the reductions, for expenditures in every other government department had increased from two (social security) to five times (housing) faster than expenditures on defense.[19]

In the end the additional extraordinary cuts—above the £4,700 million by 1983–84—were not made. One suspects the government was able to avoid them only because a Labor party study group discovered that cuts of such a magnitude—up to £1,000 million a year—would result in the loss of major export orders and as many as 50,000 jobs in aerospace, shipbuilding, and arms industries.[20] In their place the government announced a smaller additional "logistical" cut of £180 million in early 1976, and in its statement on defense for that year set the reductions for the next three years in the amount of £534 million.[21]

A succession of British governments has justified the most drastic kinds of reductions in foreign commitments and defense expenditures as a means of further expanding social services and economic welfare in Britain. In power for two of the last three terms, the leadership of the Labor party has been able to reach compromises with its own internal opposition, but the cuts, even after the compromising, have been severe. If they have not yet made Britain's armed forces "pathetic," to use the words of an American chief of staff, they may well have, as suggested by an All-Party Commons Expenditure Committee, ruined the armed forces' ability to contribute to the conventional deterrence of the Warsaw Pact, and made more likely an early resort to nuclear weapons in the event of war in Europe.[22] It goes without saying that an even more drastic loss of capability occurred in the Middle East in addition to the decline in Britain's forces in Europe. Britain is no longer able to influence developments in the Middle East through the display or use of military power.

Bilateral Policy Instruments: Military Assistance

By every measure the scope and pace of military expansion in the Middle East are astonishing. Following the quadrupling of oil prices in 1973 the oil-rich nations of the Persian Gulf began a spectacular arms build-up, in addition to the long-standing competition between the Arab states and Israel. Since 1961 the average annual rate of increase in military spending in the region has been 19.5 percent, seven times the world average of 2.9 percent in the same period.[23] The equipment is modern, sophisticated, and in total numbers approaches the 3,000 tactical aircraft and 12,250 main battle tanks at the disposal of all NATO commanders in northern Europe.[24] In 1972 alone the nations of the Middle East spent one-fourth the developing world's defense expenditures and took nearly one-third of its arms imports.[25]

Virtually all (86 percent) the major weapons supplied to developing countries come from four nations: the USSR, the United States, France, and Britain.[26] Table 13.1 shows five-year averages for their arms exports to the Middle East from 1950 to 1972. Table 13.2 displays the total value of major arms imports by Middle Eastern countries from 1950 to 1975, showing the remarkable increase that began in the late 1960s. These figures reveal much about the supply of arms to the region and about the policies of the major suppliers. The Soviet Union and the United States were the major suppliers, both worldwide and in the Middle East. Yet several important changes occurred in the relative position of the two during these years. At the outset the U.S. alone supplied half the total arms exported to developing countries. However, the Soviet share grew

TABLE 13.1

Values and Share of Exports of Major Weapons to the Middle East, 1950–72

(U.S. $ million at constant 1968 prices)

SUPPLIER:	USA	UK	USSR	FRANCE	OTHER	TOTAL*
1950–54						
$ million annual average	7	20		4	6	37
percent	17.4	54.7	0.0	10.4	17.4	100.0
1955–59						
$ million annual average	35	15	78	40	31	199
percent	17.8	7.5	39.1	19.9	15.7	100.0
1960–64						
$ million annual average	22	14	104	36	4	180
percent	12.0	7.9	57.8	20.2	2.1	100.0
1965–69						
$ million annual average	137	58	219	21	26	462
percent	29.6	12.7	47.5	4.6	5.7	100.0
1970–72						
$ million annual average	280	89	301	17	35	721
percent	38.7	12.3	41.8	2.4	4.8	100.0
1950–72						
$ million total*	1838	807	2908	554	443	6550
Percent of total	28.1	12.3	44.4	8.5	6.8	100.0

SOURCE: SIPRI, *The Arms Trade With the Third World*, rev. and abr. ed. (New York, 1975), p. 202.
Figures may not add up to total because of rounding.

rapidly after 1955, passing the U.S. in the early 1960s, after that country began to concentrate on exporting the lighter, cheaper, counter-insurgency weapons. Soviet exports reached a high in 1967 and again in the early 1970s as the Arabs rearmed themselves. The U.S. in turn greatly expanded its supplies to developing countries beginning in 1968, with much of the increase going to provide highly sophisticated weapons to Israel.[27]

TABLE 13.2
Values of Imports of Major Weapons by Middle Eastern Countries, 1950–75
(U.S. $ million at constant 1973 prices)

REGION	1950	1951	1952	1953	1954	1955	1956	1957	1958	1959	1960	1961	1962
Middle East	35	55	12	70	81	186	350	300	249	238	123	150	439
Third World	294	289	201	488	556	765	957	919	1461	920	1159	957	1302

SOURCE: SIPRI, *Yearbook, 1976,* pp. 250–51.

The export of British arms to the Middle East was overtaken and passed by both the United States and the USSR, although Britain supplied more than half the arms sent to the Middle East in the early 1950s. After a low in the late 1950s of 8 percent, Britain's share of the arms trade in the region rose steadily, and in the late 1960s and early 1970s averaged about 13 percent of the total. From 1962–67 British exports averaged $20.5 million; from 1967–72 they quadrupled to an annual average of $84.8 million.

The figures conceal a shift in favor of Egypt or, more accurately, the restitution of Egypt to a position as a recipient of British arms, alongside the Iranians, the Saudis, and others on the Gulf. The British shift toward Egypt began in the early 1970s, after Sadat succeeded Nasser and started the long quest to end Egypt's total dependence on the USSR. The most striking element of Egypt's acceptance of European arms is the initiation of arrangements for the licensed production in Egypt of British (and French) weapons financed by Saudi Arabia. In 1975, for example, Egypt and Britain were planning licensed production of 100 British "Hawk" fighters, 250 "Westland Lynx" helicopters, up to 200 of the Anglo-French "Jaguar International" long-range strike fighters, and some 10,000 of the British "Swingfire" antitank missiles. Egypt has also purchased outright substantial numbers of British helicopters and, more importantly, has bought even larger numbers of French Mirage fighters and their armaments, also with Saudi money.[28]

The Anglo-Egyptian decision in favor of licensed production remains tentative; the newlyweds appear not to have consummated the marriage. Even so, there is solid evidence that the Egyptians and Saudis are serious, and that they and the British will soon begin joint weapons

1963	1964	1965	1966	1967	1968	1969	1970	1971	1972	1973	1974	1975	TOTAL
301	296	337	336	813	962	927	1118	1350	831	1704	2260	2696	16,219
1058	914	1192	1553	1885	2059	2359	2247	2835	2673	2909	4070	4843	40,632

production on a large scale. For example, during the visit to Britain of Egyptian Foreign Minister Ismail Fahmi in mid-June 1975, the *Times* reported that Egypt had agreed in principle to buy £450 million in British arms. The same article stated that Egypt had an arms budget of £1 billion largely from Saudi Arabia and Kuwait and expected to order most of that amount from Britain and France.[29] Six months later during a summit meeting between Presidents Sadat and Giscard, the *Times* correspondent in Cairo reported that the Egyptian president had made known his determination to break his country's dependence on the USSR, and that he sought help in this from the West and especially from Britain, France, and the United States. In the joint communiqué released at the end of the visit, the two presidents announced that France would help in a major effort to build weapons factories in Egypt.[30]

Egypt and her financial backers stand to gain much by agreeing loudly on principles and moving deliberately. Like a belly-dancer they have many charms with which to please. They lure the Europeans politically and economically with the arms agreements, for the deals promise not only hundreds of millions in defense orders, but an Egypt independent of the superpowers, or at least mutually dependent on them and Britain and France as well. Egypt is pleased to heighten Israel's sense of isolation while the Europeans covet the trade and influence they see beckoning them. Egypt obviously hopes in this way to bring pressure on the Americans through the British and French, pressure that could help move Israel. The method seems to have worked, although its proof may not lie in its efficacy. Only if Egypt behaves in this way has she a shred of hope to move the Israelis and escape bondage to the USSR. The method may promise little; its alternatives promise less.

Bilateral Policy Instruments: Trade and Economic Assistance

The Middle East receives less than ten percent of British economic aid and government-backed investment. Most of the assistance goes to Commonwealth countries, with the nations of South Asia and Africa receiving the largest share. The proportion of British aid given to the Middle East has dropped significantly, falling from nearly 12 percent of the total in 1964 to 4 percent in 1975. The largest amounts have gone to Jordan over the years, with Aden and South Arabia (People's Democratic Republic of Yemen after 1968) receiving extremely large grants in the years just prior to Britain's decision to quit her bases east of Suez. Israel and Syria have received the least, leaving aside Kuwait, with essentially no aid passed to Israel for fifteen years and none to Syria since 1970. As in the case of military assistance, Britain began dramatically to increase her economic aid to Egypt after Nasser's death; the total moving from a net loss by Egypt of £740,000 in 1972, to a positive transfer of £2,855,000 in 1975.

Comparing British and United States aid to the Middle East leads to several interesting observations. U.S. aid to Syria and Libya also ceased in the early 1970s, no doubt because of major changes in the domestic and foreign policies of those two countries. The U.S. has also massively increased its aid to Sadat's Egypt: moving from no aid whatsoever in 1970 and 1971, to over one billion dollars in American economic aid for Egypt in 1976. Like the British, the Americans give much to Jordan. They, too, gave heavily to Iran through the 1960s and then curtailed aid severely.

The differences are interesting as well. Israel, for example, receives great chunks of American economic assistance while she receives none at all from Britain. The U.S., unlike the British, began in 1975 to offer aid to Syria again. The U.S. is, of course, able to grant assistance in amounts far beyond Britain's means and repeatedly outspends her ally in the region. What is striking is that despite the great difference in American and British capabilities to give aid, in many countries the U.S. is not outspending Britain. If the amounts the U.S. sends to Egypt and Israel are too huge for Britain to match, that is not the case in Iraq, Libya, Lebanon, Syria, Oman, and South Yemen. It is true that the Soviet Union has provided very large amounts of economic and especially military aid to Iraq, Syria, and Libya. Even so, the absence of American aid programs in those countries could present the British and other Europeans an opportunity to provide an alternative to dependence on either superpower.

Admittedly, the memory of European imperialism lingers in the Fertile Crescent, but, Britain has begun to move in a small way in Syria. In April 1977, British Foreign Secretary David Owen visited Syria to reopen an English language center in Damascus, closed in 1967 after the break in diplomatic relations, and to sign agreements for the exchange of scholarships, radio and television programs, and teachers.[31] Owen was the first British foreign secretary to visit Syria since the country's independence in 1946.

Bilateral trade is another obvious policy instrument. Although governments find trade more difficult to control than the economic or military assistance that comes straight from official budgets, they have effective means to cause trade to wax and wane, in tariffs and other duties, in quotas, in diplomacy, and in the grant of export credits. This is not the place for a thorough and technical analysis of either British trade policy as a whole or of her trade with the Middle East. One can, nonetheless, examine some general figures on British trade in the region and ask whether the trends they reveal are consistent with the character of British defense policy and military and economic assistance, and whether they suggest any obvious opportunities for the expansion of trade in the future. Table 13.3 shows British imports and exports to and from the Middle East in 1963, 1968, 1973, and 1977. Although this method of comparison disguises the political reasons for marked declines or increases in trade—nationalizations in Egypt, for example—it reveals the economic logic and illogic in present relations.

In Table 13.3 the countries are grouped in three categories: "Confrontation" states, those directly engaged in the Arab-Israeli conflict, Syria, Lebanon, Jordan, Israel, and Egypt; "Rejectionist" states, those opposed to all peace-making efforts, Iraq and Libya; and the "Gulf" states, Iran and those on the Arabian peninsula. The figures on trade with the Gulf states instantly show the astonishing degree to which Britain depends on petroleum imports from the Gulf countries. The figures also show that British Middle Eastern trade since 1973 differs in remarkable ways from her trade with the region before that year. The differences are so great that one must speak of the two periods separately and then attempt to explain the changes.

Britain spent more than £900 million for oil from the Gulf countries in 1973, compared with about £100 million in goods purchased from the "confrontation" states, and £200 million from Iraq and Libya, most of that for oil from Libya. As one would expect, throughout the years 1963–73, Britain's trade was in substantial deficit to both the Gulf group and the rejectionists, with each OPEC price rise adding to the imbalance. By

TABLE 13.3
British Trade with the Middle East, Selected Years, 1963–77
(£ thousand)

Country	1963 Imports	1963 Exports	1968 Imports	1968 Exports	1973 Imports	1973 Exports	1977* Imports	1977* Exports
GULF STATES								
Abu Dhabi	8,176	2,953	14,487	9,616	33,415	24,755	115,000	125,200
Bahrein	15,102	7,485	1,914	10,904	15,769	24,333	13,500	104,000
Iran	32,166	28,314	70,705	61,033	236,332	169,362	721,000	598,100
Kuwait	150,979	21,882	151,436	29,141	231,438	36,098	499,200	223,000
Oman	2	1,255	11,086	2,895	15,896	22,195	14,700	161,500
Qatar	5,694	3,587	24,349	7,197	47,744	19,410	100,700	106,700
Saudi Arabia	13,172	9,698	68,718	46,648	317,704	58,464	1,027,100	526,400
Trucial States	97	3,742	36,739	9,079	35,730	24,702	108,300	297,300
Yemen, North	147	28	8	317	428	3,159	438	24,401
Yemen, South	11,187	12,601	6,811	8,196	3,445	4,468	184	20,809
TOTAL	236,722	91,545	386,253	185,026	937,901	386,946	2,600,122	2,187,410
BALANCE	−145,117		−201,227		−550,955		−412,712	
CONFRONTATION STATES								
Egypt	8,139	33,499	10,314	12,440	23,663	27,112	77,500	176,800
Israel	17,285	23,776	43,832	88,142	69,567	187,238	149,300	244,900
Jordan	269	9,033	70	8,269	465	13,407	1,800	45,100
Lebanon	3,667	14,410	4,229	20,957	8,017	41,953	7,200	42,400
Syria	1,432	8,595	494	5,021	1,154	11,630	5,200	52,400
TOTAL	30,792	89,313	58,939	134,829	102,866	281,340	241,000	561,600
BALANCE		+58,521		+75,890		+178,474		+320,600
REJECTIONIST STATES								
Iraq	61,567	17,727	28,023	15,931	30,727	27,046	298,300	152,700
Libya	41,695	15,740	156,949	34,195	169,027	61,057	128,400	153,900
TOTAL	103,262	33,467	184,972	50,126	199,754	88,103	426,700	306,600
BALANCE	−69,795		−134,846		−111,651		−120,100	

SOURCE: Annual Statements of the Trade of the United Kingdom with Commonwealth and Foreign Countries; Overseas Trade Statistics of the United Kingdom, 1977.

*Figures are for the first eleven months of 1977 only.

1973 Britain's imports from both groups totaled £1.1 billion, but her exports only £475 million.

In her trade with the confrontation states in 1973 and before, Britain achieved a substantial surplus with every nation. This was true despite Jordan's limited economic capacity and the stagnation of Syrian-British trade. In absolute terms Syria sold less to Britain in 1973 than in 1963. In constant values, Syrian exports to Britain fell, assuming a decline in the British pound of 25 percent over that period, while British exports to Syria remained the same. In fact, Britain repeatedly sold more to Jordan than to Syria, even though Syria has twice the population of Jordan and three times the gross national product. Anglo-Egyptian trade shows favorable increases in the early 1970s, similar to the changes noted in economic and military assistance. From 1969–73 Egyptian sales to Britain increased by more than 150 percent, and Britain's exports to Egypt grew by 75 percent, although by 1973 British exports to Egypt had not regained their value in 1963.

It was British trade with Israel that was striking in this group. Israel bought more from Britain than any Arab state in the Middle East. Libya was Israel's closest Arab competitor, with only one-third the purchases from Britain. Only Iran came close, with ten times the population and five times the gross national product. In fact, in 1973 Israel bought more from Britain than Saudi Arabia, Egypt, Syria, Iraq, and Libya combined. Needless to say, Israel's trade balances ran heavily in Britain's and Europe's favor.

By November 1977, the picture had altered dramatically. The rise in oil prices had nearly trebled Britain's oil bill, with total imports from the Gulf area rising to £2,600 million. Interestingly, Britain's deficit with the Gulf actually decreased more than 25 percent during this four-year period because Gulf-state purchases from Britain rose to six-times their 1973-level, from £387 million to £2,187 million. Trade with the confrontation states had increased by about half from 1963–68, and then doubled from 1968 to 1973. During the next four years trade doubled again, despite the war-induced stagnation of Lebanese commerce. Exports to Egypt jumped from £27 million in 1973, to £177 million in 1977, and trade with Syria had finally begun to move: both imports and exports increased more than four-fold, with exports reaching £52.3 million by November 1977. Britain's trade with the rejectionists also increased sharply, with a nearly ten-fold increase in imports from Iraq and a six-fold increase in exports. Despite the higher oil price and a doubling of her export bill to Iraq and Libya, Britain's deficit to these two nations in November 1977, was £14 million lower than it had been at the end of 1968. While Britain's oil bill increased substantially, by 1977 her trade with the oil-rich nations had risen twice as fast. By 1977 her exports had risen remarkably to all three groups of countries, and, after the initially huge outflows to the oil producers in 1973–75, her export deficits to the Gulf and rejectionist group were much smaller in proportion to imports than they had been in 1973 and significantly smaller (Gulf) or about the same (rejectionist) in absolute terms.

These figures suggest several observations. First, the substantial economic and military assistance Britain extends to the Gulf states is consistent with British economic interests and the power realities in the area. Moreover, the burden of British dependence on oil imports from the area has been eased somewhat by the very large increases in exports to both the Gulf and rejectionist groups, most of which are oil producers. One sees here a mutually profitable connection that is likely to endure. If one had to anticipate a change, one would say it would occur in Anglo-Iraqi relations. Iraq has accepted French and British arms in the last three years. If Iraq should decide to allow other nations to compete with the USSR in arms and, perhaps, technical assistance, an opening would be created which the British (and French) would be eager to exploit.

Britain clearly has much to gain from trade with the confrontation states. The growth in trade with Egypt is large and should certainly be encouraged. Stagnant for more than a decade, trade with Syria has increased sharply in the years since 1973. One would expect this trend to continue, barring major political change inside Syria. The astonishing trade relationship with Israel begs to be noticed. In 1977 Israel bought more from Britain than Egypt and Syria combined. Only the enormous increase in oil revenues enabled the other Middle Eastern states to surpass Israel as Britain's best customer in the region. Even if one discounts nearly half Israel's purchases as re-exported from Britain rather than manufactured there, the economic basis remains for a close relationship between the two countries. To obtain a full picture of Israel's importance to Britain, one should add to these economic considerations a realization of Israel's decisive military role in the Middle East and the danger to British and European interests of war in the region. Today, Israel alone can initiate war against her neighbors, as was shown by her invasion of Lebanon. In this sense it is Israel and not the Arab states that destabilizes the Middle East. Moreover, in the wake of the 1973 war no European and certainly no American government can doubt that Western well-being and security would be endangered by another Arab-Israeli war. Taken together, these aspects of the current situation in the Middle East suggest that Britain's relations with Israel both require imaginative treatment and present political and economic opportunities to the British government as they seek to increase their influence in the region.

A Multilateral Policy Instrument: The European Economic Community

The nations of Western Europe are involved with developing countries—most of which are their former colonies—in numerous and remarkable ways.[32] Their relations are intimate, complex, of the greatest economic, political, and psychological importance to all parties, and, given the demands of contemporary nationalism, they are seldom discussed in public. One could not hope to disentagle these snarls of interest, need, and emotion in this short space. At the same time one cannot ignore the effects of membership in the European Economic Community on British policy in the Middle East. One way to approach this matter is to summarize the recent engagements between the European Community as such and the Middle East, to ask about the significance of those engagements, and to consider in what ways the undertakings could be made to serve British interests in the region.

At the outset one must recognize that the institution—the bureaucrats and commissioners of the EEC—have constituencies, powers, purposes, and interests that differ from those of any of the member nations. In a few ways they are larger, for they bear directly on the commerce and production of the member states, among themselves and between them and the rest of the world. In most ways they are smaller, lacking sovereignty and decisive control of fiscal and monetary policy, diplomacy, or military force. It requires only a little imagination to see that the community acts for its members by carrying out their collective decisions and, at the same time, acts upon them for ends that belong to factions of member governments or to combinations of the community and the member governments.[33] The EEC is both institution and instrument, and one may justifiably ask what happens to Britain's Middle East policy when the instrument is used, as it were, by its owners and its managers. There appear to have been two kinds of connections established between the EEC and the Middle East. They are the Euro-Arab dialog and the preferential trade agreements concluded between the community and the states in the Middle East.

The Euro-Arab dialog began during an EEC summit meeting in Copenhagen in 1973. As the oil crisis unfolded three Arab ministers arrived and demanded a hearing. The Europeans, in complete disarray, responded as best they could. Both sides agreed to hold regular conversations. The history of these talks shows the Arab side attempting to win European cooperation against Israel and the European side trying to foster the kinds of closer economic ties that will create an Arab interest in maintaining oil supplies to the community. At the conclusion of the session that ended on February 13, 1977, the Europeans refused to recognize the Palestine Liberation Organization, although the community allows PLO members to join the twenty delegations on the Arab side of the dialogs.[34] Four months later, during an EEC summit meeting, the members of the community issued a joint declaration that accepted "the need for a homeland for the Palestinian people" and supported "appropriate" participation by representatives of the Palestinians in any negotiations on the Middle East.[35]

In mid-January 1977, the EEC and Egypt, Jordan, and Syria signed agreements on trade, aid, and economic cooperation. With the conclusion of these agreements the EEC had established links with every Arab Mediterranean country except Lebanon.[36] Three weeks later the EEC and Israel concluded a similar agreement on financial aid. To Israel's annoyance the agreement had been postponed until after the conclusion of the negotiations with the Arab countries. After signing the agreement, Israel's Foreign Minister Yigal Allon criticized the community for the delay. He insisted that the amount wasn't commensurate with either Israel's very large trade with Europe or her $2,000 million overall deficit to the nations of the community. He also warned the EEC that it was "dangerous" to discuss the Arab-Israeli conflict in the Euro-Arab dialog without Israel.

Earlier and more important agreements abolishing customs duties on both sides have been signed between the community and Egypt in late 1972, and between the community and Israel in 1976.[37] These are representative of this kind of agreement between the community and Middle Eastern states. They provide for complete and rather rapid abolition of customs duties on virtually all the goods these countries ship to Europe.[38] In the case of Israel, the agreement reduced duties in Europe by 60 percent immediately, by 80 percent on January 1, 1976, and by 100 percent eighteen months later. Egypt received less sweeping reductions: 45 percent on the entry into force of the agreement, and 55 percent from January 1, 1974. Both countries granted reductions to the European members of the community. As one would suspect, Israel moved to abolition much more slowly than her far larger trading partners, while Egypt allowed only partial reductions of 30–40 percent by January 1, 1974, with duties on some textile and other machinery and some food to fall by 50 percent on January 1, 1975.[39]

The postponement of Israel's aid agreement demonstrates the effect of political considerations on the work of the European community.

Plainly, the Europeans wished to extend to Israel the same kinds of benefits granted the Arab states, but only after they had reached agreement with all the Arab governments. This is a modest use of economic influence, but the anger of the Israeli government shows how keenly it was felt. Now that major reductions in duties have been made—abolition in Israel's case—the new connections between politics and economics will have to be made over other issues: the pace and scope of further reductions, and the amount and terms of economic assistance and investment. Within the EEC Britain should concentrate her energy on these matters in an attempt to bring stability and peace to the region and to assure uninterrupted oil supplies for Western Europe.

CONCLUSION

Despite her "hands-off" approach to the Lebanese conflict, Britain does not seem to lack policy instruments with which to achieve her objectives in the Middle East. If the instruments of imperial domination and military intervention have been lost, new instruments have taken their place or old ones have become more important. These are the powers of the European Economic Community to grant preferences and economic and diplomatic support, as well as bilateral British trade and military and economic assistance to the nations of the Middle East. If only because British goals in the region have lost their imperial nature, these instruments promise much and, used in sensible ways, could make an important contribution to the interests and well-being of all parties, Britain, the Arab states, and Israel.

Established British policy in the Middle East is based on UN Resolution 242, gradual and minute alterations of rhetoric in favor of the Palestinians, and good-natured reminders to all parties to engage in "patient, quiet negotiations."[40] One may justifiably ask if this approach enables Britain to advance her interests in the most effective way. One may also ask what changes may be anticipated in British Middle Eastern policy.

British policy in the Middle East may be thought of as an example of the behavior of a "medium-sized" power in an extremely important region. Medium-sized nations have far-flung commercial, political, and security interests but lack the military and diplomatic influence they need to prevent harm to those interests or to keep the harm as small as possible. In this sense Britain is medium-sized, as is France, Germany, Japan, and, perhaps, the People's Republic of China. These nations are already trying to enlarge their capacity to influence events in the Middle East and elsewhere. As described earlier, Britain has begun to extend her trade and economic and military assistance to a number of Arab governments beyond the Gulf. The most notable example is Egypt, where trade and assistance have increased substantially. The increase in trade with Syria and Iraq suggests a change may occur in British relations with these two countries as well. Should one expect Britain's policy toward Israel to move in the same direction? Given the economic arguments in favor of close ties with Israel and the military and political evidence of Israel's willingness to resort to war and massive reprisals as a way of dealing with the Palestinians and the Arab states on her borders, one would anticipate increased economic, military, and diplomatic cooperation between Britain and Israel. Only in this way could Britain obtain the kind of influence in Israel that might persuade her to postpone the resort to war, which at present Israel alone can unleash, as she demonstrated in the invasion of southern Lebanon. This is not to argue in favor of this kind of change in Anglo-Israeli relations nor to give the author's views on the justice of any of the claims of the parties to the Arab-Israeli dispute. Rather, it is an attempt to anticipate a change in British Middle Eastern policy, a change likely to be adopted by Britain and, perhaps, by France, as a way of escaping the quandary of middle powers whose vital interests in times of crisis are left in the custody of others or exposed to chance.

Those who are tempted to see imperialism or a "go-it-alone" mentality in any recommendation for new British initiatives outside Europe must look again.[41] It in no way resembles imperialism for Britain to use aid and commerce in ways intended to foster stability and peace in a region as important to Europe as the Middle East, something she has in any case been doing for the last decade in the Gulf and has already begun to try in the eastern Mediterranean.

THE UNITED NATIONS AND THE ARAB LEAGUE

Harry N. Howard

BEGINNINGS

LEBANON was a charter member both of the Arab League (March 22, 1945) and of the United Nations. Dr. Charles Malik told a plenary session of the United Nations Conference on International Organization at San Francisco on April 28, 1945, that Lebanon was "completely ready to do its utmost part in the maintenance of international peace and security," under the United Nations then being established.[1] The San Francisco conference was designed to establish a new and effective international organization to replace the League of Nations, which had come into being following World War I, not to discuss substantive issues. Nevertheless, there was much discussion—*dans les coulisses*—of such problems as those of Palestine, the presence of Soviet troops in Iran, and of British and French forces in Syria and Lebanon.

In his statement at the plenary session of the San Francisco conference on May 2, 1945, Faris Bey al-Khouri of Syria observed that the newly formed League of Arab States, based on ties of race, language, culture, geography, and "all that goes to make a nation," could "fit in with the world organization envisaged by this conference."[2] The Arab League could serve as a regional arrangement, as outlined especially in Articles 52–54 of the United Nations Charter, although there were very serious doubts as to its possible contributions to the maintenance of international peace and security.

The Arab League was similar to other regional arrangements, such as the Organization of American States (1948) and the North Atlantic Treaty Organization (1949). In October 1952, the Arab League was given observer status by the United Nations General Assembly.[3] A special resolution of the new League of Arab States, approved by Egypt, Iraq, Saudi Arabia, and Syria, emphasized their respect for the independence and sovereignty of Lebanon "in its present frontiers," which they had recog-

269

nized "in consequence of Lebanon's adoption of an independent policy," as announced on October 7, 1943.[4]

THE FIRST TWO DECADES

Lebanon and the Palestine Issue

As already observed, the Lebanese and Syrian delegations at the United Nations Conference on International Organization brought up the question of the occupation of their countries by French and British troops, although the basic issue which involved the United Nations with Lebanon arose out of the Palestine problem with Israel, and the many thousands of Arab refugees who left, fled, or were driven out of what became the state of Israel, and came to Lebanon. As I. F. Stone has remarked, they lost their homes, their livelihood, and even their country. By 1975 it was estimated that there were some 400,000 Palestinian refugees in Lebanon, about one-half of whom lived in UNRWA centers or camps. Many of the newcomers among the refugees had fled into southern Lebanon during "Black September" 1970, after defeat by the Jordanian army. Many refugees in Lebanon were integrated into the Lebanese economy, but political integration proved impossible, because the Muslim element totaled about 95 percent of the Palestinians, and to have given them citizenship *en masse* would have upset the very delicate politico-confessional balance in Lebanon. It was clear by the 1970s, if not before, that Palestinian nationalism had become a fundamental issue in the area, and not relief and rehabilitation under the United Nations Relief and Works Agency for Palestine Refugees in the Near East, established in 1949. Moreover, it was this aspect of the problem which threatened to tear Lebanon into political shreds during 1975–78.[5]

The 1958 Conflict in Lebanon

When civil conflict broke out in Lebanon during May–September 1958, considerable use, wisely or unwisely, was made of the United Nations machinery in order to end the conflict and solve the problems which had resulted in the upheaval. The Lebanese government charged the United Arab Republic—Egypt and Syria—with infiltrating men and arms into Lebanon with the objective of overthrowing the government and forcing Lebanon into the UAR. The Council of the Arab League, which was dominated by Egypt at the time, denied the charges of intervention, called upon Lebanon to withdraw its complaint to the United Nations Security Council, urged an appeal to the various factions to stop the fighting, and proposed the establishment of an Arab League Commission to study the problem.[6] The Lebanese government maintained its position, set forth on May 22, 1958, and on June 11 the United Nations Security Council decided to send an observation group to Lebanon. The United Nations Observation Group in Lebanon (UNOGIL) was composed of some 600 military men, under the command of and direction of Galo Plaza, the former president of Ecuador, Rajeshwar Dayal, of India, and Major-General Odd Bull, of the Norwegian Air Force. UNOGIL was to investigate and report concerning this very complex situation and to ensure that there was "no illegal infiltration of personnel or supply of arms or other material across the Lebanese borders."[7]

With access only to a very small part of the Lebanese border, UNOGIL was unable to verify or to obtain direct evidence to support the charges of the Lebanese government as to infiltration into Lebanon either of men or of military equipment, as it reported from the very beginning of its operations in Lebanon. Moreover, the Lebanese government submitted little or no evidence of its own to support its position.[8] The United States was highly critical of United Nations methods, procedures, and reports and was concerned with the inferences which might be drawn from them. It strongly supported Lebanon in the United Nations but warned the Lebanese Foreign Minister, Dr. Charles Malik, privately that the evidence promised by Lebanon must support the Lebanese claims.

President Chamoun and Dr. Malik had sought to have a United Nations military force in Lebanon, and in response to an urgent appeal from President Chamoun, President Eisenhower sent some 15,000 American troops to Lebanon on July 15, the day after the overthrow of the monarchy in Iraq. Whatever the purpose of their coming, it is altogether probable that the presence of American troops and UNOGIL calmed the situation and enabled the Lebanese people to choose a successor (General Fuad Shehab) to President Chamoun in accordance with Lebanon's constitutional processes.[9] It is also conceivable that, by supporting the established order in Lebanon in 1958, the American and international intervention may have served to postpone the kinds of political and social reforms which might have prevented the collapse of the society in 1975.

In an address before the General Assembly of the United Nations on August 13, 1958,[10] President Eisenhower set forth some essential elements for a United Nations program of assistance to Lebanon, including security measures, a United Nations peace force, a regional economic development plan, and steps to avoid a new arms race in the Middle East. Ambassador Robert Murphy was sent to Lebanon during the crisis to examine and study the problems. Curiously enough, in view of the public, official American position and the open criticism of the United Nations actions in Lebanon, Ambassador Murphy agreed that much of the conflict centered on personalities and rivalries of a domestic character which had no relation to international issues. Communism played no direct or substantial role in the insurrection, although Communists, no doubt, hoped to benefit from the disorders. In Ambassador Murphy's view the primary external influences came from the United Arab Republic, although they were not determining factors in the situation.[11]

The landing of American forces brought its own difficulties in relations with members of UNOGIL. General Odd Bull thought that UNOGIL could have brought the situation under control, had it not been for the coup in Iraq on July 14, although it was also arguable that the American landings in Lebanon and the British intervention in Jordan proved a stabilizing influence. By helping to free the Lebanese situation from its external complications in General Bull's view, UNOGIL had contributed to the establishment of conditions under which the Lebanese people could arrive at a peaceful solution of their domestic problems.[12]

THE 1975–78 CONFLICT

The Renewal of Conflict

In retrospect it seems clear that the quick return of "peace and stability" in Lebanon was misleading. The writer, for instance, was told in Beirut, during 1958, that upheavals such as that through which Lebanon was then passing occurred only about once in a century, and there was, therefore, little about which to be troubled or concerned. Within two decades —not ten—Lebanon, once more, was plunged into disastrous conflict. The civil war of 1975–78, moreover, would not be as readily and easily resolved as it seemed to have been in 1958. After three years of war, Lebanese institutions seemed to have fallen apart—to have disintegrated politically and socially. Almost every governing institution collapsed and the economy was in a shambles. Estimates of the casualties varied, but they ran as high as 60,000 killed, with at least an equal number of injured and wounded, and some 750,000–1,000,000 were said to have fled the chaos.[13]

Inevitably, the conflict in Lebanon involved the Palestine issue. About one-half the 400,000 Palestinians in Lebanon were housed in UNRWA refugee centers, and the situation in Lebanon dominated UNRWA's operations during 1975–77.[14] As UNRWA Commissioner-General Sir John Rennie reported in 1976, there was much concern as to UNRWA's ability to maintain its regular program "in conditions of chronic financial instability and in a turbulent operating environment." Then the situation worsened considerably. What previous UNRWA reports to the UN General Assembly had characterized as "civil disturbances" had degenerated into an "anarchic civil war of appalling violence."[15]

In view of the dimensions of the problem and of the character of the state, the Palestine refugees were inextricably and inevitably involved. Because of the deterioration in its internal and external communications in Lebanon from September 1975 onwards, UNRWA headquarters in Beirut could no longer effectively discharge its responsibility to supervise and support its programs elsewhere in Syria and Jordan, for example. In addition, the larger-scale military activity in Lebanon and the general breakdown of law and order threatened the personal safety of the UNRWA staff and their dependents, hence a portion of the international staff was relocated in Vienna and others were sent to Amman, Jordan. In addition to Lebanon's internal problems, Israeli air raids and attacks from the sea during July, August, September, and December 1975, caused serious loss of life among refugees and damage to UNRWA installations and refugee centers and shelters.[16]

The Arab States and the Arab League

As the situation in Lebanon grew steadily worse during the latter part of 1975 and the early months of 1976, the Arab states, under the aegis of the League of Arab States, prepared to take action. In rather sharp contrast to the situation in 1958, there was no appeal for action, or even discussion, by the United Nations. Members of the Arab League, and especially Egypt, Syria, Lebanon, Jordan, Saudi Arabia, and the Palestine Liberation Organization (PLO), at times, gave much consideration to the Lebanese problem. On December 1, 1975, for example, the Egyptian government set forth a six-point program, in which it (1) called for restrictive control on the carrying of arms in Lebanese cities and towns; (2) insisted on the use of dialog and discussion between parties; (3) condemned the "irresponsible" actions of the Phalange, a right-wing Christian party under the control and direction of Pierre Gemayel; (4) condemned al-Sa'iqa, a Syrian guerrilla element, for its actions in Lebanon; (5) opposed the partition of Lebanon; and (6) regarded the attempt to "internationalize the Lebanese conflict as treason.[17] In an interview on January 7, 1976, the Foreign Minister of Syria Abdel-Halim Khaddam, told *Al-Rai Al-Am* (Kuwait) that Syria was much preoccupied with Lebanon and was seeking to facilitate a solution to its problems, and had made contacts with all parties. Syria had made it "absolutely clear" that it would not permit "the partition of Lebanon and that any attempt at partition would involve Syria's immediate intervention." Khaddam reminded his audience that Lebanon had been part of Syria historically, and that Syria would take it back "if there is any attempt at partition. . . . Lebanon must remain a single country or return to Syria."[18] Lebanese President Suleiman Frangieh reaffirmed Lebanon's sovereignty, freedom, and independence on February 7, 1976, and called for reforms, including the distribution of parliamentary representation on a 50-50 basis, although "the principle of confessional equality should be maintained as regards senior posts."[19]

First Actions of the United Nations

In response to the heavy loss of life, the destruction of property, the displacement of some thousands of persons and other human suffering, Kurt Waldheim, the secretary-general of the United Nations, appealed to member states on February 26, 1976, to contribute to an international effort to meet emergency needs, based on a request of the Lebanese government. Waldheim estimated that at least $50 million in cash and kind, would be required during the balance of 1976. The relief programs of the various United Nations agencies were coordinated by the under secretary-general for Political and General Assembly Affairs and the executive secretary of the Economic Commission for Western Asia at United Nations Headquarters in New York and within Lebanon. Initial efforts to meet the problem included a contribution valued at some $10 million from existing resources of World Food Proposals, the World Health Organization, the United Nations Children's Fund (UNICEF), and the International Committee of the Red Cross—primarily medicines, food, blankets, and clothing. Emergency assistance was undertaken by UNRWA for the most seriously affected refugees in camps, but, as the secretary-general observed: "From the outset, relief efforts were hampered by the lack of security, and the resumption of extensive fighting in March [1976] brought relief efforts within Lebanon virtually to a halt."[20]

There were other tasks which the United Nations might perform in the interest of peaceful adjustment in Lebanon. On March 20, 1976, Waldheim issued a new and urgent appeal for a cease-fire. It availed little. Without openly calling for a special session of the United Nations Security Council, the secretary-general, in a letter of March 30 to President Thomas S. Boya of Benin, noted his authority under Article 99 of the UN Charter, to "bring to the attention of the Security Council any matter which . . . may threaten the maintenance of international peace and security." Waldheim acted because "a cease-fire had now become even more urgent." He appreciated Syrian efforts to mediate, but the unfortunate fact was that the fighting continued unabated. It is interesting to note that, while Ambassador William Scranton, of the United States, and the representative of the United Kingdom agreed that a special session of the Security Council to discuss the Lebanese situation would be a "healthy thing," United Nations members of the Arab League felt that the Arabs themselves should continue to press for a resolution of the Lebanese crisis, and that the problem should not be submitted for consideration by the Security Council at that time.[21]

In the light of all these considerations, during 1976 Waldheim made a number of appeals to the Lebanese authorities and people and brought the Lebanese problem to the attention of the members of the Security Council. The Arab League also made intensive efforts to bring about a cease-fire and the reconciliation of the opposing forces and parties. But despite these efforts the horror and violence continued. Waldheim observed that the United Nations Truce Supervision Organization (UNTSO), which had been established in 1949, had been able to continue its important task of observing the cease-fire in the Lebanese-Israeli sector. He remarked in closing: "From the outset attempts to meet the humanitarian needs of the seriously affected Lebanese population have been frustrated by conditions of almost total insecurity. The international community will be faced with a monumental challenge when the situation permits the resumption of humanitarian assistance and reconstruction of the society and economy of Lebanon."[22]

President Sadat of Egypt was much concerned with events in Lebanon and discussed the problem with his National Security Council on

March 26, 1976. He urged that no time be lost if the situation were to be saved and the deterioration, which inevitably must have "dangerous repercussions" were to be halted. President Sadat observed that such repercussions would not be restricted to the damage done to Lebanon's security and the safety of its people, but also constitute a threat to the security and peace of the whole area, "resulting in serious harm to the Arab nation." In his view the only solution was "for the situation to be dealt with at the Arab level." A number of Arab countries would have to intervene with their good offices "to share in maintaining quiet and stability in Lebanon." The Arab intervention "should be accomplished by the sending of token joint Arab security forces until such times as the situation . . . [became] stable and a favorable atmosphere . . . [even] ensured for putting an end to this distressing and bloody conflict."[23]

Further Steps by the Arab League

The Lebanese conflict had changed its character by June 1, 1976, as a result of a massive Syrian intervention, although various Syrian army units, under the guise of al-Sa'iqa units, had entered Lebanon before June. On June 9–10, 1976, the Council of the League of Arab States, meeting in Cairo, asked all parties in Lebanon to cease fire immediately, and decided to place symbolic Arab security forces in Lebanon under the supervision of the secretariat of the Arab League, "in order to preserve security and stability in Lebanon." These forces were to replace those of Syria. The council also decided on the immediate dispatch of a committee, representing the Arab League Council and composed of the minister of Foreign Affairs of Bahrain, the secretary-general of the Arab League, and the chiefs of the delegations of Libya and Algeria. It was to collaborate with all parties in Lebanon, observe developments, and assure the security and stability of Lebanon. All parties in Lebanon were invited to a national reconciliation under the aegis of President-elect Elias Sarkis, in order "to safeguard the unity of the Lebanese people and its territorial integrity." The resolution also affirmed "the Arab pledge to consolidate the Palestinian revolution and to protect it against all dangers." It was to remain in permanent session in order to follow developments in Lebanon.[24]

In a message June 10 President Suleiman Frangieh, who remained in office until September 23, denounced the resolution of the Arab League as null and void. He observed that a "succession of murderous and bloody events" had afflicted Lebanon, causing the country to collapse and arousing worldwide indignation. Since that time Lebanon repeatedly had brought the problem to the attention of the Arab League which, like individual Arab states, had remained unconcerned. President Frangieh noted that the Arab League had taken action "only when the Syrian mediation, after several unsuccessful attempts at a peaceful solution, took the form of an armed intervention." The initiative of the Arab League, he said, was not in response to persistent Lebanese demands but in response to the demands of others. Lebanon refused "in respect to any matter, and particularly in respect to matters pertaining to its destiny, to submit to the will of any but its own children." Consequently, Lebanon would not "submit to a decision taken in its absence," particularly since Lebanon considered it an arbitrary verdict, not a decision. Likewise, Lebanon would not consent to any Arab country "supervising its peace and security," if such a country were "party to the war raging on its territories and contributes men and arms to the fighters and especially if such a country contributes a division to the Palestine Liberation Army." Lebanon censured the attitude of discrimination of the Arab League and declared that it would resist with all its means and resources any Arab force which entered "its territories against the will and without its prior consent, drawing attention to the numerous consequences" which would "result on the international level from this intervention."[25] On June 19 Prime Minister Rashid Karameh, a veteran Sunni leader from Tripoli, requested Syria to initiate the withdrawal of its forces "in order to prevent the renewal of the clashes, widely condemned by Arab public opinion." But he urged Mahmoud Riyadh, secretary-general of the Arab League, to speed up the implementation of the resolutions of June 9-10, which were related to this issue.[26]

Elias Sarkis, who succeeded Suleiman Frangieh as president of Lebanon on September 23, 1976, spoke of Lebanon's problems in his inaugural address. Among other things, he observed that "the bitter experience" through which Lebanon had been passing since 1975 had proved that many things needed to be changed. Democratic institutions in Lebanon, he believed, contained nothing which was sacrosanct and could not be touched if the aim were to develop them "in accordance with the needs of Lebanese society." In Sarkis's view the "really sacred things" which could "not be touched" were Lebanon's "sovereignty and its territorial and national integrity." Lebanon's relations with the Palestinian resistance, together with the resultant fighting in Lebanon, must be properly handled and based upon a foundation of frankness and trust, whereby "the sovereignty of the country and the security of all pacts and agreements would be respected to prevent any future violations." Lebanon's interests would thereby be protected and the cause of Palestine saved, in Sarkis's consideration. The new president acknowledged with gratitude "the concern expressed for our tragedy" both by the Arab League and the United Nations.[27]

Leaders of Saudi Arabia, Kuwait, Syria, Egypt, Lebanon, and the Palestine Liberation Organization, as members of the Arab League, met in a limited Arab summit conference in Riyadh October 16–18, 1976. The conference examined the situation in Lebanon and the steps and means to be taken to restore normal life, while safeguarding the sovereignty and independence of Lebanon. It announced a cease-fire and decided to strengthen the Arab peace-keeping force in Lebanon. Unanimously, the conference rejected "the partition of Lebanon in any shape or form, legal or actual, implicit or explicit and to affirm the commitment to safeguard Lebanon's national unity and territorial integrity and not to prejudice the unity of its territory or interfere in its domestic affairs in any manner." It hoped for political dialog and reconciliation in Lebanon and agreed that the Cairo Agreement of June 9–10, 1976, would soon be implemented. On October 18 the summit leaders signed a peace plan which called for an immediate cease-fire and the establishment of a 30,000-man Arab Deterrent Force, under the command of President Sarkis, with a coordinating committee composed of representatives of Saudi Arabia, Egypt, Syria, and Kuwait. A special fund was to be established for a period of six months under the general supervision of the president of Lebanon.[28] During a summit meeting of the Arab League in Cairo October 25–26, 1976, the actions taken at Riyadh were reaffirmed and the machinery for rendering assistance to Lebanon was established.[29]

By the end of the summer of 1976, some 3,000 troops of the Arab Deterrent Force had arrived in Lebanon, commanded by an Egyptian general. By mid-November some 15,000 Syrian troops were in and around Beirut, and Tripoli and Sidon were brought under control. At the end of November, it was estimated that there were no less than 30,000 Syrian troops, with some 500 tanks, in the country. This was by far the major component of what was to become the Arab Deterrent Force in Lebanon.[30] The Syrian contingent in Lebanon constituted about one-third of the Syrian armed forces. During 1976 the cost of maintaining the force in Lebanon was about $50 million per month, although the cost was reduced to some $30 million in 1977. There was no evidence that Syrian entry into Lebanon was motivated by any desire to create a "greater Syria." It may also be observed that, by the end of 1976, there were 10,000 men, composed of Libyan, Algerian, Saudi, Sudanese, and PLO troops, who had taken up positions in Lebanon as part of the Arab Deterrent Force.[31]

A LIMITED INTERNATIONAL ROLE

During the 1958 episode, the United Nations, on official request of President Chamoun, had taken action by sending UNOGIL to Lebanon for observation and reporting to the UN General Assembly, and there was considerable support for the Lebanese position, whatever the lacunae in the evidence submitted by Lebanon or gathered by UNOGIL as to external intervention on the part of the United Arab Republic. In 1975–78 this was not the case, and there was neither any formal request for specific action by the United Nations nor any formal discussion of the situation in Lebanon, although it is altogether possible that there was more external intervention during 1975–78 than in the prelude of 1958. There were a few references to the Lebanese situation during the general debate in the Thirtieth Session of the General Assembly in the fall of 1976 and during the discussion of the Arab-Israeli conflict, but little talk of specific, concrete problems.

On September 30, 1976, Secretary of State Kissinger noted that since its birth, the United Nations had been involved in the "chronic conflict in the Middle East." Each successive war had "brought greater perils, an increased danger of Great Power confrontation and more severe economic dislocations." The United States was actively engaged in the search for peace and, in Kissinger's view, the United Nations had a crucial role to play. Since the last session of the General Assembly "overwhelming tragedy" had befallen the people of Lebanon. The United States strongly supported the sovereignty, unity, and integrity of Lebanon and opposed partition of the country. The United States hoped that Lebanese affairs would soon be returned to the hands of the people of Lebanon. Kissinger declared that all United Nations members had an obligation to resolve differences, and he had no doubt that the United Nations could "play a distinct role in the reconstruction effort."[32] Foreign Secretary Crossland, of the United Kingdom, sounded much the same note on October 5. He, too, observed that from the beginning the United Kingdom had been engaged in continuous attempts to apply the principles of peaceful settlement to the Middle East.[33] Mowaffak Allaf of Syria declared that in the face of the explosive situation in Lebanon, Syria intended only to contribute constructively to the efforts aimed at putting an end to the conflict in Lebanon.[34] This was the general theme of the discussion, which never came down to the submission of concrete solutions.[35]

The Lebanese Case

On October 14, however, Ambassador Edouard Ghorra, the permanent representative of Lebanon at the United Nations, expressed the official Lebanese view concerning the tragedy which had afflicted his country.[36] He was deeply appreciative of the expressions of sympathy which Lebanon had received, and noted with satisfaction the call for the restoration of stability and peace and for United Nations assistance which had been given or promised, together with the initiative in establishing a special $50 million fund for Lebanon.

Turning to the conflict in his country, he observed that Lebanon had been in the throes of unprecedented, cruel, and tragic events for more than eighteen months. While much had been said and written concerning the origins of the fighting and about the obstacles which had prevented a settlement, a good deal of stress was wrongly placed on the internal character of the conflict, particularly in "the first phases of events." It was true, he stated, that the United Nations Charter, Article 2, paragraph 7, excluded matters falling essentially within the domestic jurisdiction of states from the purview of the organization; but Ghorra emphasized that never before had Lebanon's internal problems been of such magnitude as to generate so much violence, bloodshed, and destruction. In the Lebanese official view, had they been of the usual character, the problems could have been solved. Lebanon had been a classic example "of how various religious communities" could "live together in peace, harmony and freedom and within the framework of a democratic and progressive system of government." The only sensible way out of the difficulties was through "dialog and consensus and according to the organic law of the country." What then were the origins of the "tragic and complex events" which had disrupted Lebanese society for so many months? Ambassador Ghorra believed that the origins of Lebanon's troubles were to be found "in the web of Middle Eastern contradictions and complexities"—in the uprooting of the Palestinians, the Arab-Israeli conflict, the refusal of Israel to withdraw from Arab lands, Arab rivalries, and the assaults of Palestinians against the sovereignty of Lebanon and the security of its people. The unsettled conditions in Lebanon resulted from these factors and led to a state of tension and turbulence in the area, which inevitably affected Lebanon.

In Ghorra's view the problems were accentuated by the presence of some 400,000 Palestinians in Lebanon, among whom the Palestine revolution had established deep roots. Friction developed and intensified, and relations between the Lebanese and the Palestinians deteriorated, largely because of "constant Palestinian intervention in [its] internal affairs and intolerable encroachment on its sovereignty." The situation continued to deteriorate but seemed on the road toward solution through the Cairo Agreement of June 9–10, 1976, although fundamental issues remained unsolved. Lebanon sought to maintain its sovereignty, while the Palestinians did not, in Ghorra's view, abide by the agreement, but acted as a state within a state within a state, defied Lebanese authorities, and abused Lebanese hospitality. Moreover, after "Black September" 1970, the Palestinians sent several units of their forces into Lebanon, without the approval of the Lebanese authorities and sometimes despite them. They were accused of committing all sorts of crimes and escaped justice in the refugee centers. Only a spark was needed in such an explosive situation. Granted all that Lebanon had done in behalf of the Palestinian cause, Ghorra could not understand such behavior. He placed full responsibility for the situation on the Palestinians and their leadership. The Palestinian observer in the General Assembly was given no opportunity to reply.

In conclusion, Ambassador Ghorra felt that it was high time for an overall settlement in the Middle East by bringing about the withdrawal of Israeli forces from the occupied Arab lands and enabling the Palestinians to exercise the right of self-determination, but any delay in making peace should not impede peaceful adjustments in Lebanon. He was confident that Lebanon could and would, like Phoenix, rise again.

Waldheim's Summation

While the violence abated during 1977, there was no basic solution of fundamental issues. South Lebanon continued, at times, to be the scene of heavy fighting, with Israel openly assisting Lebanese Christians against Palestinian forces. The Lebanese conflict was not on the agenda for discussion or action in the United Nations General Assembly in the fall of 1977. Secretary-General Kurt Waldheim found little encouragement in his hope for some kind of political settlement, whether at Geneva or elsewhere. As to the situation in Lebanon, he wrote:

> In spite of the cease-fire which has put an end to the strife in Lebanon since last November, tension has persisted especially in the South of that country. While this very delicate and potentially explosive situation has

considerable international implications in the context of the Middle East problem, United Nations involvement has been confined largely to humanitarian assistance. The United Nations military observers continue to carry out their limited functions in circumstances of great difficulty and considerable danger.[37]

Waldheim thought it "vitally important," both in the interest of Lebanon and of peace in the Middle East, "that the process of conciliation between the various factions involved in this area should evolve speedily and effectively." But the process could not succeed while the fighting in the south continued. He therefore appealed to all concerned to cooperate in the efforts toward achievement of a cease-fire and a peaceful adjustment.

Looking Ahead

But the fighting did not entirely cease, even though it was not on a scale comparable to the conflict which had taken place during some nineteen months in 1975–76. Tensions persisted, particularly in south Lebanon, despite the cease-fire which had gone into effect in November 1976. While the very delicate and "potentially explosive" situation had many international implications in the "wider context of the Middle Eastern problem," it continued to be handled mostly on a regional basis—through the members of the League of Arab States. The United Nations played only a very minor political role in the Lebanese conflict, as we have seen, and confined its involvement very largely to humanitarian assistance. United Nations observers (UNTSO), of course, continued to serve their limited, but very important, functions as they had since 1949. The fact that the members of the Arab League assumed the major political role is not necessarily to reflect—one way or another—on the United Nations as an instrument for the maintenance of international peace and security. As the secretary-general of the United Nations observed on September 1, 1977, under the United Nations Charter, Article 52, "the responsibilities of the United Nations for the maintenance of international peace and security" were "complementary to, not competitive with, the efforts of regional organizations."[38] Other regional arrangements, more especially the Organization of American States, which sought a special status in the United Nations then being established, have acted in similar fashion, when members of the OAS, including the United States, did not want any intervention on the part of the United Nations.[39] In any event, most members of the United Nations were not anxious to become involved in the Lebanese conflict during 1975–77, and the Arab members were especially reluctant concerning outside intervention. The Arab governments opposed "Arabization" and "internationalization" of the conflict, although they worked to keep consideration of the problem at the "Arab level." Nevertheless, it was clear at the beginning of 1978 that the Lebanese conflict would confront the United Nations with serious problems and that the United Nations would have a very "distinct" role to play in the future, even if the character of that role was not precisely delineated.

The record of the United Nations during 1975–76, to say nothing of the past thirty years in the Arab-Israel conflict, was hardly one to inspire confidence in its ability to meet the issues of civil war or conflict. It is doubtful that it could have been otherwise. There was some hope that the United Nations machinery could be useful in leading toward peaceful adjustments, but there was little prospect in the immediate future of solving either the more general problems in the Palestine conflict or the very troubled situation in south Lebanon, where Israel had become directly involved.[40] South Lebanon had been a kind of staging area for Arab Palestinian action against Israel, and Israel had responded, from time to time, with military raids into that area.[41] Waldheim, meanwhile, continued to urge discussions at the United Nations in the latter part of November 1977, as he had done before and was to continue to do.[42]

The Lebanese war had cost some 60,000 lives and had threatened the very fabric which had held the country together. It seemed endless. Beirut was now split along confessional lines. Violence prevailed throughout the country, although not necessarily along confessional lines. There were occasional fights between the Syrian-dominated Arab Deterrent Force and the Lebanese, although without the Syrian forces, Lebanon would probably have been completely chaotic.

Al-Fatah assumed responsibility for the guerrilla attack on a bus in Tel Aviv on March 11, 1978, in which thirty-seven people were killed. Seizing on this event, Israel sent air, land, and sea forces estimated at 10,000–20,000 men, into south Lebanon, and within twenty-four hours had brought the area south of Sidon and Tyre under Israel's control. On March 19, 1978, the Security Council approved a resolution calling for an immediate cease-fire and the withdrawal "forthwith" of Israeli forces from south Lebanon.[43] At the same time a United Nations interim force was established for service in south Lebanon, at an estimated cost of some $68 million, for an initial period of six months, with provision for renewal. With the UN troops in place, Israel gradually withdrew some of its forces, and eventually completed withdrawal on June 13, 1978, but only after having heavily armed the Christian and anti-Palestinian militias, who then contested with the UN forces for the control of militarily important terrain.[44]

While fighting has subsided temporarily in southern Lebanon, tension between the Palestinians and Christians, backed by Israel, remains high. The UN forces there have unquestionably helped prevent the ugly and chronic bloodshed that occurs when local incidents blossom into firefights and artillery duels. They can do little more until the principals in Lebanon—Syria, the Palestinians and Lebanese, and Israel—together with Egypt, Jordan, the United States, and Saudi Arabia, choose to move and succeed in moving toward both a general Middle Eastern settlement and a reconstruction of Lebanon's society and government. For the short term, the Security Council has agreed to extend the stay of the UN force in the south, recognizing its immediate value and, perhaps, anticipating a constructive UN presence in the border area as part of an overall, durable peace in Lebanon and the region as a whole.

NOTES

Chapter 1—THE SOCIAL CONTEXT

1. Halim Barakat, *Lebanon in Strife: Student Preludes to the Civil War*, (Austin: University of Texas Press, 1977).

2. The Kata'ib party was founded in 1936 after Gemayel's visit to Germany on the occasion of the Olympic games that year. The party recruits its members mostly from the emerging middle-class Christian Maronites.

3. The Party of the Free Nationalists is highly amorphous and unorganized. It is known as a one-man party that is expected to disappear with the disappearance of its old founder (1958) and leader, Camille Chamoun.

4. Charles Malik, "Lebanon: Between Hope and Despair," *Monday Morning* (Beirut) 6(257)(May 16–22, 1977).

5. See *an-Nahar*, November 30, 1969, p. 10.

6. See *al-Ahad Magazine* (Beirut), January 24, 1977.

7. Malik, "Lebanon: Between Hope and Despair," *Monday Morning*, p. 16.

8. Republique Libanaise, Minstere du plan, *Besoins et possibilites de development du Liban* 1(1961):93.

9. Elie Salem, "Cabinet Politics in Lebanon," *Middle East Journal* 21(Fall 1967):496.

10. *An-Nahar*, September 7, 1968.

Chapter 2—THE PALESTINIANS

1. Quoted in *Summary of World Broadcasts (SWB)*, British Broadcasting Corporation Monitoring Service, Second Series ME/5708/A/3, January 9, 1978.

2. Voice of Palestine radio (monitored by author), Baghdad, January 8, 1978.

3. *Fiches du Monde Arabe (FMA)* (Beirut), no. 325, July 9, 1975. Figures from Ministry of Planning, Central Directorate of Statistics and Ministry of the Interior, General Directorate of Public Security.

4. *FMA*, no. 325, July 9, 1975. Original figures from Ministry of Planning, Central Directorate of Statistics and Ministry of the Interior, General Directorate of Public Security, Beirut.

5. *Ibid.*

6. Figures from UNRWA reports, summarized in *FMA*, no. 298, June 11, 1975, and from the map of UNRWA's Area of Operations, UNRWA, Amman, June 30, 1977.

7. *FMA* published the text, no. 575, October 20, 1976. A first version was given by *an-Nahar* on April 20, 1970. On September 2, 1976, the Beirut magazine *as-Sayad* published an "intimate interview" with President Frangieh in which Frangieh claimed the accords stipulated that the number of Palestinians in Lebanon should not exceed the 120,000 refugees registered with UNRWA and should have only "symbolic" light weapons in the camps. On September 6, 1976, *an-Nahar* published an interview with Abu Lynd whose version of the text was authenticated the next day by Charles Helou, no longer president of the republic.

8. Personal interviews with PFLP members.

9. All Lebanese newspapers, April 11 and 12, and May 3–17, 1973. Cf. also my dispatches to the *Christian Science Monitor* for the period.

10. *FMA*, no. 339, July 30, 1975. A new text of the Melkart Protocol, probably authentic, was published in "Horizons 80," by *L'Orient-Le Jour* (Beirut), January 1978, pp. 66–67.

11. *Falastin al-Thawra* (Beirut), May 28, 1973.

12. *FMA*, no. 345. August 6, 1975.

13. Author's observations and conversations with al-Fatah and PFLP leaders.

14. *FMA*, no. 418, December 23, 1975.

15. All Lebanese newspapers, December 17, 1975.

16. United Press International, January 6, 1976.

17. Israel radio in English, January 20, 1976.

18. John Bulloch, *Death of a Country, The Civil War in Lebanon* (London: Weidenfeld and Nicolson, 1977), p. 115.

19. *FMA*, no. 532, September 1, 1976.

20. Cf. my report to ABC Radio News, March 26, 1976, from Damascus.

21. Israel radio (monitored by author), March 11, 1976.

22. *FMA*, no. 610, April 6, 1977.

23. Bulloch, *Death of a Country*, p. 131.

24. *FMA*, no. 634, May 18, 1977.

25. Author's dispatch to the *Christian Science Monitor*, July 16, 1976.

26. Personal interview with Hassan Sabry al-Kholy and Red Cross representatives.

27. *Al-Ahram* (Cairo), September 7, 1976.

28. *FMA*, nos. 690, July 13, 1977, and 694, July 20, 1977.

29. Private interview with Camille Chamoun in Beirut, April 28, 1977.

30. *Reuters*, Beirut, January 22, 1978.

Chapter 3—THE LIMITS OF MILITARY POWER: Syria's Role

1. See A. H. Hourani, *Syria and Lebanon* (London: 1946), passim.

2. As recently as February 1977, President al-Assad resorted to a most interesting argumentation in a press interview, *al-Rai al-Amm* (Kuwait), February 9, 1977: Syria gave up four (Muslim) provinces in order to prevent the French from establishing a (Christian) sectarian state in Lebanon. "Thus," he said, "the Lebanon of today was established on a basis of participation and Syria will not accept partition in any form."

3. See A. Kelidar, "Religion and State in Syria," *Asian Affairs* 61(n.s. 5) (1974):16–22. The evolution of the Lebanese Shi'a community's cooperation with the 'Alawi communities in Lebanon and Syria was reported extensively in the Lebanese press. See, for instance, *al-Hayat*, July 7, 1973.

4. On Syria's regional policy in the early 1972, see M. Kerr, "Hafiz Assad and the Changing Patterns of Syrian Politics," *International Journal* 28(4)(1975): 689–706; M. Maoz, *Syria under Hafiz al-Assad: New Domestic and Foreign Policies*, Jerusalem Papers on Peace Problems, no. 15, 1975; and I. Rabinovich, "Continuity and Change in the Syrian Ba'th Regime," in I. Rabinovich and H. Shaked, eds., *From June to October* (New Brunswick, N.J., 1977), and "Phases in Syria's Policy in the Arab Israeli Conflict Since the October War" in the Shiloah Center's volume *Between War and Settlement* (Hebrew edition, Tel Aviv, 1977, English edition forthcoming, 1978).

5. Indeed, the most articulate exposition of the risks with which the Lebanese civil war presented Syria in 1975 was made by Assad himself in his July 20, 1976 speech, mentioned and analyzed below.

6. F. Stoakes, "The Supervigilantes: The Lebanese Kata'ib Party as Builder, Surrogate and Defender of The State," *Middle Eastern Studies* 2(October 1975): 215–31.

7. On the coordination of Syrian policy with the U.S., see J. Bulloch, *Death of a Country* (London: Weidenfeld and Nicolson, 1977), pp. 107–108; W. B. Quandt, *Decade of Decisions* (Berkeley: University of California Press, 1977), pp. 282–83; and A. Kelidar, *Lebanon: The Collapse of a State*, Conflict Studies (London)(August 1976), p. 13. This is the place to note that the "conspiratorial theory" explanations of Syria's policy in Lebanon have so far failed to be anchored in concrete evidence. See, for instance, F. Maughrabi and Naseer Aruri, eds., *Lebanon: Crisis and Challenge in the Arab World* (Detroit: Association of Arab American University Graduates, Special Report, no. 1, January 1977).

8. These themes were developed later in an interview granted by President al-Assad to British journalist Patrick Seale and published in the London *Observer* on March 6, 1977.

9. The first Lebanese leader to point in public to the real significance of a political solution imposed by Syria was Raymond Edde. His views were published by *al-Nahar* on January 28, 1976.

10. Radio Damascus, April 1, 1976.

11. The best study to date of Syria's military campaigns in Lebanon is a Hebrew-language article "The Syrian invasion of Lebanon: Military moves as a Political Instrument," *Ma'arachot*, July 1977.

12. Radio Damascus, July 20, 1976. The reports of domestic unrest in Syria are surveyed in I. Rabinovich, "Syria" in Colin Legum, ed., *Middle East Contemporary Survey, 1976–1977* (New York: Homes and Meier, 1978).

13. Kelidar, *Lebanon*; and cf. *New York Times*, August 31, 1977.

14. See D. Dishon, "The Lebanese War—an All-Arab Crisis," *Midstream* (January 1977):25–32.

15. See *al-Watan al-Arabi* (Paris), September 23, 1977.

16. Radio Damascus, July 20, 1976.

17. Radio Damascus, September 20, 1976.

18. *Al-Sayyad*, September 9, 1976.

Chapter 4—THE MILITARY DIMENSION

1. I am indebted to Walter S. Pullar for research assistance.

2. *Lebanese Parties and Militias*, U.S. Department of State, Bureau of Intelligence and Research, Report No. 200, November 10, 1975.

3. This included a large number of kidnappings and vendettas for personal reasons which frequently characterized the breakdown of law and order.

4. Some 5,000 troops were reportedly engaged at Zagharta, and on September 15 the army moved into Tripoli where the first clash occurred with the leftists. The bitter reaction virtually neutralized the army as an instrument of central authority. Premier Rashid Karameh later detailed a strong army force to seize a shipload of illegal weapons for the Christians. The regulars were turned back by a single Phalangist roadblock. *International Herald Tribune*, November 7, 1975.

5. *New York Times*, September 9, 15; October 26, 1975.

6. *Ibid.*, October 22; November 6, 29; December 3, 1975.

7. *International Herald Tribune*, December 31, 1975.

8. *New York Times*, January 7, 9, 16, 19, 20, 1975: They also gained the northern approaches to Tripoli, advancing over the northern Lebanese border.

9. After several weeks of heavy fighting for the camp Tel al-Za'atar, the rightists sustained a series of reversals and accepted a Syrian-sponsored ceasefire. *New York Times*, January 7, 9, 16, 1975.

10. *Strategic Survey*, International Institute for Strategic Studies, 1976, p. 87.

11. *International Herald Tribune*, May 3, 1976.

12. *Ibid.*, March 10, 1976.

13. *Foreign Broadcast Information Service (FBIS)*, March 11, 1976; *New York Times*, March 14, 1976.

14. *Strategic Survey*, IISS, 1976, p. 87.

15. *International Herald Tribune*, June 12, 1976.

16. *Ibid.*, March 24, 1976.

17. *Ibid.*, March 22, 1976.

18. *New York Times*, April 2, 9, 1976.

19. *Strategic Survey*, IISS, 1976, p. 87.

20. Casualties now surpassed 18,500 killed and 40,000 wounded, *International Herald Tribune*, May 3, 1976.

21. Galia Golan, *The Soviet Union and the PLO*, Adelphi Paper, no. 131, 1977.

22. *Washington Post*, June 2, 1976.

23. *International Herald Tribune*, July 7, 11, 1976.

24. *Washington Post*, June 7, 1976.

25. *New York Times*, June 21, 1976; and *International Herald Tribune*, June 25, 1976.

26. *International Herald Tribune*, July 25; August 12, 15, 18, 29; September 2, 6, 14, 1976.

27. *New York Times*, September 28, 29, 1976.

28. *Ibid.*, October 18, 24, 1976.

29. *Ibid.*, October 27, 1976.

30. Henry Kissinger, news conference, Hartford, Ct., October 27, 1976, *Department of State Bulletin*, November 22, 1976. According to Middle Eastern News Agency (MENA), January 3, 1977, official statistics were 63,875 killed, 217,593 wounded, and 7,800 missing.

31. Trevor N. Dupuy, *Elusive Victory: The Arab-Israeli Wars, 1947–74*, (Indianapolis: Bobbs Merrill, 1977), see charts; and Anthony H. Cordesman, "How Much is Too Much?," *Armed Forces Journal International*, October 1977.

32. *New York Times*, November 15, 21, 1976.

33. MENA, February 12, 1977.

34. *New York Times*, February 26, 1977.

35. In factional fighting between the two rejectionist factions more than 100 were reportedly killed from June 9 to mid-July.

36. Palestinian Press Service (WAFA), June 1, 1977. In reality this was merely an up-grading of the training levels of Fatah units that were not subordinated to Syria. They were expected to ultimately have a higher proficiency than the rejectionist guerrillas.

37. Since the beginning of the October 1976 cease-fire, the heavy fighting in the border area had forced nearly 100,000 to evacuate their homes, many for the second and third times, compounding Lebanon's own refugee problem.

38. *International Herald Tribune*, May 28, 1977.

39. The Beirut Christian Daily, *Le Reveil*, July 31, criticized the latest scheme as impractical in part because the rightists refused to withdraw from villages that were legitimately theirs.

40. WAFA, August 24, 1977.

41. *Le Reveil*, August 27, 1977.

42. *International Herald Tribune*, November 10, 1977; see also *International Herald Tribune*, November 8, 9, 12–13, 1977, and WAFA same dates. There was widespread speculation at the time that Israel's disproportionately heavy retaliation was timed to influence the Arab Foreign Ministers' Meeting November 12–13.

43. *International Herald Tribune*, May 19, 1976.

44. *Washington Post*, July 21, 1976.

45. *International Herald Tribune*, May 19, 1976.

46. *Washington Post*, July 21, 1976; *International Herald Tribune*, October 11, 22, 1976. According to an interview with a former Israeli Cabinet minister, Israel supplied $100 million to the rightists since May 1976, including 12,000 rifles, 5,000 machine guns, and 110 tanks. Some Israeli officers served as advisors in northern Lebanon, and about 1,500 rightists were trained in Israel, *Time*, August 22, 1977.

47. *International Herald Tribune*, August 27, 1976; and *Christian Science Monitor* July 20, 1976.

48. *Ibid.*, August 18, 1976.

49. *Ibid.*, September 29, 1976; and *Financial Times*, October 18, 1976.

50. It is somewhat easier to estimate the amount of arms transferred into third countries from where they were reshipped to Lebanon. For example, the Soviet Union supplied Libya with $158 million of arms in 1973, and $209 million in 1974; Iraq received $341 million in 1973, and $356 million in 1974; Syria received $724 million in 1973, and $465 million in 1974. *World Military Expenditures and Arms Transfers, 1965-1974*, U.S. Arms Control and Disarmament Agency Report to Congress, 1974; and Roger F. Pajak, "Soviet Military Aid to Iraq and Syria," *Strategic Review*, Winter 1976.

51. *Los Angeles Times*, June 13, 1978.

Chapter 5—ISRAEL

1. Note the text of the 1969 Cairo Accords in Walid Khadduri, ed., *International Documents on Palestine: 1969* (Beirut: Institute for Palestine Studies, 1972).

2. See A. Yaniv, "P.L.O. A Profile," Israel Universities Study Group for Mideast Affairs (August 1974).

3. It must be remembered that the Christian Community as a whole has not actively collaborated with Israel. Israel's ties are with the Maronite Christians through its support of two out of three of the Maronite private armies—the Phalangists, led by Pierre Gemayal, and the "Tigers," led by Camille Chamoun. The third Maronite militia, led by former President Suleiman Frangieh, is supported

by Syria. The Greek Orthodox community, the second-largest Christian community in Lebanon, has not taken an active anti-Palestinian/Muslim, pro-Israeli position.

4. The "good fence" yielded intelligence and began the overt connection between Israel and the anti-Palestinian/Muslim groups in southern Lebanon. It is also the first time Israel has made direct contact with Arabs as an ally rather than a conqueror.

5. See *Washington Post*, April 11, 1977, p. 18.

6. *Christian Science Monitor*, April 14, 1977, p. 7.

7. See *New York Times*, May 29, 1977, p. 11; and *Washington Post*, May 28, 1977, p. 10.

8. *Washington Post*, August 16, 1977, p. A.

9. *Washington Post*, September 3, 1977, p. 11.

10. See *New York Times*, February 26, 1978, p. 11.

11. *Foreign Broadcast Information Service (FBIS)* 5(43)(March 2, 1978), p. G1.

12. *FBIS* 5(48)(March 10, 1978), p. N1.

13. *Ibid.*

14. *Ibid.*

15. Dial Torgerson, "Israel's Thrust into Lebanon: Was it Simply Blind Revenge or Calculated Self-Defense?" *Los Angeles Times*, March 26, 1978, Part VI, p. 12. See also *New York Times*, March 30, 1978, p. 12.

16. Interview on IDF Radio, 1005 GMT, March 18, 1978, as reported in *FBIS* 5(54)(March 20, 1978), p. N18.

17. *Time*, April 13, 1978. *Time* put the number of refugees at 265,000, with 100,000 in Sidon alone.

18. See the reports in *Time*, March 27, 1978, especially pp. 26–27.

19. *Ibid.*, p. 29. The *Times* of London on March 21 reported that only 300 inhabitants were left in Tyre out of a population of 60,000. See also the eyewitness report by Robert Fisk of the Israeli air and naval bombardment of Tyre, London *Times*, March 20, 1978. A ten-minute rocket attack on Damour was reported in the *Times* on March 16. When it ended the town was "mostly rubble."

20. *Times*, March 15, 1978: this report, from the *Times's* correspondent in Jerusalem, stated that Israeli military headquarters on March 14 announced that the attack on Lebanon was not a reprisal but was intended to protect Israel against Palestinian attack from Lebanese territory by destroying the terrorist bases there.

21. *FBIS* 5(59)(March 27, 1978), p. N9.

22. According to Israeli Defence Minister Weizman, when it was clear that a UN presence was imminent "we had to decide where it would be best for the UN force to be stationed—on the banks of the Litani or someplace else." He added it "was decided that it is better for a UN force to be stationed on the Litani, and that's how we got there, so that UN soldiers would be situated there." *New York Times*, May 7, 1978, p. 3. Weizman was even more explicit about this subject in

an earlier interview: "The entire area [of southern Lebanon] except for the Tyre strip, is clear of terrorists now. This gives the United Nations a better opening position for the prevention of the return of the terrorists into the region. If we had stopped the operation at an earlier stage, when the area was swarming with terrorists, we could not have proved that the terrorists have returned to the region and that the UN force has not fulfilled its job." *FBIS* 5(58)(March 24, 1978), p. N1, from *Ma'ariv*, March 24, 1978.

23. *Los Angeles Times*, March 15, 1978, p. 6. See *New York Times*, March 17, 1978, p. 10, for the text of the U.S. statement on the Israeli invasion. Sources close to Israel's Ministry of Defence say that the orders on the campaign did not refer to a security strip of 10 km (6.2 miles), but specified the key points to be taken by the IDF (i.e., Bint Jubayl, al-Khiyyam, etc.) which were about 4–8 km from the border. This strip is reminiscent of a clause in the Chtaura agreement which specified that all Palestinian forces should withdraw to a line 10 km from the Israeli border. At that time the U.S. appeared satisfied with the agreement, but Israel was not. It may be that, in speaking of this strip Israel was trying to satisfy Washington, and that the 10 km strip would still fulfill the objective of unifying the Christian enclaves.

24. At a U.S. State Department news conference, for example, Secretary of State Cyrus Vance was quoted as saying that the U.S. would persevere in its quest for a Middle East peace settlement despite the "substantial obstacles" resulting from differences with Prime Minister Begin which Vance said had "slowed down" the negotiating efforts. *New York Times*, March 25, 1978, p. 3.

25. The text of the Vance letter to O'Neill is in *New York Times*, April 6, 1978, p. 14.

26. See, for example, the interview with Senator Abraham Ribicoff in the *Wall Street Journal*, March 13, 1978, p. 1; and Jacob Javits' criticism of Israel's vaguely worded response to questions submitted by Secretary of State Vance concerning Israel's position on a final settlement. Javits called the Israeli response the "wrong signal at the wrong time." *Washington Post* (June 22, 1978), p. A1. Equally worrisome to Israel was the position Ribicoff took in favor of the U.S. aircraft sales to Saudi Arabia and Egypt—sales which Israel adamantly opposed. Ribicoff's support of the package of 200 warplanes to Saudi Arabia, Egypt, and Israel was credited with influencing the votes of liberal Democrats such as Culver, Bumpers, Eagleton, and Inouye, among others, and with winning over such Republicans as Bellmon and Mathias.

27. *Los Angeles Times*, March 19, 1978, p. 6.

28. *New York Times*, March 25, 1978, pp. 1, 3.

29. See, for example, *Washington Post*, August 23, 1977, p. 9, concerning U.S. State Department inquiries into possible violations of U.S. law by Israel in using U.S.-supplied weapons during the campaign in southern Lebanon.

30. See *Los Angeles Times*, April 9, 1978, p. 1; see also *New York Times*, April 6, 1978, pp. 1, 14.

31. *FBIS* 5(58)(March 24, 1978), p. N3, from *Ma'ariv*, March 24, 1978, pp. 24, 31.

32. *Ibid.*, (54), (March 20, 1978), p. N18, from an interview on IDF Radio in Hebrew, March 18, 1978.

33. *Ibid.*

34. *Ibid.*, (58), (March 24, 1978), p. N2, from *Ma'ariv*, March 24, 1978, pp. 24, 31.

35. A fairly detailed, unclassified account of these encounters appears in *Time*, August 14, 1978, pp. 21-22. Another account of Jordanian-Israeli contacts appears in *The Economist*, January 22, 1977, p. 60. See also Arnaud de Borchgrave, "Dayan's Secret," *Newsweek*, October 3, 1977, p. 43.

36. See *Washington Post*, November 10, 1977, p. 1.

Chapter 6—SAUDI ARABIA

1. David E. Long, "King Faysal's World View," a paper presented at Conference on King Faisal sponsored by the University of Southern California, May 1978, p. 3.

2. *Ibid.*, p. 10.

3. From a speech given in Riyadh on January 21, 1963, reprinted in "Prince Faysal Speaks" (Saudi Arabia, n.d.), p. 12.

4. Joint statement on Talks in Riyadh, Cairo Voice of the Arabs, 1130 GMT, April 23, 1975, in *Foreign Broadcast Information Service (FBIS)*.

5. *Ibid.*

6. On May 23 President Suleiman Frangieh announced the formation of Lebanon's first and only military government. The prime minister was Rifai, 76, who had retired as head of the Internal Security Forces in 1962. Real power rested with army commander Ghanim, who became defense minister, and Chief of Staff Nasarallah, who became interior minister. *Reuters* report by Andrew Waller, Beirut, May 23, 1975.

7. The cabinet had one Sunni (Karameh), one Shi'ah ('Adil Usayran), one Druze (Majid Arslan), one Maronite (Camille Chamoun), one Catholic (Philippe Tagla), and one Greek Orthodox (Ghassan Tueini).

8. Beirut Radio Broadcast, July 2, 1975, in *FBIS*, July 20, 1975.

9. Edward Sheehan, *The Arabs, Israelis and Kissinger* (New York: Reader's Digest Press, 1976), Appendix 8, p. 25.

10. Syria's opponents—Lebanese rightists, some Palestinians, Iraqis, and Egyptians among others—took every opportunity to portray Assad as having imperial ambitions in Lebanon.

11. Syrian official statement, October 14, 1975, *FBIS*.

12. See *New York Times*, December 1975.

13. *Black Cross, A Portfolio of the Conspiracy Against Lebanon*, Arab Socialist Union, Nassaritt Organization, Beirut, 1976.

14. The Israelis had reaffirmed their inhumanity and brutality in Arab

minds by their air strikes on Palestinian camps on December 2. See *New York Times*, December 3, 1975.

15. See the seventeen-point Frangieh-Assad plan as published following their meeting in Damascus, February 16, 1976.

16. Jalloud visited Damascus just days before the Riyadh meeting was cancelled and reportedly strongly urged the Syrians not to meet with the Egyptians.

17. Most units were Syrian, but Libyan, Sudanese, Somali, and Saudi elements participated. The participation of Saudi troops and the Saudi provision of transport for the Sudanese again illustrated the Saudi desire to take a more activist role in Arab affairs.

18. Beirut Radio in *FBIS*, June 27, 1976, Jalloud press conference.

19. Moscow Radio Commentary in *FBIS*, June 25, 1976.

20. The Syrians instead gambled that the Israelis would not attack and moved second-tier units off the Golan.

21. The Libyans were furious when they learned that Assad was willing to accept Sinai II. Qadhafi withdrew his representative from Damascus. Radio Tripoli in *FBIS*, October 13, 1976.

22. Cairo MENA in *FBIS*, August 19, 1976, reporting on a visit to Riyadh where Sadat made this commitment.

23. Saudi News Agency announcement in *FBIS*, October 18, 1976.

Chapter 7—EGYPT

1. U.S. Department of State, Bureau of Public Affairs, Office of Media Services, press release, "Agreement between Egypt and Israel," September 1, 1975, p. 1.

2. *An-Nahar Arab Report*, June 28, 1976, p. 3.

3. *Ibid.*, September 22, 1975.

4. *Ibid.*, October 6, 1975, p. 3.

5. Article I of the Agreement between Egypt and Israel, see note 1.

6. *An-Nahar Arab Report*, September 15, 1975, pp. 3–4.

7. For a summary of Palestinian-Egyptian relations see R. D. McLaurin, Mohammed Mughisuddin, and Abraham Wagner, *Foreign Policy Making in the Middle East* (New York: Praeger, 1977), pp. 74–79.

8. *The Arab World*, February 6, 1974, pp. 11–12.

9. *An-Nahar Arab Report*, October 27, 1975, p. 2.

10. *Ibid.*, April 19, 1976.

11. *Foreign Broadcast Information Service (FBIS)*, April 12, 1976, pp. D-7–D-8.

12. *FBIS*, April 13, 1976, p. D-1.
13. *Ibid.*
14. *An-Nahar Arab Report*, January 26, 1976, p. 3.
15. *FBIS*, April 23, 1976, p. D-7.
16. *Ibid.*

Chapter 8—THE HASHEMITE KINGDOM OF JORDAN

Apart from the references below, this chapter is based upon a number of detailed discussions with senior officials in the Jordanian government. We are grateful to them for their time and insights.

1. The following projections give some idea of the manpower base and related areas, based on current demographic trends.

JORDANIAN MANPOWER BASE

	1975	1985	2005
Total Population (millions)	2.65	3.81	7.98
Dependence Ratio	1.02	1.04	1.06
Male Labor Force (millions)	.591	.828	1.699

It is important to note that the projected population increase, given extremely limited natural resources, would greatly reduce the standard of living in the kingdom. A fertility reduction program would ultimately further shrink the manpower base from the figures given above. These data were supplied by the Center for Advanced Research, Chapel Hill, North Carolina. We are grateful to Edward E. Azar for his assistance in developing the data.

2. It was the Saudis who drove the Hashemites—the Sherif Husain—from the Arabian peninsula in the process of uniting what is now Saudi Arabia.

3. William B. Quandt, "Lebanon 1958 and Jordan 1970," *The Use of the Armed Forces as a Political Instrument*, by Barry M. Blechman and Stephen S. Kaplan (Washington, D.C.: Brookings Institution, 1976), pp. x–39ff; and Marvin Kalb and Bernard Kalb, *Kissinger* (Boston: Little, Brown, 1974), pp. 203–206.

4. The famous and appropriate title used by Malcolm Kerr: *The Arab Cold War*, 3rd. ed. (New York and London: Oxford University Press, 1971).

5. See Paul A. Jureidini and William E. Hazen, *The Palestinian Movement in Politics* (Lexington, Mass.: Heath, 1976); and William B. Quandt, Fuad Jabber,

and Ann Mosely Lesch, *The Politics of Palestinian Nationalism* (Berkeley: University of California Press, 1973).

6. R. D. McLaurin, Mohammed Mughisuddin, and Abraham R. Wagner, *Foreign Policy Making in the Middle East* (New York: Praeger, 1977), pp. 256–57.

7. Details on the civil war are available in Paul A. Jureidini and William E. Hazen, *Six Clashes: An Analysis of the Relationship Between the Palestinian Guerrilla Movement and the Governments of Jordan and Lebanon* (Kensington, Md.: American Institutes of Research, 1971).

8. See Hassan Badri, Taha el Magdoub, Mohammed Dia el Din Zohdy, and Trevor N. Dupuy, *The Ramadan War, 1973* (Colorado Springs: Westview Press, 1977); Trevor N. Dupuy, *The Middle East War of October of 1973 in Historical Perspective* (Dunn Loring, Va.: Historical Evaluation and Research Organization, 1976); Chaim Herzog, *The War of Atonement* (Boston: Little, Brown, 1975); Walter Z. Laqueur, *Confrontation: The Middle East War and World Politics* (London: Wildwood House, 1974); Riad N. el-Rayyes and Dunia Nahas, eds., *The October War: Documents, Personalities, Analyses and Maps* (Beirut: An-Nahar, 1974); Zeev Schiff, *October Earthquake* (Tel Aviv: University Publishing Projects, 1974) and *The Yom Kippur War, 1973* (Colorado Springs: Westview Press, 1977); Lester A. Sobol, ed., *Israel and the Arabs: The October 1973 War* (New York: Facts on File, 1974); Sunday Times Insight Team, *Insight on the Middle East War* (London: Times News, 1974); and Lawrence L. Whetten, *The Canal War: Four-Power Conflict in the Middle East* (Cambridge, Mass.: MIT Press, 1974).

9. Sir John Bagot Glubb, *A Soldier With the Arabs* (New York: Harper, 1957), *passim.*

10. This is not to say the social or other cultural belief systems are the same. Indeed, the cultural traditions of the Jordanians and the Palestinians are remarkable for their differences.

11. See P. J. Vatikiotis, "The Politics of the Fertile Crescent," *Political Dynamics in the Middle East*, Paul Y. Hammond and Sidney S. Alexander, eds., (New York: Elsevier, 1972), Chapter 7; and Richard F. Nyrop, et al., *Area Handbook for the Hashemite Kingdom of Jordan* (Washington, D.C.: American University, Foreign Area Studies, 1974), pp. 73–76.

12. McLaurin, Mughisuddin, and Wagner, *Foreign Policy Making*, pp. 231–41.

13. See the chapter in this book by Halim Barakat; cf. Paul A. Jureidini and William E. Hazen, *Lebanon's Dissolution: Futures and Consequences* (Alexandria, Va.: Abbott Associates, 1976).

14. Sources in note 11.

15. See P. J. Vatikiotis, "Politics and the Military in Jordan," *The Military and Politics in Five Developing Nations*, John P. Lovell, ed., (Kensington, Md.: American Institutes for Research, 1970), Chapter 3.

16. The city-dwelling elites provide the leading ultranationalists, of whom the late Wasfi Tal is an example.

17. Principally, the Majahs.

18. E.g., the Tuqans, Tals, and Rifais.

19. However, it is important to note that more than a decade has passed since Amman last ruled the territory. Many changes have taken place since that time, including, particularly, the Jordanian civil war and the continued rise in Palestinian consciousness. Both processes have deeply affected the political perspectives and expectations of the Palestinian people living in the West Bank, most of whom clearly do not seek Jordanian rule (but do wish to be free of Israeli occupation). It is certainly possible that the palace, recognizing the demographic and attitudinal realities, might choose not to press for the return of the West Bank. See R. D. McLaurin, Edward E. Azar, Suhaila Haddad, and Emile A. Nakhleh, *Ethnic Conflict in Regional Conflict: Demographic, Attitudinal, and Communications Factors in Israeli Governance of Arabs in Israel and the Occupied Territories* (Alexandria, Va.: Abbott Associates, 1977), especially Chapters 2 and 4.

20. Note 6 above.

21. See Edward R. F. Sheehan, *The Arabs, Israelis, and Kissinger: A Secret History of Diplomacy in the Middle East* (New York: Reader's Digest Press, 1976), for some contemporary serious and tragicomic insights into these expectations.

22. Among the most recent examples was the HAWK missile dispute of 1975 in which the U.S. Congress blocked the sale of an advanced U.S. surface-to-air missile to Jordan. After discussions about modifying the number and mobility of launchers, a stalemate ensued. Jordan then threatened to acquire a Soviet system; the King even visited Moscow in the course of the negotiations. Eventually, the governments of the United States and Jordan were able to come to terms on the sale.

23. Compare, for example, the data below.

COOPERATIVE DIMENSIONS OF INTERACTION
BETWEEN JORDAN AND SELECTED EUROPEAN STATES*

1946–50	753
1951–55	852
1956–60	1,825
1961–65	1,404
1966–70	2,200
1971–75	617

SOURCE: Conflict and Peace Data Bank (COPDAB), Center for Advanced Research, Chapel Hill, N.C.
*Belgium, France, Germany (F.R.G.), Italy, the Netherlands, and the United Kingdom

24. The blockade/boycott to which Jordan was subjected as a result of the civil war was, for example, only selectively implemented in fact by Syria. Airline routing and other informally cooperative interactions began to grow.

25. Cf. McLaurin, Mughisuddin, and Wagner, *Foreign Policy Making in*

the Middle East, Chapter 6; and Paul A. Jureidini, "The Abating Threat of War," *International Interactions* 3(3)(1977), *passim.*

26. The assumption of both governments is that should there be another Arab-Israeli war, Israel will attempt to attack Syria *around* the Golan rather than *through* the heavily defended heights, that is, will attack through Lebanon or Jordan. Consequently, Jordanian-Syrian cooperation is built upon the concept of joint defense of northern Jordan as an attack route to Syria. Syria will provide the air defense cover, Jordan the ground forces to close this avenue to the Israeli Defense Forces. To this end, the two countries have begun to coordinate plans, military codes and communications, ranks, and have conducted joint exercises. See "Completing the Eastern Front," *An-Nahar Arab Report* 7(5)(February 2, 1976), Backgrounder; Fehmi Saddy, *The Eastern Front: Implications of the Syrian/ Palestinian/Jordanian Entente and the Lebanese Civil War* (Alexandria, Va.: Abbott Associates, 1976), pp. 13–16. Cf. Juan de Onis, "Hussein Says Jordan Will Protect Syria," *New York Times,* July 11, 1975, p. 2; Jim Hoagland, "Jordan Gets Pledge of Syrian Air Cover," *Washington Post,* May 14, 1975, p. A1.

27. Jordan has provided some military advisors and forces to some of the Gulf countries as a means of expressing interest and concern in the area, as an alternative to the sheikhdoms turning to Iraq or Saudi Arabia, and in order to demonstrate to both Iran and Saudi Arabia the sincerity of Jordan's interest in the region.

28. Amman has been considerably more flexible in this respect than its larger neighbor to the south, but in general both governments view revolutionary ideologies as somewhat dubious allies to their monarchical forms of government.

29. Nyrop, et al., *Area Handbook,* p. 164.

30. Note 3 above.

31. Yehoshafat Harkabi, *Arab Strategies and Israel's Response* (New York: Free Press, 1977), p. 136.

32. Cf. note 26 above.

33. The issue here is not the justification of these actions. Rather, it can be argued that they would not have been taken in earlier years.

34. Enver M. Khoury, *The Crisis in the Lebanese System: Confessionalism and Chaos* (Washington, D.C.: American Institutes for Public Policy Research, July 1976), pp. 46–47; and John Bulloch, *Death of a Country* (London: Weidenfeld and Nicolson, 1977), p. 95.

35. The minority 'Alawi regime in Damascus was more concerned than the Jordanian government for a variety of reasons, not the least of which was the specter of renewed religious friction in Syria as a function of the confessional aspects of the Lebanese strife.

36. See Hafez al-Assad's lengthy defense of the Syrian action, *FBIS,* July 21, 1976, pp. H-1–23.

37. *An-Nahar Arab Report and Memo* 1(25)(June 21, 1976), Chronology.

38. Reports from the October War suggest that the quality of Iraqi troops was perhaps the poorest of the major combatants.

Chapter 9—THE ARAB-ISRAELI CONFLICT

1. While Israel claimed that Resolution 242 allowed her to retain those occupied lands which she deemed essential to her security, the Arabs insisted that she must withdraw from all occupied territories. The great preponderance of UN members held that Israel had to withdraw from all or nearly all of these territories. Even the United States position was that only "insubstantial alterations" in the pre-1967 borders could be allowed. *U.S. Department of State Bulletin*, 62 (January 5, 1970):7ff.

2. *Christian Science Monitor*, March 9, 1972.

3. *Middle East Intelligence Survey* (Tel Aviv), April 1, 1973, p. 2; and personal interviews with Palestinians in Beirut during the first week of August 1971.

4. *Department of State Bulletin*, 63 (August 10, 1970):176; *New Middle East* (London), July, 1972, p. 5; *New York Times*, February 26, 1971.

5. See Fred J. Khouri, *The Arab-Israeli Dilemma*, 2nd ed. (Syracuse: Syracuse University Press, 1976), pp. 361–69; Malcolm H. Kerr, ed., *The Elusive Peace in the Middle East* (Albany: State University of New York Press, 1975), pp. 63–82, 286–99.

6. *Le Monde* reported on November 6, 1973, that after analyzing the regional and international situation, al-Fatah leaders concluded that it would be in the best interests of the Palestinians to accept a compromise settlement which allowed for the existence of Israel. The *New York Times* reported on June 9, 1974, that while moderate Palestinian leaders had concluded that their goal for a secular, democratic state was "no longer feasible," they could not state this publicly because of internal political considerations. On February 19, 1974, al-Fatah, Sa'iqa, and the Popular Democratic Front for the Liberation of Palestine approved a document calling for the establishment of a Palestinian state in areas to be evacuated by Israel in the event of a peace settlement; and on June 8, 1974, the PLO National Council voted overwhelmingly to authorize the PLO leader, Yasir Arafat, to attend a Geneva Conference provided that Palestinian rights were recognized as a major issue to be resolved. (*New York Times*, February 21 and June 9, 1974; *Journal of Palestine Studies*, Summer, 1974, pp. 224ff and Winter, 1975, pp. 164–71, 174ff; Edward R. F. Sheehan, "How Kissinger Did It: Step by Step in the Middle East," *Foreign Policy*, Spring 1976, pp. 47, 69ff.

7. According to Terence Smith of the *New York Times* (July 13, 1975), Israel's strategy was to "buy time." A senior Israeli official told *Time* (September 22, 1975, p. 34) that it had been Israel's strategy since the 1967 war to stall for time and that Israel considered a stalemate to be to her advantage. Also see *Newsweek*, February 9, 1976, p. 32.

8. As early as November 5, 1973, even close friends of Israel in Western Europe voted for a European Economic Community resolution calling for an Israeli withdrawal from all occupied lands and for recognition of the "legitimate rights" of the Palestinians (*New York Times*, November 7, 1973). Even Abba

Eban and other Israelis conceded that the Palestinian issue was basic to the whole Arab-Israeli problem (*New Outlook* (Tel Aviv), July–August, 1975, pp. 2ff and September 1975, p. 9ff).

9. *New Outlook*, July–August 1975, p. 2. Also see footnote 7.

10. Kamal S. Salibi, *Crossroads to Civil War* (Delmar: Caravan Books, 1976), pp. 92, 97, 121.

11. *Ibid.*, p. 160; *New York Times*, August 13, 1977; and personal interviews with Maronite leaders and their followers in Beirut between June and August 1958; in the period 1961 to 1964, when the author was a visiting professor at the American University of Beirut; and during August–September 1969, July–August 1971, January 1975, and November 1977.

12. Salibi, *Crossroads to Civil War*, pp. 89ff. Personal discussions with PLO officials and representatives to the UN, as well as other Palestinians, especially during the fall 1974 UN General Assembly session and in Beirut in January 1975.

13. Salibi, *Crossroads to Civil War*, p. 9; Michael Hudson, *The Precarious Republic Revisited: Reflections on the Collapse of Pluralist Politics in Lebanon* (Washington, D.C.: Center for Contemporary Arab Studies, Georgetown University, 1977), p. 11.

14. *New York Times*, September 22 and 26, 1977.

15. Hudson, *The Precarious Republic Revisited*, p. 28.

16. Salibi, *Crossroads to Civil War*, pp. 127, 151.

17. Hudson, *The Precarious Republic Revisited*, p. 11; *New York Times*, September 1, 1977.

18. Egypt and the U.S. had actually made their own secret agreement in which the U.S. promised to continue efforts to work out another Syrian-Israeli accord and to insure Palestinian participation in any Middle East settlement (*New York Times*, March 3, 1976). But this was not divulged until months later.

19. Hudson, *The Precarious Republic Revisited*, p. 15.

20. *Christian Science Monitor*, November 9, 1976; *New York Times*, September 1, 1977. Also interviews with Palestinian officials and representatives in New York at various times since the end of the civil war—especially during the UN General Assembly sessions in the fall of 1976 and 1977; and interviews with Palestinians in Damascus and Beirut in the middle of November 1977.

21. *New York Times*, May 26, 28, and June 3, 1978; *Middle East Intelligence Survey*, April 1–15, 1978, p. 1; personal interviews with PLO representatives, May and June 1978.

22. *Middle East Intelligence Survey*, December 1–15, 1977, p. 135.

23. *New York Times*, January 12, 1978. Similar views were expressed by the president and foreign minister of Lebanon to the author in interviews held in Beirut during the third week of November 1977.

24. *New York Times*, January 12, 1978. *Lebanese-American Journal*, December 26, 1977. Similar views were expressed to the author by several Maronite leaders during the third week of November 1977 in Beirut.

25. Camille Chamoun, former president of Lebanon, was one of the main

leaders in the movement for establishing some kind of a separate Christian entity. Interview with Chamoun on November 19, 1977.

26. Ever since the 1974 Rabat Conference, King Hussein has officially held that only the PLO could negotiate for the Palestinians and that the Palestinians should have their own state. Under proper circumstances, however, he probably would consider being involved in negotiating the future of the West Bank and he would welcome some kind of union between his own country and a future Palestine entity.

27. Interview with President Sadat at Ismailia on November 28, 1977. Also a letter of November 30, 1977, from President Sadat to the author.

28. *New Outlook*, September–October, 1976, p. 2.

Chapter 10—INTER-ARAB RELATIONS

1. Special acknowledgments go to Paul Jureidini and Ronald D. McLaurin for providing essential source materials for this chapter as well as a substantive critique of an earlier draft, and to Edward Haley for critique and editorial advice.

2. Text of the Protocol in Mohammad Khalil, *The Arab States and the Arab League: A Documentationary Record* (Beirut: Khayats, 1962)2:54. The same assurance was later inserted in the Arab League Pact under Article 8 where each member state undertook to respect "as the exclusive concerns" of other member states their respective "systems of government," and to "abstain from any action calculated to change established system of government." Text of the Pact in Helen Miller Davis, *Constitutions, Electoral Laws, Treaties of States in the Near and Middle East* (Durham, N.C.: Duke University Press, 1953), pp. 529–30.

3. See Kamal S. Salibi, *Crossroads to Civil War: Lebanon 1958–1976* (Delmar, N.Y.: Caravan Books, 1976), pp. 24–26 on Lebanon's position regarding participation in the UAC.

4. See John K. Cooley, "Beirut Shake-up Hints Guerrilla Ban," *Christian Science Monitor*, July 2, 1969, p. 2.

5. Cited in Paul A. Jureidini and William E. Hazen, *The Palestinian Movement in Politics* (Lexington, Mass.: Lexington Books, 1976), p. 69. Although the agreement was to remain top secret, a Beirut newspaper, *an-Nahar*, published what it claimed was the true text. The paper was taken to task by the Lebanese government for revealing secret information, but the contents were never officially denied. It appears in translation in Jureidini and Hazen, *The Palestinian Movement in Politics*, pp. 68–69. It was later published in *al-Bayraq*, a Beirut newspaper, and is allegedly the full text. It appears in translation in *SWASIA* 3 (21)(March 19, 1976):2.

6. See Samih Farsoun and Walter Carroll, "Civil War in Lebanon: Sect, Class and Imperialism," *Monthly Review* 28(2)(June1976):28–29 for a discussion of the Palestinian national movement and the Lebanese left.

7. See Salibi, *Crossroads to Civil War*, pp. 75–77, for a detailed discussion of the Lebanese groups covered and the impact this had on Lebanese politics.

8. For example, in December 1973 during a brief visit by Secretary of State Kissinger to Lebanon, President Frangieh urged Kissinger to create a Palestinian state with all dispatch so that the several hundred thousand Palestinians living in Lebanon would leave and allow the country to live in peace. See Edward R. F. Sheehan, *The Arabs, Israelis, and Kissinger* (New York: Reader's Digest Press, 1976), p. 101.

9. *Foreign Broadcast Information Service (FBIS)* 5(51)(March 14, 1975):N2. Israeli Chief of Staff Mordechai Gur emphasized the new priority assigned to the Syrian front and warned of the possibility of renewed fighting that "might develop into one of the largest armed forces battles ever."

10. See Chapter 2, by John Cooley, in this volume. See also *MERIP Report*, No. 44, for a discussion of the array of forces at the outset of the conflict.

11. An informative discussion and analysis of the stages through which the Lebanese war passed is done by Farsoun and Carroll, "The Civil War in Lebanon: Sect, Class, and Imperialism," *Monthly Review* 28(2)(June 1976):31–32. The authors' analysis converges very closely with John Cooley's first-hand observations on when the fighting shifted from a Palestinian-Lebanese Christian rightist conflict to a war between strictly Lebanese factions.

12. See R. D. McLaurin, Mohammed Mughisuddin and Abraham R. Wagner, *Foreign Policy Making in the Middle East* (New York: Praeger, 1977), Chap. 6, for a description and analysis of Syria's foreign policy.

13. The general strategy of the Eastern Front was revealed for the first time in a backgrounder on September 9, 1975, by Syrian Foreign Minister Abdel Halim Khaddam. Khaddam announced that Syria had begun planning for the establishment of a defensive line from Ras al-Nakoura on the Lebanese coastal border with Israel to the Gulf of Aqaba in southern Jordan. That was the first official reference by Syria to the inclusion of Lebanon in a unified defensive strategy. See *an-Nahar Arab Report* 7(5)(February 2, 1976):1, backgrounder.

14. See *New York Times*, March 9, 1975, p. 3.

15. *Middle East Monitor* 5(6)(March 15, 1975); and *FBIS* 5(45)(March 6, 1975):A9.

16. See the official communiqué, translation in BBC Summary of World Broadcasts (June 14, 1975), reprinted in *SWASIA* 2 (25) (June 27, 1975):2.

17. Henry Tanner "Syria and Jordan to Coordinate Policies," *New York Times*, June 13, 1975, p. 3. It is not certain that a joint military command was actually agreed upon in June or August. The military implications of a Syrian-Jordanian rapproachment however, were not lost on Israel. Defense Minister Shimon Peres observed that Israel now faced a "hostile arch" along its northern and eastern borders as a result of Syrian-Jordanian collaboration. *Jerusalem Post*, June 15, 1975, p. 2.

18. See *FBIS* 5(43)(March 4, 1975):G1; *FBIS* 5(52)(March 15, 1975):G2; *FBIS* 5(63)(April 1, 1975):G1.

19. These images that Egypt wished to cultivate in Washington and the

Arab world respectively emerged more clearly in President Sadat's historic peace initiative to Jerusalem in November 1977.

20. Egypt terminated its military aid to the Phalangists after their forces overran two Muslim areas, Karantina and Maslakh, and dealt with the inhabitants of these areas in an extremely brutal manner. After this bloodbath Egyptian aid to the Phalangists became untenable as it would have implied support for Christian rightist, anti-Muslim policies.

21. For an analysis of this period see Salibi, *Crossroads to Civil War*, pp. 120–29. Salibi makes a persuasive case to suggest that the resumption of hostilities was caused mainly by a number of domestic factors.

22. See, for example, a speech by President Assad July 20, 1976, as reported in *FBIS* 5(141)(July 21, 1976):H-1, H-28. See also radio broadcasts monitored by *FBIS* 5(185)(September 23, 1975):G2; press conference by Syrian Foreign Minister Abdel Halim Khaddam, September 25, 1975, as reported in *FBIS* 5(188) (September 26, 1975):G2; and charges by Zuheir Moshin, head of the PLO Military Department and leader of the Syrian-controlled al-Sa'iqa guerrilla organization, of Egyptian efforts to intensify the strife with American and Israeli blessing as reported in *FBIS* 5(190)(September 30, 1975):A2.

23. See *an-Nahar Arab Report* 6(41)(October 13, 1975):2–3. References to Israeli troop movement are found in *FBIS* 5(193)(October 3, 1975):G3, and 5(201) (October 16, 1975):H3. Interviews the author had with sources close to Syrian and Israeli officialdom (and who wish to remain anonymous) support allegations that Israel was contemplating an offensive against Syria through Lebanon in September–October of 1975.

24. *An-Nahar Arab Report* 6(45)(November 10, 1975):2.

25. Much of this section draws heavily on Fehmi Saddy, *The Eastern Front: Implications of the Syrian/Palestinian Entente and the Lebanese Civil War* (Alexandria, Va.: Abbott Associates, Inc., 1977). This is a report prepared by Abbott Associates for the Office of the Assistant Secretary of Defense (International Security Affairs). See also the analysis by Eric Rouleau, "Syria in the Quagmire," *Le Monde* (June 1, 1976), p. 5; translation in *SWASIA* 3(24)(June 18, 1976):1.

26. See *FBIS* 5(15)(January 22, 1976):G5–G6; and the *New York Times*, January 23, 1976, p. 1, for summary and discussion of the agreement respectively.

27. *FBIS* 5(15)(January 22, 1976):G3.

28. See Henry Tanner, "Syrian Move Into Lebanon Laid to a Rift with Leftists," *New York Times*, April 16, 1976, pp. 1, 5.

29. *Defense and Foreign Affairs Weekly Report on Strategic Middle Eastern Affairs* 2(3)(January 19, 1977).

30. *Ibid.*, 2(40)(October 27, 1976).

31. See *New York Times*, July 27, 1976, p. 2. The shipments were described as being just large enough to help keep the Palestinian forces going and to keep the Syrian forces bogged down there.

32. See *New York Times*, March 31, 1976, pp. 1, 10.

33. *Defense and Foreign Affairs Weekly Report on Strategic Middle Eastern Affairs* 2(40)(October 27, 1976).

34. See James F. Clarity, "Troop Movements by Iraq Stir Concern in Damascus," *New York Times*, June 11, 1976, pp. 1, 14.

35. See *an-Nahar Arab Report and Memo* 2(8)(February 20, 1978), p. 7.

36. *Ibid.*

37. *New York Times*, February 20, 1976, p. 4.

38. *Ibid.*, February 16, 1976, p. 12.

39. Francis Ofner, "Fear of Consequences Keeps Israel, Syria Out of Lebanon," *Christian Science Monitor*, November 3, 1976, p. 1.

40. *Ibid.*

41. *Washington Post*, January 24, 1976, p. A13.

42. See, for example, Francis Ofner, "Syria's Maneuvering Goes Unchallenged," *Christian Science Monitor*, April 22, 1976, pp. 1, 5. There were unconfirmed reports that Syria and Israel, with the U.S. acting as intermediary, arranged a deal that allowed Syria to intervene in Lebanon in exchange for Syrian renewal of the UN peace-keeping forces on the Golan Heights and a promise to stay out of southern Lebanon. See the *Christian Science Monitor*, May 5, 1976, p. 9; and *The Economist*, April 17, 1976, p. 43.

43. *New York Times*, January 23, 1976, p. 3.

44. Joseph Kraft, "Syria and the P.L.O.," *Washington Post*, January 12, 1976, p. A19.

45. *Washington Post*, February 3, 1976, p. A13.

46. *New York Times*, February 1, 1976, p. E4.

47. *Ibid.*, June 2, 1976, p. K4.

48. David Binder, "Envoy Says U.S. Erred in Beirut Policy," *New York Times*, May 27, 1976, p. 3.

49. *Washington Post*, February 28, 1976, p. A12; *Le Matin an-Nahar Arab Report* 7(7)(February 16, 1976): pp. 2–3.

50. See the *Washington Post*, February 2, 1976, p. A11.

51. The idea of the Eastern Front as either a war or peace strategy is developed by Saddy, *The Eastern Front*, pp. 37–42.

52. *An-Nahar Arab Report and Memo* 1(21)(September 12, 1977):9.

53. See Henry Tanner, "Egypt and P.L.O. Said to Resolve Policy Quarrel," *New York Times*, May 6, 1976, pp. 1, 9.

54. See for example, Meron Medzini, "The Middle East: Restoring a Dream," *Los Angeles Times*, March 22, 1978, Pt. II, p. 7, for an articulation of the argument in favor of a third Egyptian-Israeli agreement.

Chapter 11—THE SOVIET UNION

1. Cf. William E. Griffith, "Soviet Influence in the Middle East," *Survival* (January/February 1976):8.

2. A good survey of Soviet Middle Eastern policy that examines both

strengths and weaknesses is Robert O. Freedman, *Soviet Policy Toward the Middle East Since 1970* (New York: Praeger, 1975). Among other points, Freedman emphasized the dilemma the Soviets repeatedly encounter when giving substantial arms supplies to a country without receiving control over the recipient's domestic or foreign policies. The greater Soviet military and political presence in the region has also brought the risk of becoming directly involved in an Arab-Israeli war, perhaps with the United States. In addition, the Soviets have generally not been able to protect or promote the local Communist parties in their protégé states.

3. For a comprehensive discussion of Soviet diplomacy during the period between the end of the October War and the Golan agreement see Galia Golan, *Yom Kippur and After* (Cambridge, 1977), pp. 129–250.

4. At the end of the October War, UNSC Resolutions 338 and 339 made the U.S. and the USSR co-chairmen of the Geneva Middle East Peace Conference. Negotiations for both the Egyptian and Syrian disengagement agreements technically took place under a Geneva Conference mandate. The Soviet Union, in its capacity as conference co-chairman, participated in the meetings of Geneva Conference members called to formalize both the Sinai I and Golan accords.

5. During the 1973 clashes between the PLO and the Lebanese army, the Soviets had adopted an even-handed policy and encouraged a peaceful settlement of differences between the Palestinian and Lebanese authorities.

6. The 1958 U.S. intervention in the fighting was certainly a factor in Soviet thinking as it has always been in the context of troubles in Lebanon.

7. Moscow certainly wanted to avoid the weakening of Palestinian political-military prestige. Concurrently, however, the USSR's past experience with PLO obstreperousness and unpredictability argued against an outcome in Lebanon which would provide the PLO with a clearcut victory over the forces which up to then had kept the Palestinians in check. Syria, no less than the USSR, meanwhile, probably also saw Syrian interests as dictating some measure of control over Lebanon's approach to the Arab-Israeli conflict. And Assad certainly wanted to avoid a situation which would put the initiative over issues of war and peace into the hands of the PLO or its allies in Lebanon.

8. *Pravda* on October 3, for example, stated that the fighting afforded "no grounds for interference in Lebanese affairs by outsiders, particularly Israel." Other reporting and comment, meanwhile, contended that Israel was conspiring with Lebanese rightists, particularly the Phalange, in order to prepare a combined assault against the PLO and leftist-Muslim forces. *Pravda*, October 3, 1976; Radio Moscow, October 24, 1976, in Foreign Broadcast Information Service (*FBIS*), *Daily Report: Soviet Union*, October 25, 1976; and Radio Moscow, November 2, 1976, in *FBIS*, November 3, 1976.

9. Radio Moscow, November 2, 1976, in *FBIS*, November 3, 1976.

10. There were several reports during January that Palestinian forces had become actively engaged in the fighting, primarily in trying to break the Christian blockades at several of the larger Palestinian refugee camps.

11. Middle East expert Ye. Primakov told Radio Moscow listeners, for ex-

ample, that the "important thing" about the agreement was that it had stopped the fighting and that Syrian, Palestinian, and Lebanese "representatives had virtual control over events." He made no mention of a Syrian or Palestinian military involvement and suggested that the cease-fire had thwarted efforts to "provoke" the PLO into taking on an active military role in the fighting. Radio Moscow, February 13, 1976, in *FBIS*, February 1976; and Radio Moscow February 2, 1976, in *FBIS*, February 3, 1976.

12. The immediate pretext for Sadat's action was Soviet refusal to permit India to provide spare parts for Egypt's deteriorating fleet of MIG-21 aircraft.

13. As a result of the expulsion from Egyptian ports, Syria became the only country in the Eastern Mediterranean providing ready access to port facilities for the Soviet Mediterranean squadron. Moscow had failed to obtain corresponding privileges in Libya despite its increasing ties with Qadhafi, and Yugoslavia, the only state in the area offering naval servicing facilities to the USSR, had laws severely restricting their use.

14. During the spring the Soviet Union sought through diplomacy to expand its increasingly narrow base of support in the Arab world by trying to improve relations with Jordan. The effort failed, however, despite signs of promise, when King Hussein finally refused to accept a military supply relationship with the USSR following his visit to Moscow in June. See Robert O. Freedman, "The Soviet Union and the Civil War in Lebanon," unpublished paper prepared for the Annual Meeting of the Middle East Studies Association, New York, NY, November 1977, pp. 33–34.

15. Soviet media, for example, publicized statements by Arafat and the leader of the Lebanese Communist party emphasizing their support for a negotiated settlement of the crisis. Concurrently, in what was probably an effort to encourage unity among its increasingly divided friends, Moscow also increased publicity for claims that the U.S. was preparing to interfere in the situation. Radio Moscow, April 2, 1976, in *FBIS*, April 5, 1976; and TASS dispatch April 3, 1976, in *FBIS*, April 6, 1976.

16. Freedman, "The Soviet Union and the Civil War in Lebanon," p. 13.

17. *Pravda*, April 7, 1976, in *FBIS*, April 8, 1976.

18. Kosygin visited Iraq May 29–31 and Syria May 31–June 4.

19. Moscow put forth two authoritative statements on the Middle East in early 1976, each calling for a resumption of the Geneva Conference. Brezhnev had made the first during his address to the 25th Congress of the CPSU in February. The second was issued in the form of a TASS statement on the Middle East on April 28. See Freedman, "The Soviet Union and the Civil War in Lebanon," pp. 9–10, 16–17.

20. The Soviet-Iraqi communiqué stated that both sides stressed that the right solution to the crisis in Lebanon could be achieved only "by the Lebanese people themselves." Radio Moscow, May 31, 1976, in *FBIS*, June 1, 1976.

21. There was no Soviet public support for Assad's military action during the talks with the Soviet leader. Nor, however, did Moscow publicly refute

Syria's step. For several days following the talks, in fact, Soviet media withheld opinion, a fairly good indication that Moscow was undecided about how to respond.

22. TASS dispatch, June 9, 1976, in *FBIS*, June 10, 1976.

23. The most notable gesture was Moscow's acquiescence in the opening of a PLO office in Moscow in mid-June.

24. Gerd Linde, *Das sowjetisch-Syrische Verhaltis vor dem Hintergrund der Libanon-Krise* (Cologne: 1977), pp. 20–22.

25. Criticism of Assad personally was generally avoided, and there was no real hint from Moscow that it saw developments in Syria taking on the characteristics that it had so sharply criticized in Egypt.

26. The Soviet ambassador in Beirut on at least one occasion specifically denied that the Soviet Union was delivering arms to the factions in Lebanon. Paris, AFP dispatch in English, July 16, 1976.

27. The new public position was set forth in an authoritative "Observer" article in *Pravda* on September 8.

28. Roving Ambassador Vinogradov visited Damascus on September 20, PLO Political Department Chief Qaddumi was in Moscow September 15–17, and Arafat was reported as meeting with the Soviet ambassador in Beirut on several occasions during mid-September. Although little information is available on these talks, the failure of the communiqué following Qaddumi's talks in Moscow to mention a demand for Syrian withdrawal suggested that Moscow was pressing this point with the Palestinians as the basis for compromise with Syria. Moscow, meanwhile also continued to insist on the protection of Palestinian rights in Lebanon.

29. Moscow reacted to the new fighting with still another TASS statement criticizing Syria. However, the statement indicated no return to the USSR's earlier position demanding Syrian withdrawal from Lebanon, even clearer evidence that Moscow now acquiesced in the Syrian presence there.

Chapter 12—THE UNITED STATES

1. For a detailed analysis of the domestic origins of the crisis see Michael C. Hudson, *The Precarious Republic* (New York: Random House, 1968), pp. 108–16.

2. Enver M. Koury, *The Crisis in the Lebanese System* (Washington, D.C.: American Enterprise Institute, 1976), pp. 44–45.

3. *New York Times*, May 6, 1975.

4. *Ibid.*, March 31, 1976.

5. After the Lebanese crisis eased, this "sitrep" continued to be prepared daily, its substantive scope broadened to embrace the Arab-Israel complex of

problems. Along with a general round-up of major world issues, it forms the core of the secretary's daily briefing.

6. Who exacted bribes for opening the barriers, the most acceptable form of which was small-arms ammunition, readily procurable on the Beirut black market. Interview with Ambassador L. Dean Brown, August 2, 1977.

7. Secret, that is, except from readers of newspapers. The text was promptly leaked to the Israeli press, and full details of the understanding were published by the *New York Times* on September 10, 1975.

8. Figure cited by Koury, *The Crisis in the Lebanese System*, p. 43.

9. For an interesting statement of the secretary's personal view of the Palestinians see John G. Stoessinger, *Henry Kissinger: The Anguish of Power* (New York: Norton, 1976), pp. 201–203.

10. *New York Times*, November 28, 1975; *Christian Science Monitor*, August 17, 1976.

11. *New York Times*, November 28, 1975.

12. *Ibid.*, July 26, 1975.

13. *Christian Science Monitor*, July 20, 1976.

14. *New York Times*, December 16, 1975.

15. *Ibid.*

16. *Ibid.*, March 31 and April 1, 1976.

17. *Ibid.*, May 6, 1976.

18. *Ibid.*, May 12, 1976.

19. The American ambassador in Damascus was, as a result of the persistent public opposition of the United States, for a time refused access to senior Syrian officials. Interview with Ambassador Brown, August 2, 1977.

20. *New York Times*, May 27, 1976.

21. E.g., "One Invasion that the U.S. Approves," *U.S. News and World Report*, June 14, 1976, p. 66.

22. *Christian Science Monitor*, November 24, 1976.

23. *New York Times*, June 30, 1976.

24. President Ford, who canceled election campaign appearances to preside over the planning, which involved the highest military and national security officials, was gratuitously accused of "over-dramatizing" the situation for reasons of domestic political tactics.

25. Press Release No. 464, Department of State, September 23, 1976.

26. *New York Times*, December 16, 1976.

27. E.g., *Christian Science Monitor*, August 17, 1976.

28. *New York Times*, March 16, 1978.

29. *Christian Science Monitor*, March 16, 1978.

30. *New York Times*, March 16, 1978.

31. Text in *New York Times*, March 20, 1978.

32. The American question and the deadlock in the Israeli government over their response are discussed in the *Los Angeles Times*, June 16, 1978. The Is-

raeli response—essentially that after five years the future of the West Bank and Gaza will be open to negotiations by "the parties" and the representatives of the Arabs in the occupied areas elected according to the provisions of the Begin government's local autonomy plan—is in *Los Angeles Times*, June 19, 1978.

Chapter 13—BRITAIN AND THE MIDDLE EAST

1. For an account of the Lebanese crisis of 1958 and the American and British landings, see R. F. Wall, "The Middle East," *Survey of International Affairs, 1956-1958* (London: Oxford University Press, 1962), especially pp. 364-78, 392-400.

2. See Philip Darby, *British Defense Policy East of Suez, 1947-1969* (London: Oxford University Press, 1973); Joseph Frankel, *British Foreign Policy, 1945-1973* (London: Oxford University Press, 1975); and P. Edward Haley, "Britain and the Middle East," in Tareq Ismael, ed., *The Middle East in World Politics* (Syracuse, N.Y.: Syracuse University Press, 1974).

3. The Euro-Arab dialog is discussed in the London *Times*, February 10, 11, 14, 1977.

4. *Ibid.*, June 30, 1977.

5. The French government sent a former foreign minister as mediator and offered to send a peace-keeping force to Lebanon. Neither were taken seriously by any of the parties. *Ibid.*, April 8, May 22, 1976.

6. See especially Alvin Z. Rubinstein, "Assessing Influence as A Problem in Foreign Policy Analysis," in Alvin Z. Rubinstein, ed., *Soviet and Chinese Influence in the Third World* (New York: Praeger, 1975), pp. 1-22.

7. If Egypt set such conditions she would not have been the first to act in this way, nor would it have been the first time another statesman had required Britain to be less than she was before he would give his consent to a new, joint initiative. DeGaulle is alleged to have told an adviser he would permit Britain to join the EEC, but not until she was "completely naked." See Stanley Hoffmann, *Decline or Renewal: France Since the 1930s* (New York: Viking, 1974).

8. Statement on the Defense Estimates, 1966: Part I, "The Defence Review," Cmnd. 2901 (London, February 1966); Part II, "Defence Estimates, 1966-67," Cmnd. 2902 (London, February 1966).

9. When they took office in 1970, the Conservatives boasted they would actually spend less on defense than the previous administration. They did. See "Supplementary Statement on Defense Policy, 1970."

10. International Institute for Strategic Studies, *The Military Balance, 1977-1978* (London, 1977), p. 98.

11. *Ibid.*, p. 76.

12. "Statement on the Defense Estimates, 1975," Cmnd. 5976 (London, March 1975), p. 40.

13. *Ibid.*, pp. 7–15. The first chapter in this statement contains the Defense Review. British forces would remain in Hong Kong, Gibraltar, Belize, and the Falkland Islands. See also London *Times*, March 20, 1975.

14. London *Times*, April 16, 1975, July 23, 1971.

15. "Statement on the Defence Estimate, 1975," pp. 5–6. The Labour government's figure showed that Soviets outnumbered NATO forces in the Eastern Atlantic in surface ships, submarines, and combat aircraft, while Soviet forces on NATO's central front possessed substantially more soldiers, and more than twice the number of tanks, field guns, and tactical aircraft.

16. The controversies may be followed in the London *Times*, especially December 1, 5, 1975, January 15, February 6, 11, March 18, April 1, June 19, July 23, 1976, and May 13, 1977.

17. See, for example, the statement by the Conservative spokesman on defense, Ian Gilmore, to the National Defence College, reported in the London *Times*, June 19, 1976.

18. This was the position of Chancellor of the Exchequer Dennis Healy, who asked for another £1,300 million reduction in defense spending in the period 1977–78, in addition to the £4,700 million already decided. See London *Times*, December 5, 1975.

19. R. Bacon, W. Eltis, *Britain's Economic Problem: Too Few Producers* (London: Macmillan, 1976), Table 58, cited in James Bellini, Geoffrey Pattie, *A New World Role for the Medium Power: The British Opportunity* (London: Royal United Services Institute for Defence Studies, 1977), excerpted in *Survival*, September/October 1977, pp. 217–24, at p. 220.

20. *Survival*, January 15, 1976.

21. Statement on the Defence Estimates, 1976, Cmnd. 6432, p. 18.

22. This is ironic, of course, because the rationale for letting go east of Suez and in the Mediterranean is to enable Britain to concentrate on Europe and the North Atlantic. The remarks by the American officer, General George Brown, were cited in a London *Times* editorial January 11, 1977. The All-Party Committee report, Paper 254, is cited in the *Times* March 18, 1977. See also the articles on defense spending on March 25 and 29, 1977.

23. Stockholm International Peace Research Institute (SIPRI), *Yearbook, 1976*, pp. 62–63. The authors of the SIPRI studies suggest that the arms race in the Middle East is out of control, p. 71.

24. *Ibid.*, p. 65. Tactical aircraft numbered 2,300 and main battle tanks 10,500 in the Middle East at the end of 1975.

25. Stockholm International Peace Research Institute (SIPRI), *The Arms Trade With the Third World*, rev. and abr. ed. (New York, 1975), p. 33.

26. *Ibid.*, p. 12.

27. *Ibid.*, p. 20.

28. SIPRI, *Yearbook, 1974,* "Arms Trade Register," p. 223; *Yearbook, 1975,* "Arms Trade Register," pp. 254–55. See also *New York Times,* March 2, 1978.

29. The *Times* of London, June 13, 1975.

30. *Ibid.,* December 15, 1975. Earlier in the year Egypt, Saudi Arabia, Qatar and United Arab Emirates announced a £4,000 million plan to set up an Arab armaments industry. See also the reports on January 24, 29, February 10, May 16, June 12, November 4, 8, December 12, 15, 1975, and April 6, 1976.

31. London *Times,* April 28, 1977.

32. The Lomé Convention (February 28, 1975) is an example of the complexity and importance of these relations. It is a five-year agreement on trade, aid, and industrial cooperation between the nine and forty-six African, Caribbean, and Pacific countries. Virtually all the goods from these countries are to be allowed free access to the European market. See London *Times,* May 11, 1975. This convention replaced the earlier Yaounde agreement with nineteen African countries. It also promised £1,700 million to be given in aid by the European Development Fund by 1980.

33. The best-publicized examples of resistance to the community are General deGaulle's various collisions with everyone over common agricultural and defense policies. They are discussed in Edward L. Morse, *Foreign Policy and Interdependence in Gaullist France* (Princeton, N.J.: Princeton University Press, 1973); Alfred Grosser, *French Foreign Policy Under DeGaulle* (Boston: Little, Brown, 1967); and in Hoffmann, *Decline and Renewal,* and John Newhouse, *DeGaulle and the Anglo-Saxons* (New York: Viking, 1970).

34. London *Times,* February 14, 1977.

35. *Ibid.,* June 30, 1977; see also May 22, 1976.

36. *Ibid.,* January 19, 1977.

37. European Communities No. 1 (1975). Agreement between the European Economic Community and the Arab Republic of Egypt, December 18, 19, 1972 (entered into force, November 1, 1973), Cmnd. 5926; European Communities No. 136 (1975), Agreement between the European Economic Community and the State of Israel.

38. There are exceptions and ceilings after which duties may be reintroduced. See, for examples, Protocol 1 to the Israeli agreement, European Communities No. 136 (1975), pp. 12–27.

39. Israel agreed to abolish duties on most items during the years 1980–85. Cmnd. 6249, p. 28.

40. See, for example, the extemporaneous remarks of Foreign Minister Owen at an Inter-Parliamentary Union British Group in Westminster Hall, House of Commons, February 28, 1978. Transcript in author's possession.

41. See F. S. Northedge, "Britain's Peace in the Changing World," in Michael Leifer, ed., *Constraints and Adjustments in British Foreign Policy* (London: Allen and Unwin, 1972), pp. 192–207.

Chapter 14—THE UNITED NATIONS AND THE ARAB LEAGUE

1. For convenience see especially the Department of State, *The United Nations Conference on International Organization. San Francisco, California, April 25–June 26, 1945. Selected Documents* (Washington, D.C.: USGPO, 1946), pp. 298–300.

2. *Ibid.*, p. 395. In general see also Robert W. MacDonald, *The League of Arab States: A Study in the Dynamics of Regional Organization* (Princeton, N.J.: Princeton University Press, 1965), 290 pp.

3. See Department of State, *American Foreign Policy, 1950–1955: Basic Documents* (Washington, D.C.: USGPO, 1957), I, pp. 1243–59.

4. Muhammad Khalil, *The Arab States and the Arab League: A Documentary Record*, vol. I *Constitutional Developments*, vol. II *International Affairs* (Beirut: Khayats, 1962), I, pp. 105–109; II, pp. 55 ff.

5. See Fahim Qubain, *Crisis in Lebanon* (Washington, D.C.: Middle East Institute, 1961), p. 243; Kamal Salibi, *Crossroads to Civil War: Lebanon, 1958–1975* (New York: Caravan Books, 1976), p. 178. See also Rosemary Sayigh, "The Struggle for Survival: The Economic Conditions of the Palestinian Refugees in Lebanon," *Journal of Palestine Studies* (hereafter cited as *JPS*), 7 (2) (Winter 1978):101–19.

6. Khalil, *International Affairs*, pp. 191–96.

7. It is probable that the Iraqi revolt of July 14, 1958, had more to do with the American show of force in Lebanon than events in Lebanon and the appeal of President Chamoun. Among other things, see Department of State, *American Foreign Policy: Current Documents 1958* (Washington, D.C.: USGPO, 1958), pp. 937–1067.

8. See UN Docs. S/4040, 4052, 4085, 4100, 4114; *American Foreign Policy 1958: Current Documents*, 952–68, 975–80, 1039–42, 1056–67, 1064–67. See also Fred J. Khouri, "UN Peacekeeping in the Middle East," *Journal of South Asian and Middle Eastern Studies* 1(1)(Fall 1977):97–117.

9. *American Foreign Policy: Current Documents*, 1032–39.

10. *Ibid.*

11. See Robert Murphy, *Diplomat Among Warriors* (Garden City, N.Y.: Doubleday, 1964), p. 404. See also Major-General Odd Bull, *War and Peace in the Middle East: The Experiences and Views of a UN Observer* (Boulder, Colo.: Westview Press, 1977), Chapter I. Bull indicates that Admiral Holloway complained of the effrontery of President Chamoun in trying to use the American Sixth Fleet for his own personal purposes.

12. *Ibid.*, pp. 14, 20. It is conceivable that the handling of the Lebanese problem in 1958, granted all the limitations involved, served to hamper Waldheim's efforts in 1975–77. As General Bull records in his memoir, UNOGIL's functions were only to observe and report. I should question, in any event, the ability of UNOGIL to formulate and carry out the necessary reforms.

13. *The Washington Post*, September 22, 1977.

14. Norman F. Howard, "Upheaval in Lebanon," *Current History* 70(402) (January 1976):5-9, 36; "Tragedy in Lebanon," *ibid.* 72(423)(January 1977):1-5, 3032. See also Michael Hudson, "The Lebanese Crisis," *JPS*, 4(3-4)(Spring/Summer 1976):109-12.

15. See the *Annual Report* of UNRWA for 1974-75 in U.N. Doc. A/9613 and Corr. 1; A/10013 and Corr. 1; UNRWA, *Palestine Refugees Today, Newsletter No. 83* (March 1977) p. 23.

16. U.N. Doc. (A/31/13), pars. 1-3.

17. *JPS* 5(3-4)(Spring/Summer 1976):264-65.

18. *Ibid.*, p. 268.

19. *Ibid.*, pp. 269-71.

20. *Report of the Secretary-General on the Work of the Organization, 16 June 1975-15 June 1976. General Assembly, Official Records, Thirty-First Session,* Supplement 1(A/31/1), pp. 139-40, pars. 44-46.

21. *Introduction to the Report of the Secretary-General on the Work of the Organization 1976* (New York: United Nations), pp. 9-10.

22. *Ibid.*

23. *JPS* 5(3-4)(Spring/Summer 1976):273-74.

24. *JPS* 6(1)(Autumn 1976):169-70.

25. *Ibid.*, pp. 170-71. See also the inaugural address of President Hafez Assad on July 26, 1976. *Ibid.*, p. 177.

26. *Ibid.*, p. 171.

27. *Ibid.* 6(2)(Winter 1977):189-91.

28. *Ibid.*, pp. 191-94.

29. *Ibid.*, p. 194.

30. *JPS* 6(2)(Winter 1977):191-92; *Why Syria Invaded Lebanon.* Merip Report No. 51; Norman F. Howard, "Tragedy in Lebanon," *Current History*, 72(423) (January 1977):30. See also the Department of State, Bureau of Public Affairs, Office of Media Services, *Selected Documents No. 4. U.S. Policy in the Middle East, November 1974-February 1976* (Washington, D.C.: USGPO, 1977), pp. 95-97.

31. *Review of Recent Developments in the Middle East,* Hearings before the Subcommittee on Europe and the Middle East of The Committee on International Relations, House of Representatives, Ninety-fifth Congress, First Session, June 8, 1977 (Washington, D.C.: USGPO, 1977) p. 128. See especially pp. 56-60.

32. Official Records, Thirty-first Session, Plenary Meetings, *Vol. 1 of 3 Records of the Thirty-Second Meeting, September 21-October 14, 1976,* p. 119.

33. *Ibid.*, pp. 310-13, October 5, 1976.

34. *Ibid.*, pp. 252-57.

35. *Ibid.* See also statements of Mr. Meguid (Egypt) and Yigal Allon (Israel), pp. 423-27, 585-94.

36. *Ibid.*, pp. 601, 605, 616-17.

37. See *Report of the Secretary-General of the United Nations on the Work of the Organization 1977* (New York: United Nations, 1977), pp. 9-11.

38. *Ibid.*

39. See especially James M. Markham, "The War that Won't Go Away," *New York Times Magazine*, October 9, 1977, pp. 33, 45, 48, 52, 54. See also *The Washington Post*, November 15, 1977.

40. See the *New York Times*, November 15, 1977.

41. On November 25, 1977, by a vote of 102–4–29 (US), the UN General Assembly condemned Israel's invasion of south Lebanon which, at the time, looked like an attempt on the part of Israel to achieve its ambitions in south Lebanon up to the Litani River.

42. *New York Times*, November 30, 1977.

43. See especially the Lebanese and Israeli communications to the United Nations, March 15, 17, 1978, in UN Docs. S/12606, 12607, and the secretary-general's report of March 19, 1978 (S/12611). The Security Council Resolution is embodied in S/425, of March 19, 1978. The Israeli forces struck from the sea south of Sidon on June 9, 1978, just four days before their promised withdrawal, *Washington Post, New York Times*, June 10, 1978.

44. On June 14 UN Secretary-General Waldheim sharply criticized Israel for turning over control of the southernmost areas along the border to Lebanese Christian militia forces. See *New York Times*, June 15, 1978.

INDEX

Ford, Gerald, 42, 230, 233, 236
France, 87, 236, 250, 252, 256–59, 268
Frangieh, Suleiman: 8, 75, 118, 144, 156,
   172, 195, 213, 232, 234–36; private
   militia, 4, 236; military government,
   35; and Palestinian resistance movement, 37; and "constitutional declaration," 38, 62; and al-Ahdab's "television coup," 40; flees Baabda, 40; on
   Palestinians in Lebanon, 32; pleads
   Palestinian case at UN, 33; and Syrian regime, 61–62; "new national
   charter," 62; and Syrian presence in
   Lebanon, 93; Iraqi pressure on, 189;
   refusal to resign, 237; and Arab
   League role, 276–77. See also Damascus Pact
Frangieh, Tony, 4
Free Nationalists, 4, 8. See also National
   Liberal Party; Camille Chamoun

Gaza, 164
Gemeyel, Amin, 4. See also Pierre
   Gemeyel
Gemeyel, Bashir, 4, 43. See also Pierre
   Gemeyel
Gemeyel, Pierre, 4, 15, 18, 33–34, 37, 49–
   50, 61, 117, 121, 140, 204–205.
Geneva Middle East Peace Conference,
   96, 163, 166, 193. See also Soviet
   Union
Germany, Federal Republic of, 268
Ghanem, General Iskander, 32
Ghorra, Edouard, 280
Godley, G. McMurtrie, 232, 235
Golan Heights, 32
"Good Fence." See Israel, "open fence"
   policy
Great Britain. See Britain
Greater Syria, 7, 68–69
"Green Line," 41–42, 44
Gulf Organization for Development in
   Egypt, 130
Gur, Lieutenant General Mordechai, 86,
   100, 102–103, 109

Habbash, George, 31, 33, 43, 127
Haddad, Major Saad, 53, 90, 99
Hassan, al-, Khaled, 46, 126
Hawatmeh, Nayyaf, 32–33, 141

Hawk, William, 43
Helou, Charles, 180
Higher Military Committee, 191
Hoefliger, Jean, 44–45
Hoss, Selim, 50
Hussein, King: 40, 108, 147, 149, 154,
   167, 199; and Palestinians, 140, 162,
   228–29, 245; and Israel, 52, 151; and
   West Bank, 151, 153; and Syria, 152,
   201–202, 229; and Camille Chamoun,
   155; and Suleiman Frangieh, 156; and
   Eastern Front, 187; and U.S., 236

ibn Abdul Wahhab, Muhammad, 114
Iran, 249, 261
Iraq: 129, 134, 136, 153, 164, 166, 173,
   198, 216, 218, 260–61; political support for leftists, 41, 193, 237; Syrian
   hegemony in Lebanon, 63, 65; anti-
   Syrian forces in Lebanon, 65; military
   aid to rejectionists, 88; aid to Lebanese factions, 127; sends troops to
   Lebanon, 138, 193–94; support for
   Palestinians, 206; and Sinai II, 211;
   and PLO, 221; and Riyadh accords,
   222–23; 1958 coup, 226, 271–72
Iraq Petroleum Company, 225
Islam, 114–15
Israel: 111, 163–64, 166, 168, 209, 261,
   284; raids into Lebanon, 4, 17–19,
   31–32, 86, 92–94, 97, 110, 186, 196;
   aid to Christians, 19, 45–46, 48, 50,
   81, 85, 87, 90, 92–94, 96, 98–100,
   106–112, 166, 197, 235, 284; objectives of intervention, 20, 81, 107–108;
   and Syrian intervention, 38–39, 50,
   93, 99, 198, 239; use of cluster
   bombs, 28, 53, 90; Rent-a-car raid,
   31–32, 196; "open fence" policy,
   45–46, 48, 81, 92, 94, 97; and Lebanese ports, 47, 87; and Lebanese peace-
   keeping force, 48–49; "red line," 49,
   85, 196; threatens intervention, 49;
   attacks Palestinian camps, 50, 235–36;
   invasion of southern Lebanon, 51,
   89–90, 97–106, 168, 186, 246, 284;
   withdrawal from Lebanon, 53, 90;
   and Army of South Lebanon, 53; and
   IDF, 85–86; US pressure, 86, 104,
   106, 198; policy on terrorism, 96,
   100–101; constraints on actions in

United States (*cont.*)
   Lebanon, 230; and PLO, 233; and
   Hafez Assad, 238; and traditional
   Arab regimes, 244; and King Hussein,
   245; and Middle East policy, 245–47;
   and Anwar Sadat, 246; and UN, 247,
   275; aid to Middle East, 256–58, 260;
   and Jordan, 260; and Libya, 260. *See
   also* Chapter 12

Vance, Cyrus, 21, 247
Vanguards of Lebanon's Arab Army, 66

Waldheim, Kurt, 53, 282
Wavell Camp, 29, 43
Weizman, Chaim, 247
Weizman, Ezer, 106, 109–110
West Bank, 147, 151, 153, 164, 171

Yamani, Zaki, 120
Yarmouk Brigade, 143
Yemen, People's Democratic Republic of,
   134, 136, 260

Zagharta, 75

LEBANON IN CRISIS

was composed in 10-point Compugraphic Palatino and leaded two points
by Metricomp, Inc.,
with display type in Typositor Fantail
by Dix Typesetting Co. Inc.;
printed on 50-pound Warren Smooth Eggshell,
Smyth-sewn and bound over boards in Columbia Bayside Vellum,
also adhesive bound with laminated paper covers,
by Maple-Vail Book Manufacturing Group, Inc.;
and published by

SYRACUSE UNIVERSITY PRESS
SYRACUSE, NEW YORK 13210